BEASTARS

BEASTARS

Volume 4

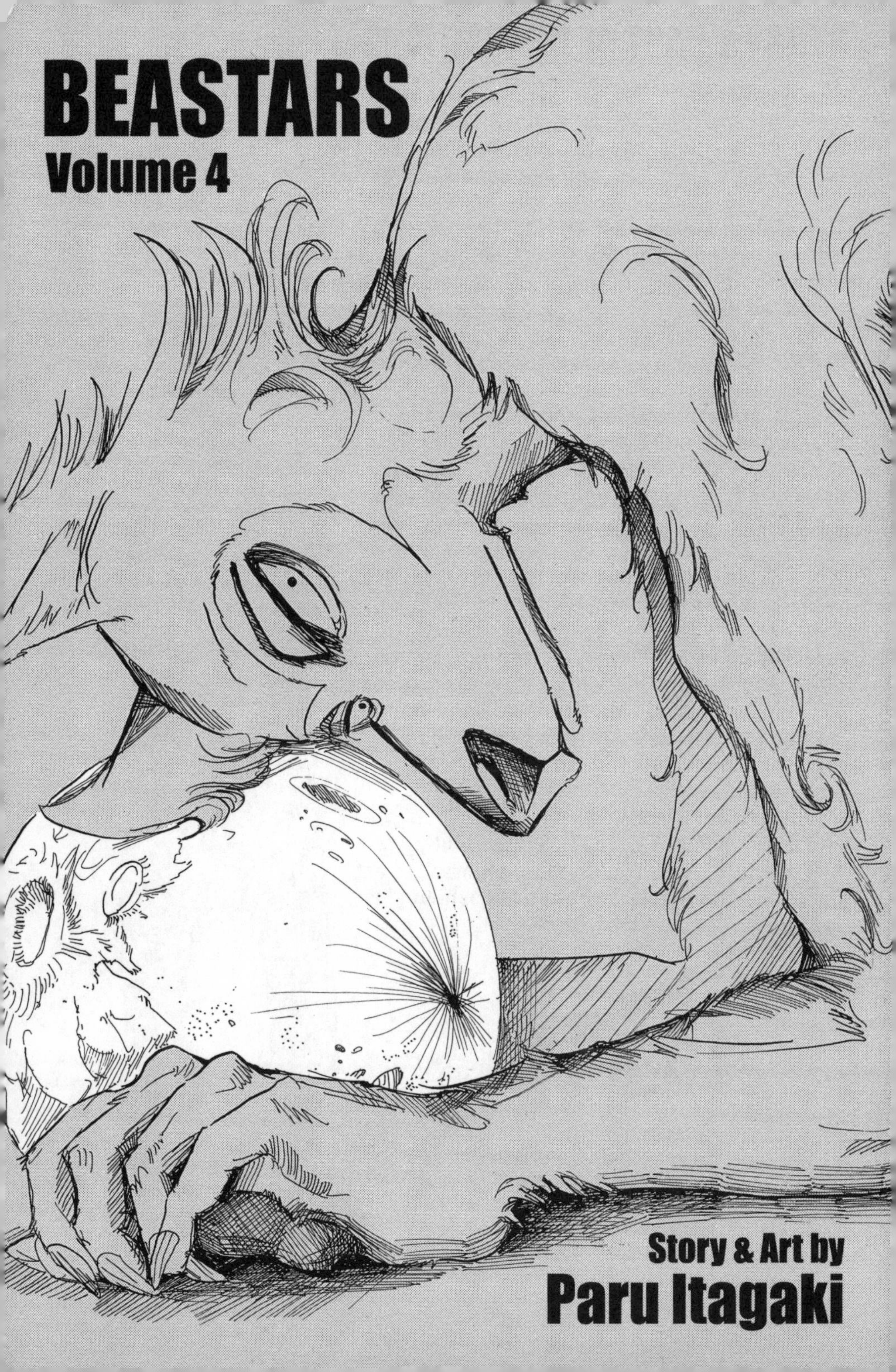

Story & Art by

Paru Itagaki

STORY & CAST OF CHARACTERS

Cherryton Academy is an integrated boarding school for a diverse group of carnivores and herbivores. Recently, Tem, an alpaca member of the Drama Club, was slain and devoured on campus. The murderer has yet to be identified, and everyone's nerves are on edge.

The summer Meteor Festival is fast approaching, and the Drama Club is busy making decorations and preparing for the festival dance. After news reports of the murder of a Thomson's gazelle by a wolf-led pack of Canidae, gray wolf Juno is bullied by her classmates. Legoshi comes to her rescue, then learns that she is a new member of the Drama Club.

Legoshi and three other carnivores from the Drama Club go into town to discuss their role in the festival. On their way back to campus, they accidentally wander into the black market where meat from funeral homes and hospitals is sold.

When Bill tries to get Legoshi to pool his money with the others so they can buy (and bite off) the finger of a street beggar, Legoshi flees. He is picked up by Mr. Panda, the self-proclaimed psychologist of the black market, who proceeds to diagnose Legoshi. Mr. Panda tells the young wolf that his attraction to dwarf rabbit Haru is merely the sublimated instincts of a predator.

On his way out of the black market, Legoshi runs into bald eagle Aoba, who has been waiting for him to return. Aoba couldn't bring himself to eat the meat of an herbivore either. Legoshi begins to cry...

Legoshi

★ Gray wolf ♂
★ High school second-year
★ Member of the Drama Club production crew
★ Physically powerful yet emotionally sensitive
★ Struggles with his identity as a carnivore

B E A S T A R S

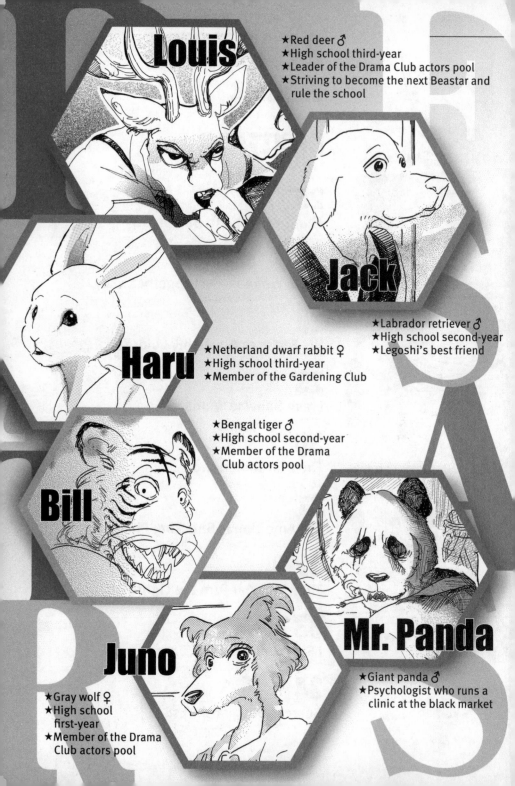

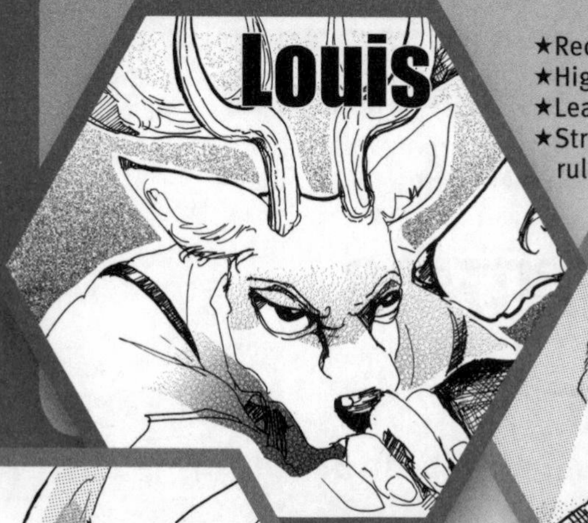
Louis

★Red deer ♂
★High school third-year
★Leader of the Drama Club actors pool
★Striving to become the next Beastar and rule the school

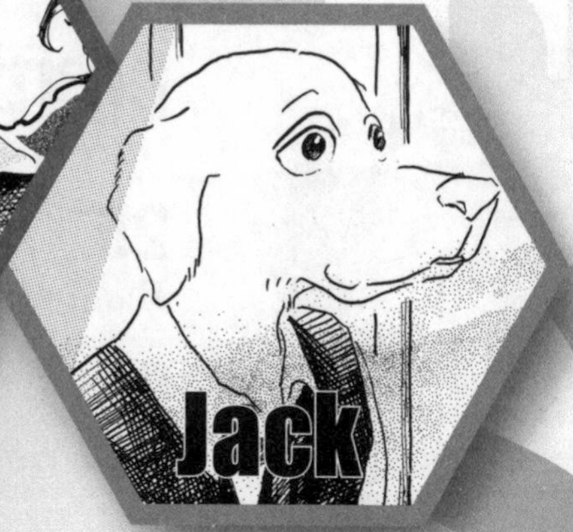
Jack

★Labrador retriever ♂
★High school second-year
★Legoshi's best friend

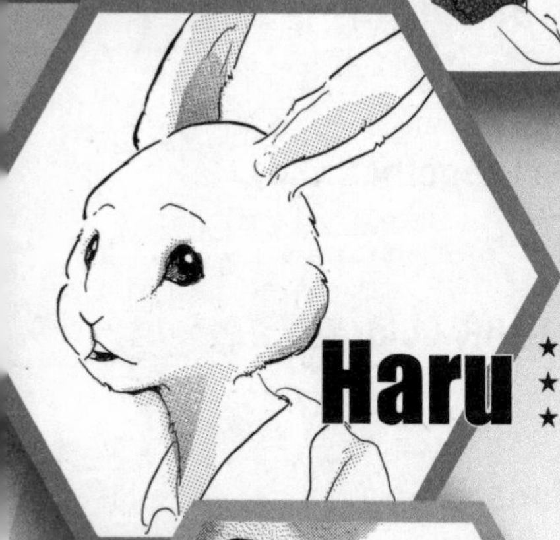
Haru

★Netherland dwarf rabbit ♀
★High school third-year
★Member of the Gardening Club

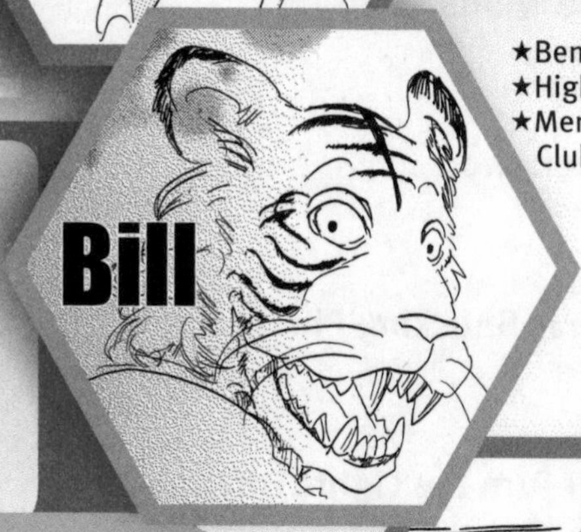
Bill

★Bengal tiger ♂
★High school second-year
★Member of the Drama Club actors pool

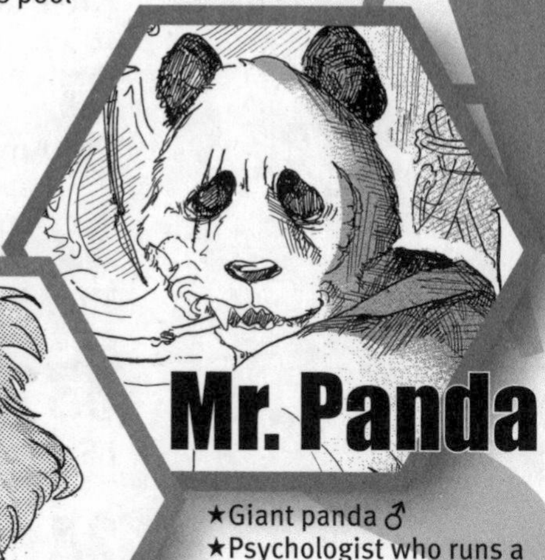
Mr. Panda

★Giant panda ♂
★Psychologist who runs a clinic at the black market

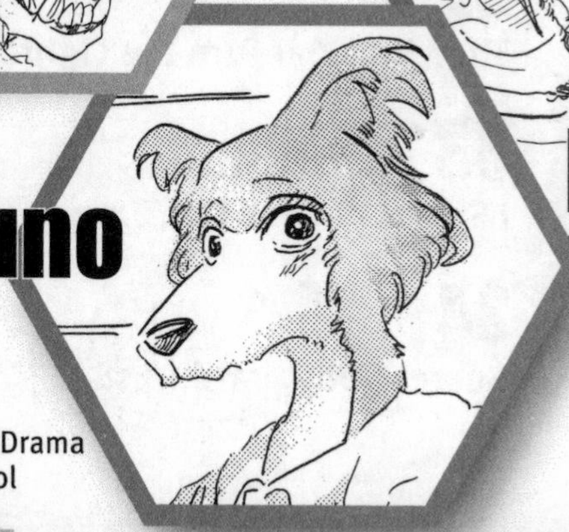
Juno

★Gray wolf ♀
★High school first-year
★Member of the Drama Club actors pool

BEASTARS
Volume 4

CONTENTS

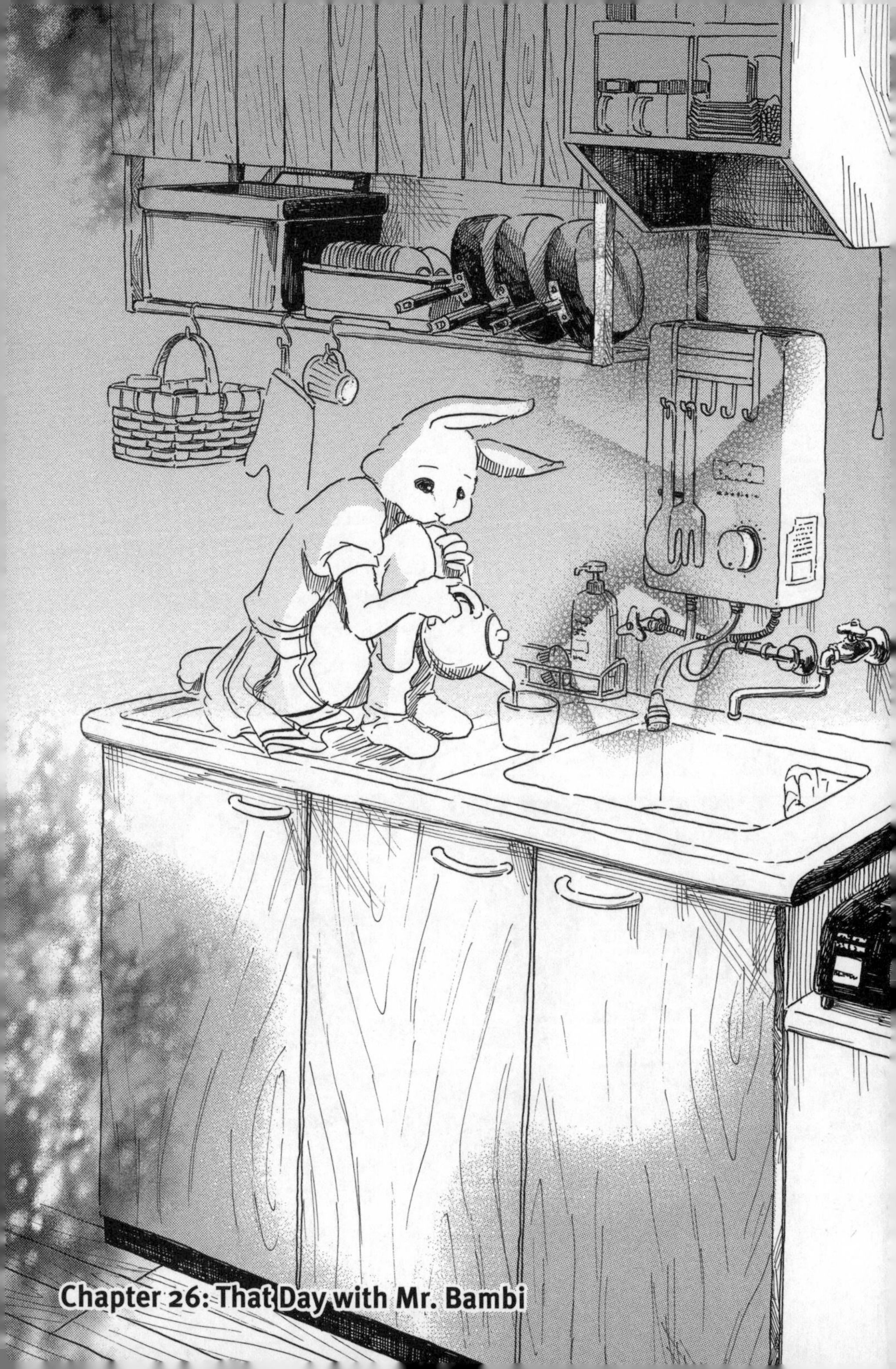

Chapter 26: That Day with Mr. Bambi

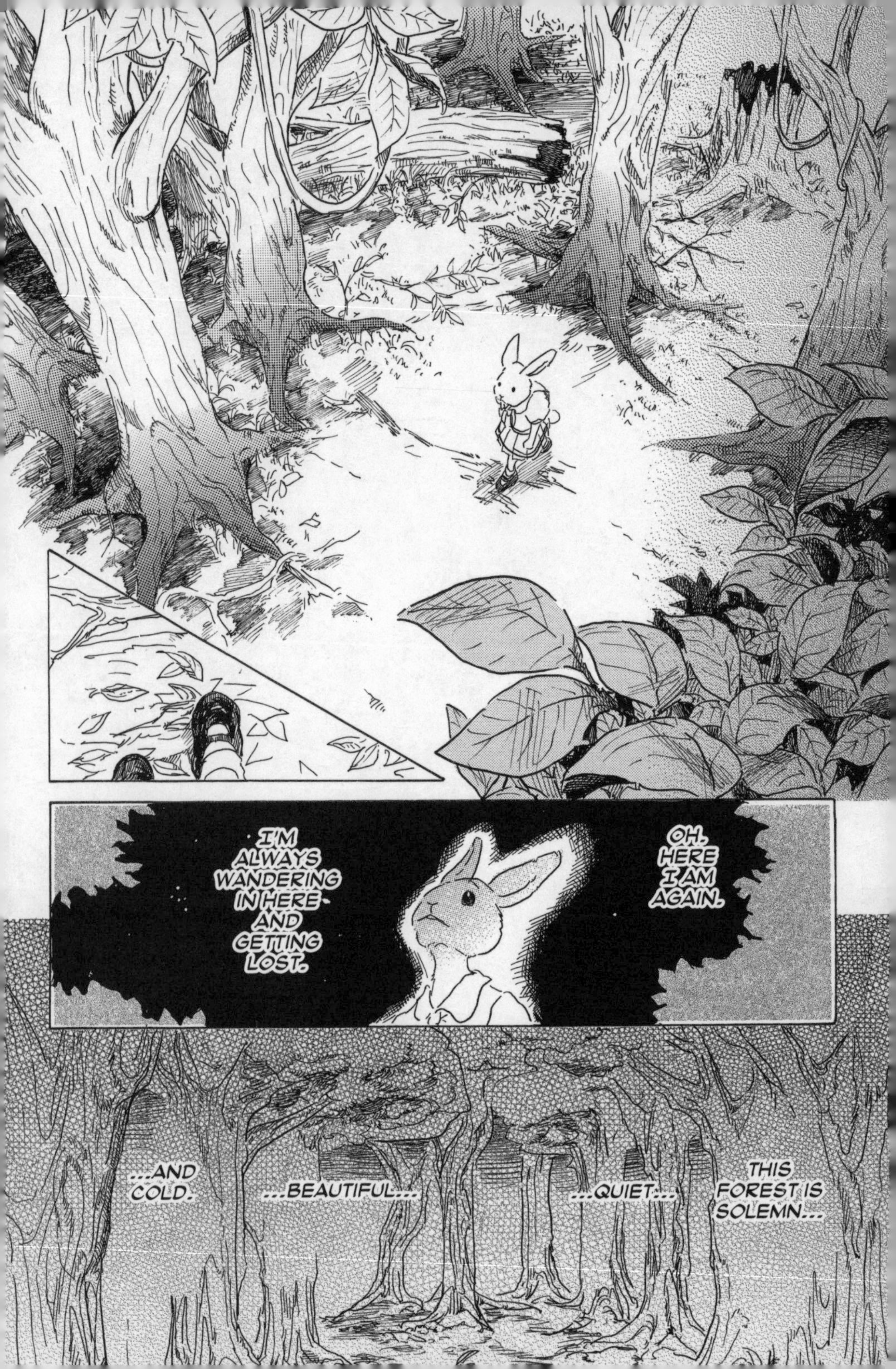
OH. HERE I AM AGAIN.
I'M ALWAYS WANDERING IN HERE AND GETTING LOST.
THIS FOREST IS SOLEMN...
...QUIET...
...BEAUTIFUL...
...AND COLD.

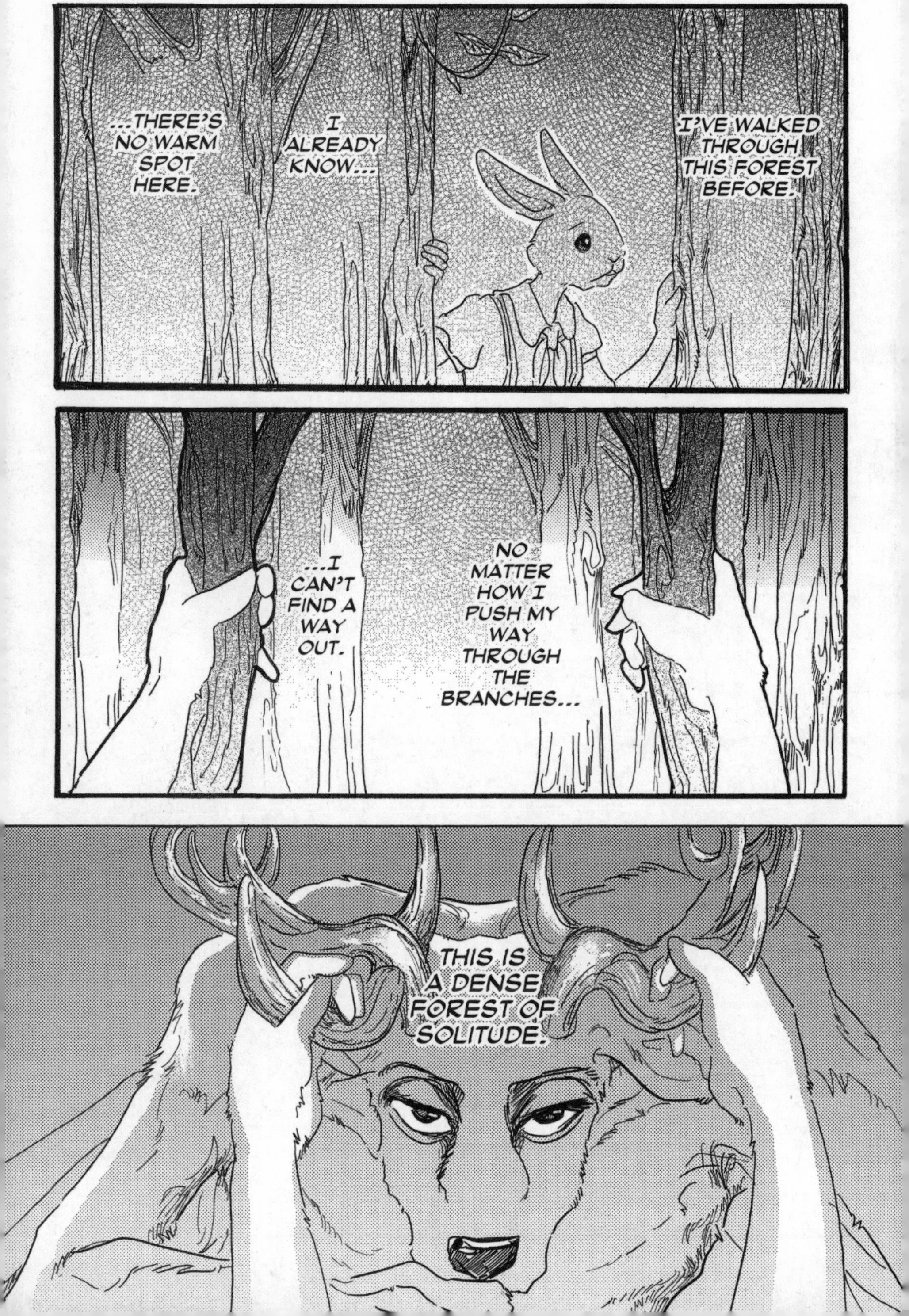
I'VE WALKED THROUGH THIS FOREST BEFORE.
I ALREADY KNOW...
...THERE'S NO WARM SPOT HERE.
NO MATTER HOW I PUSH MY WAY THROUGH THE BRANCHES...
...I CAN'T FIND A WAY OUT.
THIS IS A DENSE FOREST OF SOLITUDE.

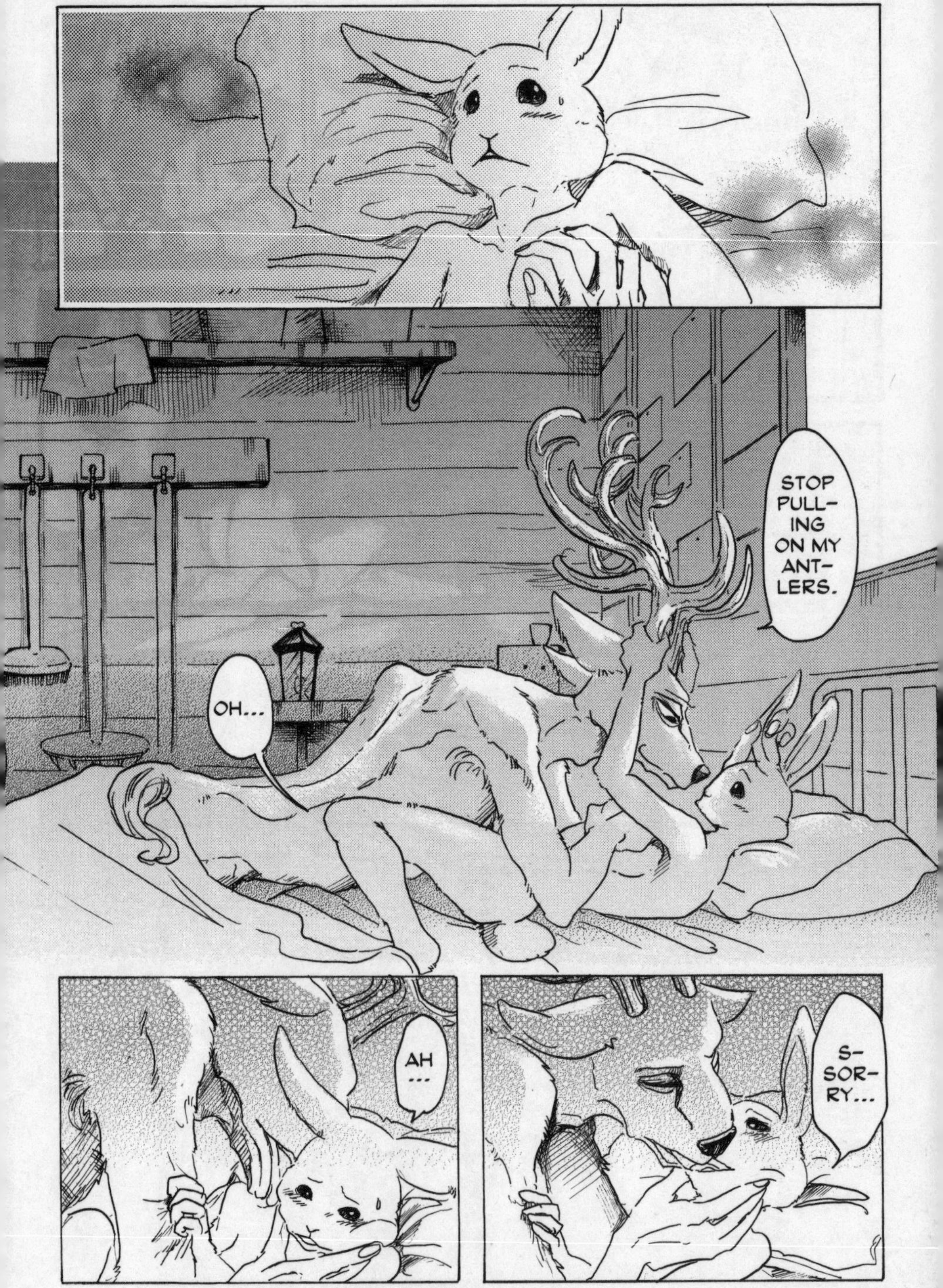
STOP PULL-ING ON MY ANT-LERS.
OH...
S-SOR-RY...
AH ...

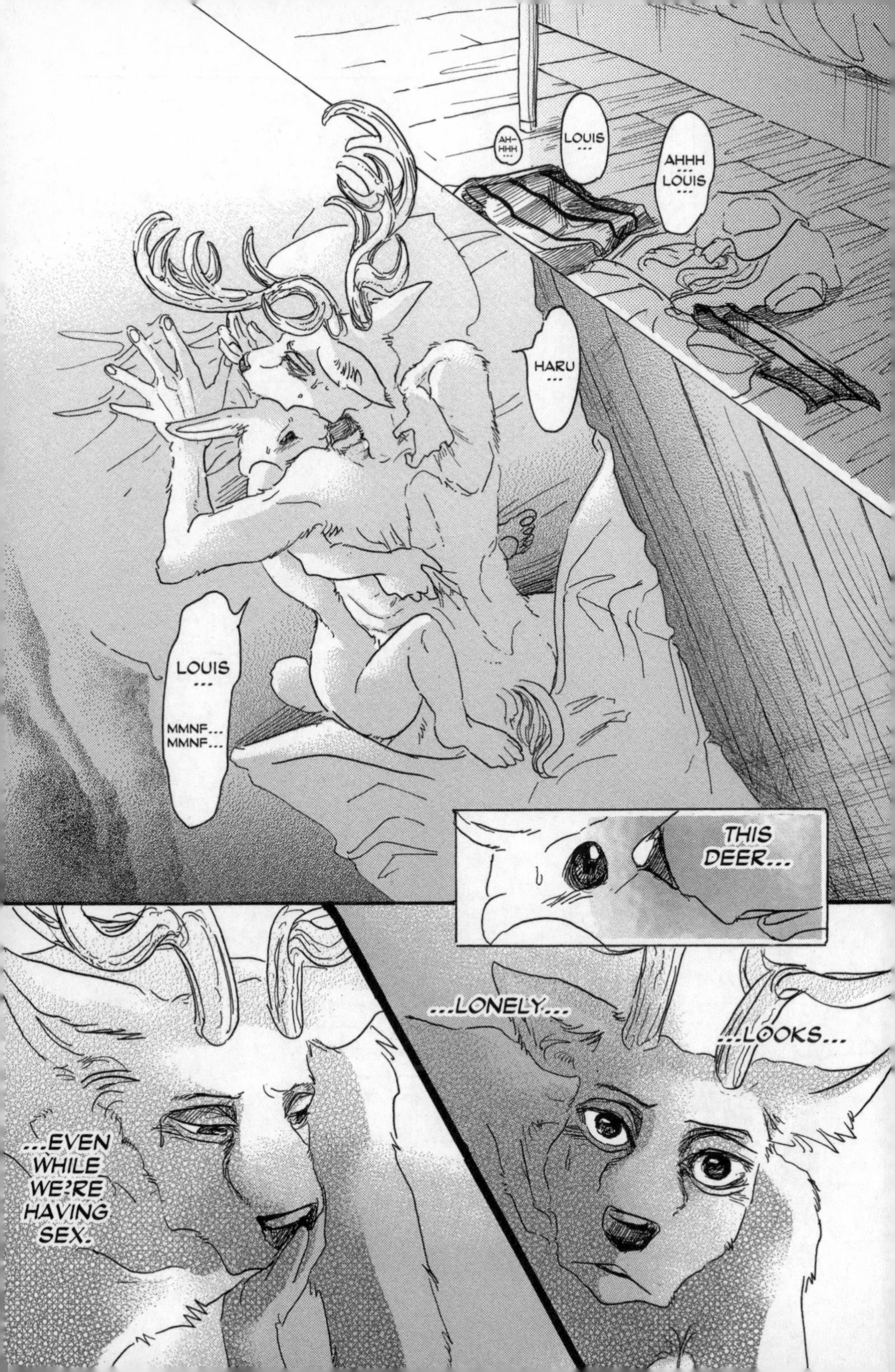
AHHH... LOUIS...
LOUIS...
AH-HHH...
HARU...
LOUIS... MMNF... MMNF...
THIS DEER...
...LOOKS...
...LONELY...
...EVEN WHILE WE'RE HAVING SEX.

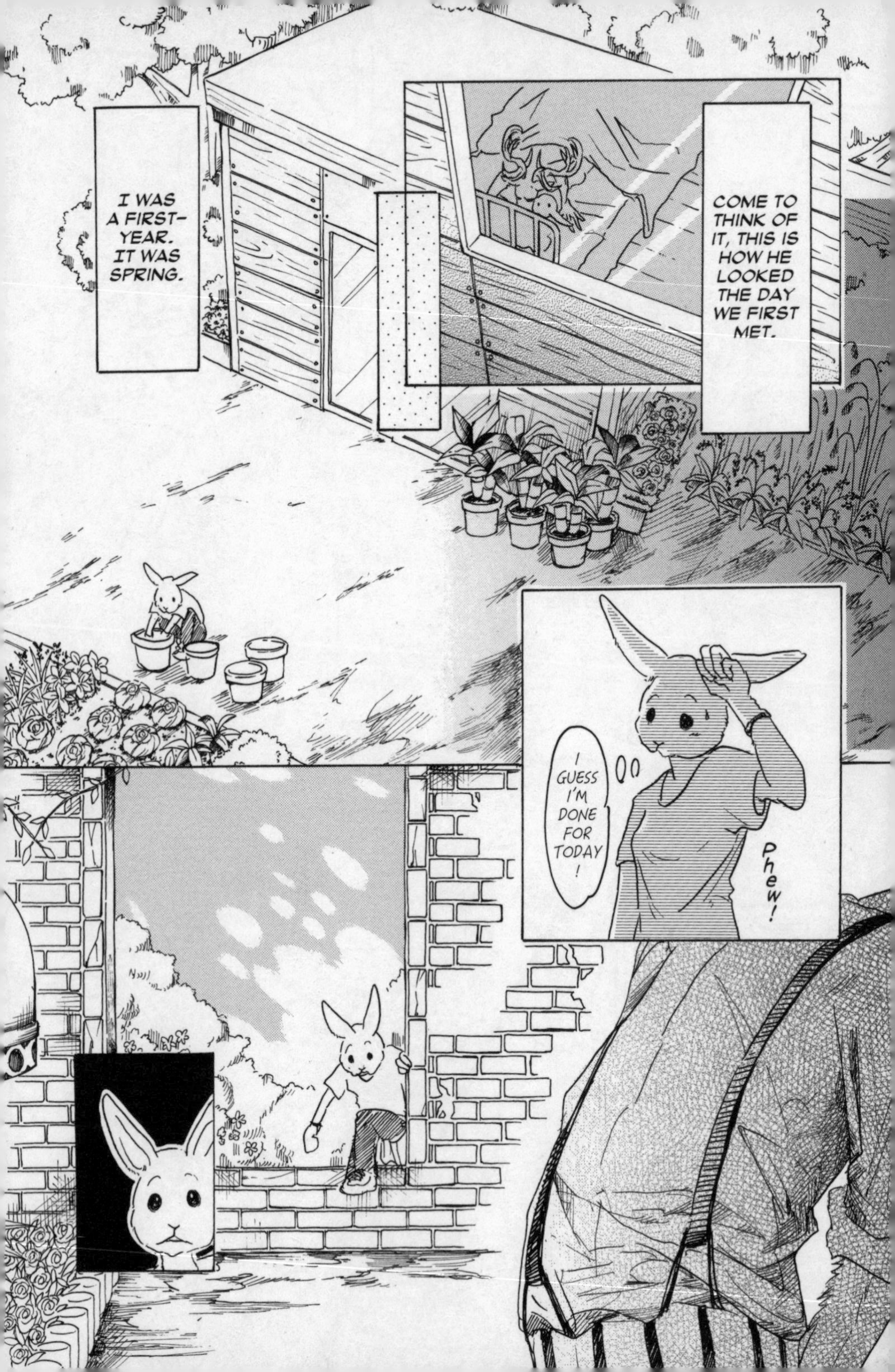
COME TO THINK OF IT, THIS IS HOW HE LOOKED THE DAY WE FIRST MET.
I WAS A FIRST-YEAR. IT WAS SPRING.
I GUESS I'M DONE FOR TODAY!
Phew!

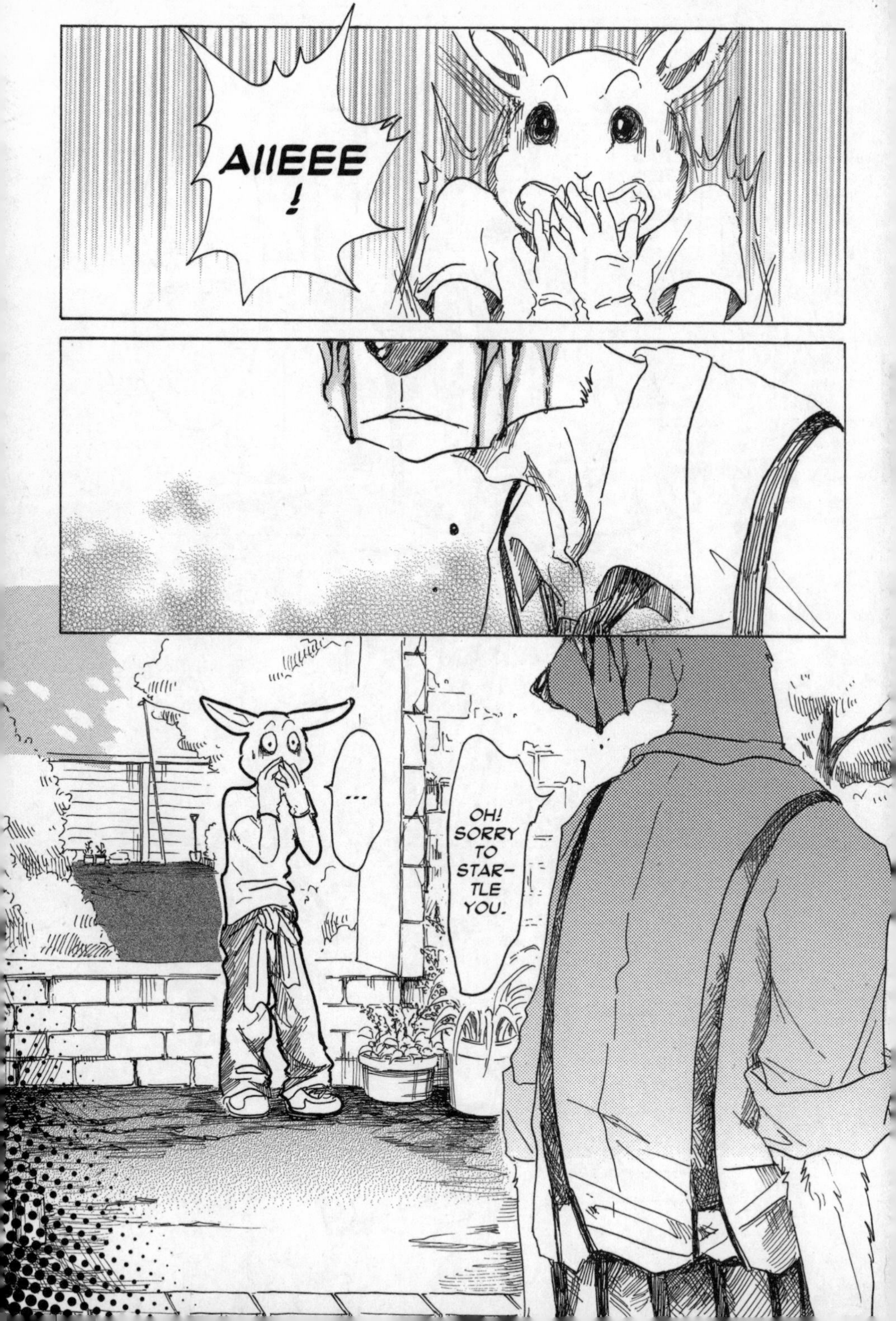
AIIEEE!
OH! SORRY TO STARTLE YOU.
...

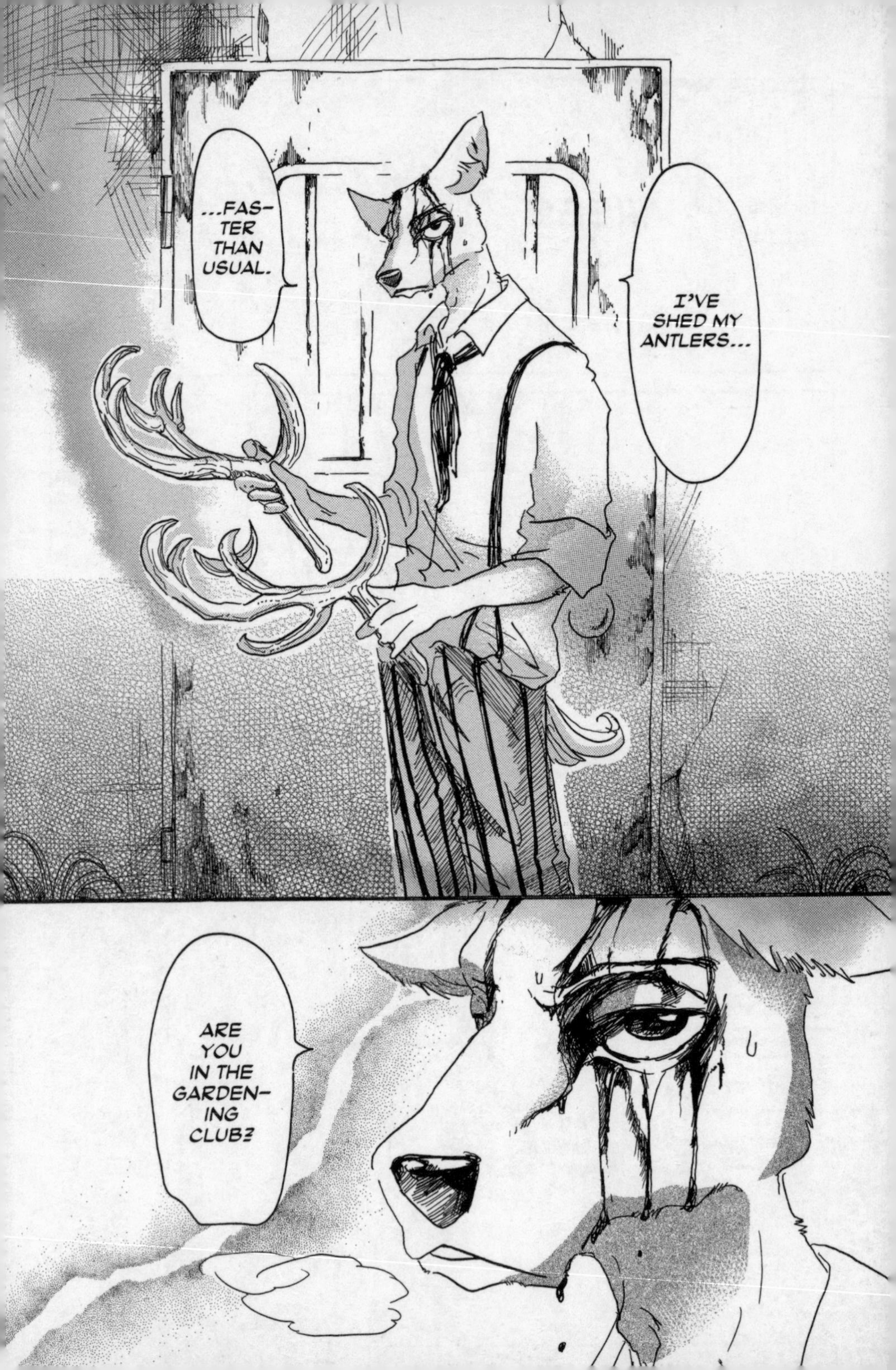
I'VE SHED MY ANTLERS...
...FASTER THAN USUAL.
ARE YOU IN THE GARDENING CLUB?

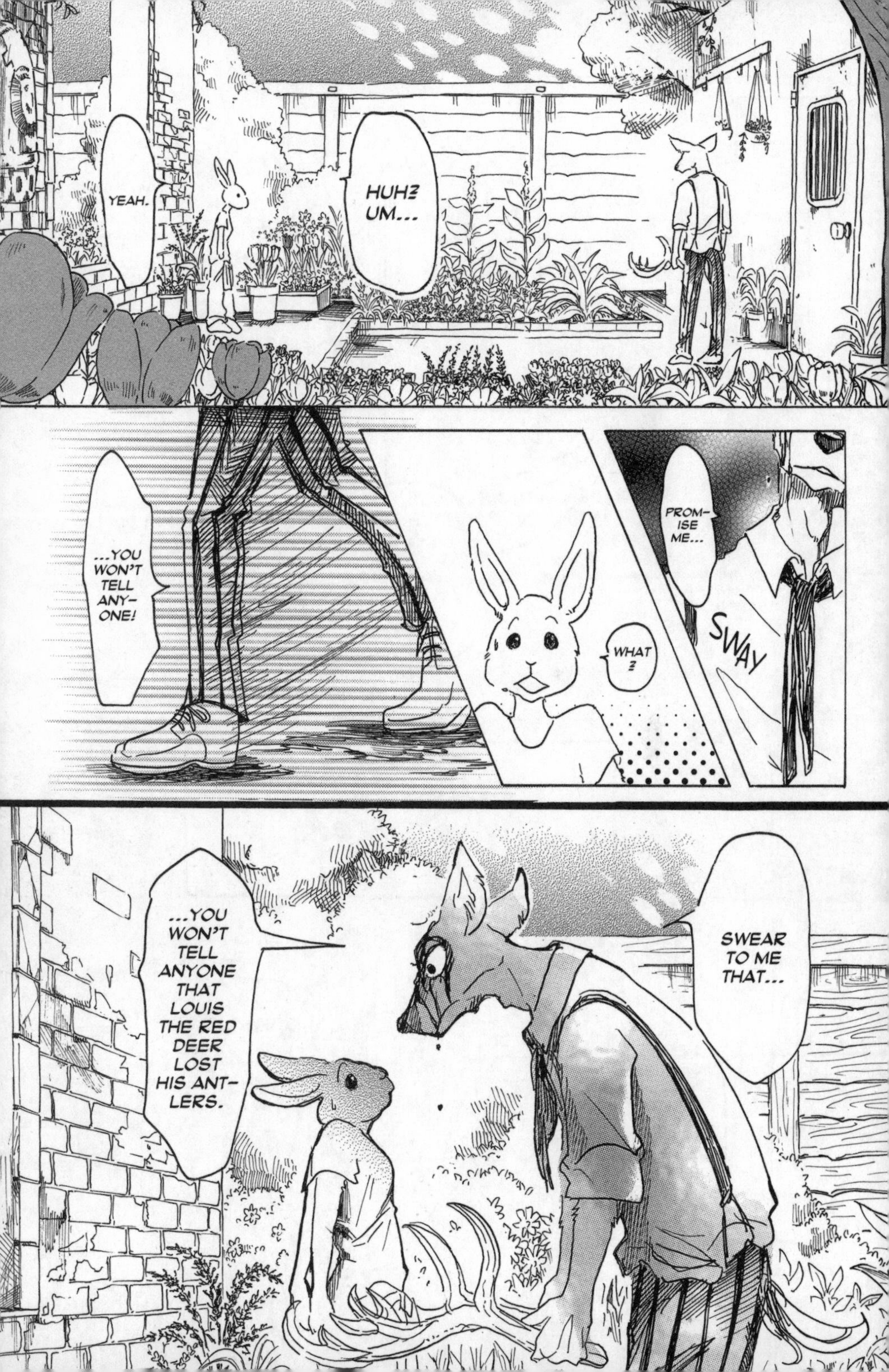
HUH? UM...
YEAH.
PROMISE ME...
SWAY
WHAT?
...YOU WON'T TELL ANYONE!
SWEAR TO ME THAT...
...YOU WON'T TELL ANYONE THAT LOUIS THE RED DEER LOST HIS ANTLERS.

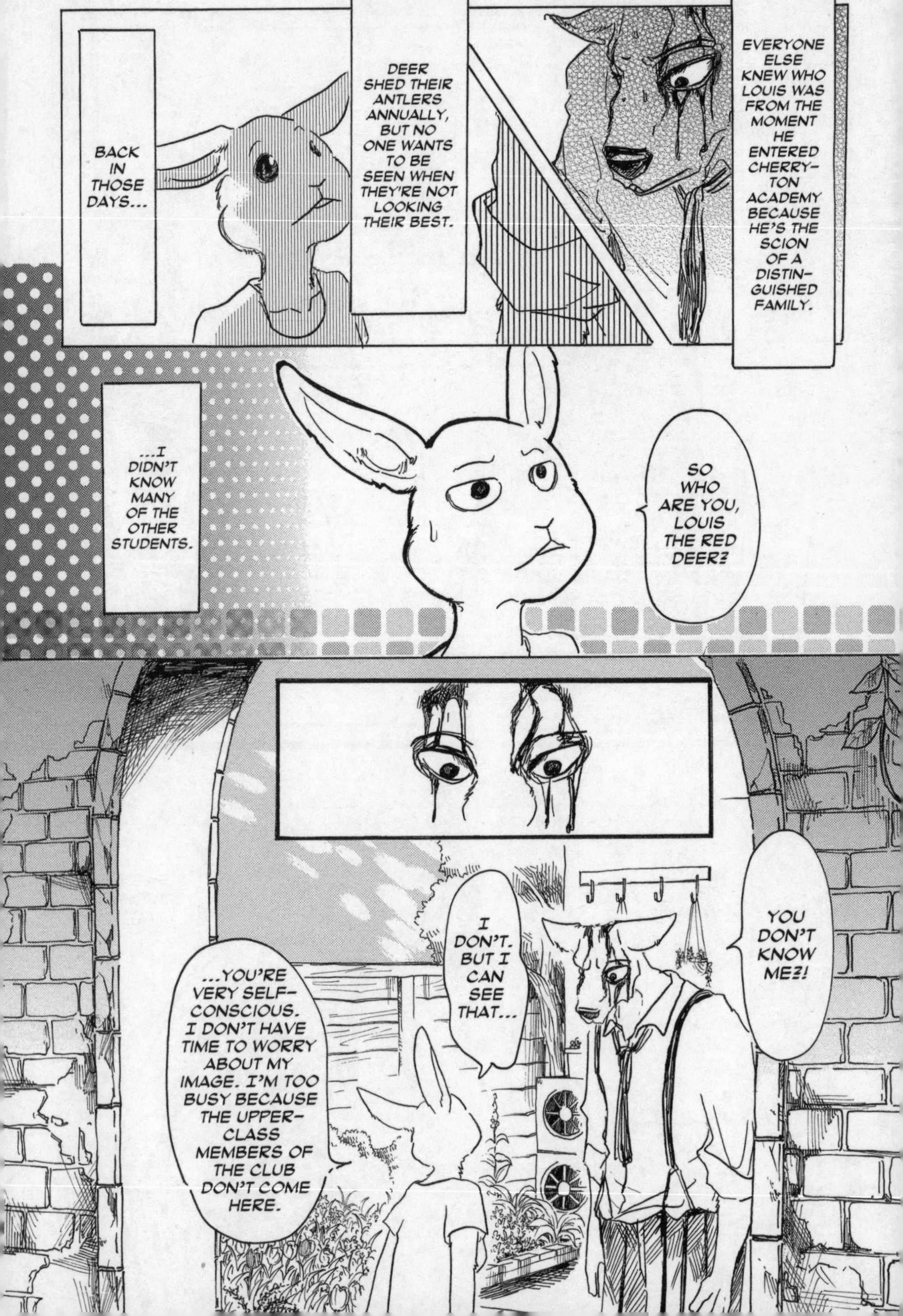
EVERYONE ELSE KNEW WHO LOUIS WAS FROM THE MOMENT HE ENTERED CHERRYTON ACADEMY BECAUSE HE'S THE SCION OF A DISTINGUISHED FAMILY.
DEER SHED THEIR ANTLERS ANNUALLY, BUT NO ONE WANTS TO BE SEEN WHEN THEY'RE NOT LOOKING THEIR BEST.
BACK IN THOSE DAYS...
SO WHO ARE YOU, LOUIS THE RED DEER?
...I DIDN'T KNOW MANY OF THE OTHER STUDENTS.
YOU DON'T KNOW ME?!
I DON'T. BUT I CAN SEE THAT...
...YOU'RE VERY SELF-CONSCIOUS. I DON'T HAVE TIME TO WORRY ABOUT MY IMAGE. I'M TOO BUSY BECAUSE THE UPPER-CLASS MEMBERS OF THE CLUB DON'T COME HERE.

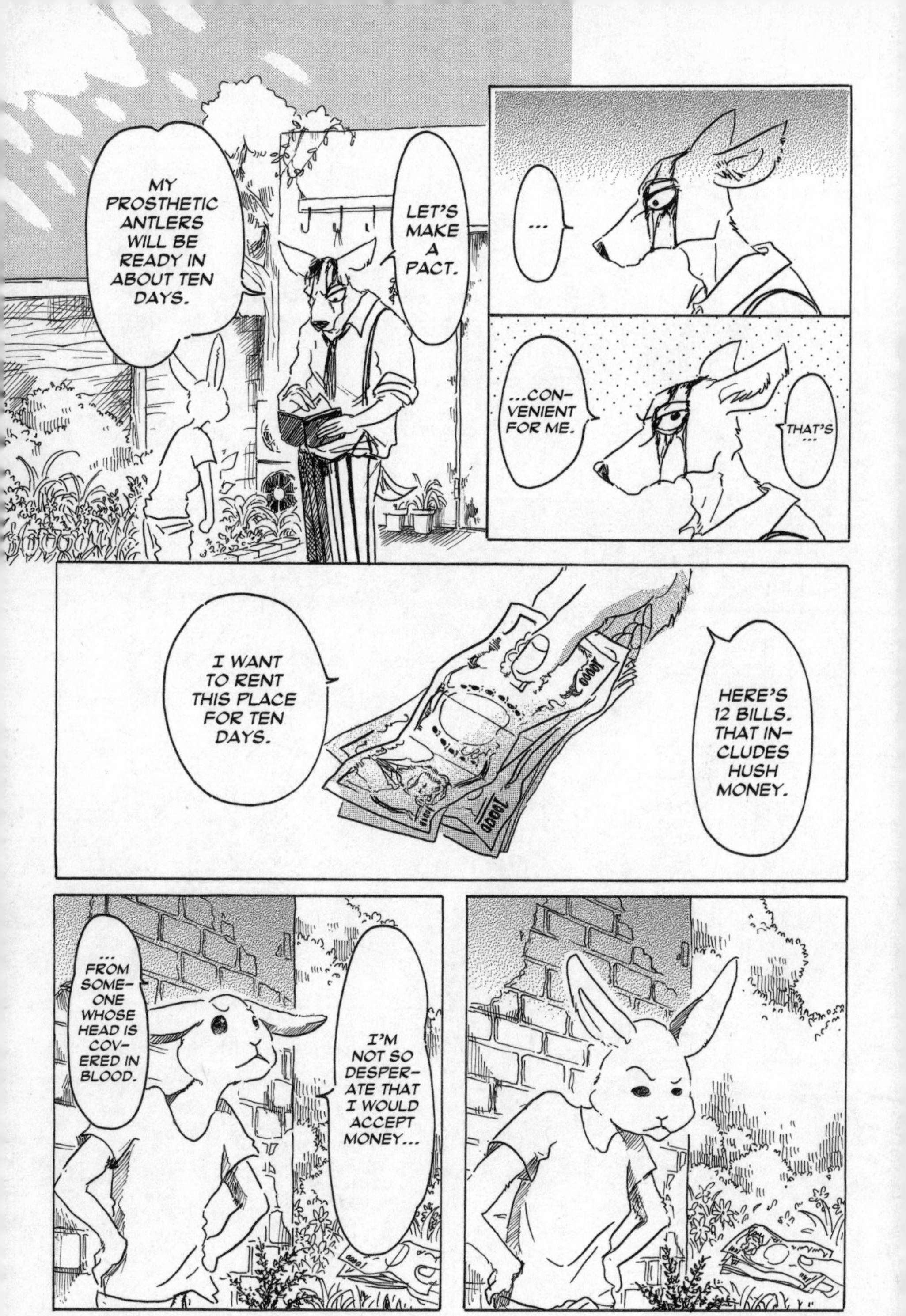
...
THAT'S...
...CON-VENIENT FOR ME.
LET'S MAKE A PACT.
MY PROSTHETIC ANTLERS WILL BE READY IN ABOUT TEN DAYS.
HERE'S 12 BILLS. THAT IN-CLUDES HUSH MONEY.
I WANT TO RENT THIS PLACE FOR TEN DAYS.
I'M NOT SO DESPER-ATE THAT I WOULD ACCEPT MONEY...
...FROM SOME-ONE WHOSE HEAD IS COV-ERED IN BLOOD.

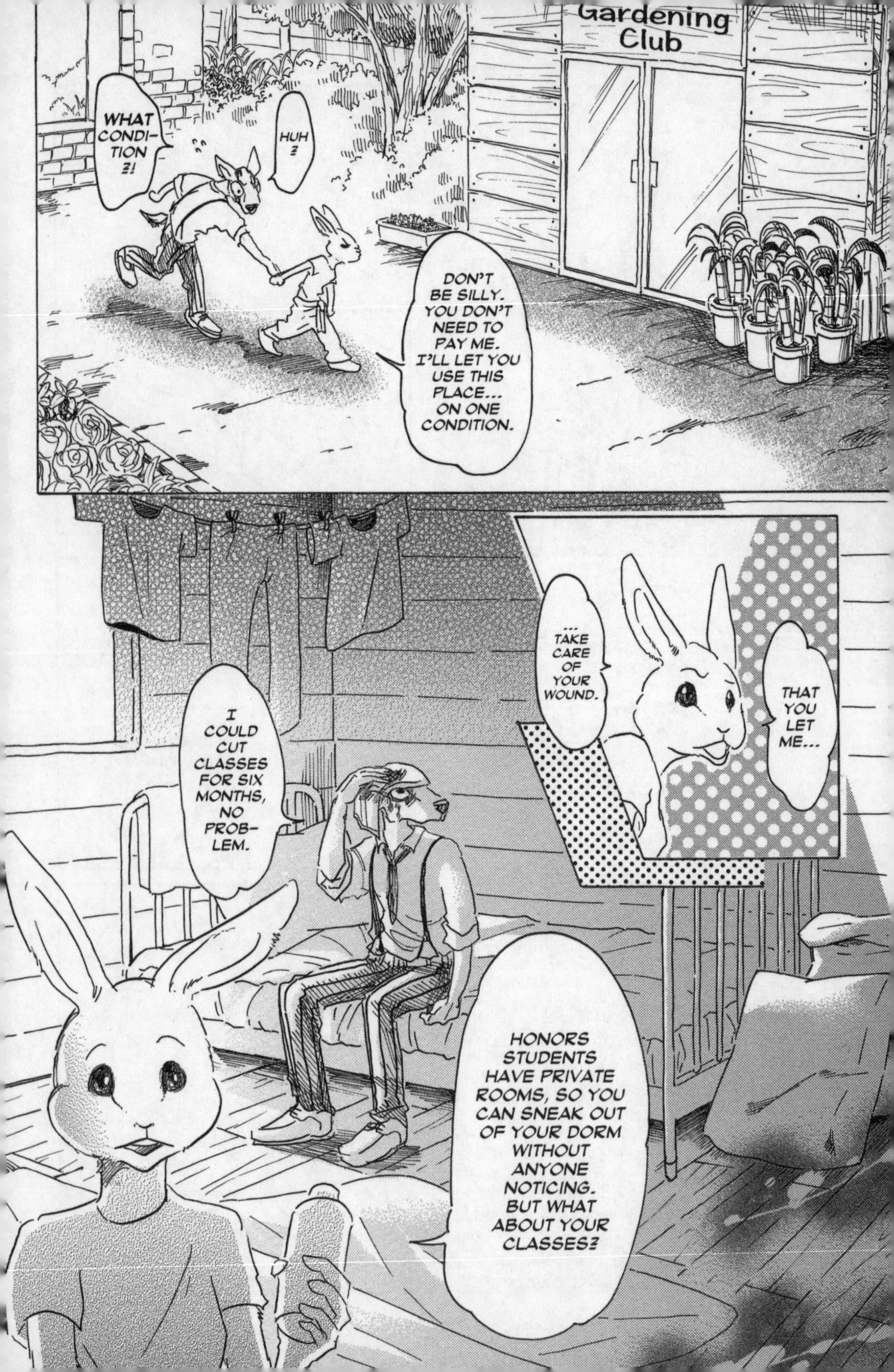

Gardening Club
DON'T BE SILLY. YOU DON'T NEED TO PAY ME. I'LL LET YOU USE THIS PLACE... ON ONE CONDITION.
HUH?
WHAT CONDITION?!
THAT YOU LET ME...
...TAKE CARE OF YOUR WOUND.
HONORS STUDENTS HAVE PRIVATE ROOMS, SO YOU CAN SNEAK OUT OF YOUR DORM WITHOUT ANYONE NOTICING. BUT WHAT ABOUT YOUR CLASSES?
I COULD CUT CLASSES FOR SIX MONTHS, NO PROB-LEM.

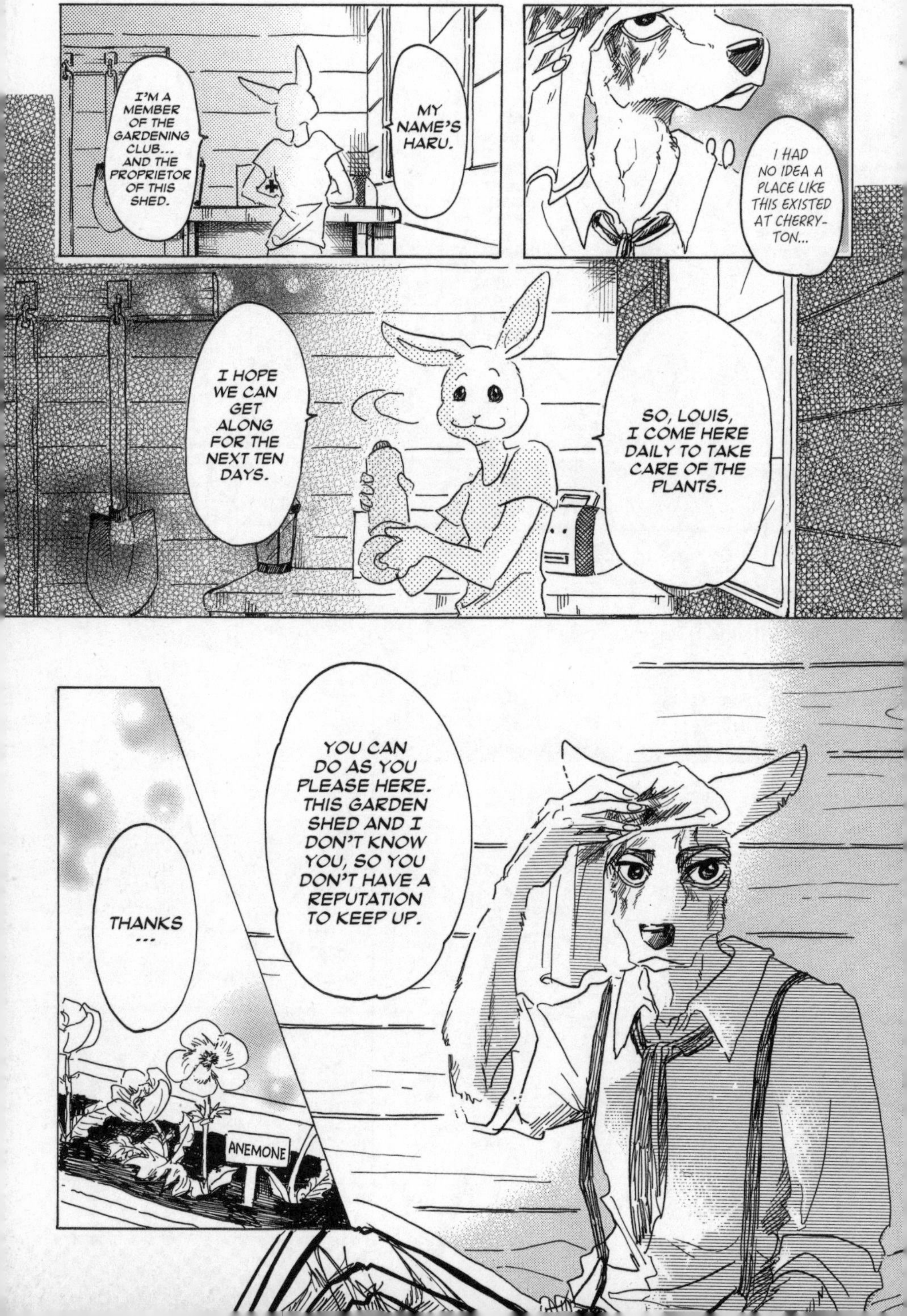
I HAD NO IDEA A PLACE LIKE THIS EXISTED AT CHERRY-TON...
MY NAME'S HARU.
I'M A MEMBER OF THE GARDENING CLUB... AND THE PROPRIETOR OF THIS SHED.
SO, LOUIS, I COME HERE DAILY TO TAKE CARE OF THE PLANTS.
I HOPE WE CAN GET ALONG FOR THE NEXT TEN DAYS.
YOU CAN DO AS YOU PLEASE HERE. THIS GARDEN SHED AND I DON'T KNOW YOU, SO YOU DON'T HAVE A REPUTATION TO KEEP UP.
THANKS ...
ANEMONE

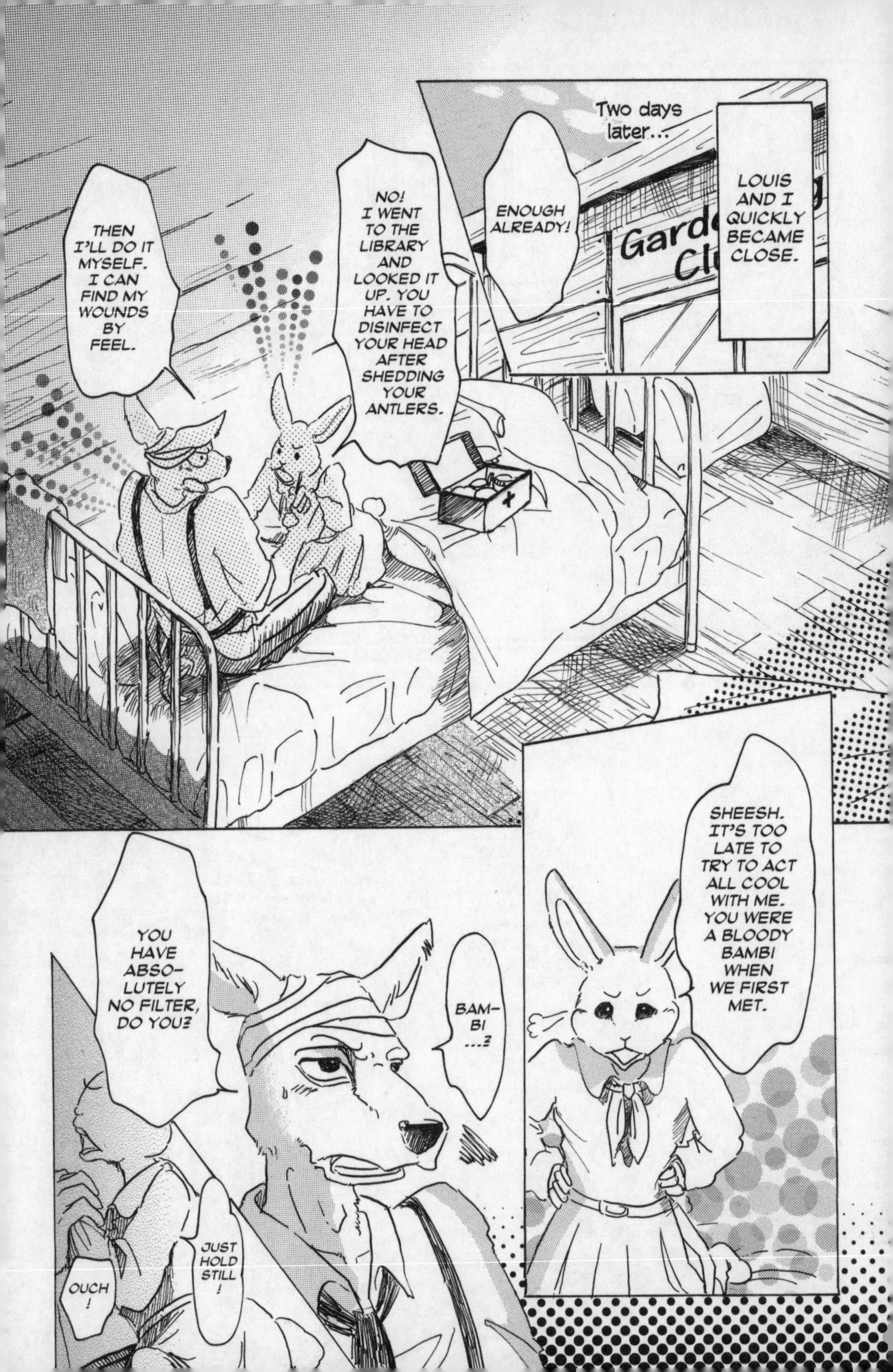
LOUIS AND I QUICKLY BECAME CLOSE.
Two days later...
ENOUGH ALREADY!
NO! I WENT TO THE LIBRARY AND LOOKED IT UP. YOU HAVE TO DISINFECT YOUR HEAD AFTER SHEDDING YOUR ANTLERS.
THEN I'LL DO IT MYSELF. I CAN FIND MY WOUNDS BY FEEL.
SHEESH. IT'S TOO LATE TO TRY TO ACT ALL COOL WITH ME. YOU WERE A BLOODY BAMBI WHEN WE FIRST MET.
BAM-BI ...?
YOU HAVE ABSO-LUTELY NO FILTER, DO YOU?
JUST HOLD STILL!
OUCH!

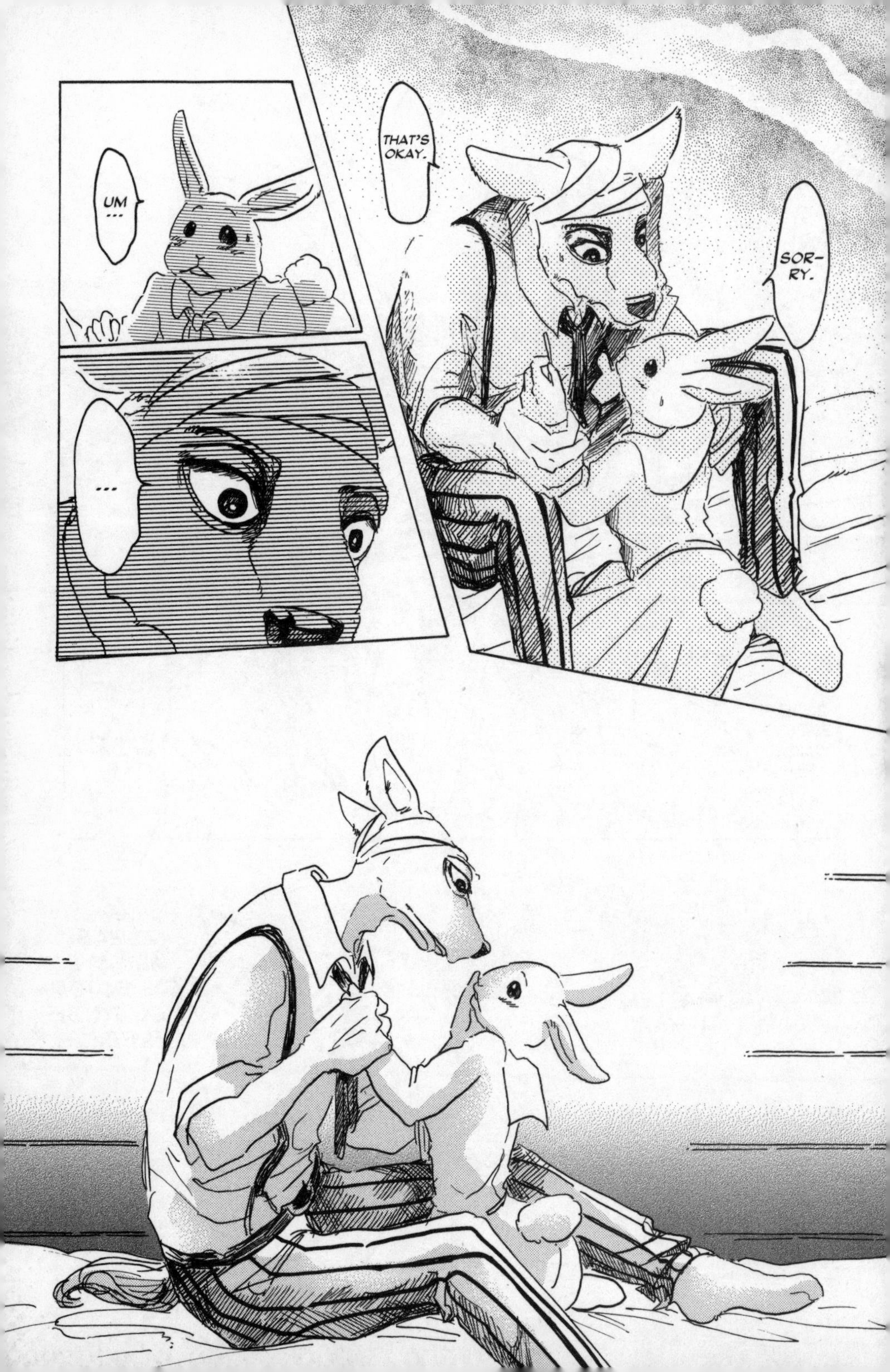

SOR-RY.
THAT'S OKAY.
UM...
...

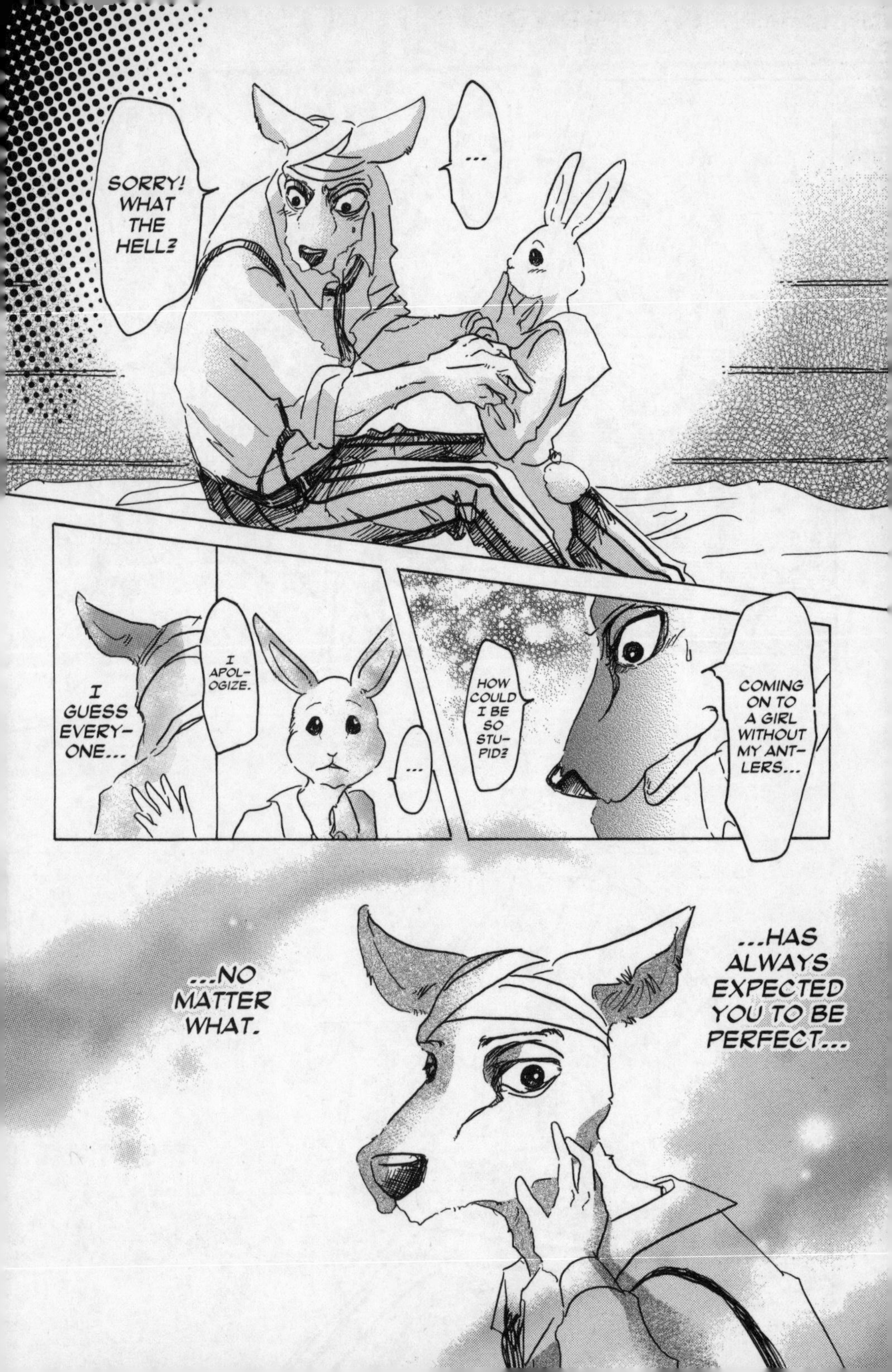

...
SORRY! WHAT THE HELL?
COMING ON TO A GIRL WITHOUT MY ANTLERS...
HOW COULD I BE SO STUPID?
I APOLOGIZE.
...
I GUESS EVERYONE...
...HAS ALWAYS EXPECTED YOU TO BE PERFECT...
...NO MATTER WHAT.

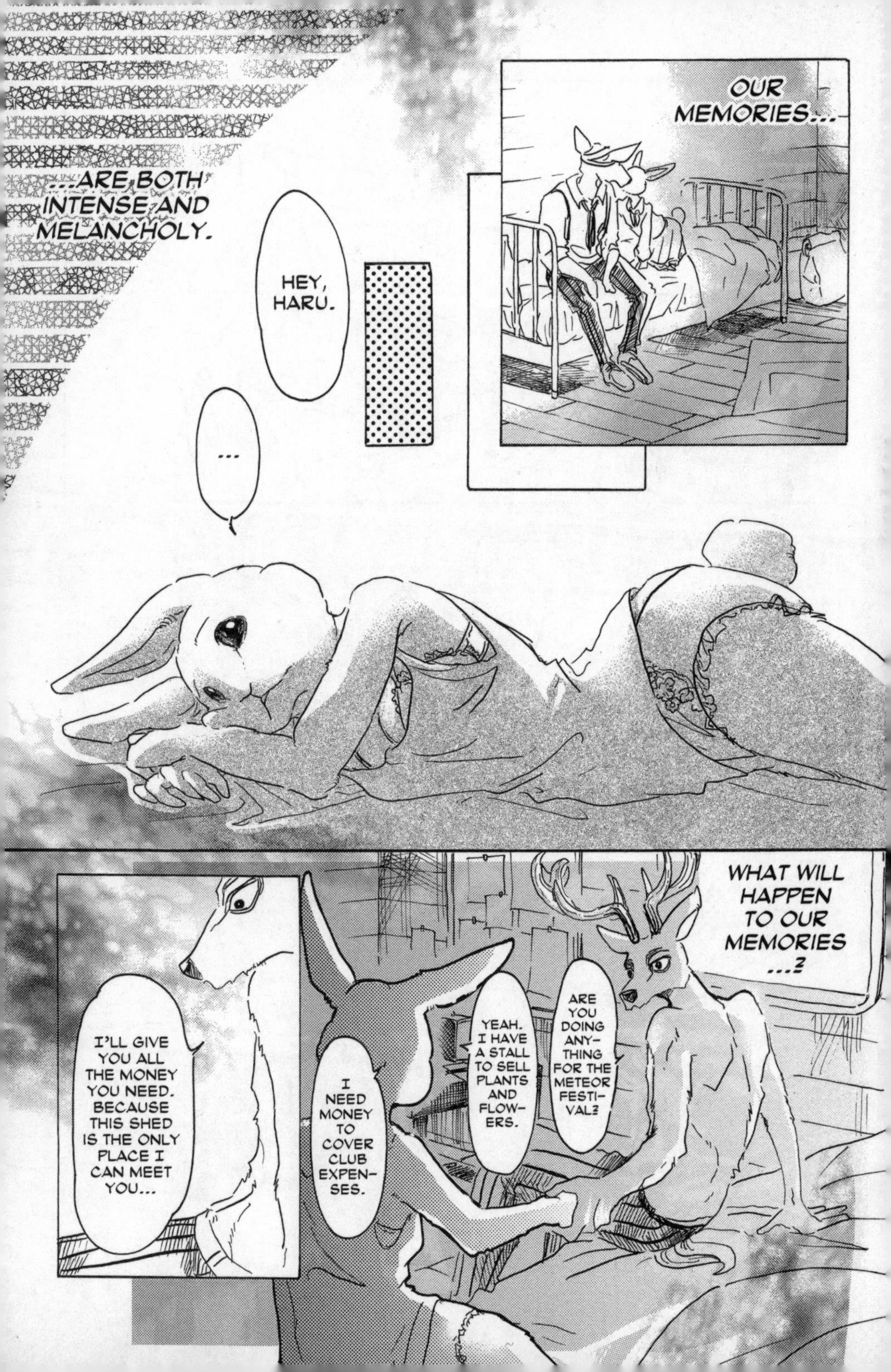
OUR MEMORIES...
...ARE BOTH INTENSE AND MELANCHOLY.
HEY, HARU.
...
WHAT WILL HAPPEN TO OUR MEMORIES ...?
ARE YOU DOING ANY-THING FOR THE METEOR FESTI-VAL?
YEAH. I HAVE A STALL TO SELL PLANTS AND FLOW-ERS.
I NEED MONEY TO COVER CLUB EXPEN-SES.
I'LL GIVE YOU ALL THE MONEY YOU NEED. BECAUSE THIS SHED IS THE ONLY PLACE I CAN MEET YOU...

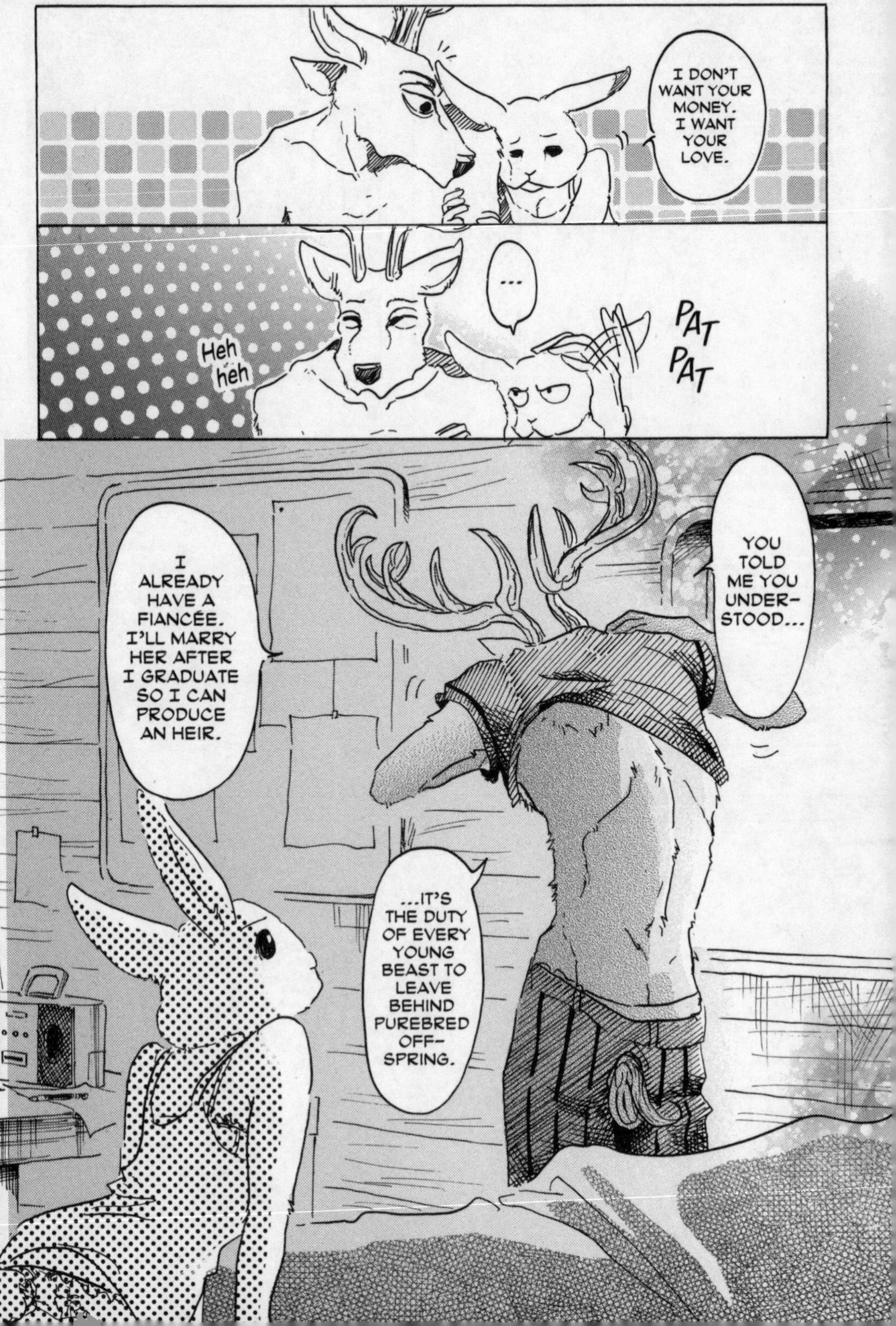
I DON'T WANT YOUR MONEY. I WANT YOUR LOVE.
PAT PAT
...
Heh heh
YOU TOLD ME YOU UNDER-STOOD...
I ALREADY HAVE A FIANCÉE. I'LL MARRY HER AFTER I GRADUATE SO I CAN PRODUCE AN HEIR.
...IT'S THE DUTY OF EVERY YOUNG BEAST TO LEAVE BEHIND PUREBRED OFF-SPRING.

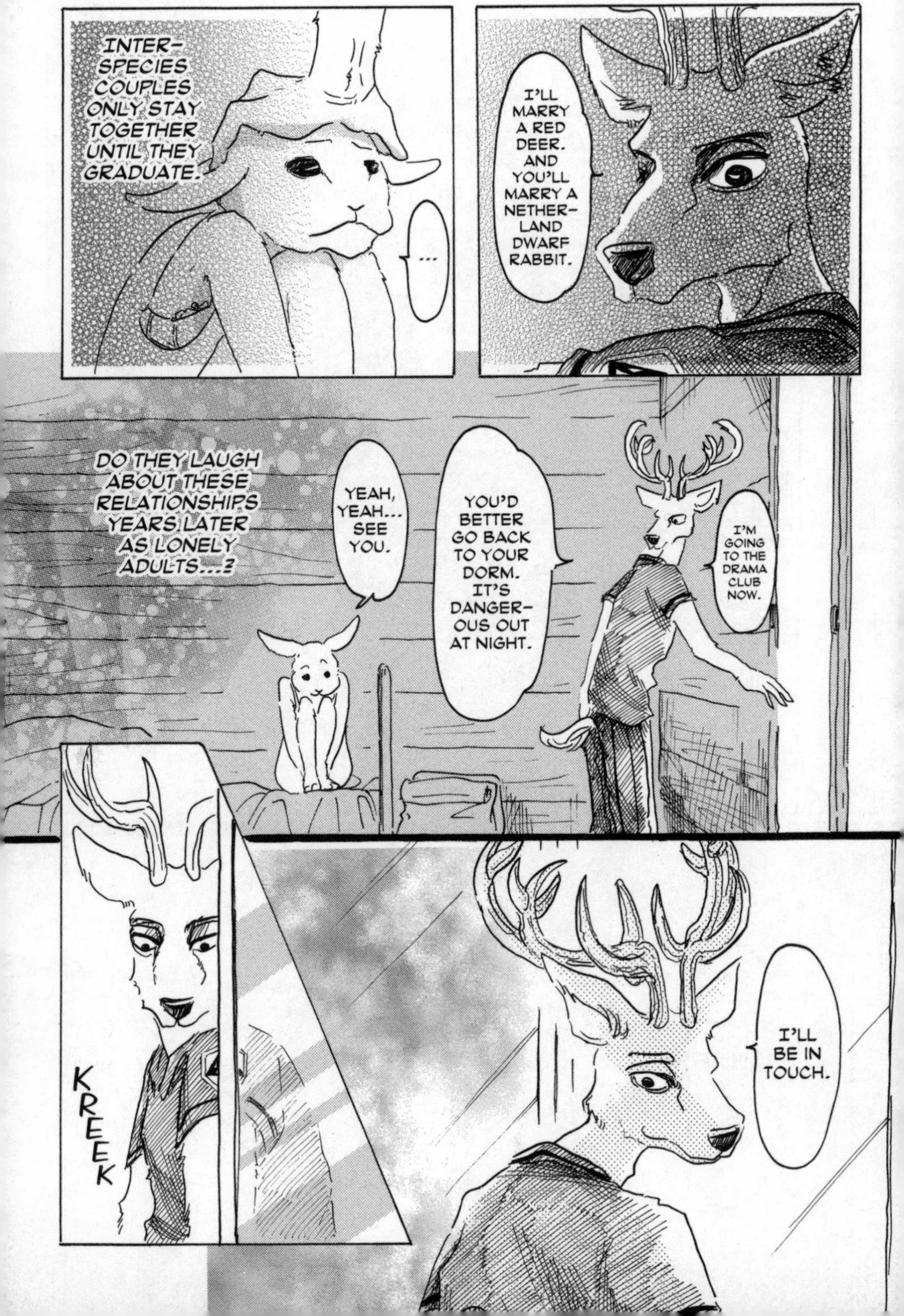
I'LL MARRY A RED DEER. AND YOU'LL MARRY A NETHER-LAND DWARF RABBIT.
INTER-SPECIES COUPLES ONLY STAY TOGETHER UNTIL THEY GRADUATE.
...
I'M GOING TO THE DRAMA CLUB NOW.
YOU'D BETTER GO BACK TO YOUR DORM. IT'S DANGER-OUS OUT AT NIGHT.
YEAH, YEAH... SEE YOU.
DO THEY LAUGH ABOUT THESE RELATIONSHIPS YEARS LATER AS LONELY ADULTS...?
I'LL BE IN TOUCH.
KREEK

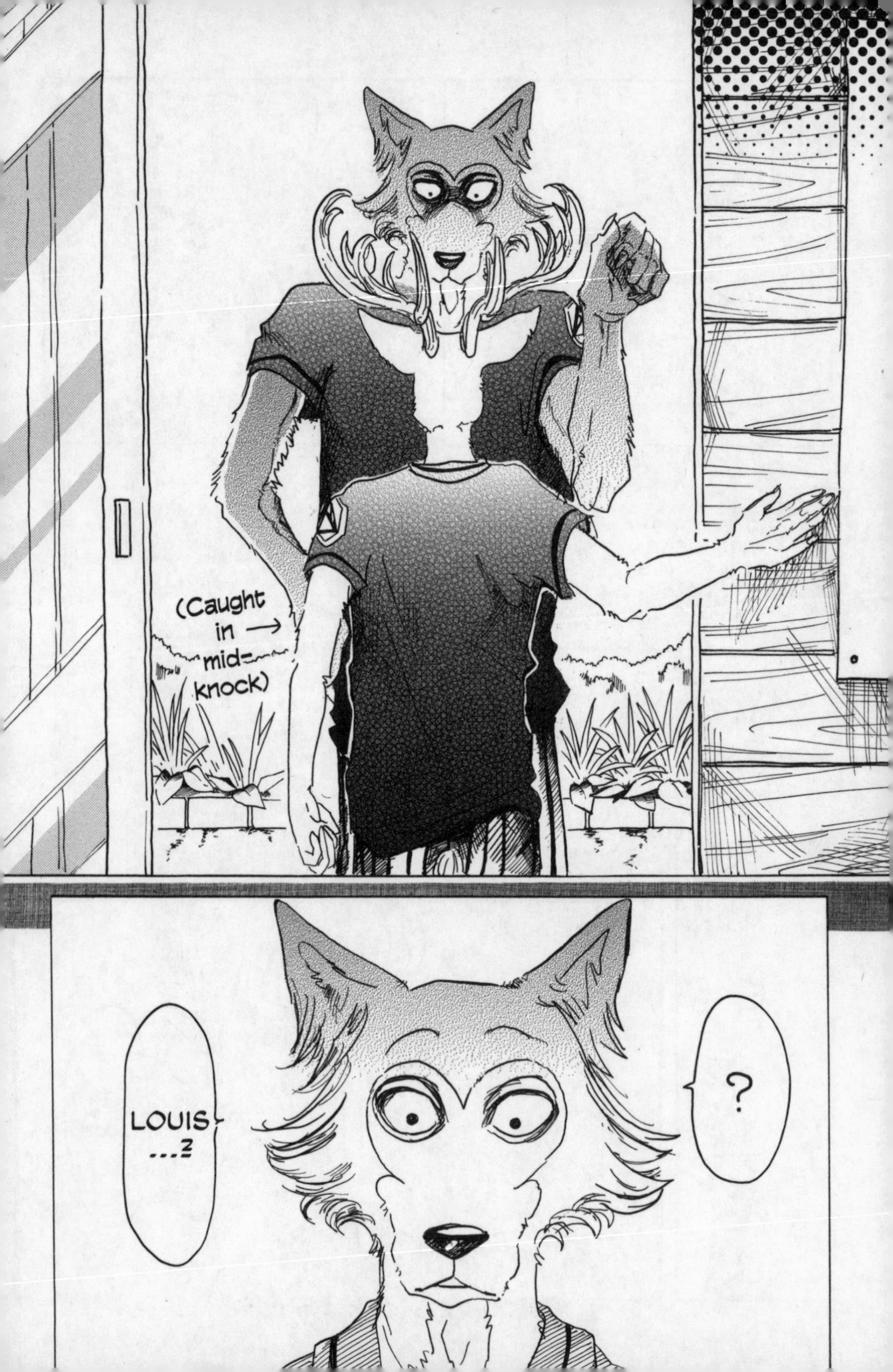
(Caught in mid-knock)
?
LOUIS ...?

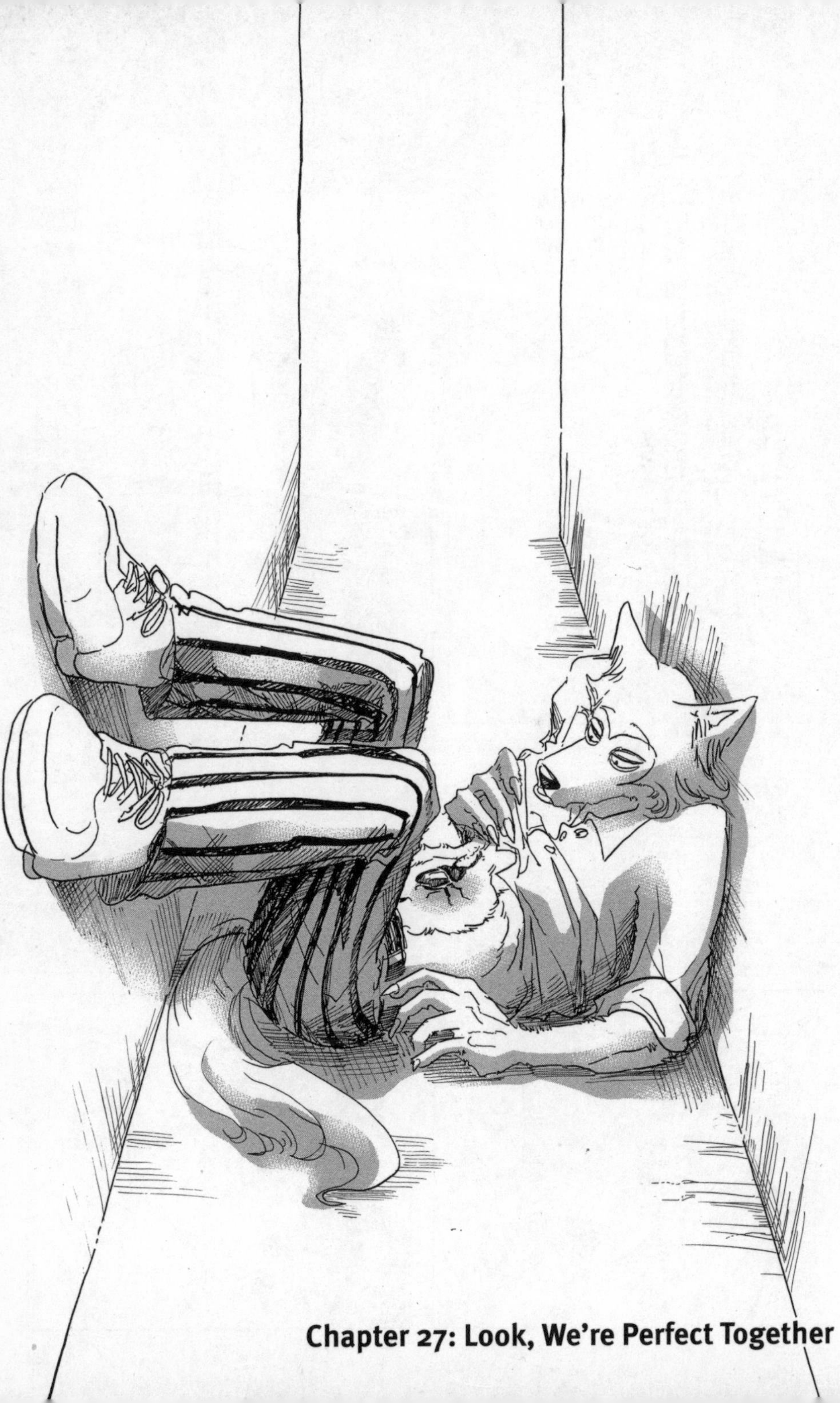

Chapter 27: Look, We're Perfect Together

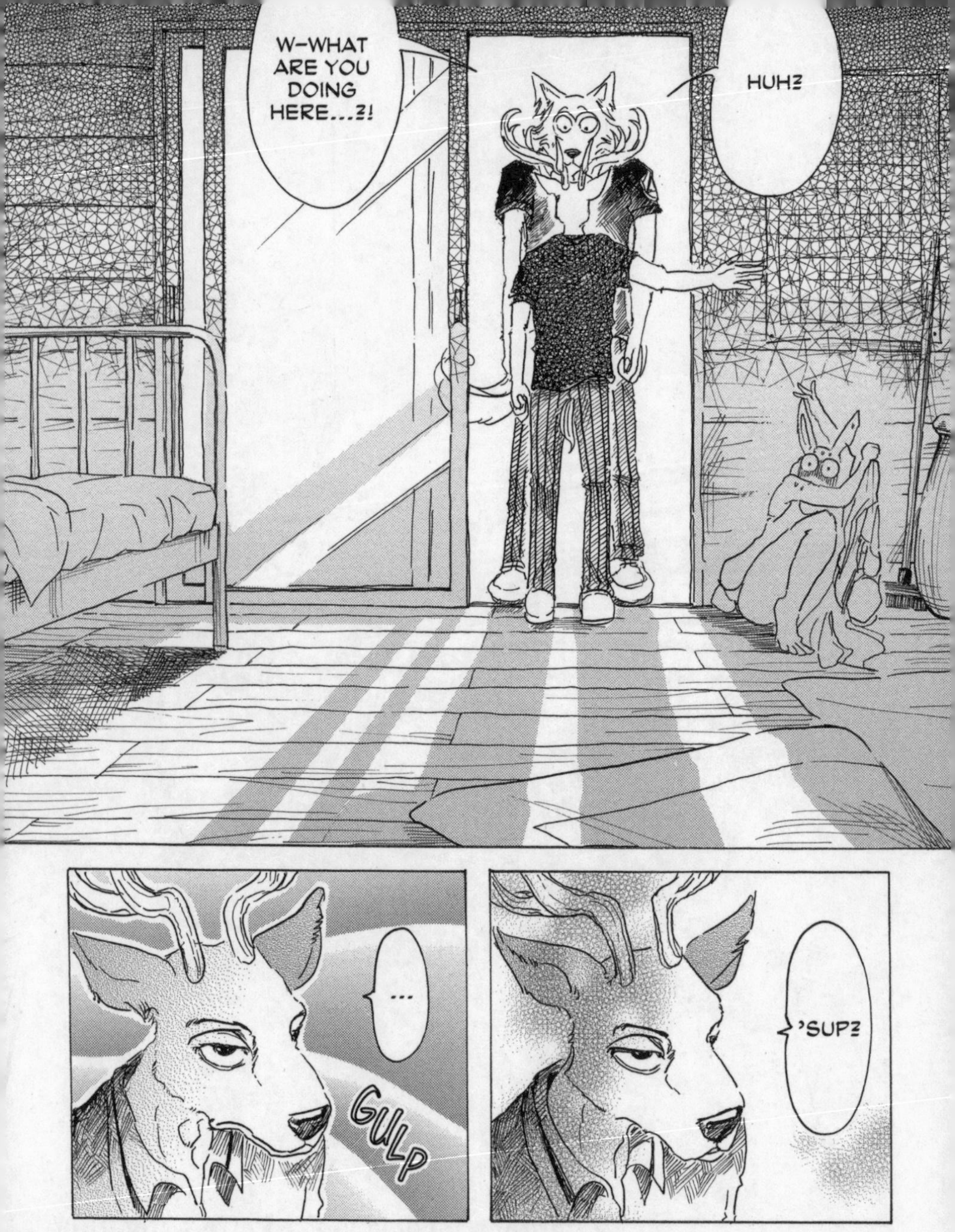
HUH?
W-WHAT ARE YOU DOING HERE...?!
'SUP?
...
GULP

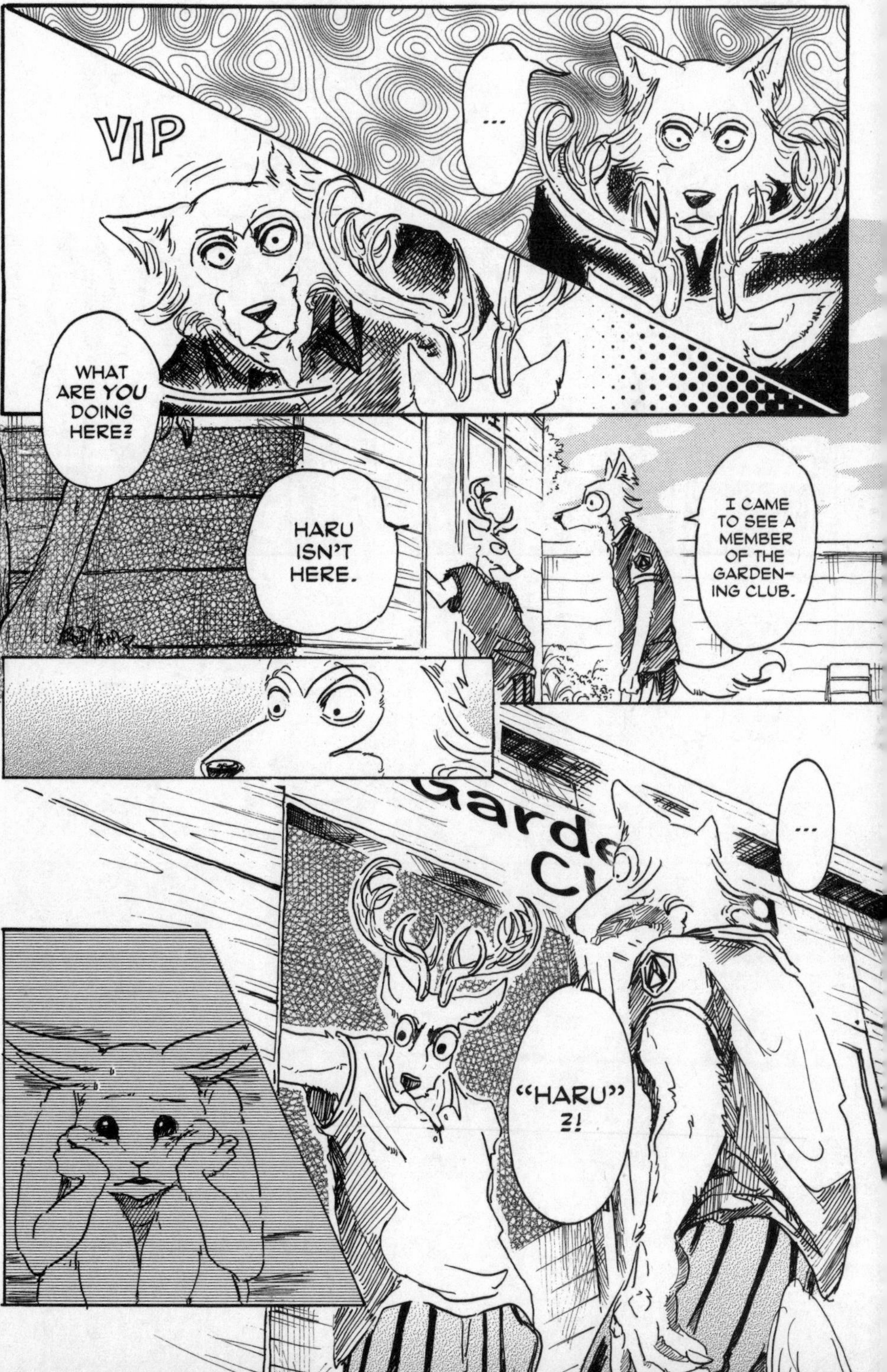
...
VIP
WHAT ARE YOU DOING HERE?
I CAME TO SEE A MEMBER OF THE GARDEN-ING CLUB.
HARU ISN'T HERE.
...
"HARU" ?!

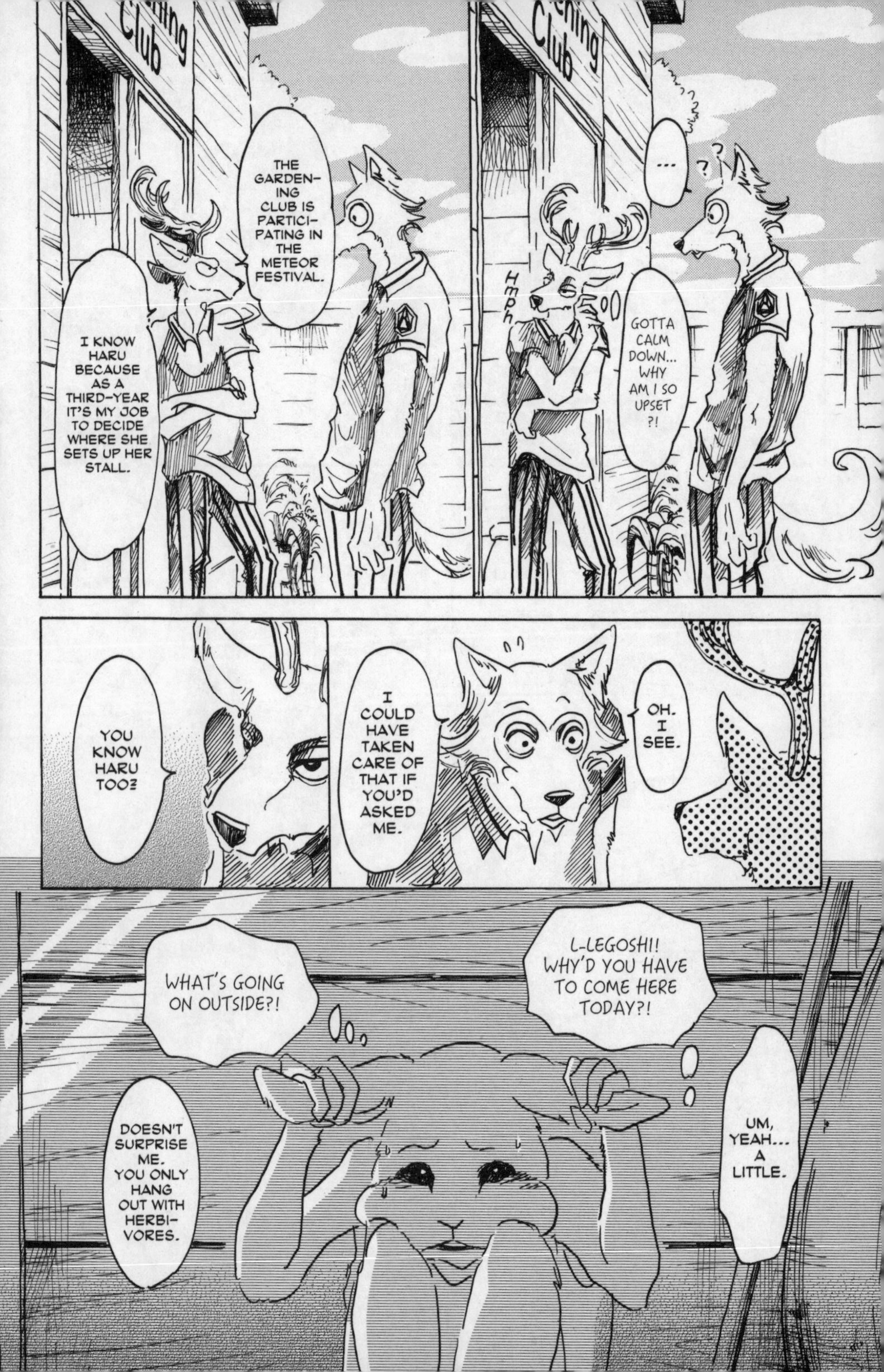
...
Hmph
GOTTA CALM DOWN... WHY AM I SO UPSET?!
THE GARDENING CLUB IS PARTICIPATING IN THE METEOR FESTIVAL.
I KNOW HARU BECAUSE AS A THIRD-YEAR IT'S MY JOB TO DECIDE WHERE SHE SETS UP HER STALL.
OH. I SEE.
I COULD HAVE TAKEN CARE OF THAT IF YOU'D ASKED ME.
YOU KNOW HARU TOO?
L-LEGOSHI! WHY'D YOU HAVE TO COME HERE TODAY?!
UM, YEAH... A LITTLE.
WHAT'S GOING ON OUTSIDE?!
DOESN'T SURPRISE ME. YOU ONLY HANG OUT WITH HERBIVORES.

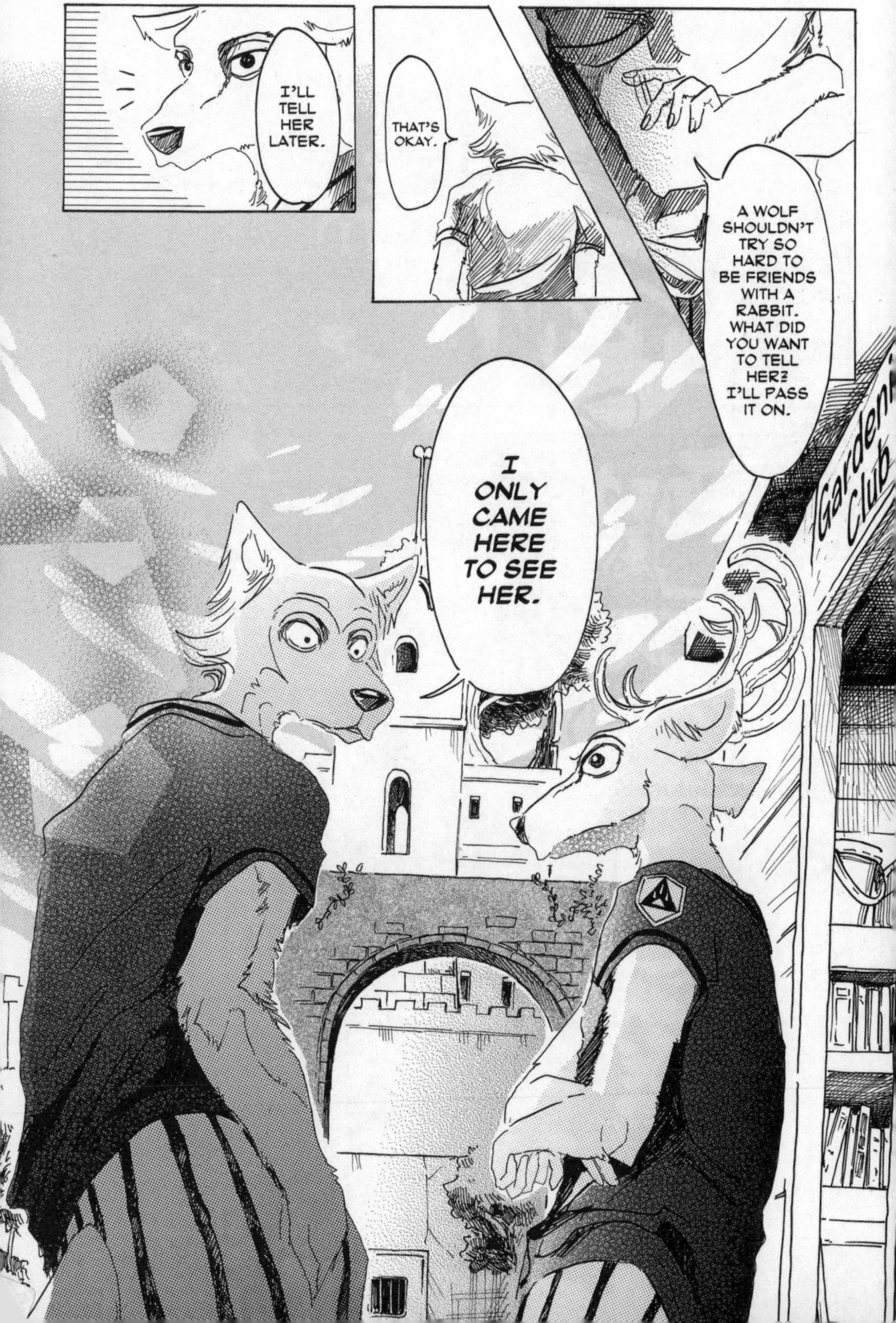
A WOLF SHOULDN'T TRY SO HARD TO BE FRIENDS WITH A RABBIT. WHAT DID YOU WANT TO TELL HER? I'LL PASS IT ON.
THAT'S OKAY.
I'LL TELL HER LATER.
I ONLY CAME HERE TO SEE HER.

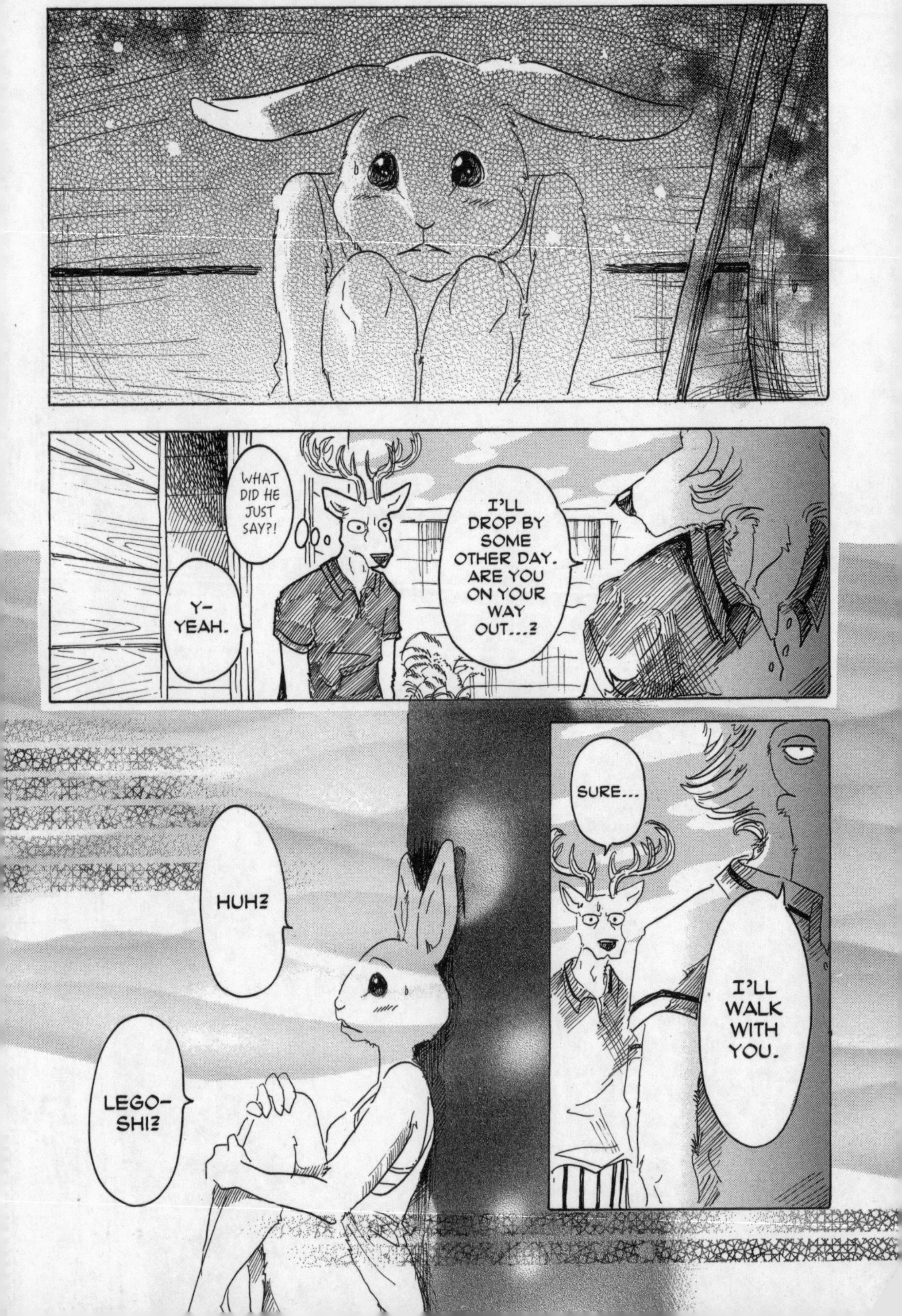
I'LL DROP BY SOME OTHER DAY. ARE YOU ON YOUR WAY OUT...?
WHAT DID HE JUST SAY?!
Y-YEAH.
SURE...
I'LL WALK WITH YOU.
HUH?
LEGO-SHI?

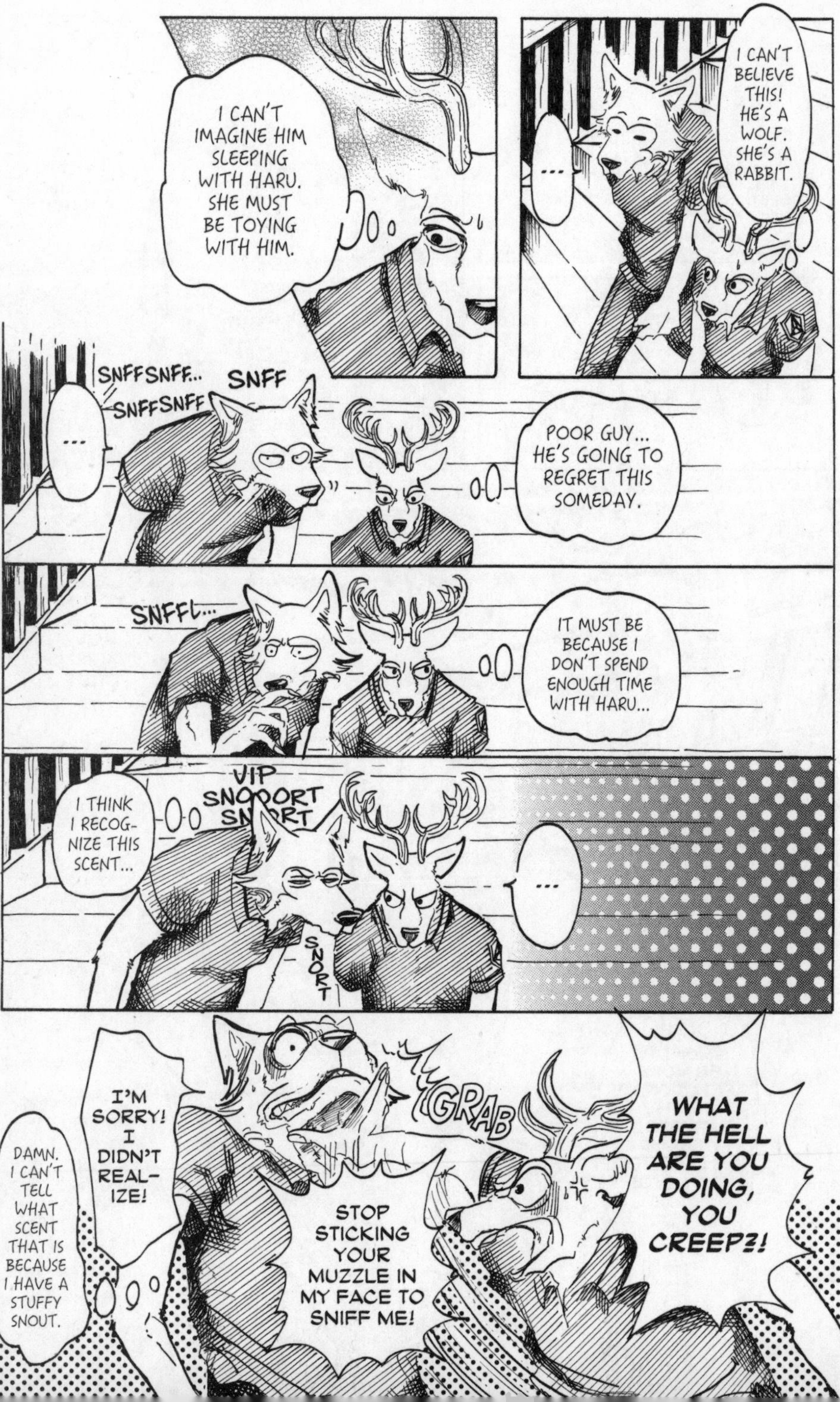
I CAN'T BELIEVE THIS! HE'S A WOLF. SHE'S A RABBIT.
...
I CAN'T IMAGINE HIM SLEEPING WITH HARU. SHE MUST BE TOYING WITH HIM.
POOR GUY... HE'S GOING TO REGRET THIS SOMEDAY.
SNFF
SNFFSNFF...
SNFFSNFF
...
IT MUST BE BECAUSE I DON'T SPEND ENOUGH TIME WITH HARU...
SNFFL...
...
VIP
SNOOORT
SNORT
I THINK I RECOGNIZE THIS SCENT...
SNORT
WHAT THE HELL ARE YOU DOING, YOU CREEP?!
GRAB
STOP STICKING YOUR MUZZLE IN MY FACE TO SNIFF ME!
I'M SORRY! I DIDN'T REALIZE!
DAMN. I CAN'T TELL WHAT SCENT THAT IS BECAUSE I HAVE A STUFFY SNOUT.

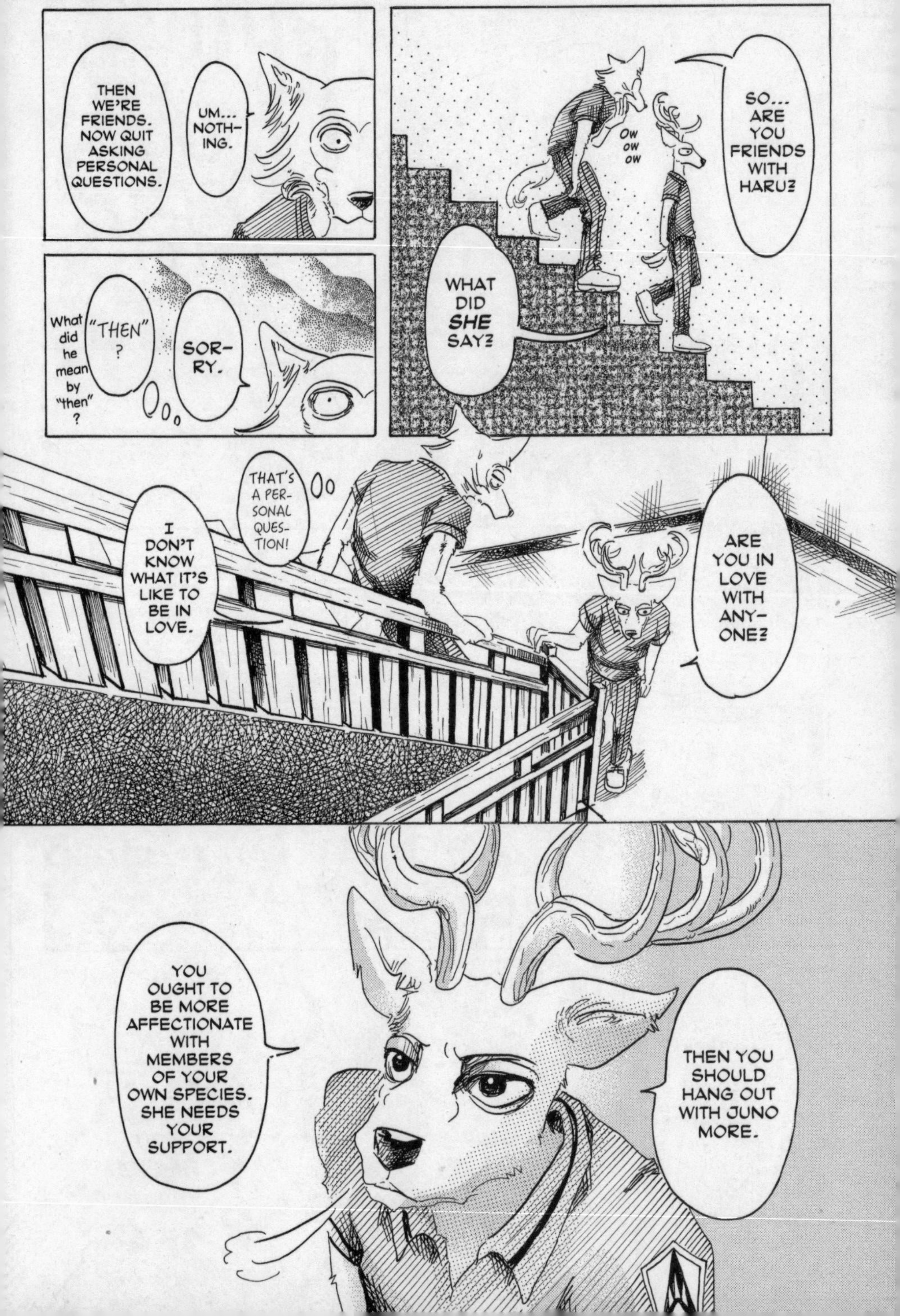
SO... ARE YOU FRIENDS WITH HARU?
OW OW OW
WHAT DID SHE SAY?
UM... NOTHING.
THEN WE'RE FRIENDS. NOW QUIT ASKING PERSONAL QUESTIONS.
SORRY.
"THEN"?
What did he mean by "then"?
ARE YOU IN LOVE WITH ANYONE?
THAT'S A PERSONAL QUESTION!
I DON'T KNOW WHAT IT'S LIKE TO BE IN LOVE.
THEN YOU SHOULD HANG OUT WITH JUNO MORE.
YOU OUGHT TO BE MORE AFFECTIONATE WITH MEMBERS OF YOUR OWN SPECIES. SHE NEEDS YOUR SUPPORT.

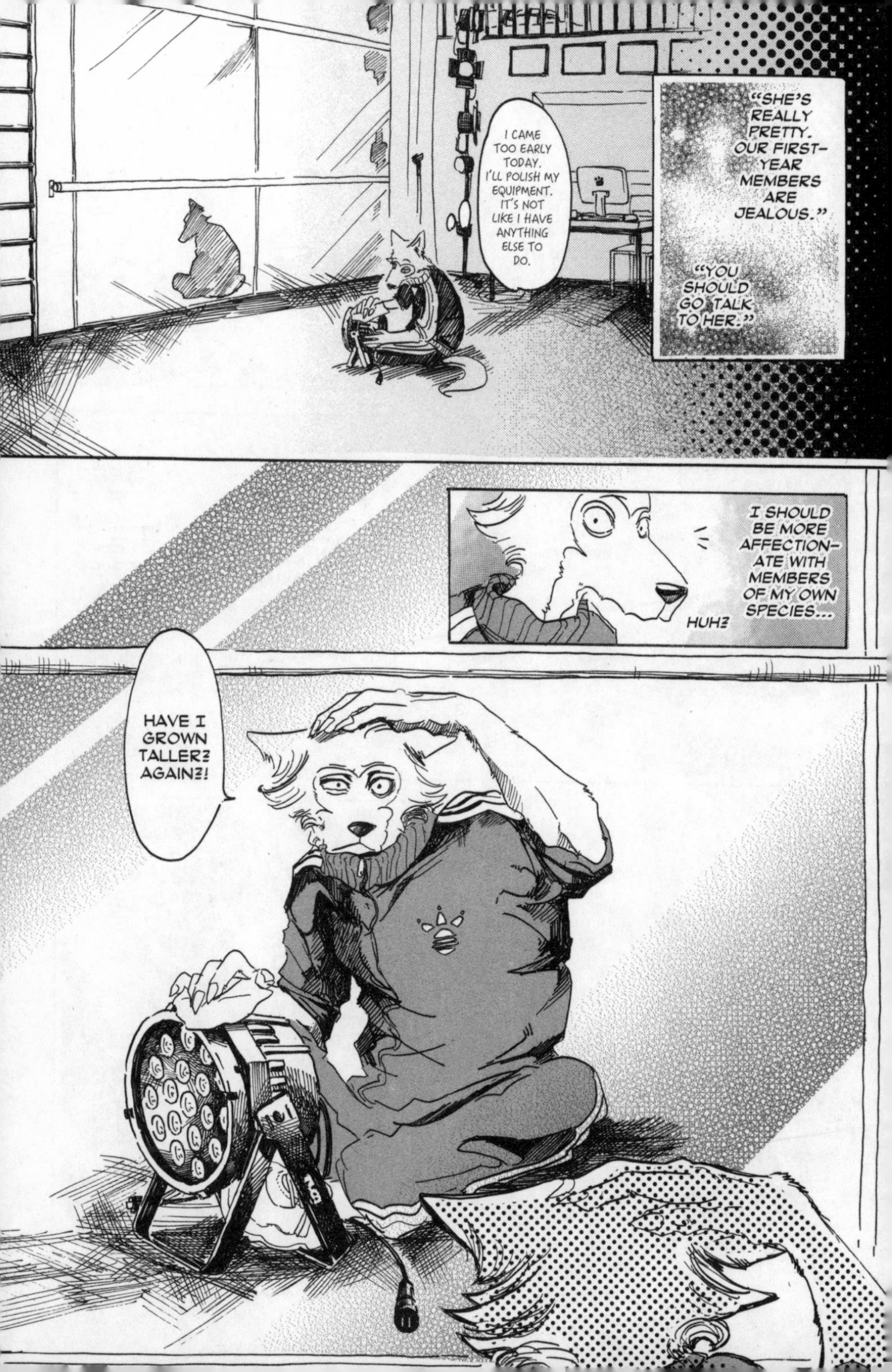
"SHE'S REALLY PRETTY. OUR FIRST-YEAR MEMBERS ARE JEALOUS."
"YOU SHOULD GO TALK TO HER."
I CAME TOO EARLY TODAY. I'LL POLISH MY EQUIPMENT. IT'S NOT LIKE I HAVE ANYTHING ELSE TO DO.
I SHOULD BE MORE AFFECTION-ATE WITH MEMBERS OF MY OWN SPECIES...
HUH?
HAVE I GROWN TALLER?! AGAIN?!

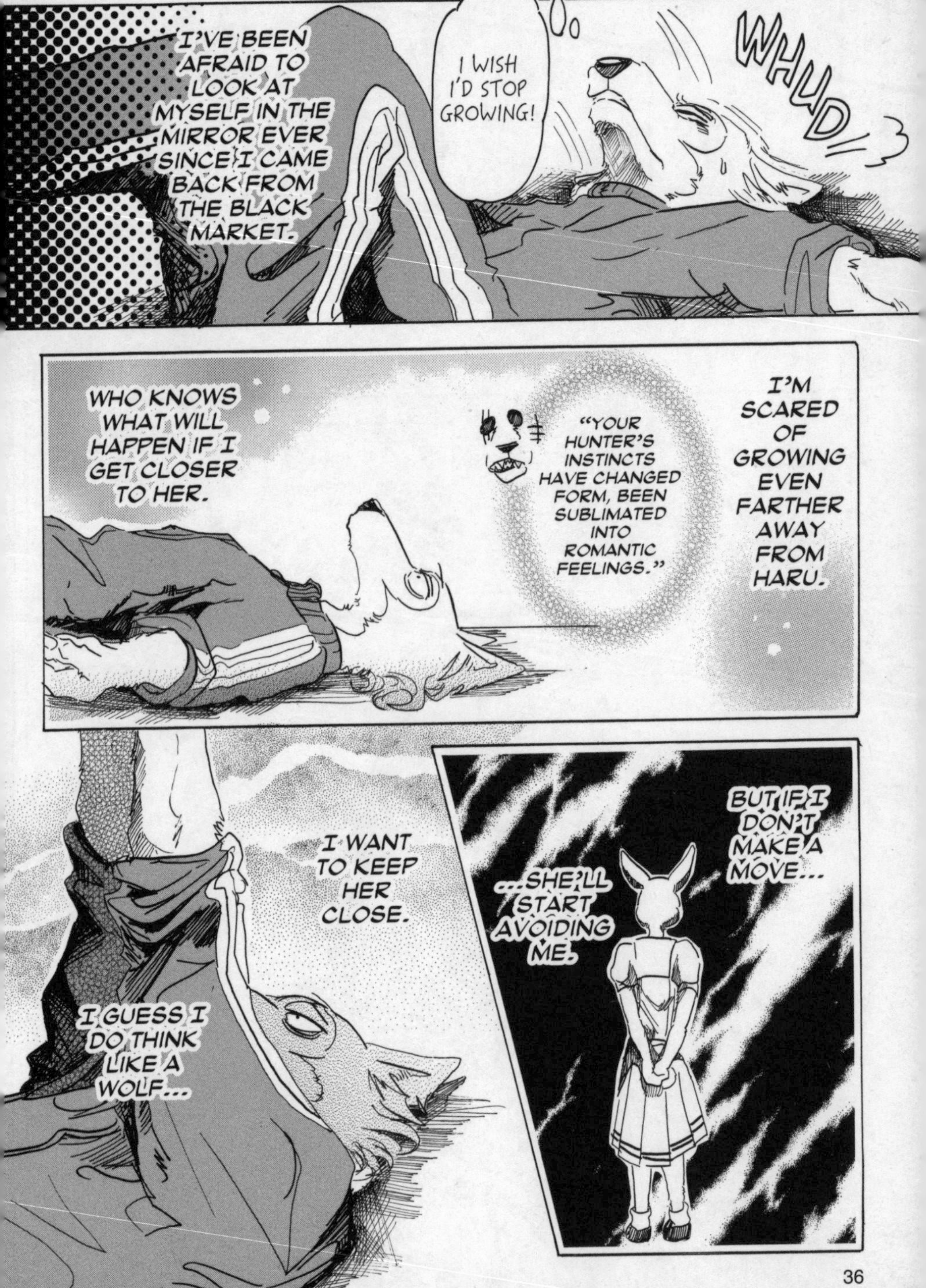
WHUD
I WISH I'D STOP GROWING!
I'VE BEEN AFRAID TO LOOK AT MYSELF IN THE MIRROR EVER SINCE I CAME BACK FROM THE BLACK MARKET.
I'M SCARED OF GROWING EVEN FARTHER AWAY FROM HARU.
"YOUR HUNTER'S INSTINCTS HAVE CHANGED FORM, BEEN SUBLIMATED INTO ROMANTIC FEELINGS."
WHO KNOWS WHAT WILL HAPPEN IF I GET CLOSER TO HER.
BUT IF I DON'T MAKE A MOVE...
...SHE'LL START AVOIDING ME.
I WANT TO KEEP HER CLOSE.
I GUESS I DO THINK LIKE A WOLF...

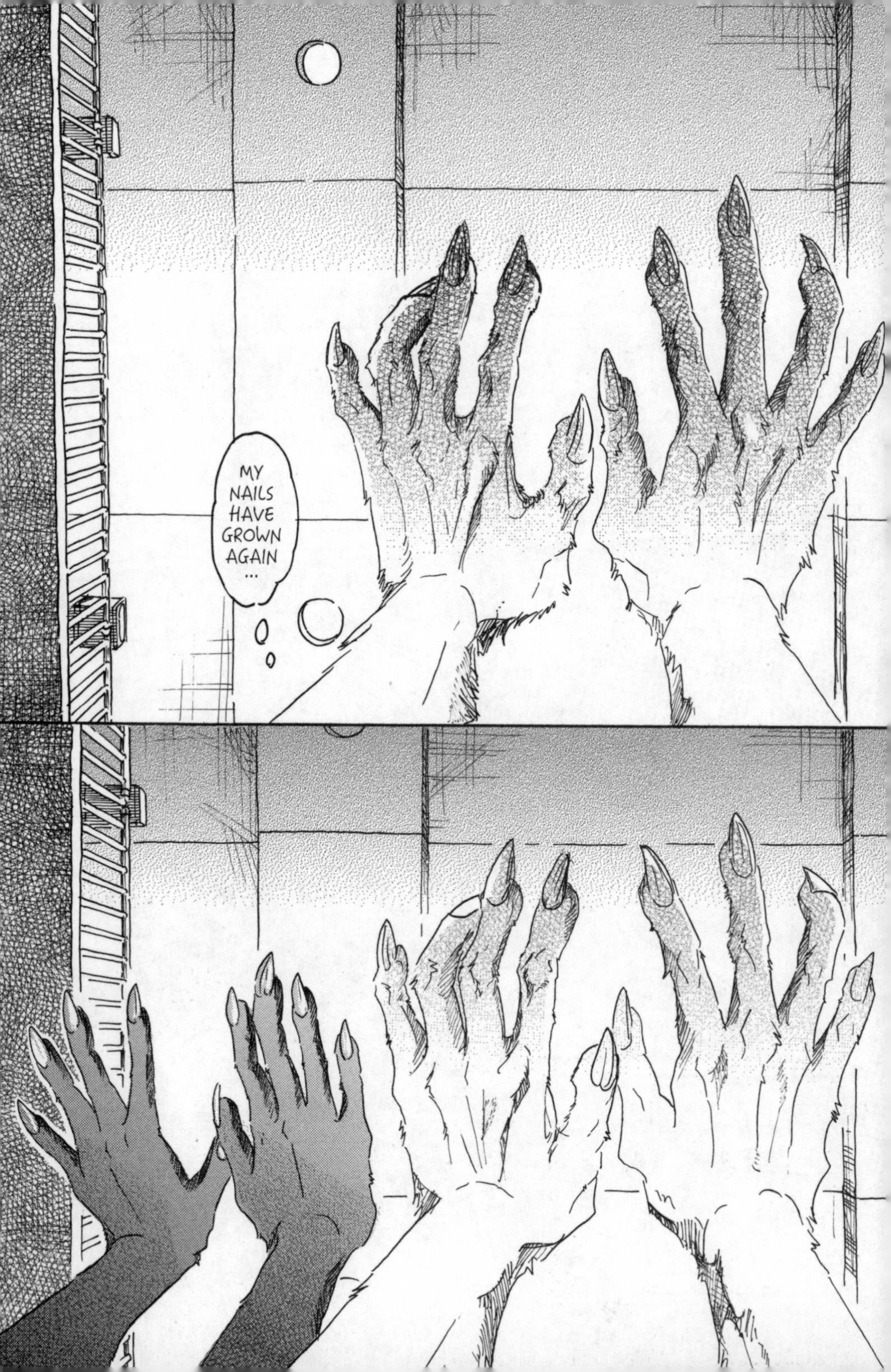
MY NAILS HAVE GROWN AGAIN ...

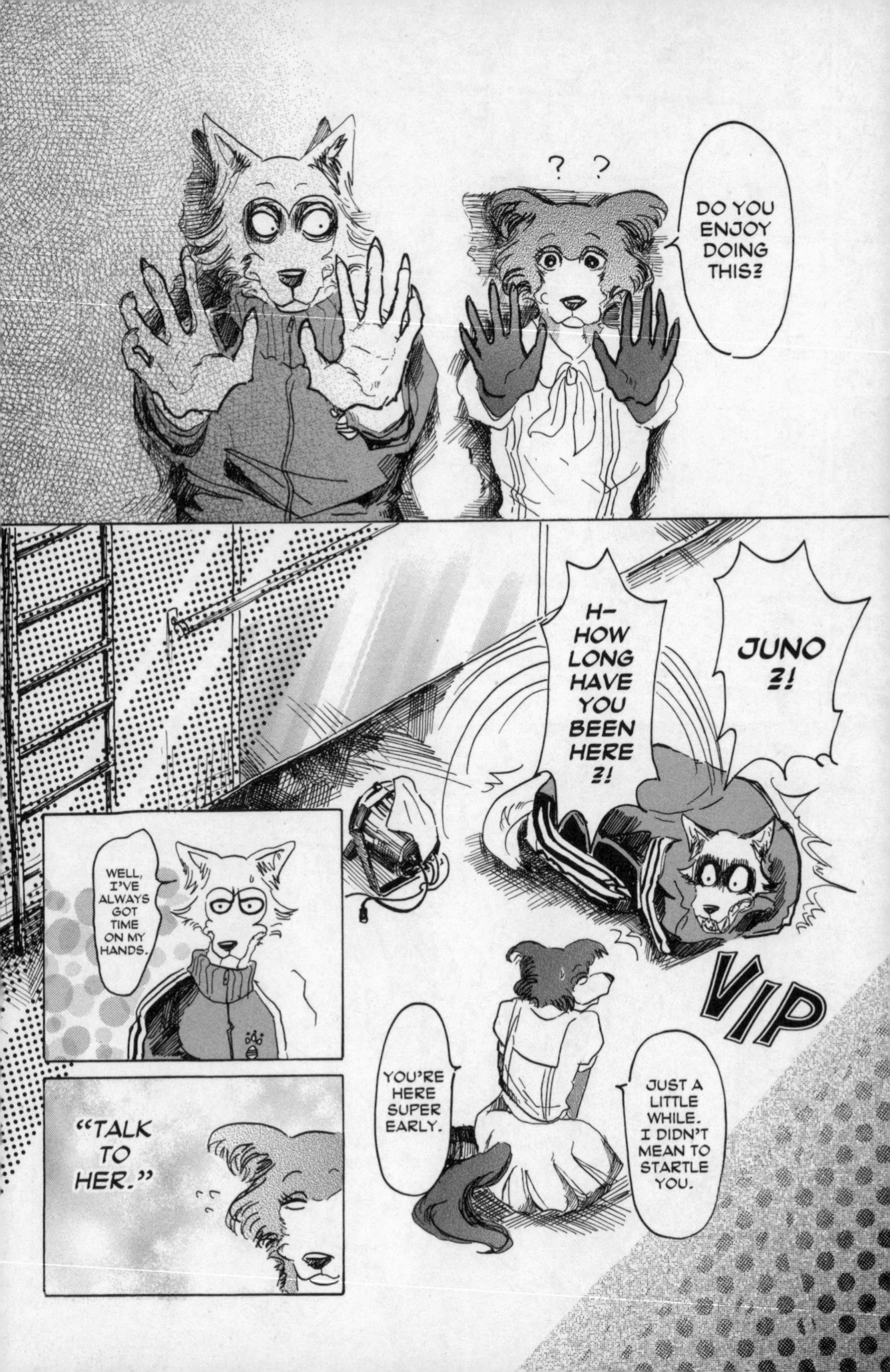

? ?
DO YOU ENJOY DOING THIS?
JUNO?!
H-HOW LONG HAVE YOU BEEN HERE?!
VIP
JUST A LITTLE WHILE. I DIDN'T MEAN TO STARTLE YOU.
YOU'RE HERE SUPER EARLY.
WELL, I'VE ALWAYS GOT TIME ON MY HANDS.
"TALK TO HER."

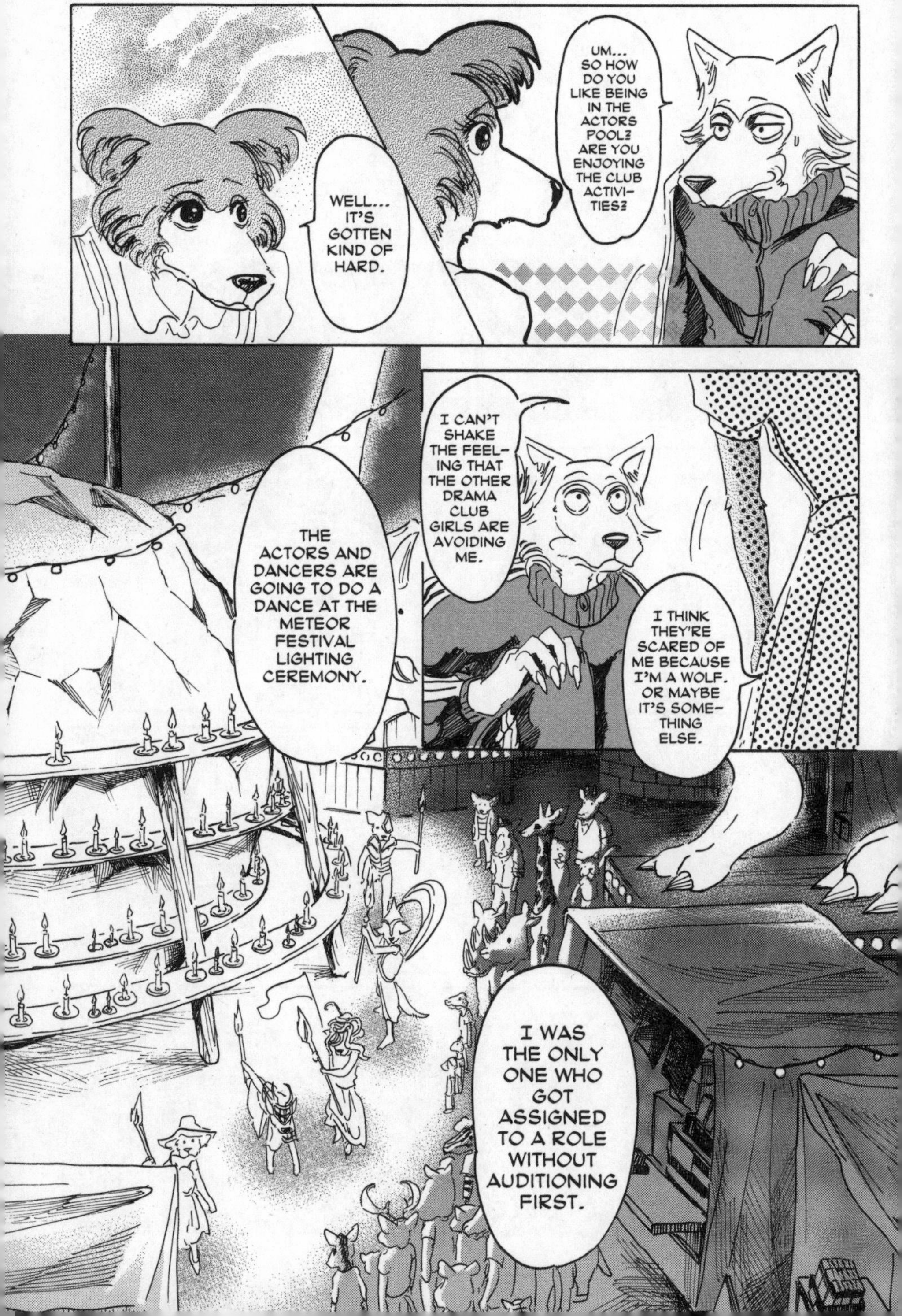
UM... SO HOW DO YOU LIKE BEING IN THE ACTORS POOL? ARE YOU ENJOYING THE CLUB ACTIVITIES?
WELL... IT'S GOTTEN KIND OF HARD.
I CAN'T SHAKE THE FEELING THAT THE OTHER DRAMA CLUB GIRLS ARE AVOIDING ME.
I THINK THEY'RE SCARED OF ME BECAUSE I'M A WOLF. OR MAYBE IT'S SOMETHING ELSE.
THE ACTORS AND DANCERS ARE GOING TO DO A DANCE AT THE METEOR FESTIVAL LIGHTING CEREMONY.
I WAS THE ONLY ONE WHO GOT ASSIGNED TO A ROLE WITHOUT AUDITIONING FIRST.

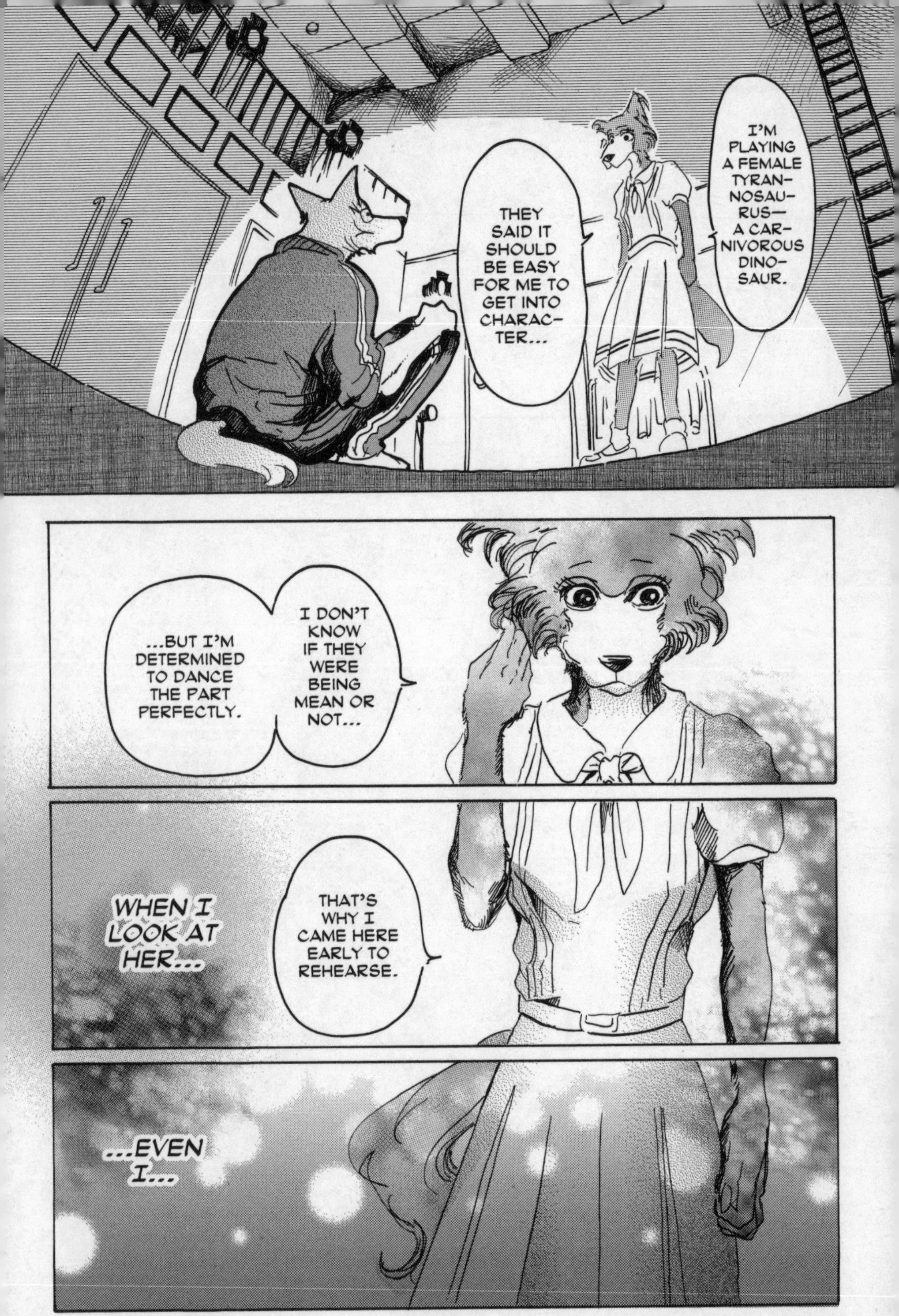
I'M PLAYING A FEMALE TYRANNOSAURUS—A CARNIVOROUS DINOSAUR.
THEY SAID IT SHOULD BE EASY FOR ME TO GET INTO CHARACTER...
I DON'T KNOW IF THEY WERE BEING MEAN OR NOT...
...BUT I'M DETERMINED TO DANCE THE PART PERFECTLY.
THAT'S WHY I CAME HERE EARLY TO REHEARSE.
WHEN I LOOK AT HER...
...EVEN I...

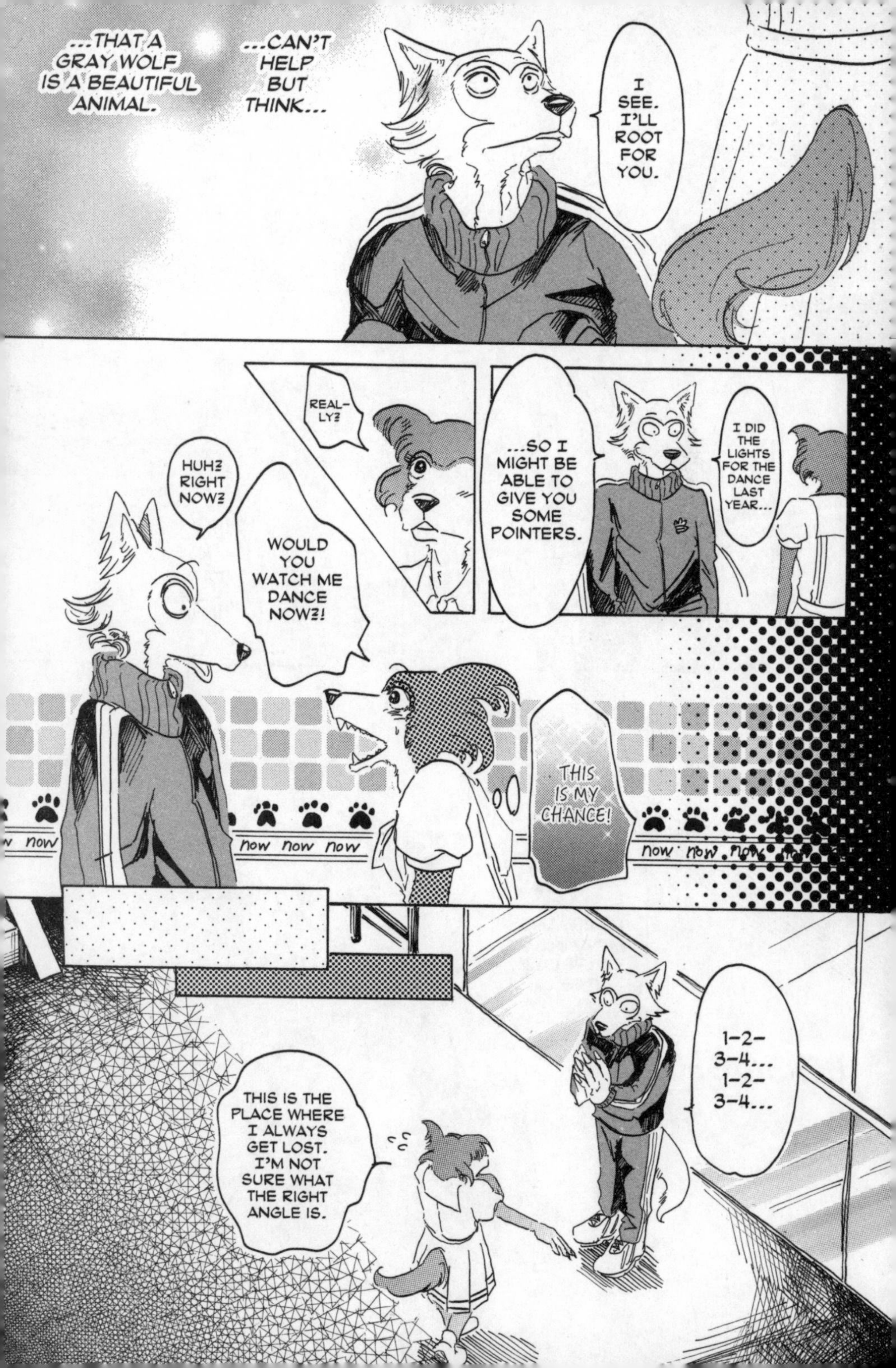
I SEE. I'LL ROOT FOR YOU.
...CAN'T HELP BUT THINK...
...THAT A GRAY WOLF IS A BEAUTIFUL ANIMAL.
I DID THE LIGHTS FOR THE DANCE LAST YEAR...
...SO I MIGHT BE ABLE TO GIVE YOU SOME POINTERS.
REAL-LY?
WOULD YOU WATCH ME DANCE NOW?!
HUH? RIGHT NOW?
THIS IS MY CHANCE!
now now now now
now now now
now now
1-2-3-4... 1-2-3-4...
THIS IS THE PLACE WHERE I ALWAYS GET LOST. I'M NOT SURE WHAT THE RIGHT ANGLE IS.

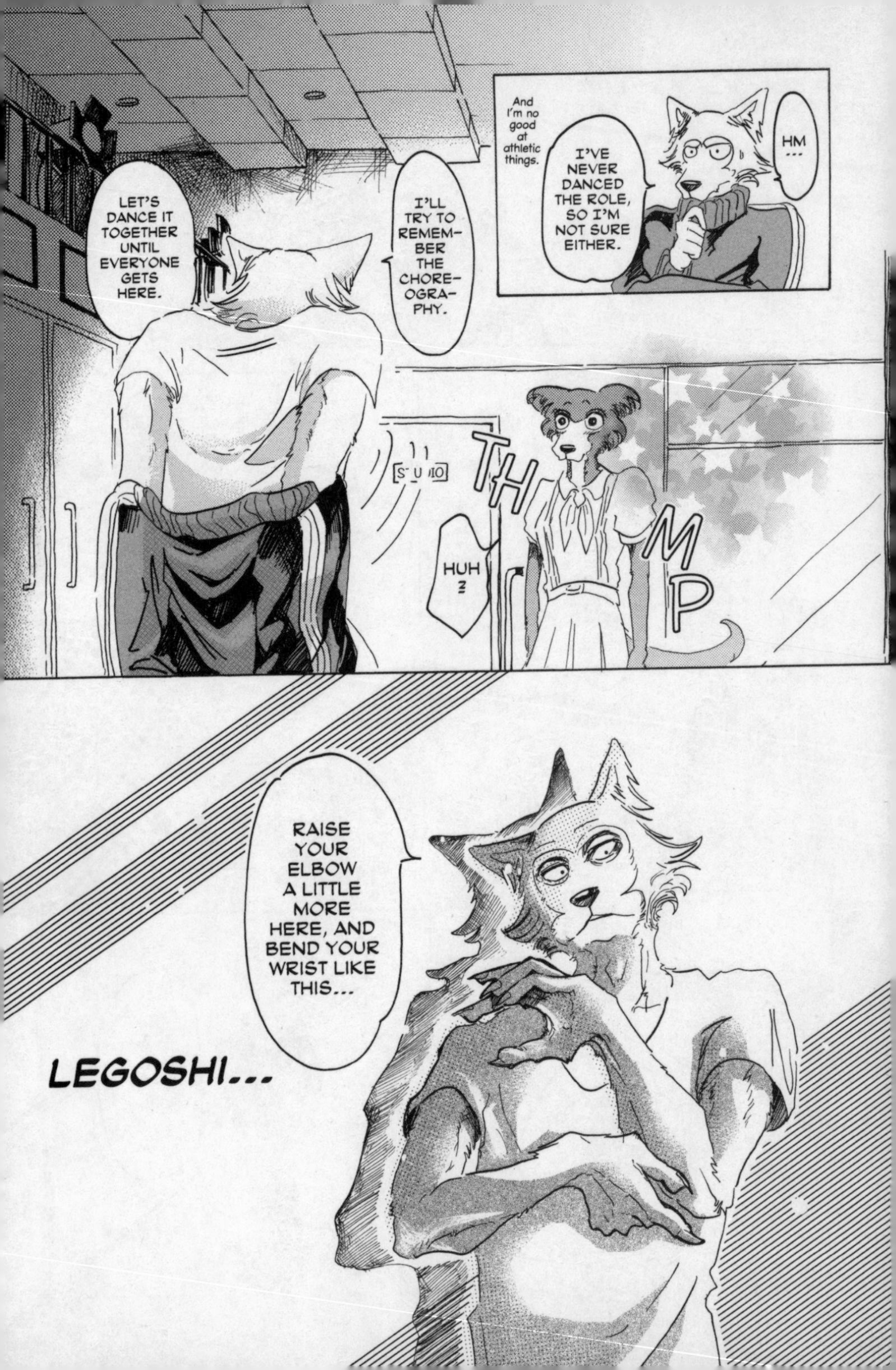
HM...
I'VE NEVER DANCED THE ROLE, SO I'M NOT SURE EITHER.
And I'm no good at athletic things.
I'LL TRY TO REMEMBER THE CHOREOGRAPHY.
LET'S DANCE IT TOGETHER UNTIL EVERYONE GETS HERE.
THUMP
HUH?
RAISE YOUR ELBOW A LITTLE MORE HERE, AND BEND YOUR WRIST LIKE THIS...
LEGOSHI...

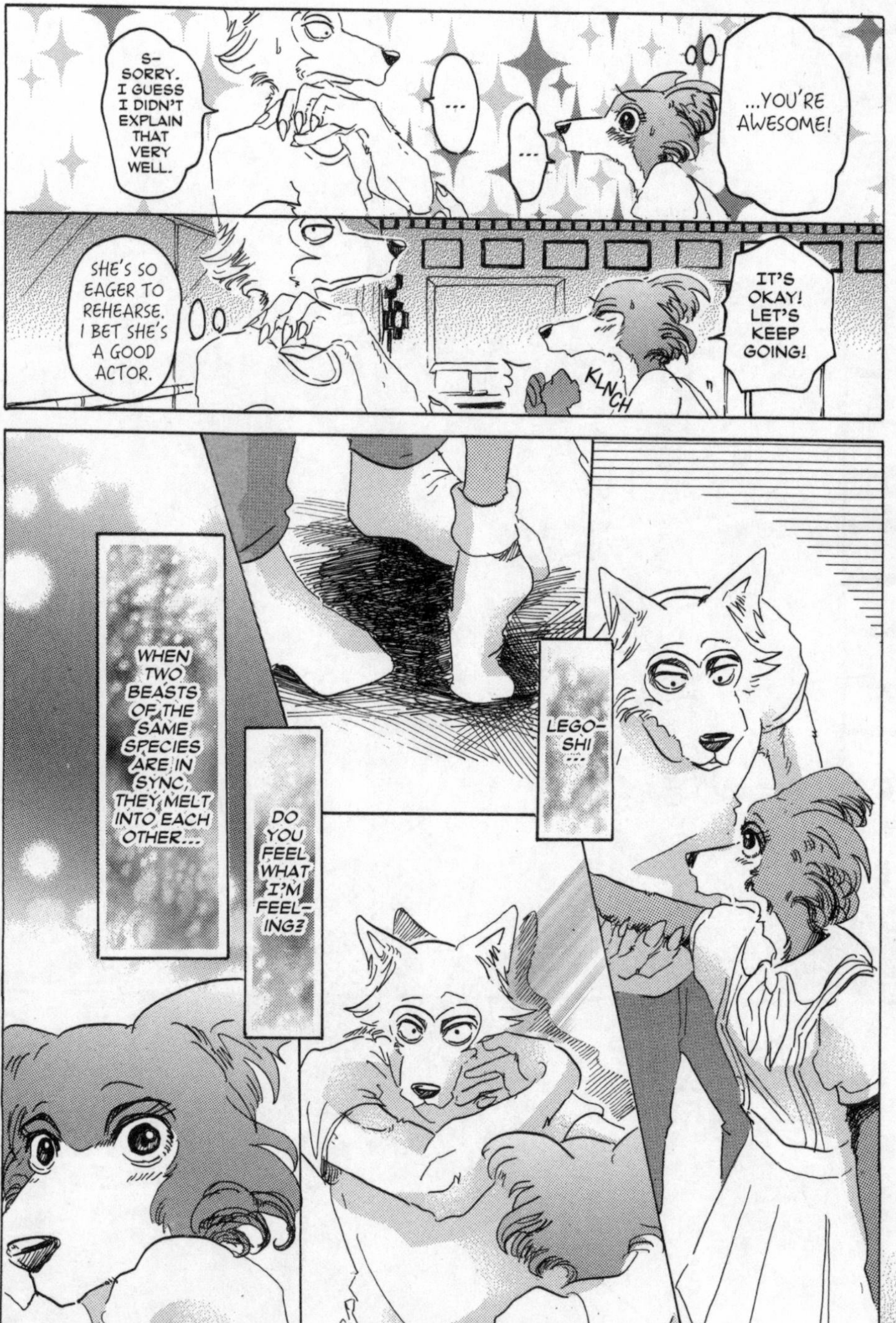
...YOU'RE AWESOME!
...
...
S-SORRY. I GUESS I DIDN'T EXPLAIN THAT VERY WELL.
IT'S OKAY! LET'S KEEP GOING!
KLNCH
SHE'S SO EAGER TO REHEARSE. I BET SHE'S A GOOD ACTOR.
LEGO-SHI...
WHEN TWO BEASTS OF THE SAME SPECIES ARE IN SYNC, THEY MELT INTO EACH OTHER...
DO YOU FEEL WHAT I'M FEEL-ING?

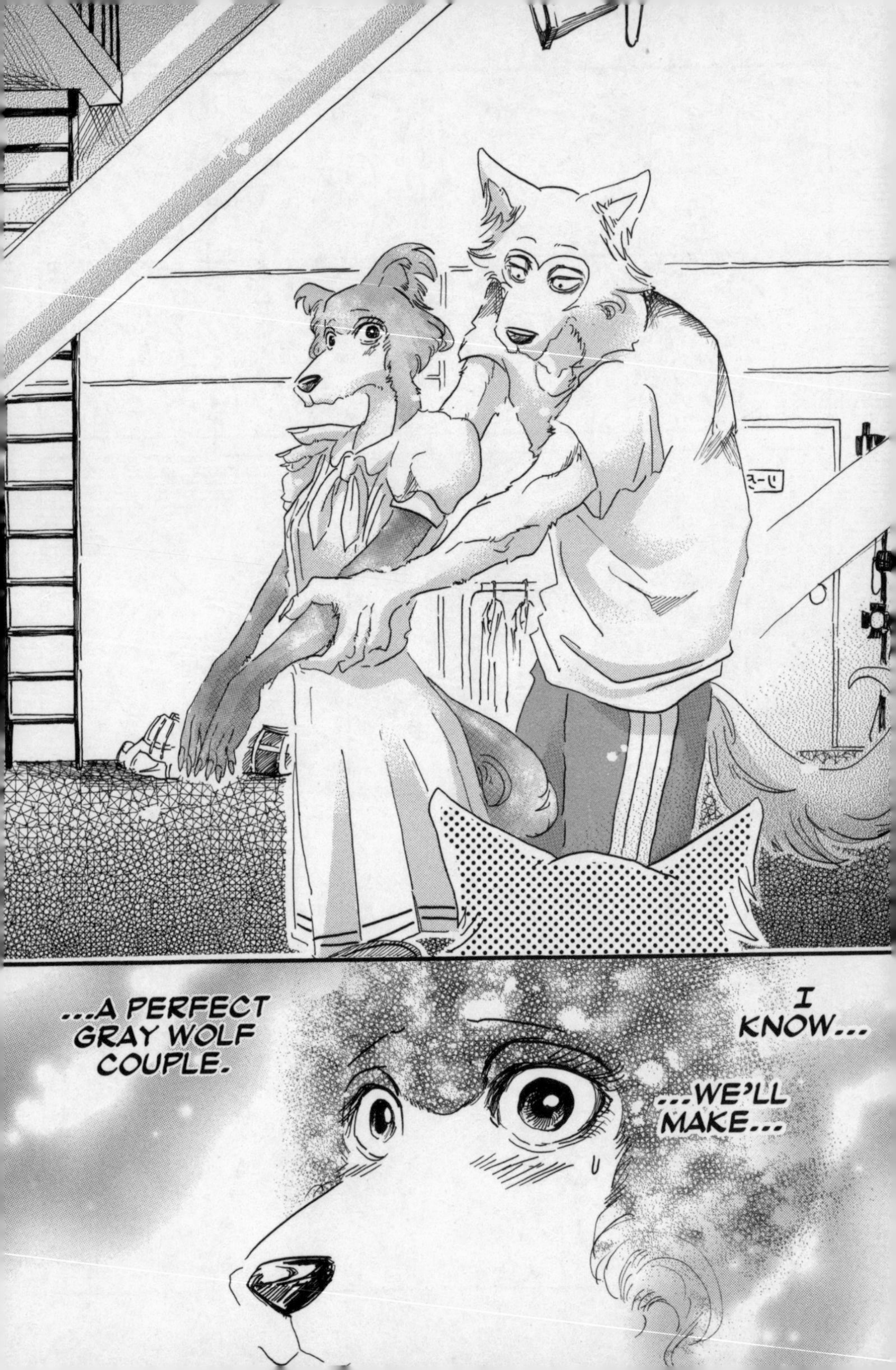
I KNOW...
...WE'LL MAKE...
...A PERFECT GRAY WOLF COUPLE.

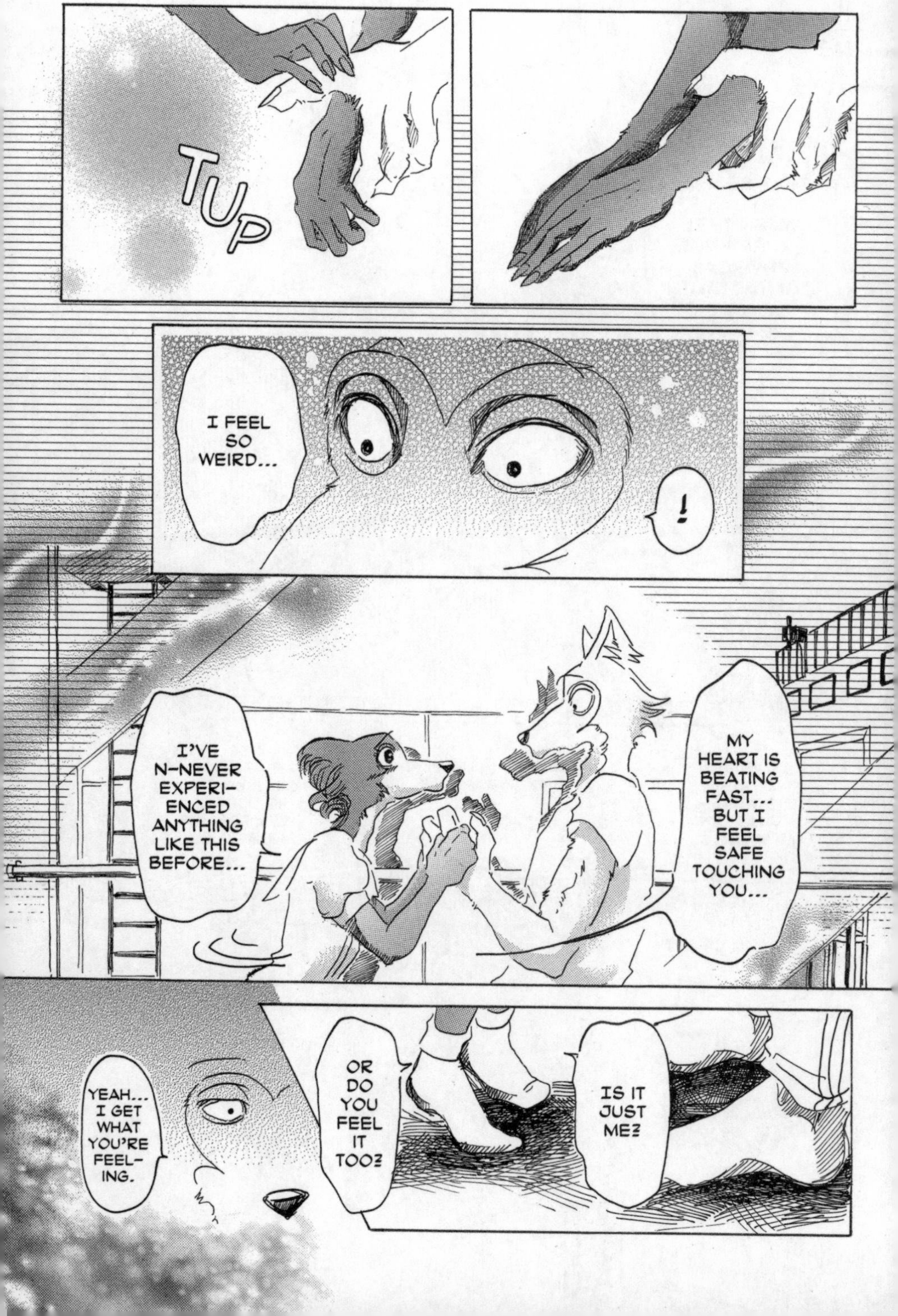
TUP
!
I FEEL SO WEIRD...
MY HEART IS BEATING FAST... BUT I FEEL SAFE TOUCHING YOU...
I'VE N-NEVER EXPERIENCED ANYTHING LIKE THIS BEFORE...
IS IT JUST ME?
OR DO YOU FEEL IT TOO?
YEAH... I GET WHAT YOU'RE FEELING.

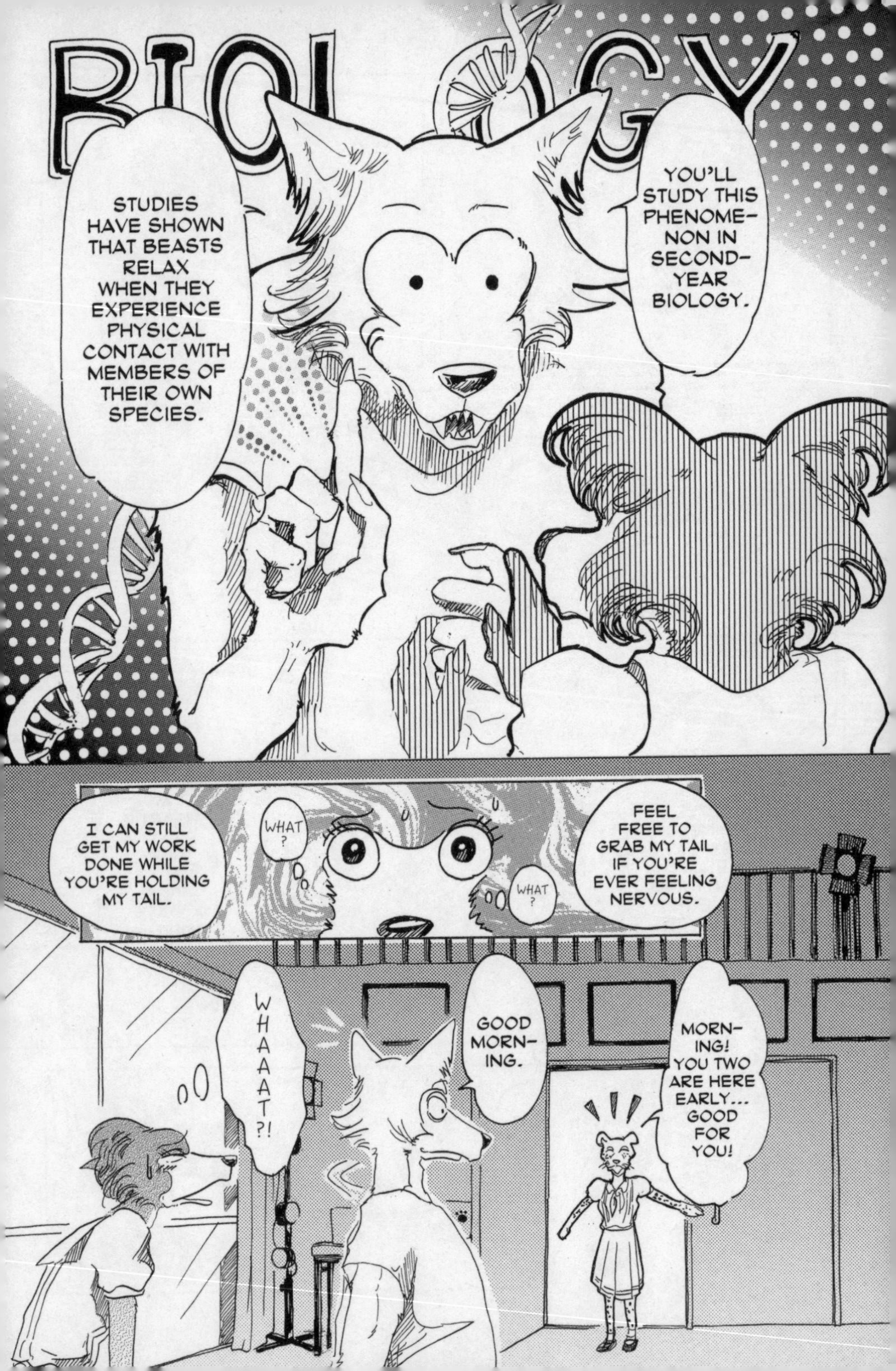
BIOLOGY
YOU'LL STUDY THIS PHENOMENON IN SECOND-YEAR BIOLOGY.
STUDIES HAVE SHOWN THAT BEASTS RELAX WHEN THEY EXPERIENCE PHYSICAL CONTACT WITH MEMBERS OF THEIR OWN SPECIES.
FEEL FREE TO GRAB MY TAIL IF YOU'RE EVER FEELING NERVOUS.
WHAT?
WHAT?
I CAN STILL GET MY WORK DONE WHILE YOU'RE HOLDING MY TAIL.
MORNING! YOU TWO ARE HERE EARLY... GOOD FOR YOU!
GOOD MORNING.
WHAAAT?!

Chapter 28: His Feelings Are Richly Colored

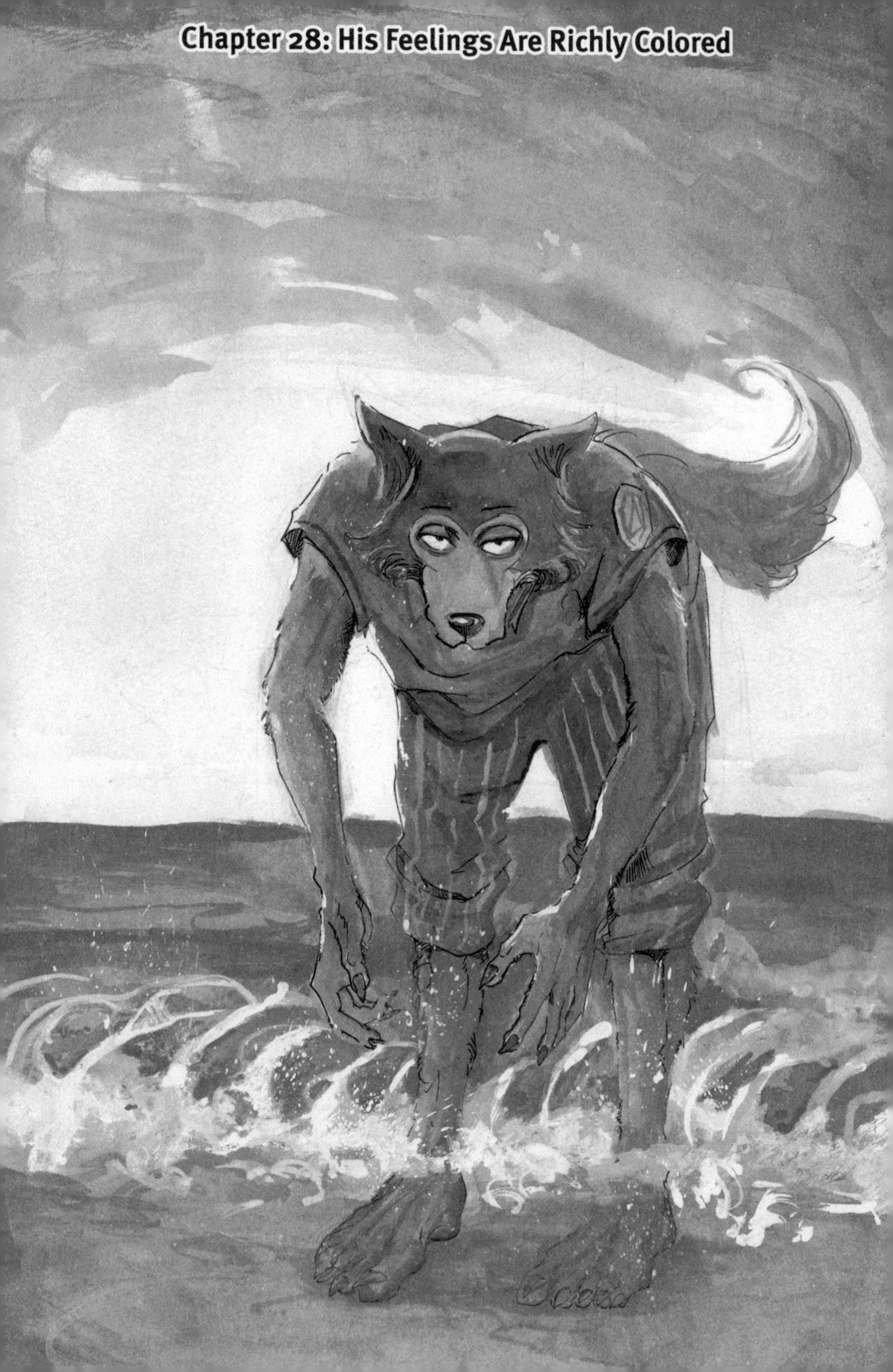

**BEASTARS
Vol. 4**

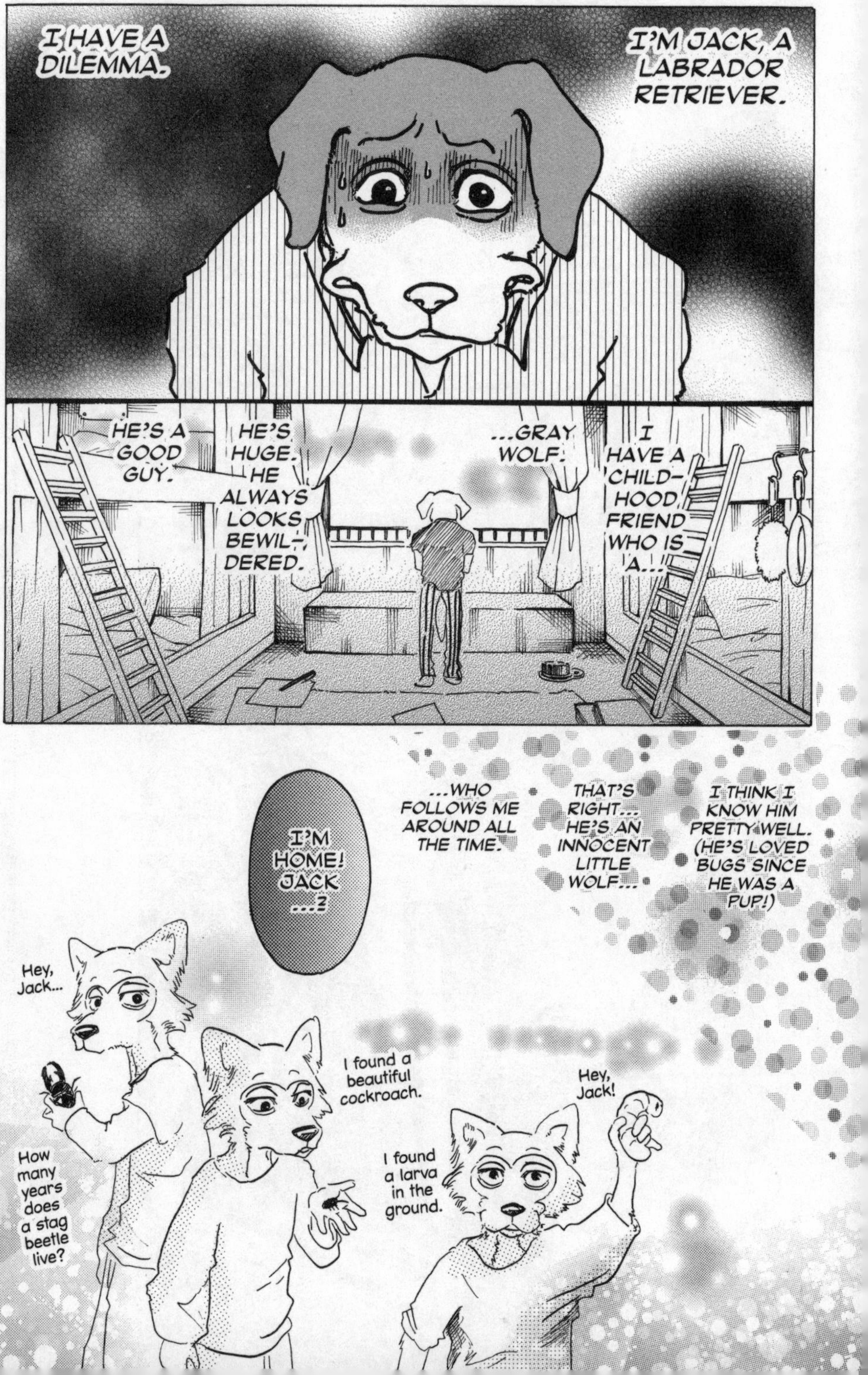
I'M JACK, A LABRADOR RETRIEVER.
I HAVE A DILEMMA.
I HAVE A CHILDHOOD FRIEND WHO IS A...
...GRAY WOLF.
HE'S HUGE. HE ALWAYS LOOKS BEWILDERED.
HE'S A GOOD GUY.
I THINK I KNOW HIM PRETTY WELL. (HE'S LOVED BUGS SINCE HE WAS A PUP!)
THAT'S RIGHT... HE'S AN INNOCENT LITTLE WOLF...
...WHO FOLLOWS ME AROUND ALL THE TIME.
I'M HOME! JACK ...?
Hey, Jack!
I found a larva in the ground.
I found a beautiful cockroach.
Hey, Jack...
How many years does a stag beetle live?

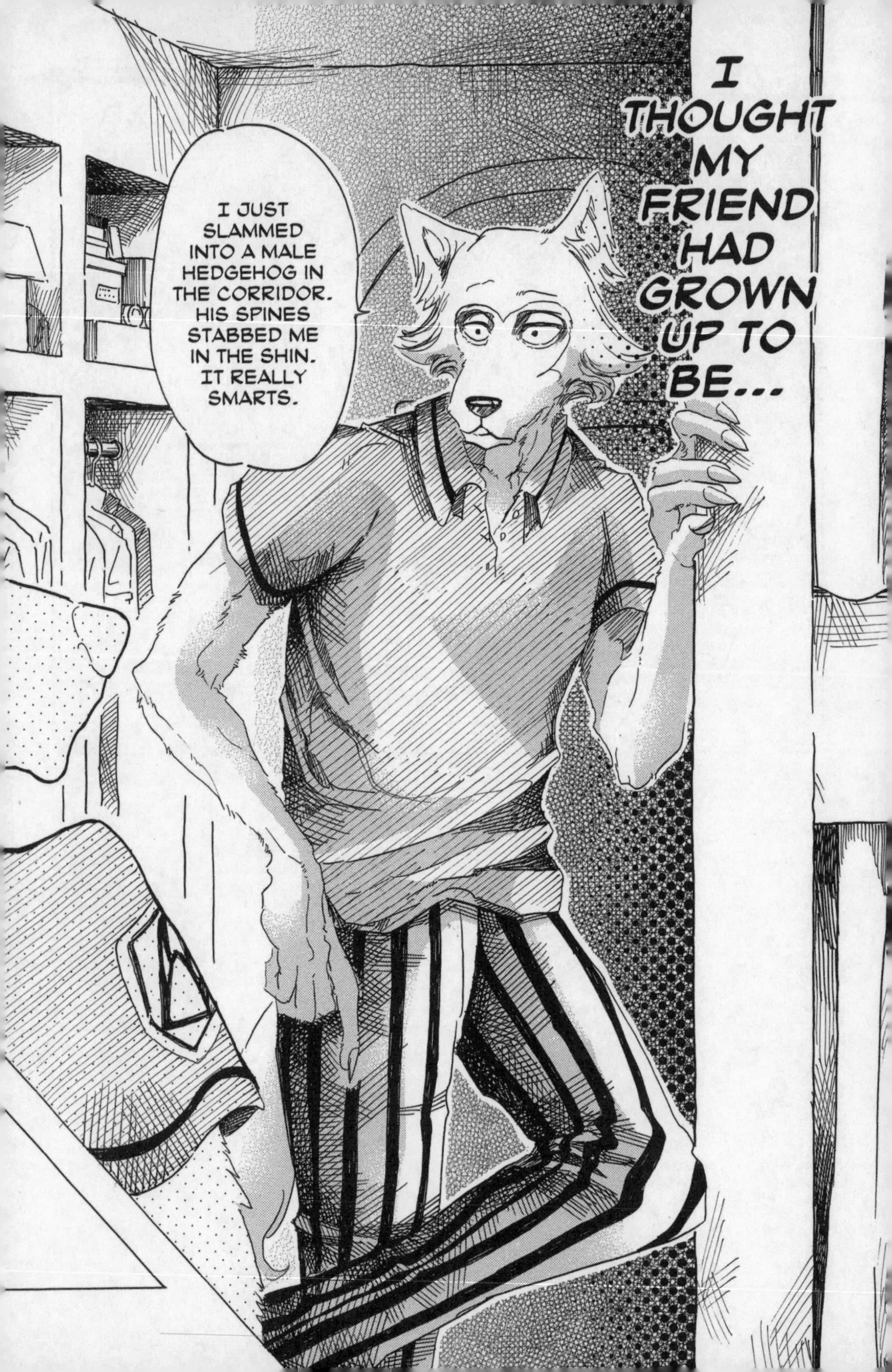
I THOUGHT MY FRIEND HAD GROWN UP TO BE...
I JUST SLAMMED INTO A MALE HEDGEHOG IN THE CORRIDOR. HIS SPINES STABBED ME IN THE SHIN. IT REALLY SMARTS.

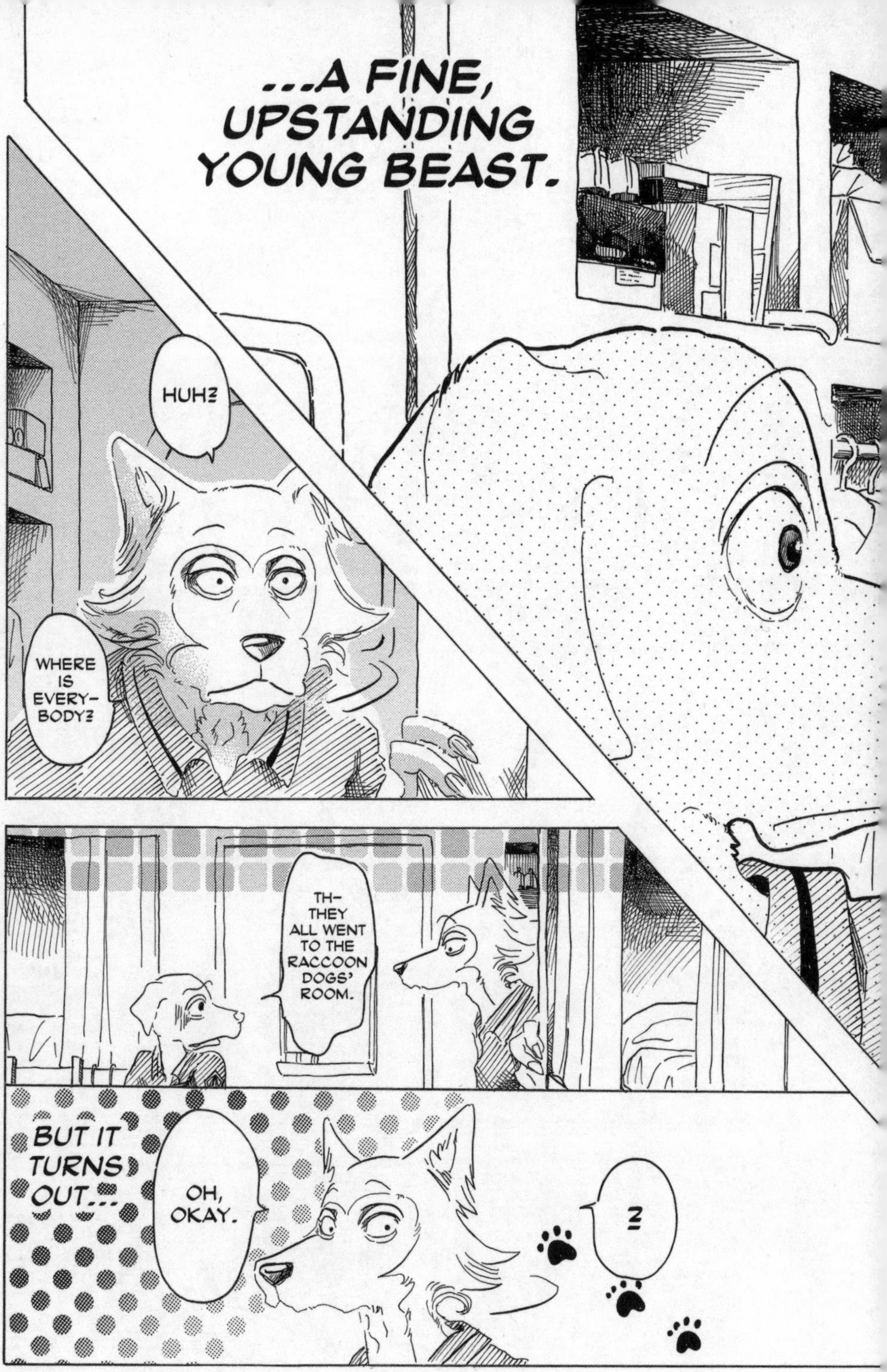
...A FINE, UPSTANDING YOUNG BEAST.
HUH?
WHERE IS EVERY-BODY?
TH-THEY ALL WENT TO THE RACCOON DOGS' ROOM.
?
OH, OKAY.
BUT IT TURNS OUT...

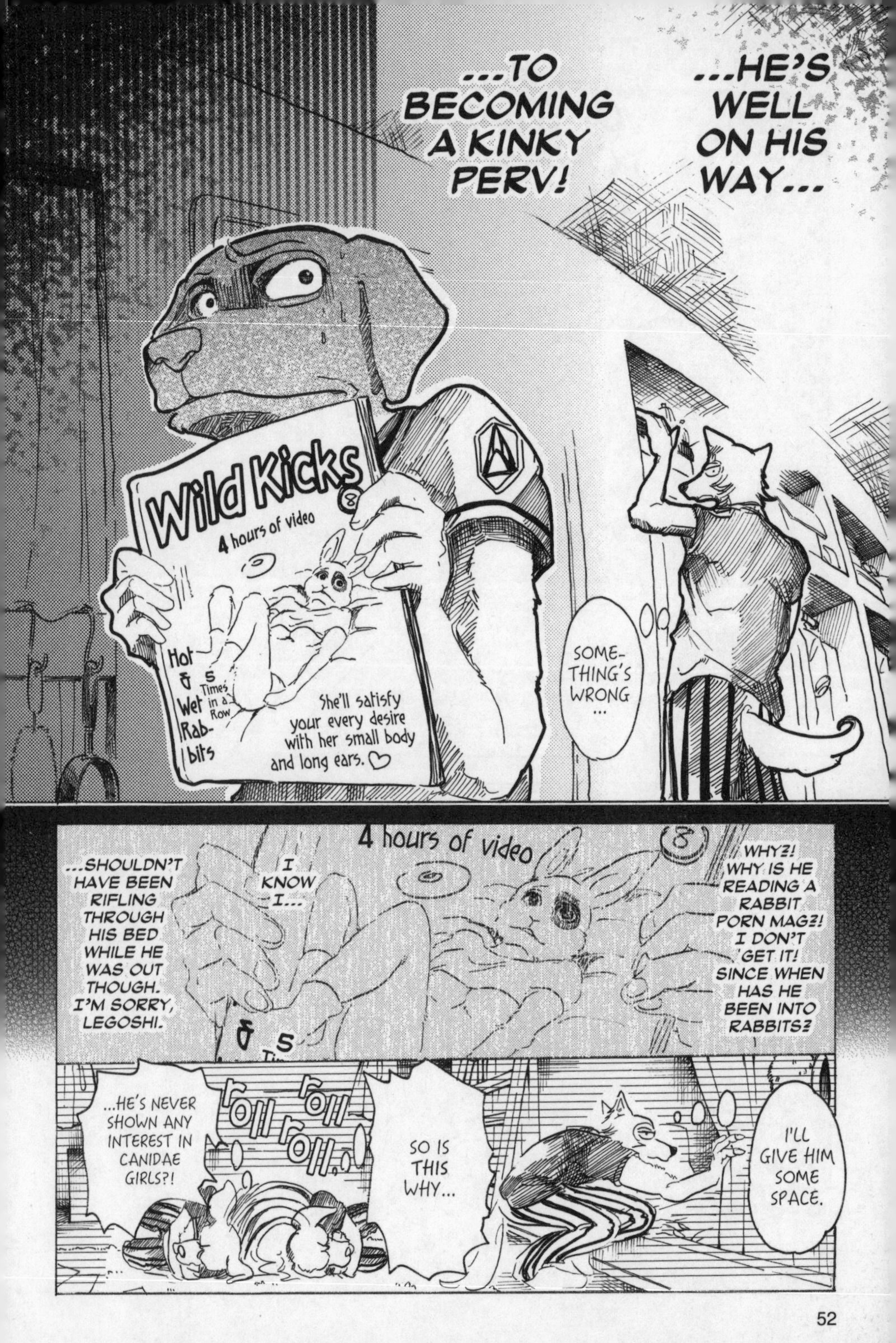
...HE'S WELL ON HIS WAY...
...TO BECOMING A KINKY PERV!
SOME-THING'S WRONG ...
Wild Kicks
8
4 hours of video
Hot & Wet Rab-bits
5 Times in a Row
She'll satisfy your every desire with her small body and long ears. ♡
WHY?! WHY IS HE READING A RABBIT PORN MAG?! I DON'T GET IT! SINCE WHEN HAS HE BEEN INTO RABBITS?
4 hours of video
I KNOW I...
...SHOULDN'T HAVE BEEN RIFLING THROUGH HIS BED WHILE HE WAS OUT THOUGH. I'M SORRY, LEGOSHI.
I'LL GIVE HIM SOME SPACE.
SO IS THIS WHY...
roll roll roll
...HE'S NEVER SHOWN ANY INTEREST IN CANIDAE GIRLS?!

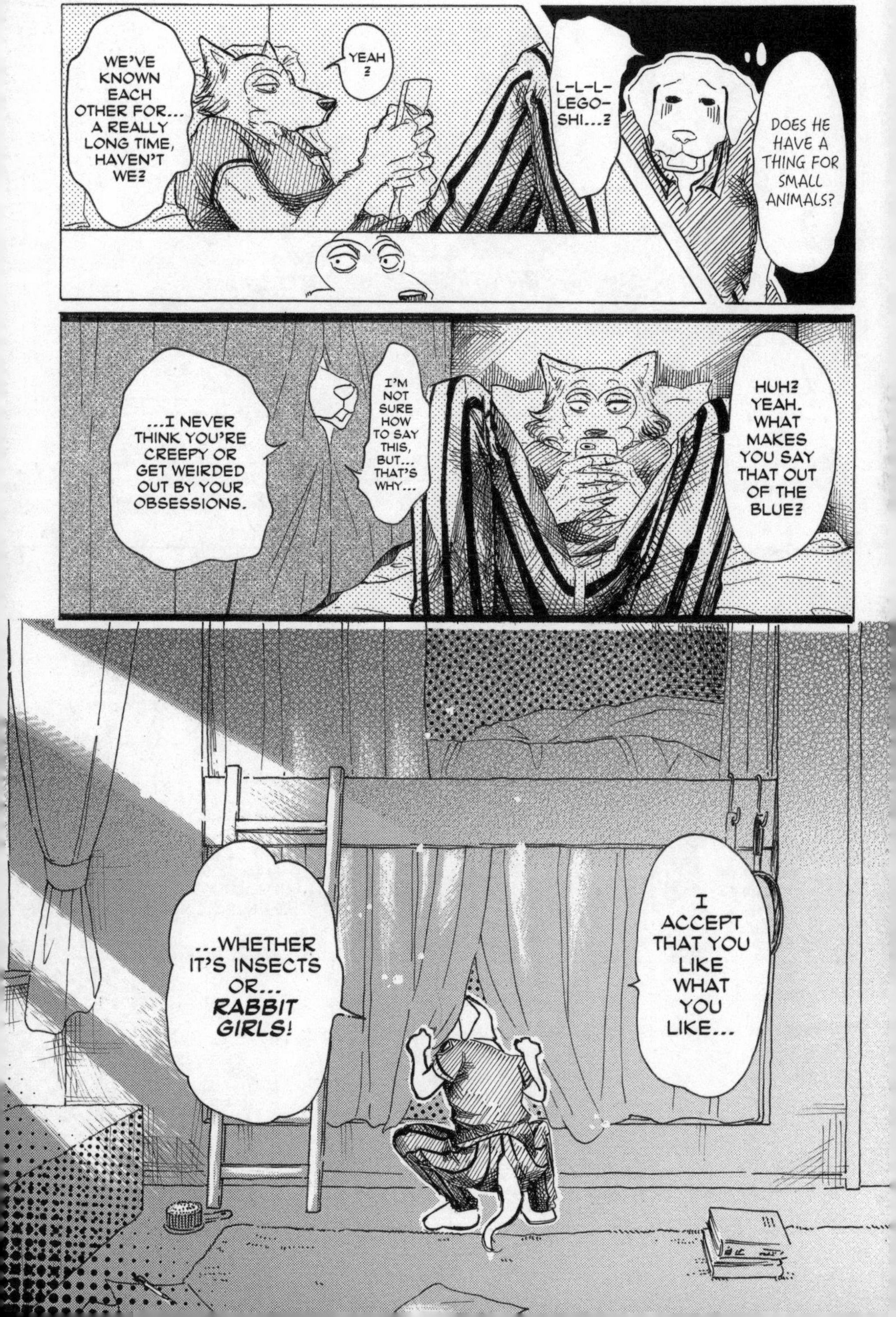
L-L-L-LEGO-SHI...?
DOES HE HAVE A THING FOR SMALL ANIMALS?
WE'VE KNOWN EACH OTHER FOR... A REALLY LONG TIME, HAVEN'T WE?
YEAH?
HUH? YEAH. WHAT MAKES YOU SAY THAT OUT OF THE BLUE?
I'M NOT SURE HOW TO SAY THIS, BUT... THAT'S WHY...
...I NEVER THINK YOU'RE CREEPY OR GET WEIRDED OUT BY YOUR OBSESSIONS.
I ACCEPT THAT YOU LIKE WHAT YOU LIKE...
...WHETHER IT'S INSECTS OR... ***RABBIT GIRLS!***

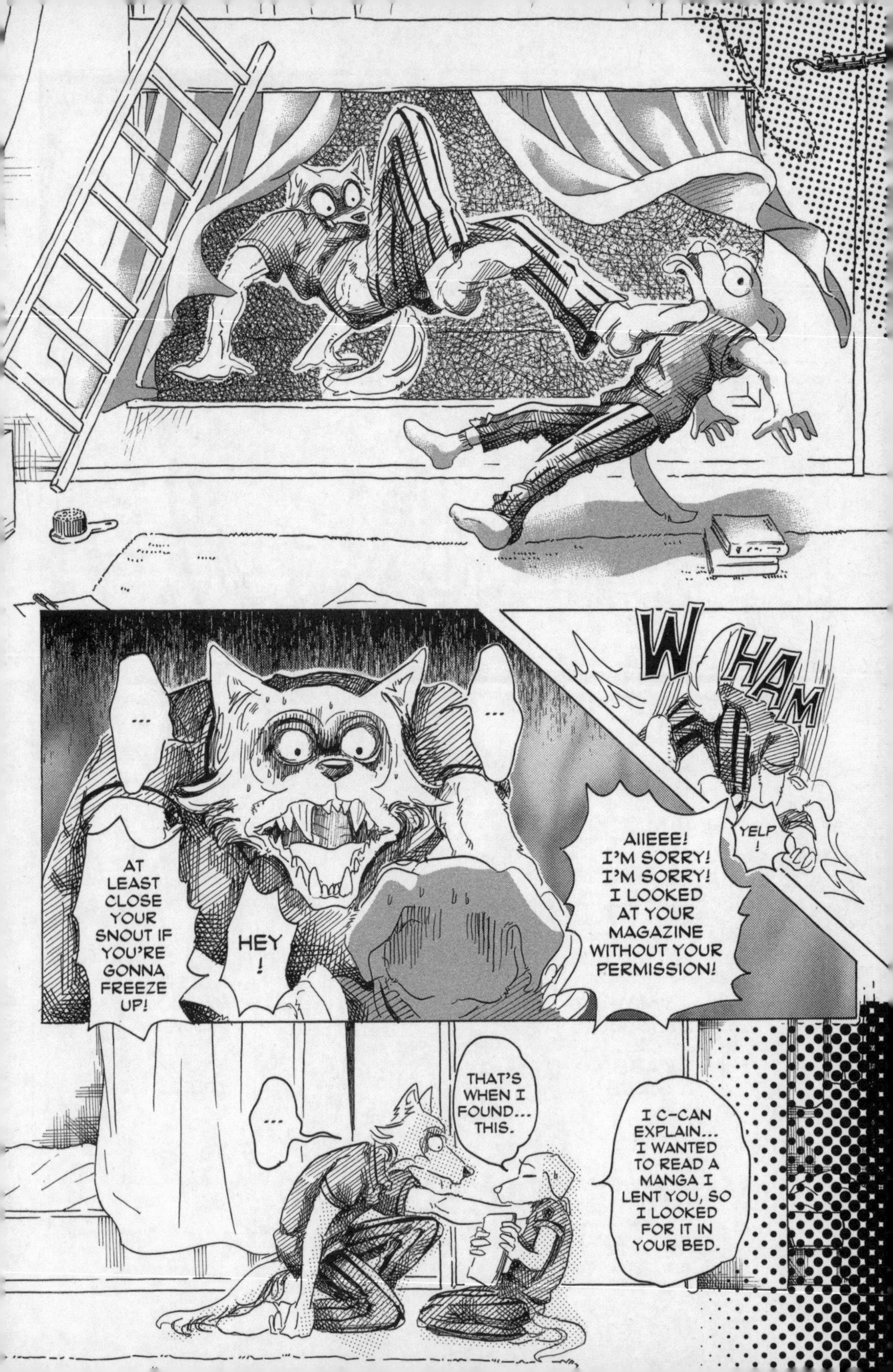
WHAM
YELP!
AIIEEE! I'M SORRY! I'M SORRY! I LOOKED AT YOUR MAGAZINE WITHOUT YOUR PERMISSION!
...
...
HEY!
AT LEAST CLOSE YOUR SNOUT IF YOU'RE GONNA FREEZE UP!
I C-CAN EXPLAIN... I WANTED TO READ A MANGA I LENT YOU, SO I LOOKED FOR IT IN YOUR BED.
THAT'S WHEN I FOUND... THIS.
...

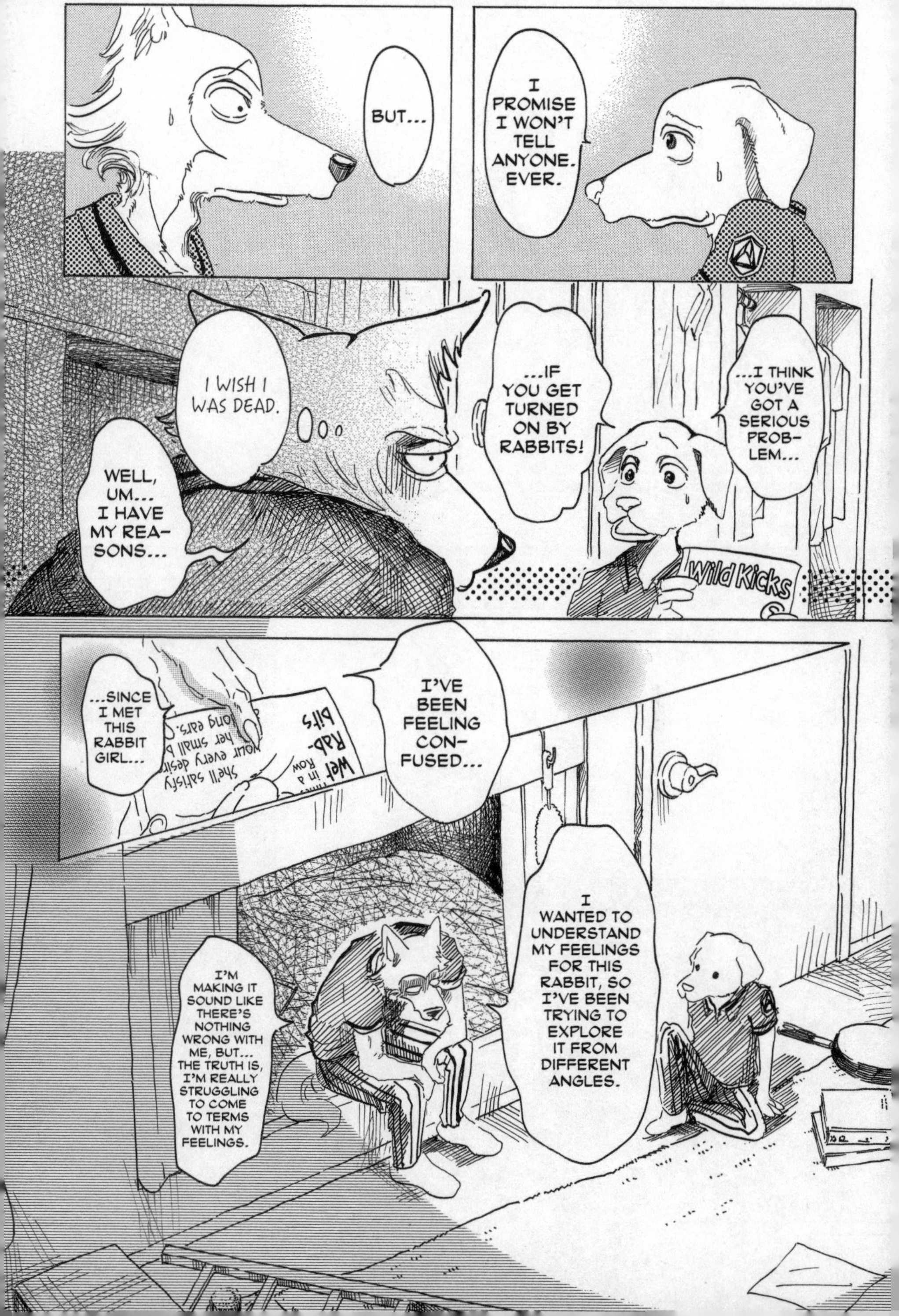
I PROMISE I WON'T TELL ANYONE. EVER.
BUT...
...I THINK YOU'VE GOT A SERIOUS PROB-LEM...
...IF YOU GET TURNED ON BY RABBITS!
I WISH I WAS DEAD.
WELL, UM... I HAVE MY REA-SONS...
Wild Kicks
I'VE BEEN FEELING CON-FUSED...
...SINCE I MET THIS RABBIT GIRL...
I WANTED TO UNDERSTAND MY FEELINGS FOR THIS RABBIT, SO I'VE BEEN TRYING TO EXPLORE IT FROM DIFFERENT ANGLES.
I'M MAKING IT SOUND LIKE THERE'S NOTHING WRONG WITH ME, BUT... THE TRUTH IS, I'M REALLY STRUGGLING TO COME TO TERMS WITH MY FEELINGS.

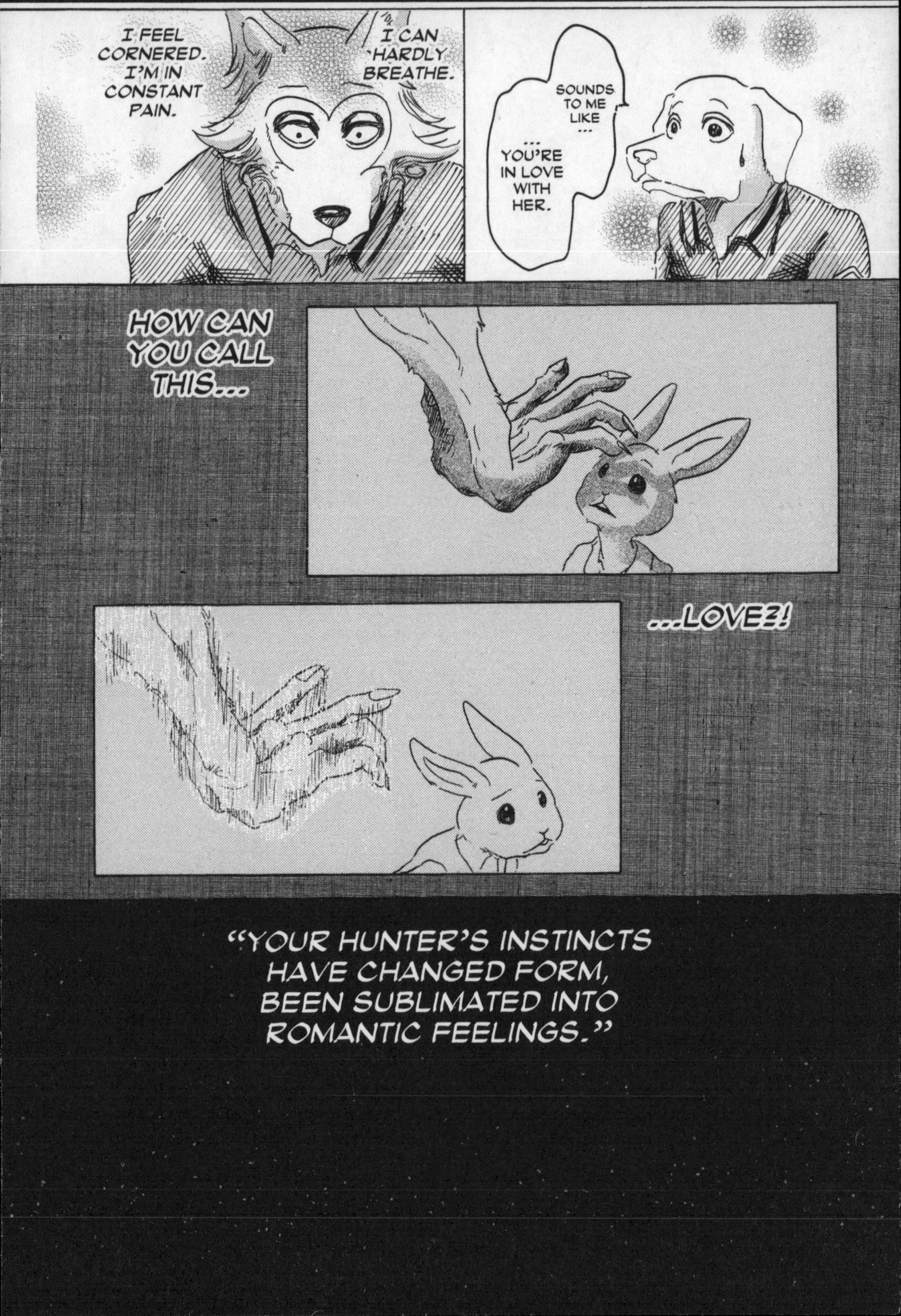
SOUNDS TO ME LIKE ...
... YOU'RE IN LOVE WITH HER.
I CAN HARDLY BREATHE.
I FEEL CORNERED. I'M IN CONSTANT PAIN.
HOW CAN YOU CALL THIS...
...LOVE?!
"YOUR HUNTER'S INSTINCTS HAVE CHANGED FORM, BEEN SUBLIMATED INTO ROMANTIC FEELINGS."

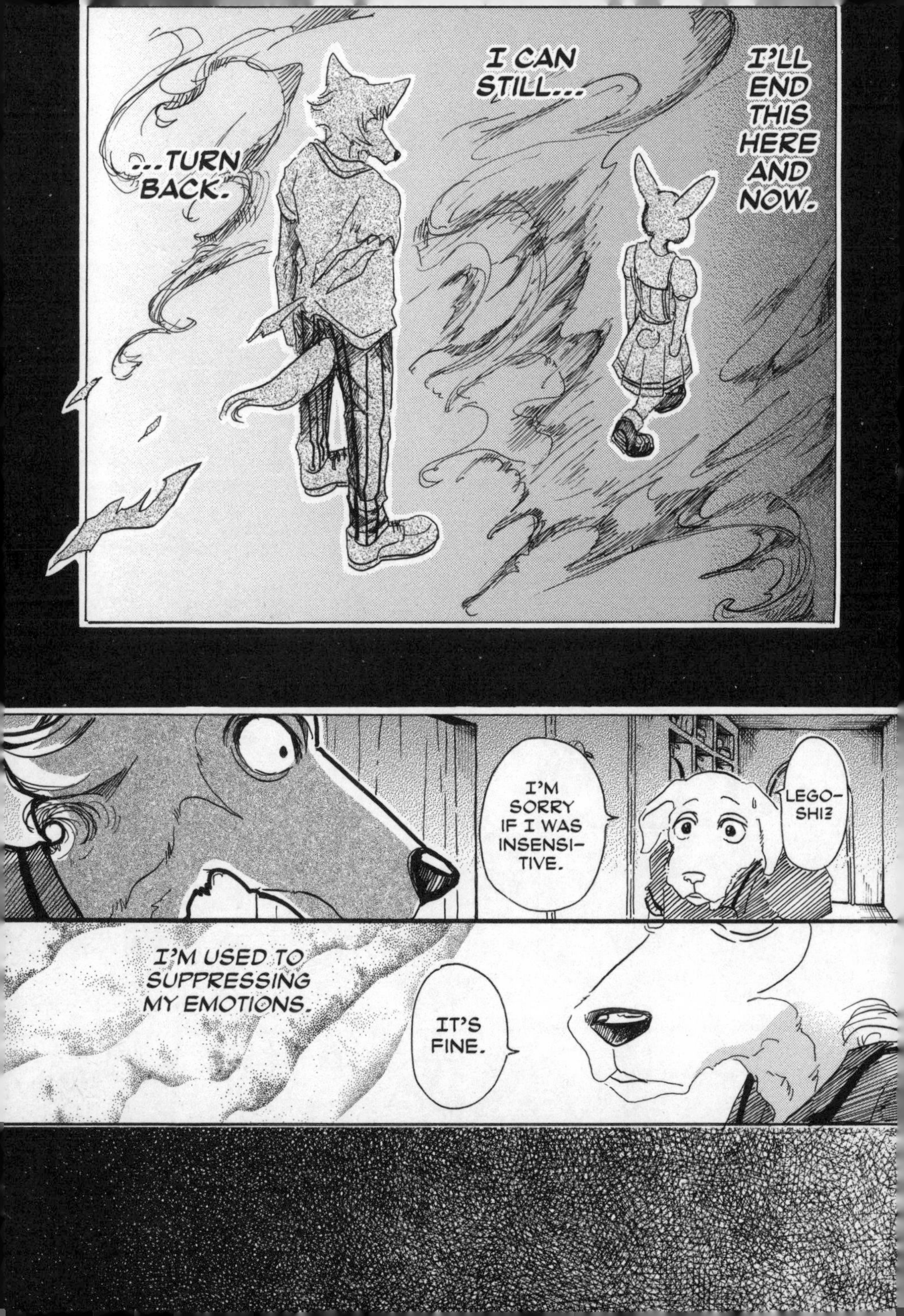
I'LL END THIS HERE AND NOW.
I CAN STILL...
...TURN BACK.
LEGO-SHI?
I'M SORRY IF I WAS INSENSI-TIVE.
IT'S FINE.
I'M USED TO SUPPRESSING MY EMOTIONS.

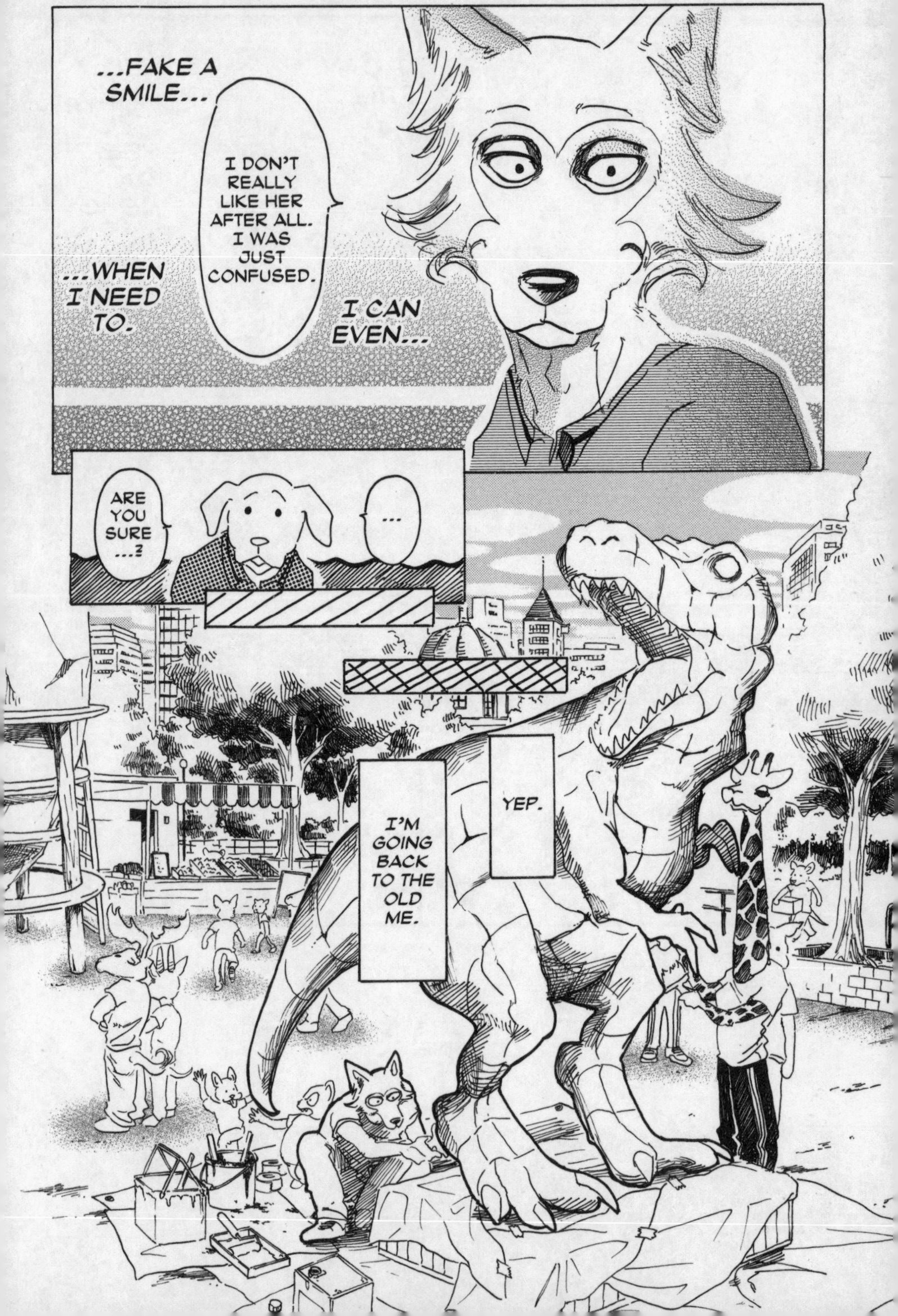
I CAN EVEN...
...FAKE A SMILE...
...WHEN I NEED TO.
I DON'T REALLY LIKE HER AFTER ALL. I WAS JUST CONFUSED.
...
ARE YOU SURE...?
YEP.
I'M GOING BACK TO THE OLD ME.

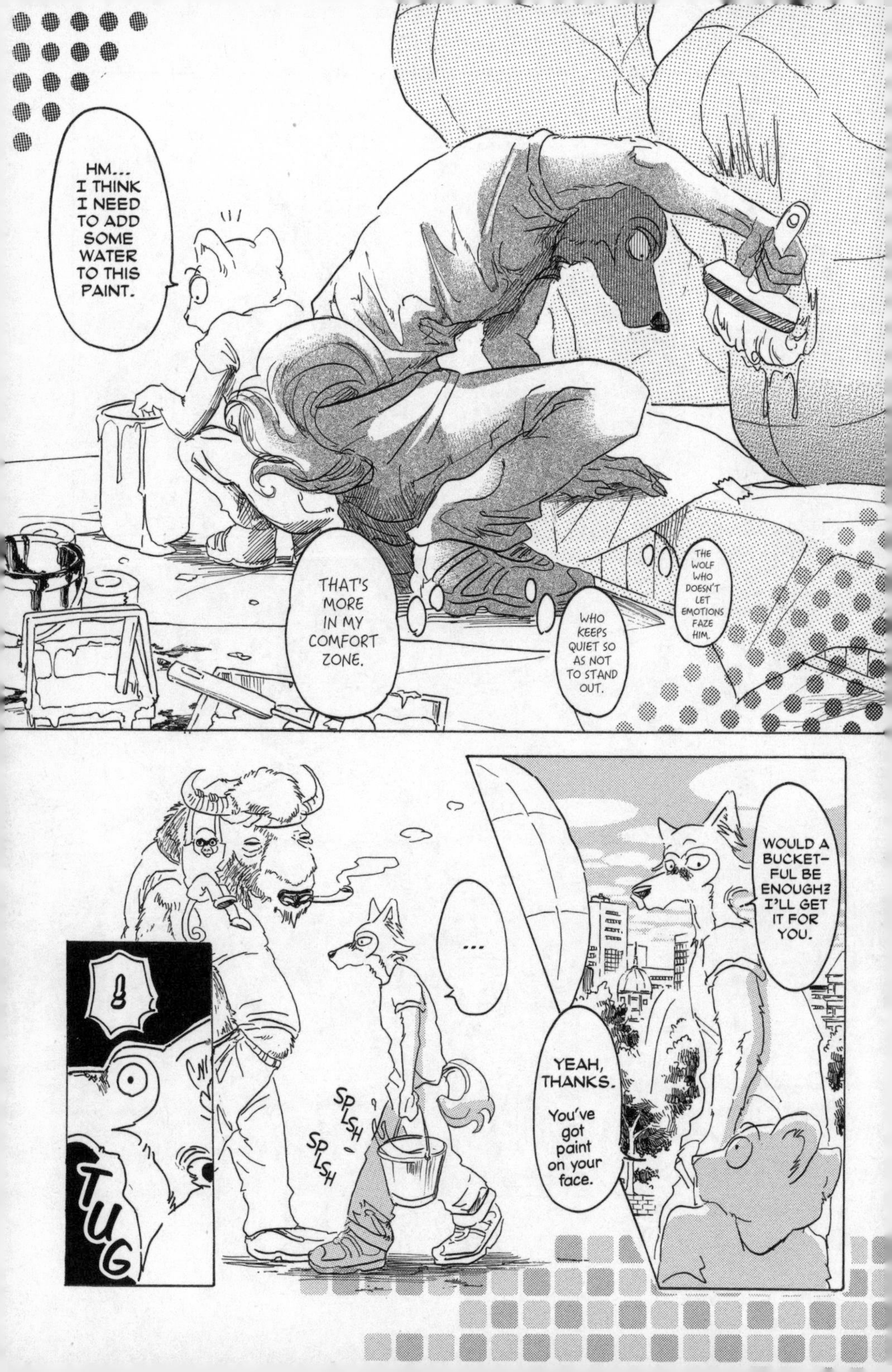
HM... I THINK I NEED TO ADD SOME WATER TO THIS PAINT.
THE WOLF WHO DOESN'T LET EMOTIONS FAZE HIM.
WHO KEEPS QUIET SO AS NOT TO STAND OUT.
THAT'S MORE IN MY COMFORT ZONE.
WOULD A BUCKET-FUL BE ENOUGH? I'LL GET IT FOR YOU.
YEAH, THANKS.
You've got paint on your face.
...
SPLSH
SPLSH
!
TUG

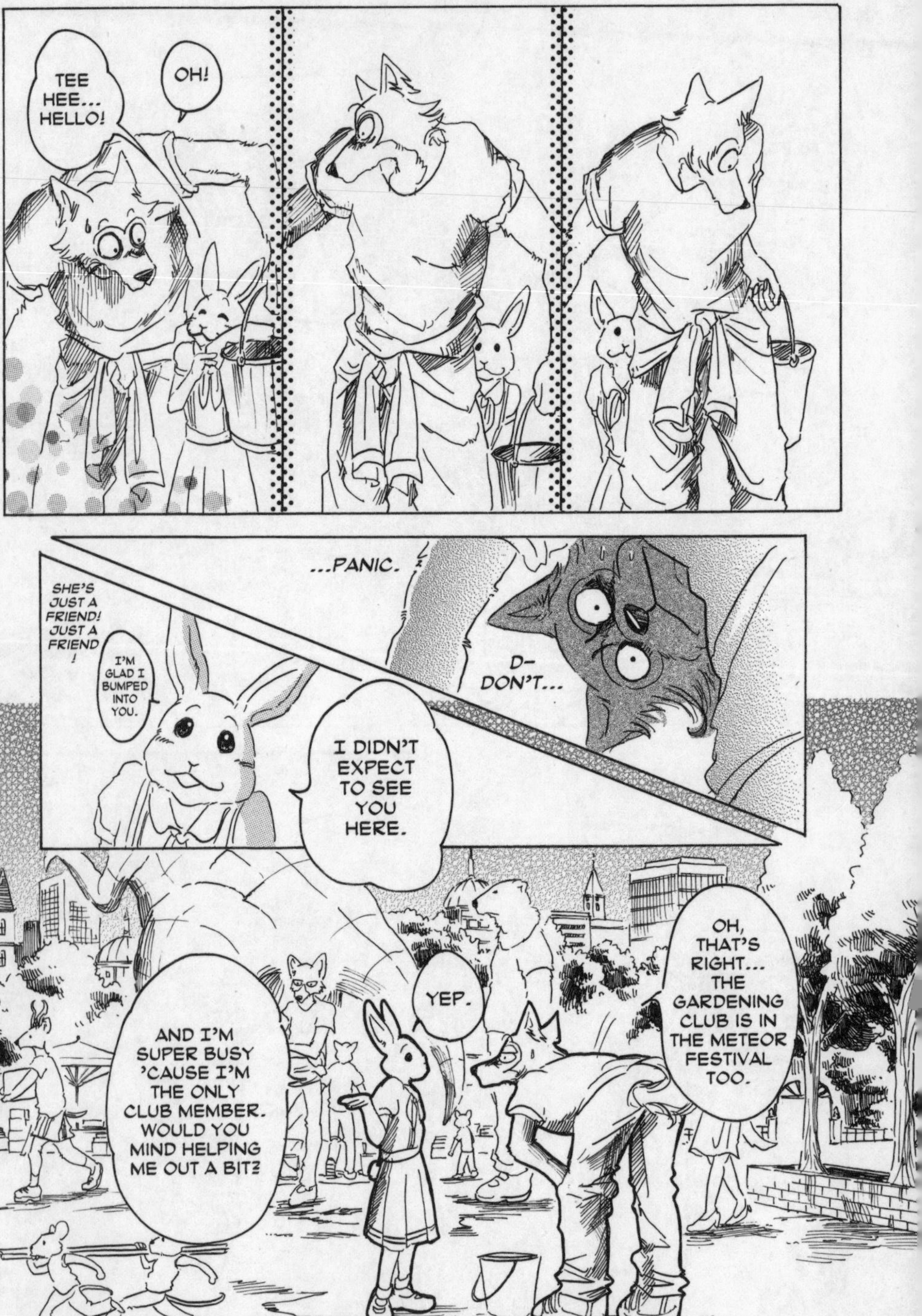
OH!
TEE HEE... HELLO!
...PANIC.
D- DON'T...
I DIDN'T EXPECT TO SEE YOU HERE.
I'M GLAD I BUMPED INTO YOU.
SHE'S JUST A FRIEND! JUST A FRIEND!
OH, THAT'S RIGHT... THE GARDENING CLUB IS IN THE METEOR FESTIVAL TOO.
YEP.
AND I'M SUPER BUSY 'CAUSE I'M THE ONLY CLUB MEMBER. WOULD YOU MIND HELPING ME OUT A BIT?

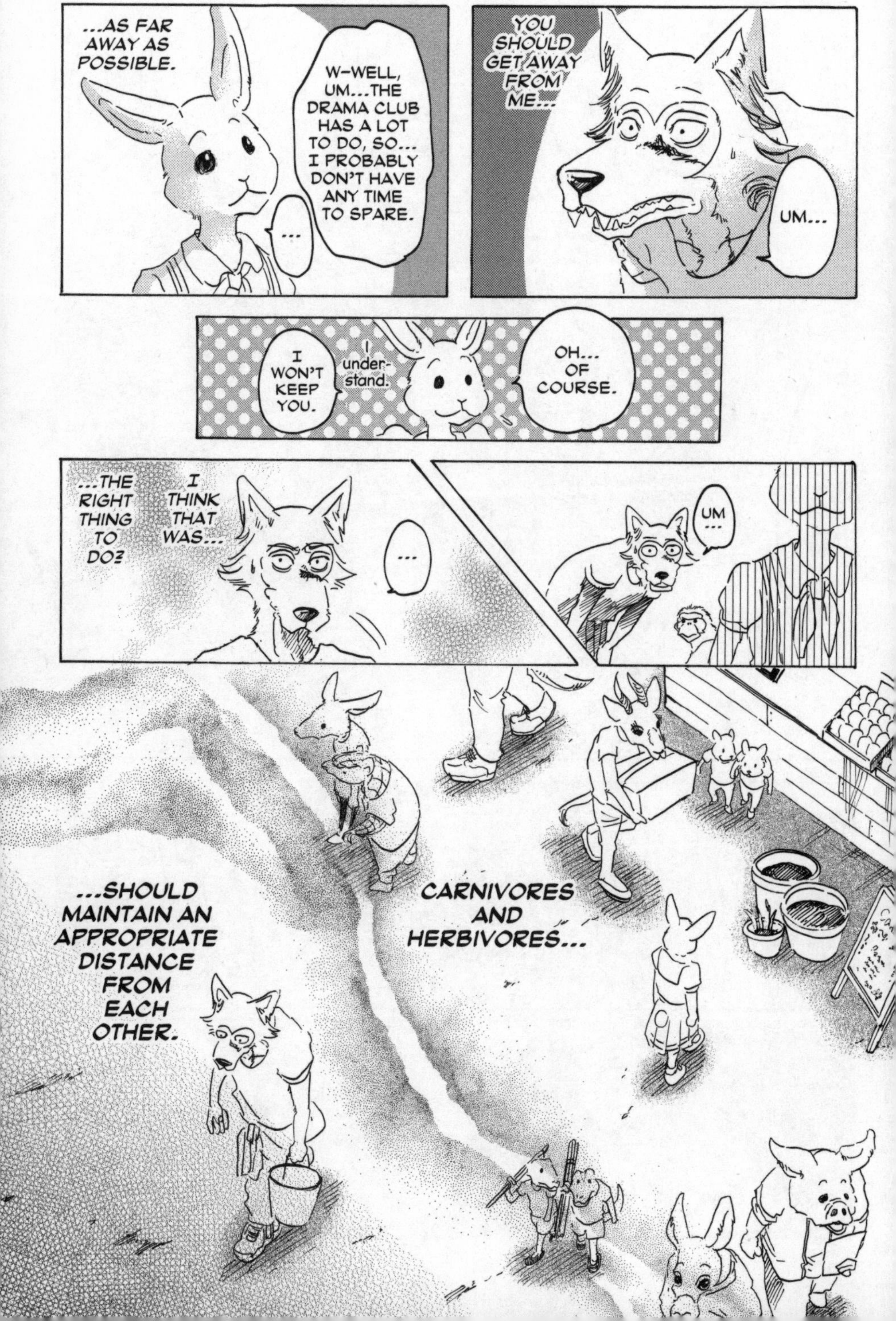
UM...
YOU SHOULD GET AWAY FROM ME...
...AS FAR AWAY AS POSSIBLE.
W-WELL, UM...THE DRAMA CLUB HAS A LOT TO DO, SO... I PROBABLY DON'T HAVE ANY TIME TO SPARE.
...
OH... OF COURSE.
I understand.
I WON'T KEEP YOU.
UM ...
...
I THINK THAT WAS...
...THE RIGHT THING TO DO?
CARNIVORES AND HERBIVORES...
...SHOULD MAINTAIN AN APPROPRIATE DISTANCE FROM EACH OTHER.

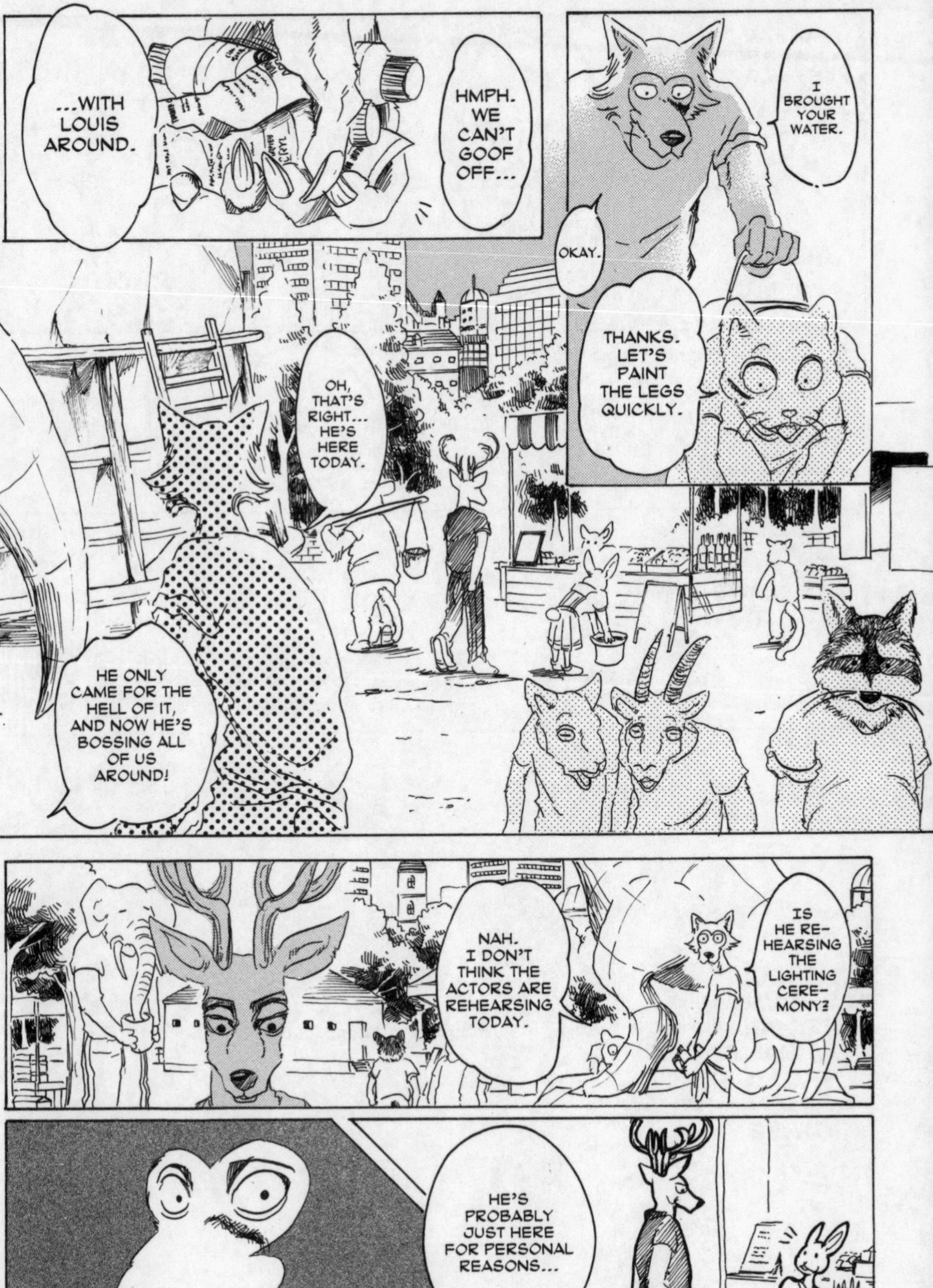
I BROUGHT YOUR WATER.
OKAY.
THANKS. LET'S PAINT THE LEGS QUICKLY.
HMPH. WE CAN'T GOOF OFF...
...WITH LOUIS AROUND.
OH, THAT'S RIGHT... HE'S HERE TODAY.
HE ONLY CAME FOR THE HELL OF IT, AND NOW HE'S BOSSING ALL OF US AROUND!
IS HE REHEARSING THE LIGHTING CEREMONY?
NAH. I DON'T THINK THE ACTORS ARE REHEARSING TODAY.
HE'S PROBABLY JUST HERE FOR PERSONAL REASONS...

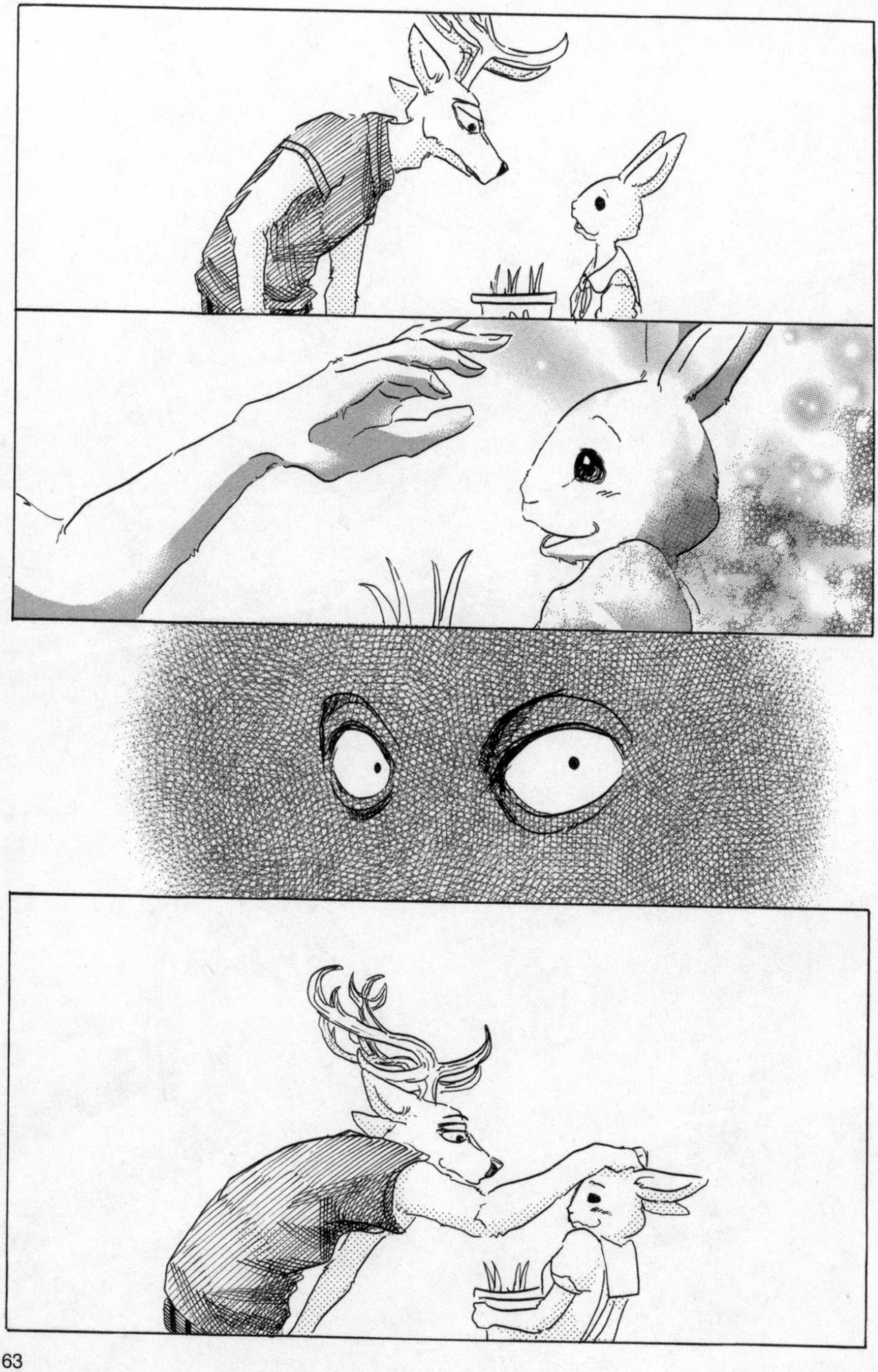

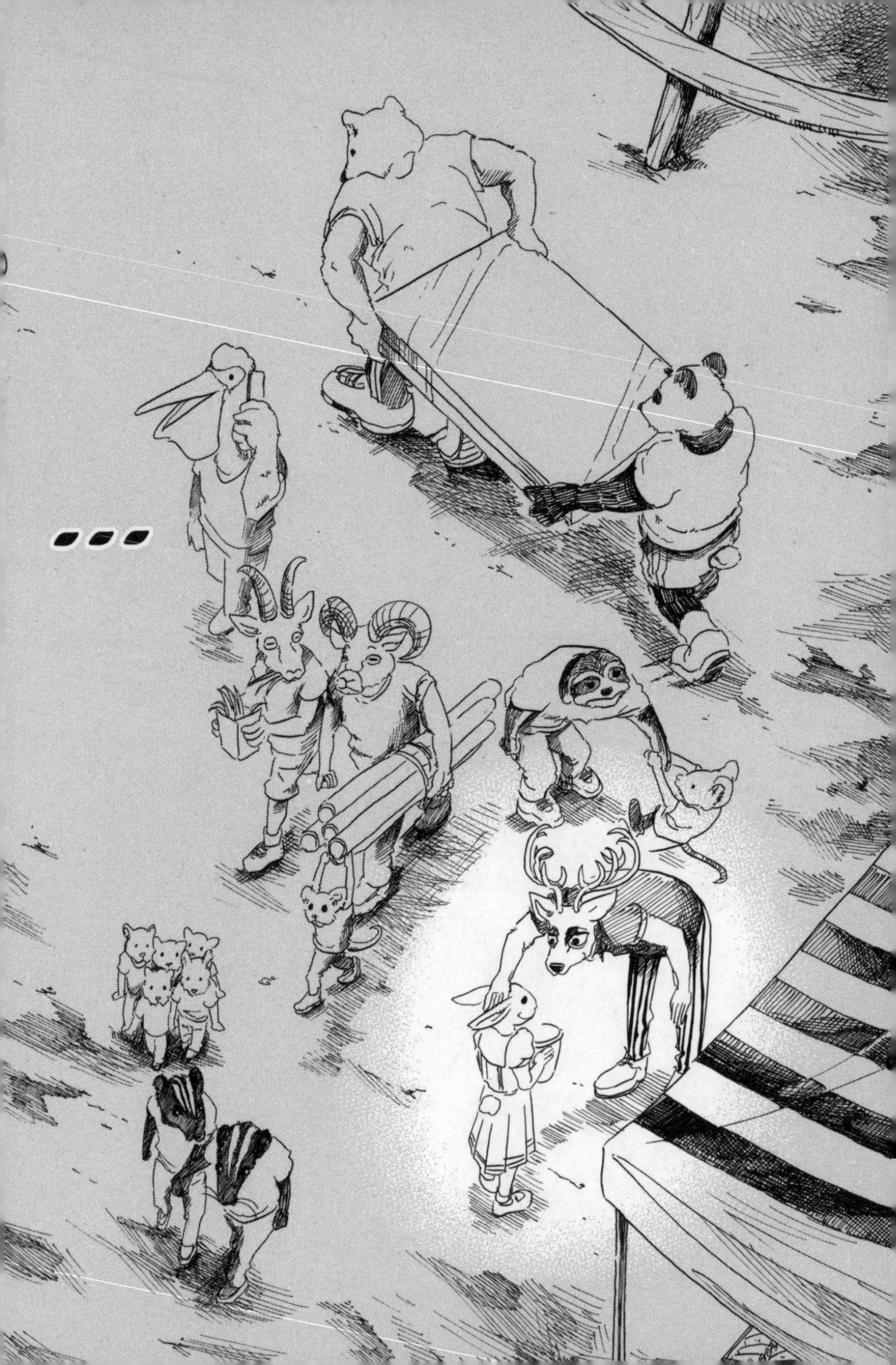
...

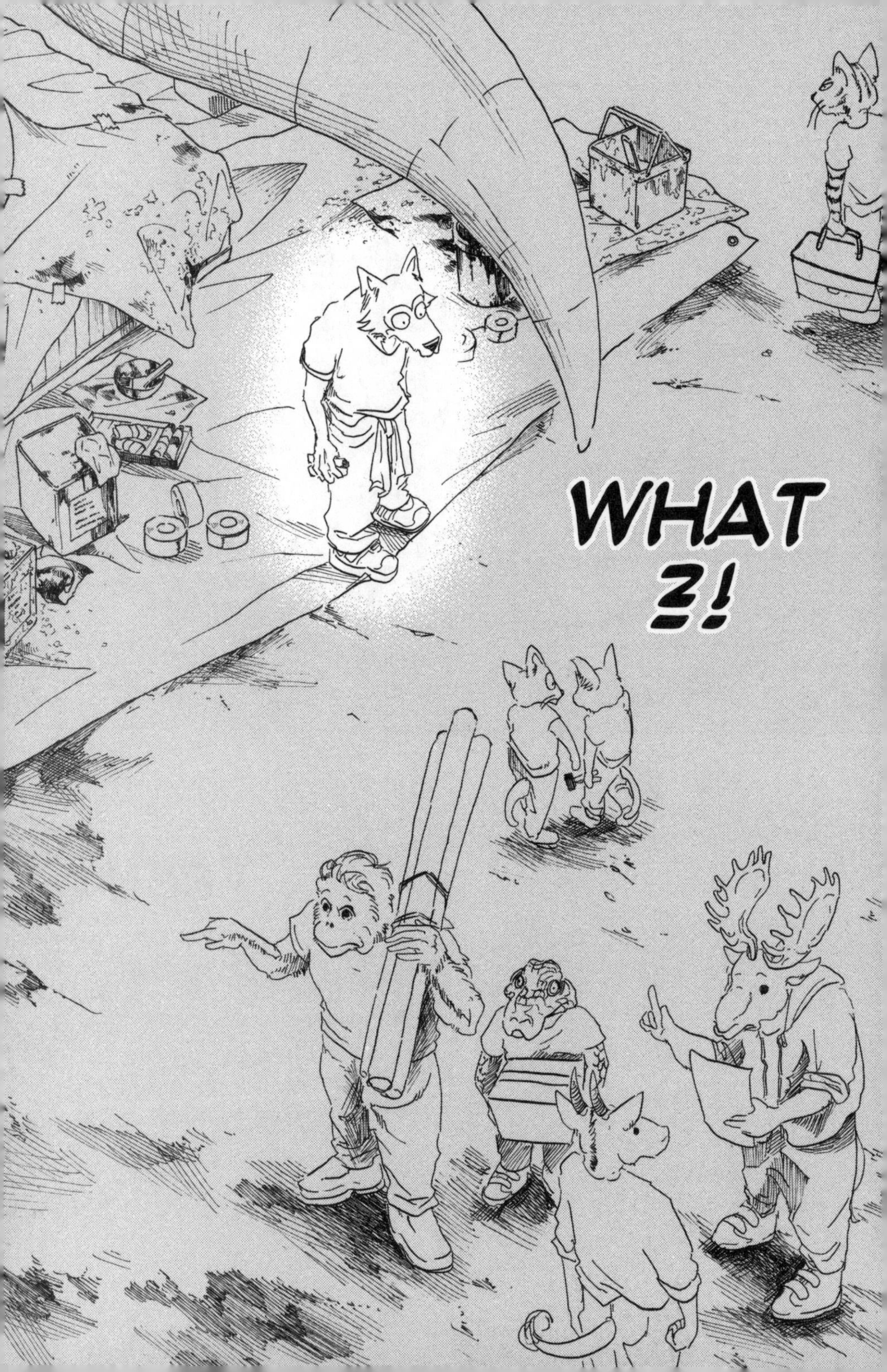
WHAT
?!

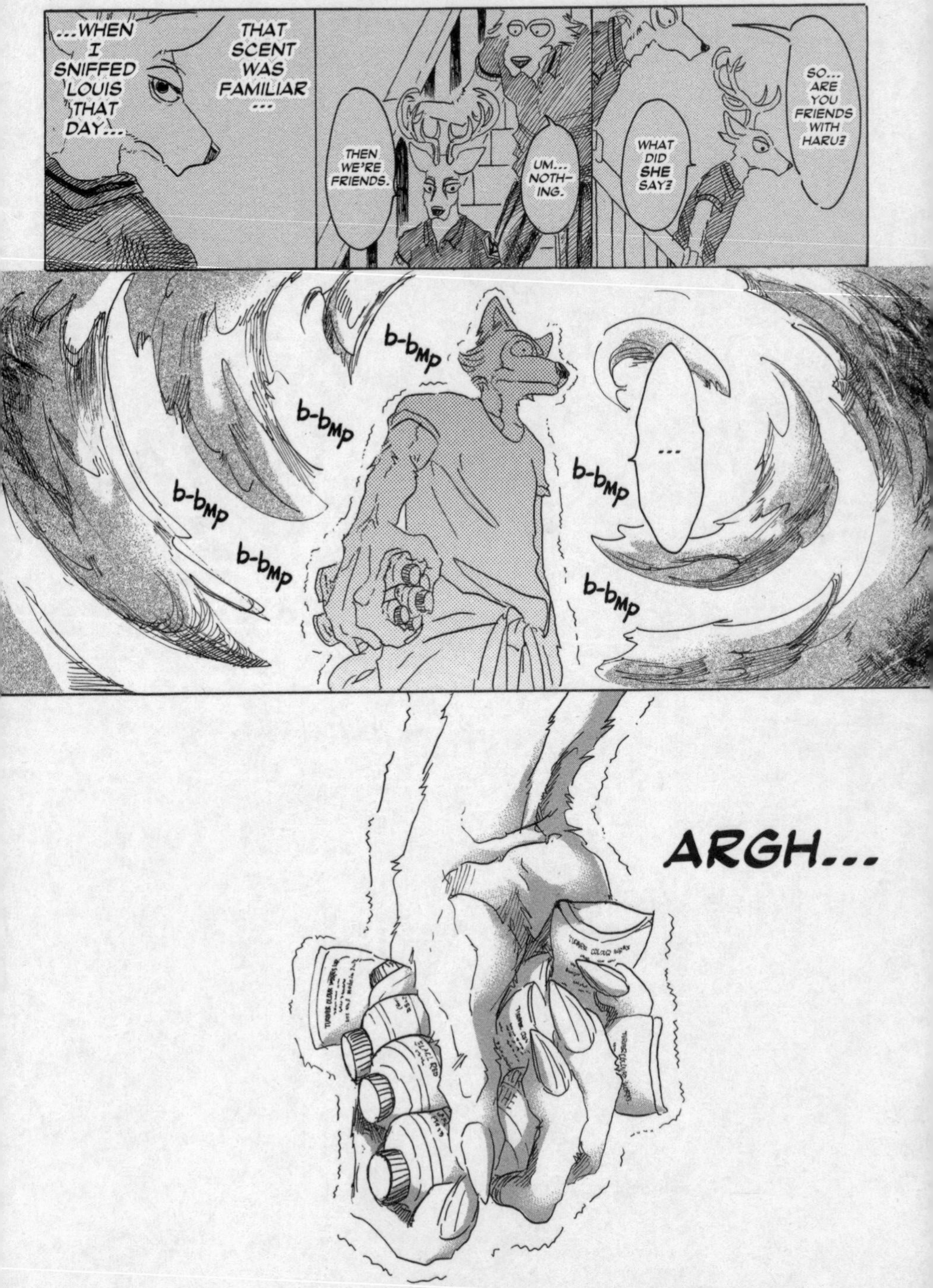
SO... ARE YOU FRIENDS WITH HARU?
WHAT DID SHE SAY?
UM... NOTHING.
THEN WE'RE FRIENDS.
THAT SCENT WAS FAMILIAR...
...WHEN I SNIFFED LOUIS THAT DAY...
b-bmp
...
b-bmp
b-bmp
b-bmp
b-bmp
b-bmp
ARGH...

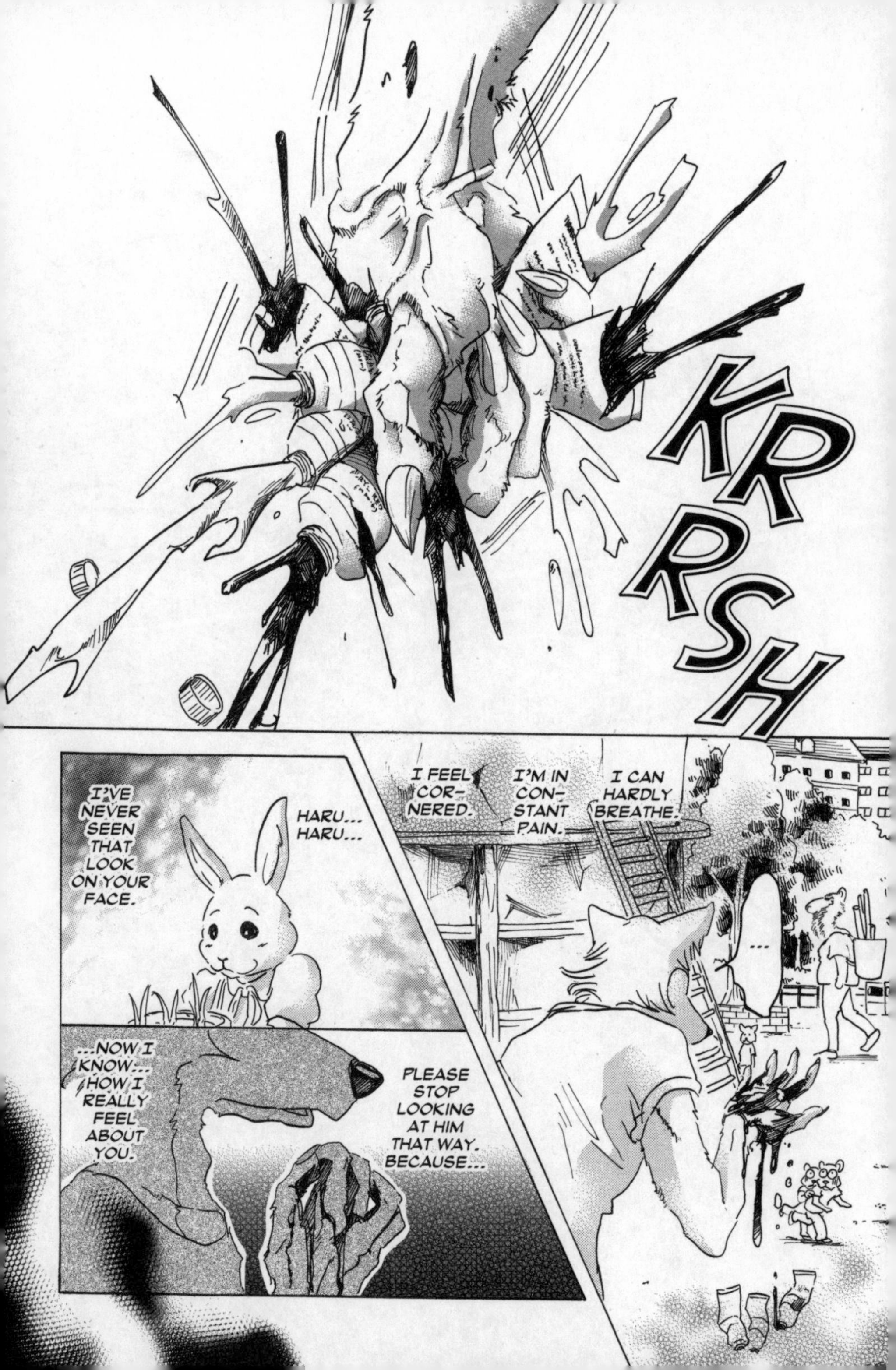
KRRSH
I CAN HARDLY BREATHE.
I'M IN CON-STANT PAIN.
I FEEL COR-NERED.
...
HARU... HARU...
I'VE NEVER SEEN THAT LOOK ON YOUR FACE.
PLEASE STOP LOOKING AT HIM THAT WAY. BECAUSE...
...NOW I KNOW... HOW I REALLY FEEL ABOUT YOU.

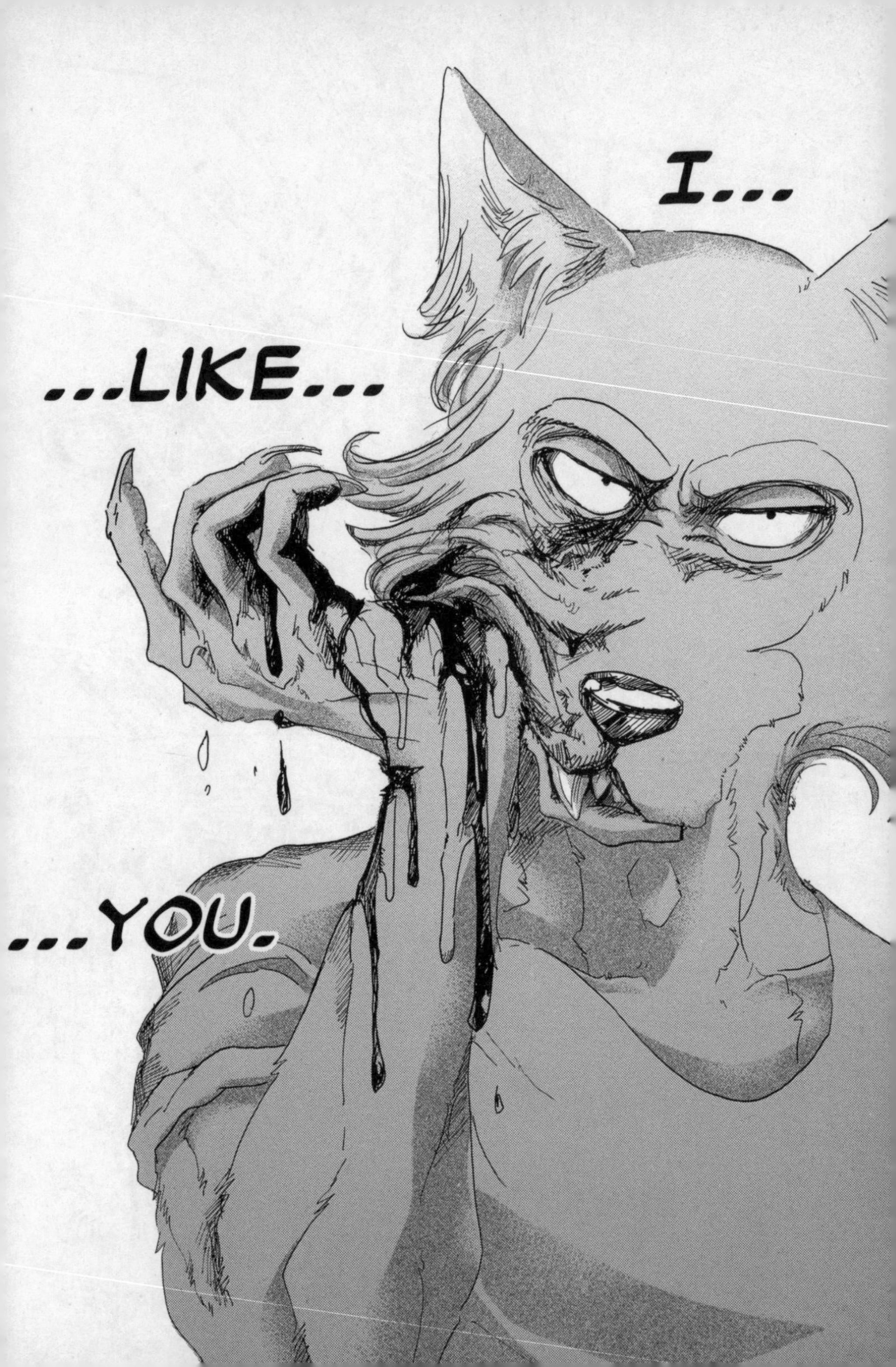
I...
...LIKE...
...YOU.

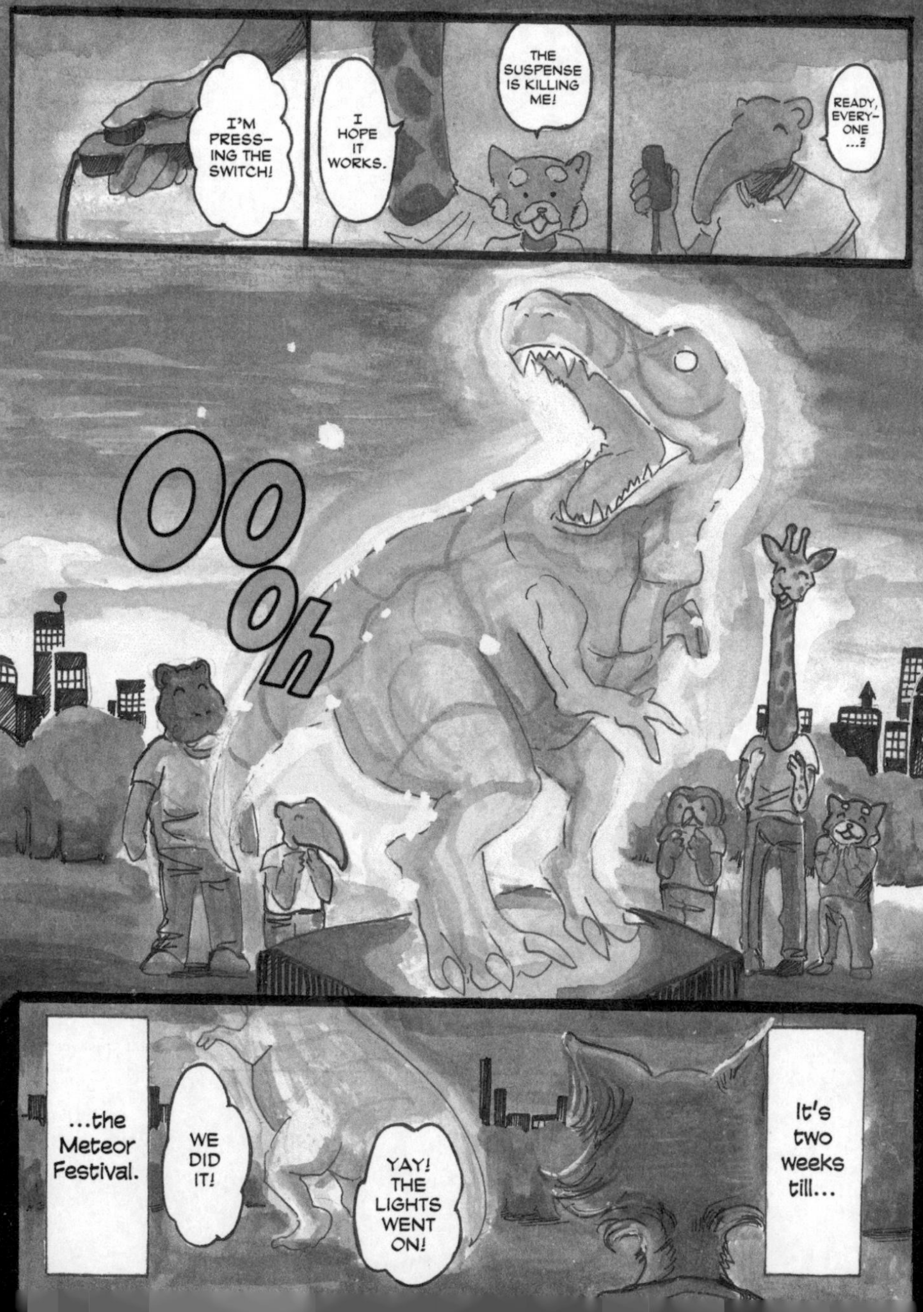
READY, EVERY-ONE ...?
THE SUSPENSE IS KILLING ME!
I HOPE IT WORKS.
I'M PRESS-ING THE SWITCH!
Ooooh
It's two weeks till...
YAY! THE LIGHTS WENT ON!
WE DID IT!
...the Meteor Festival.

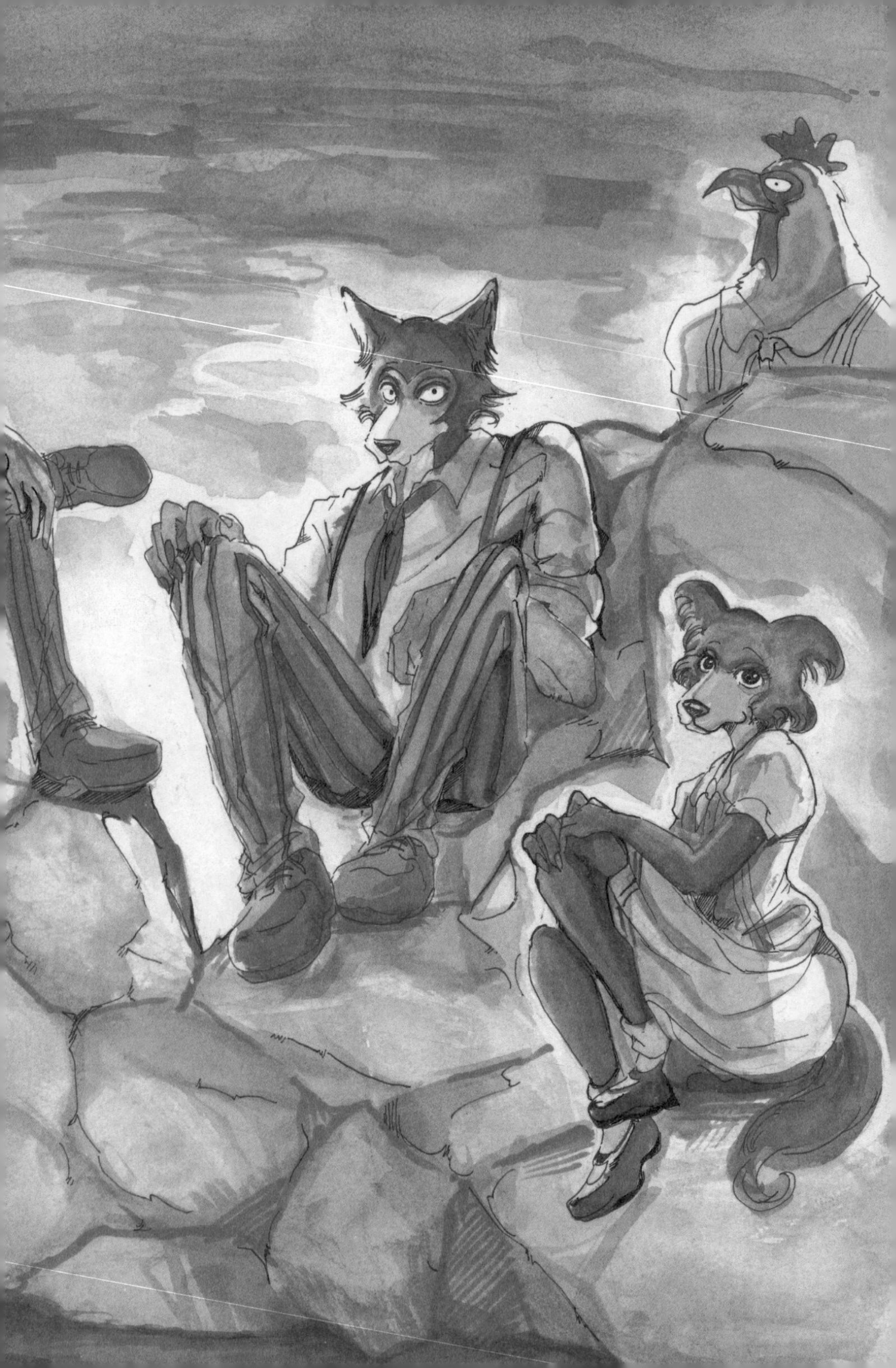

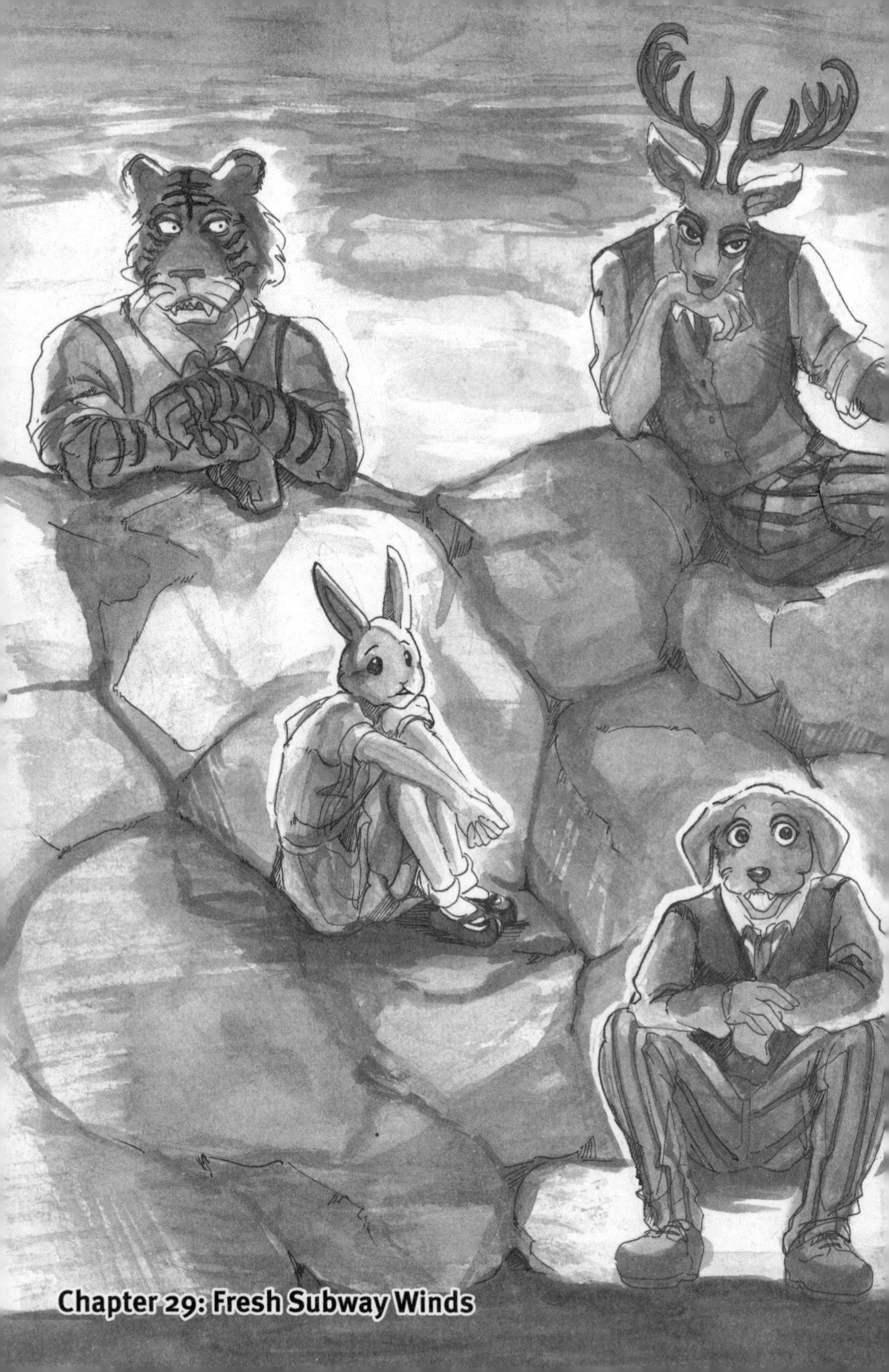

Chapter 29: Fresh Subway Winds

BEASTARS
Vol. 4

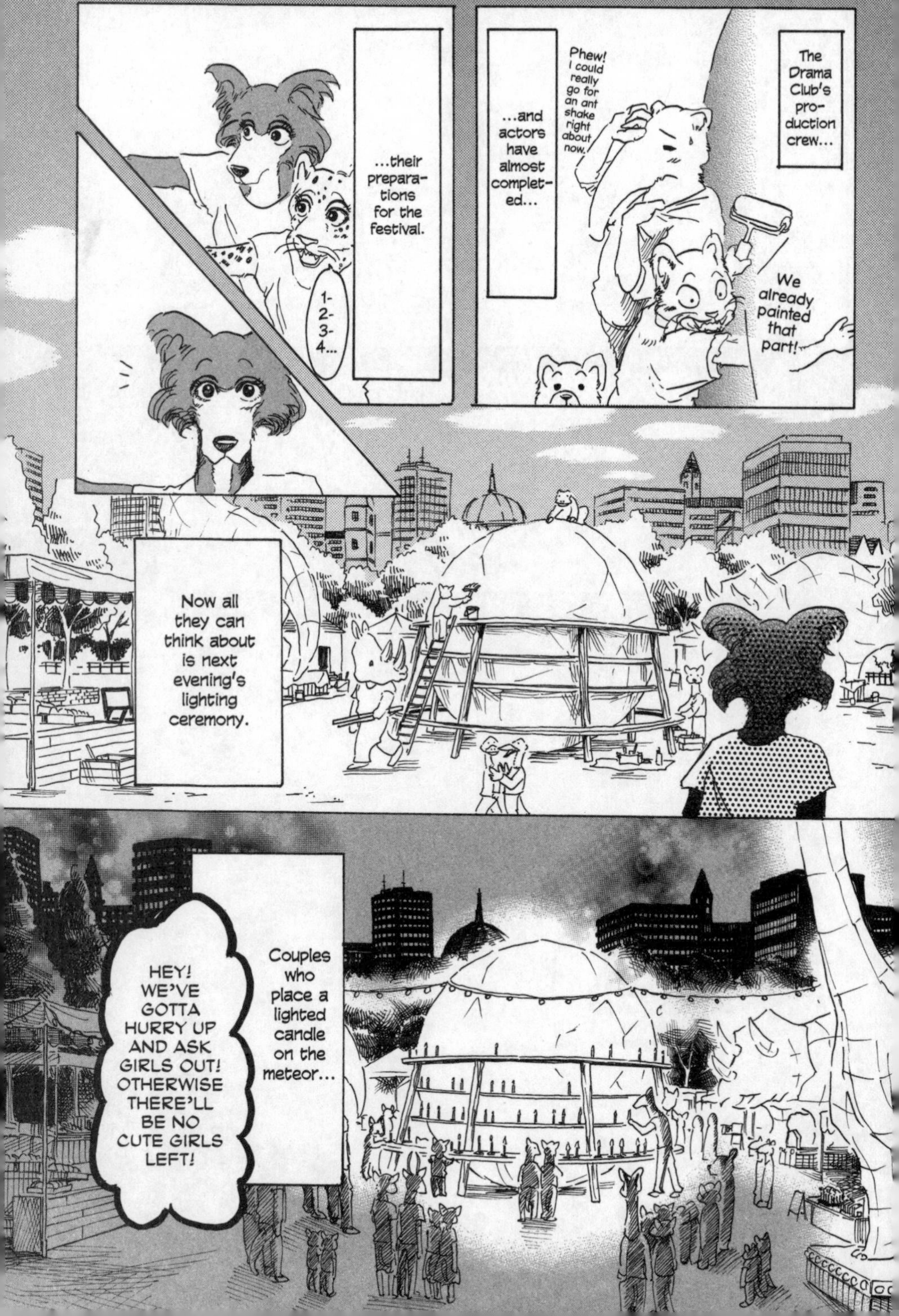

The Drama Club's production crew...
Phew! I could really go for an ant shake right about now.
...and actors have almost completed...
We already painted that part!
...their preparations for the festival.
1-2-3-4...
Now all they can think about is next evening's lighting ceremony.
Couples who place a lighted candle on the meteor...
HEY! WE'VE GOTTA HURRY UP AND ASK GIRLS OUT! OTHERWISE THERE'LL BE NO CUTE GIRLS LEFT!

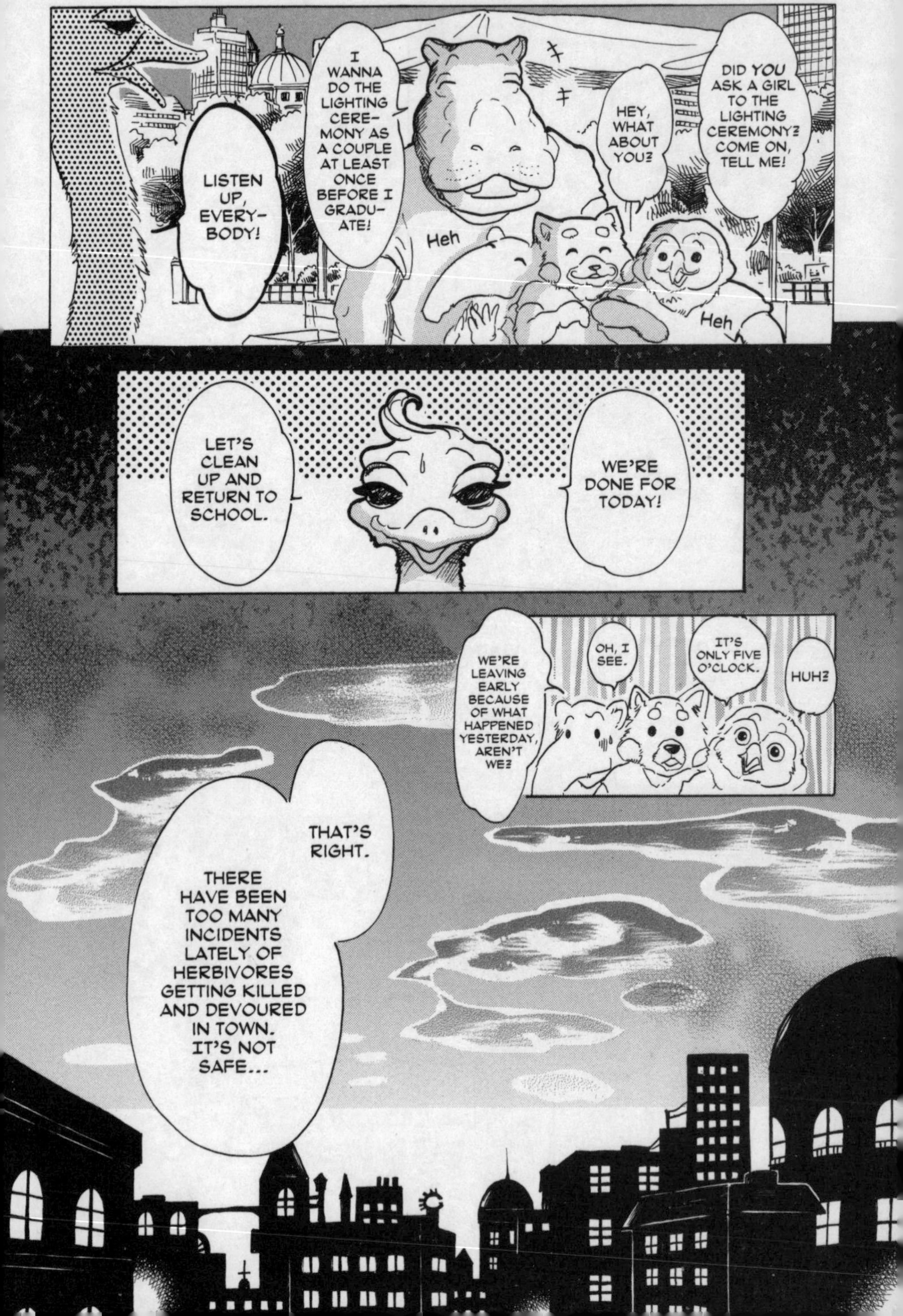
DID YOU ASK A GIRL TO THE LIGHTING CEREMONY? COME ON, TELL ME!
HEY, WHAT ABOUT YOU?
I WANNA DO THE LIGHTING CEREMONY AS A COUPLE AT LEAST ONCE BEFORE I GRADUATE!
Heh
Heh
LISTEN UP, EVERYBODY!
WE'RE DONE FOR TODAY!
LET'S CLEAN UP AND RETURN TO SCHOOL.
HUH?
IT'S ONLY FIVE O'CLOCK.
OH, I SEE.
WE'RE LEAVING EARLY BECAUSE OF WHAT HAPPENED YESTERDAY, AREN'T WE?
THAT'S RIGHT.
THERE HAVE BEEN TOO MANY INCIDENTS LATELY OF HERBIVORES GETTING KILLED AND DEVOURED IN TOWN. IT'S NOT SAFE...

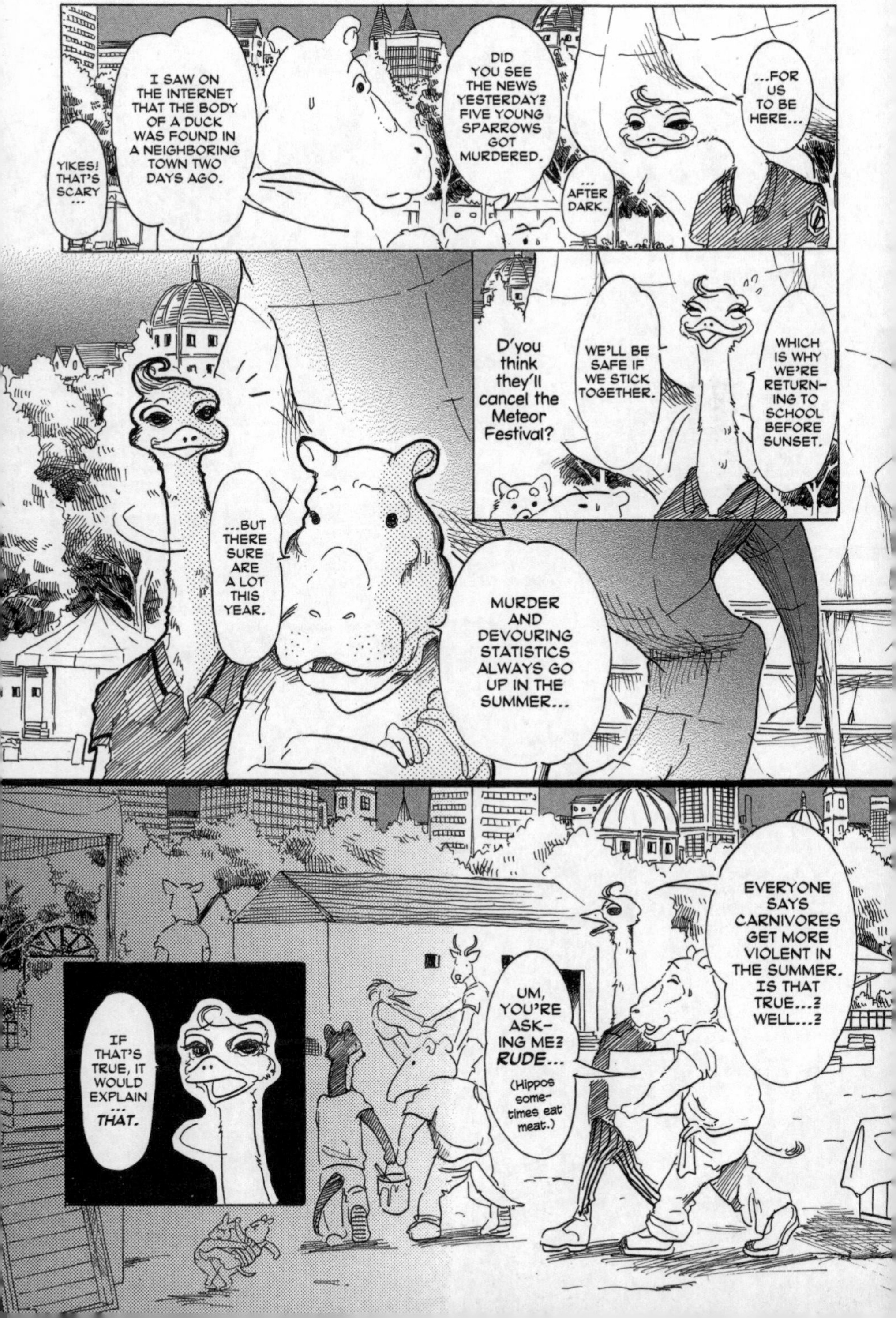

...FOR US TO BE HERE...
...AFTER DARK.
DID YOU SEE THE NEWS YESTERDAY? FIVE YOUNG SPARROWS GOT MURDERED.
I SAW ON THE INTERNET THAT THE BODY OF A DUCK WAS FOUND IN A NEIGHBORING TOWN TWO DAYS AGO.
YIKES! THAT'S SCARY...
WHICH IS WHY WE'RE RETURNING TO SCHOOL BEFORE SUNSET.
WE'LL BE SAFE IF WE STICK TOGETHER.
D'you think they'll cancel the Meteor Festival?
MURDER AND DEVOURING STATISTICS ALWAYS GO UP IN THE SUMMER...
...BUT THERE SURE ARE A LOT THIS YEAR.
EVERYONE SAYS CARNIVORES GET MORE VIOLENT IN THE SUMMER. IS THAT TRUE...? WELL...?
UM, YOU'RE ASKING ME? *RUDE*...
(Hippos sometimes eat meat.)
IF THAT'S TRUE, IT WOULD EXPLAIN... *THAT.*

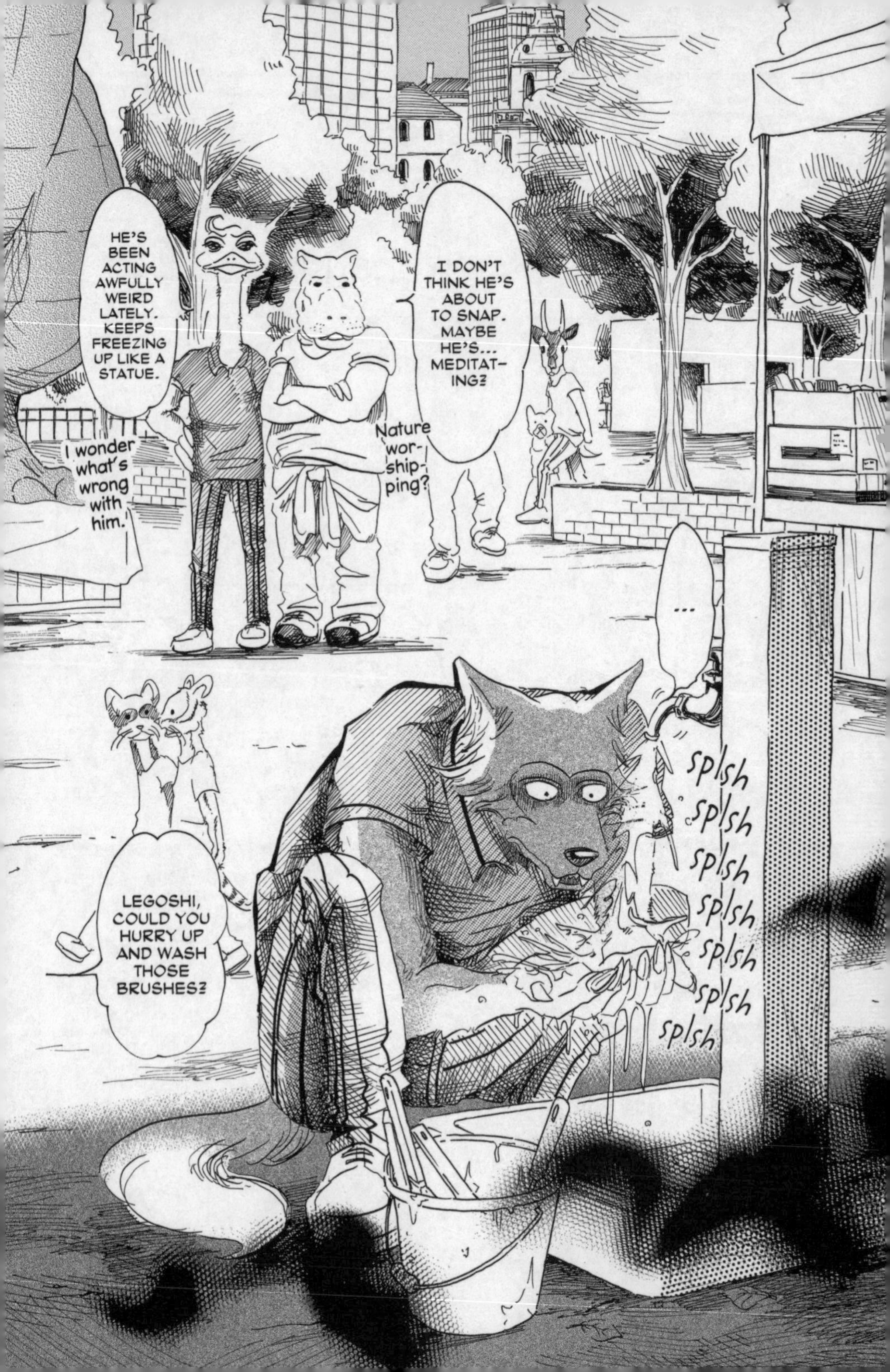
I DON'T THINK HE'S ABOUT TO SNAP. MAYBE HE'S... MEDITATING?
HE'S BEEN ACTING AWFULLY WEIRD LATELY. KEEPS FREEZING UP LIKE A STATUE.
Nature worshipping?
I wonder what's wrong with him.
...
splsh splsh splsh splsh splsh splsh splsh
LEGOSHI, COULD YOU HURRY UP AND WASH THOSE BRUSHES?

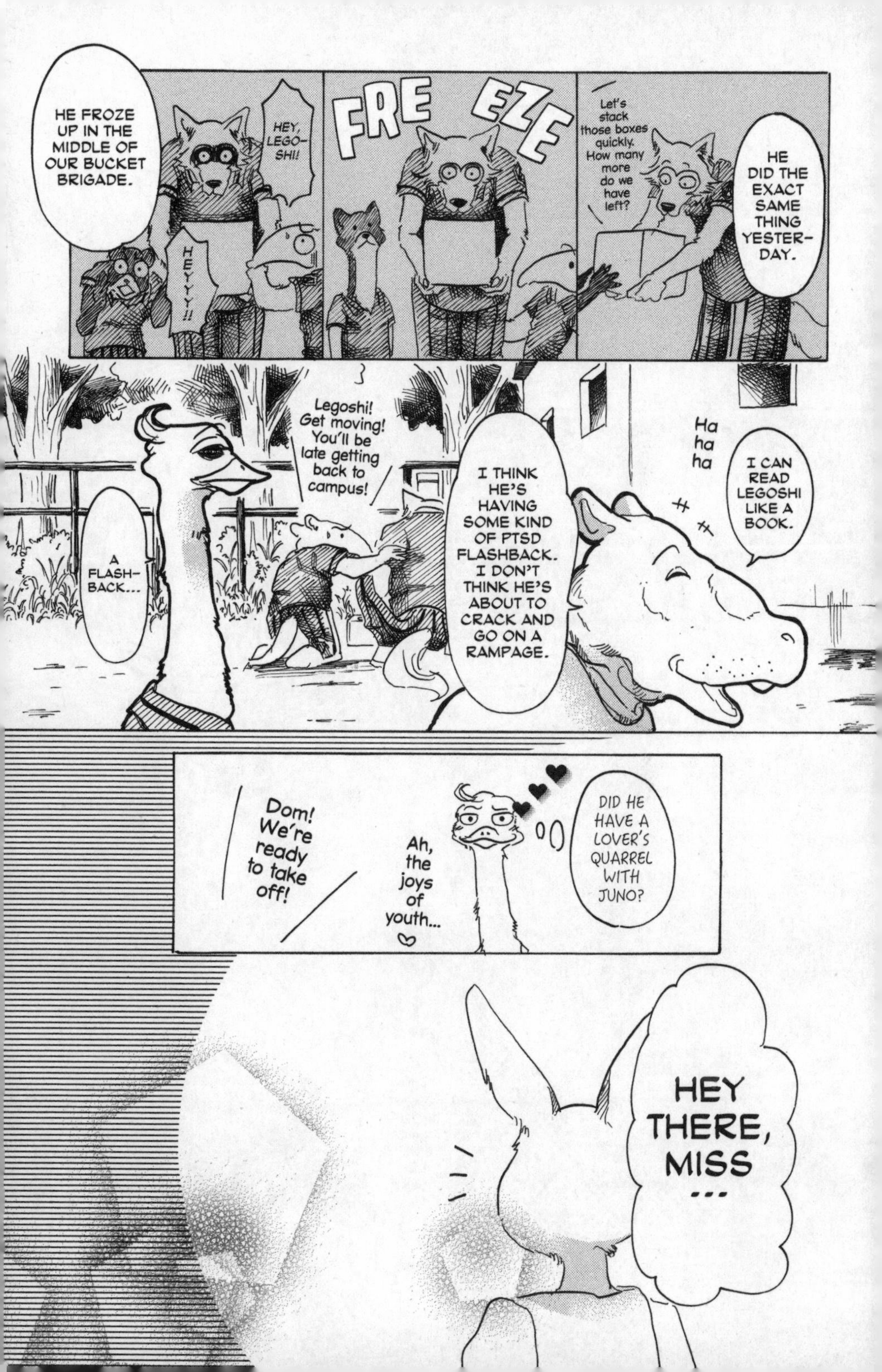
Let's stack those boxes quickly. How many more do we have left?
HE DID THE EXACT SAME THING YESTERDAY.
FREEZE
HEY, LEGOSHI!
HEYYY!!
HE FROZE UP IN THE MIDDLE OF OUR BUCKET BRIGADE.
I CAN READ LEGOSHI LIKE A BOOK.
Ha ha ha
I THINK HE'S HAVING SOME KIND OF PTSD FLASHBACK. I DON'T THINK HE'S ABOUT TO CRACK AND GO ON A RAMPAGE.
Legoshi! Get moving! You'll be late getting back to campus!
A FLASHBACK...
DID HE HAVE A LOVER'S QUARREL WITH JUNO?
Ah, the joys of youth...
Dom! We're ready to take off!
HEY THERE, MISS ...

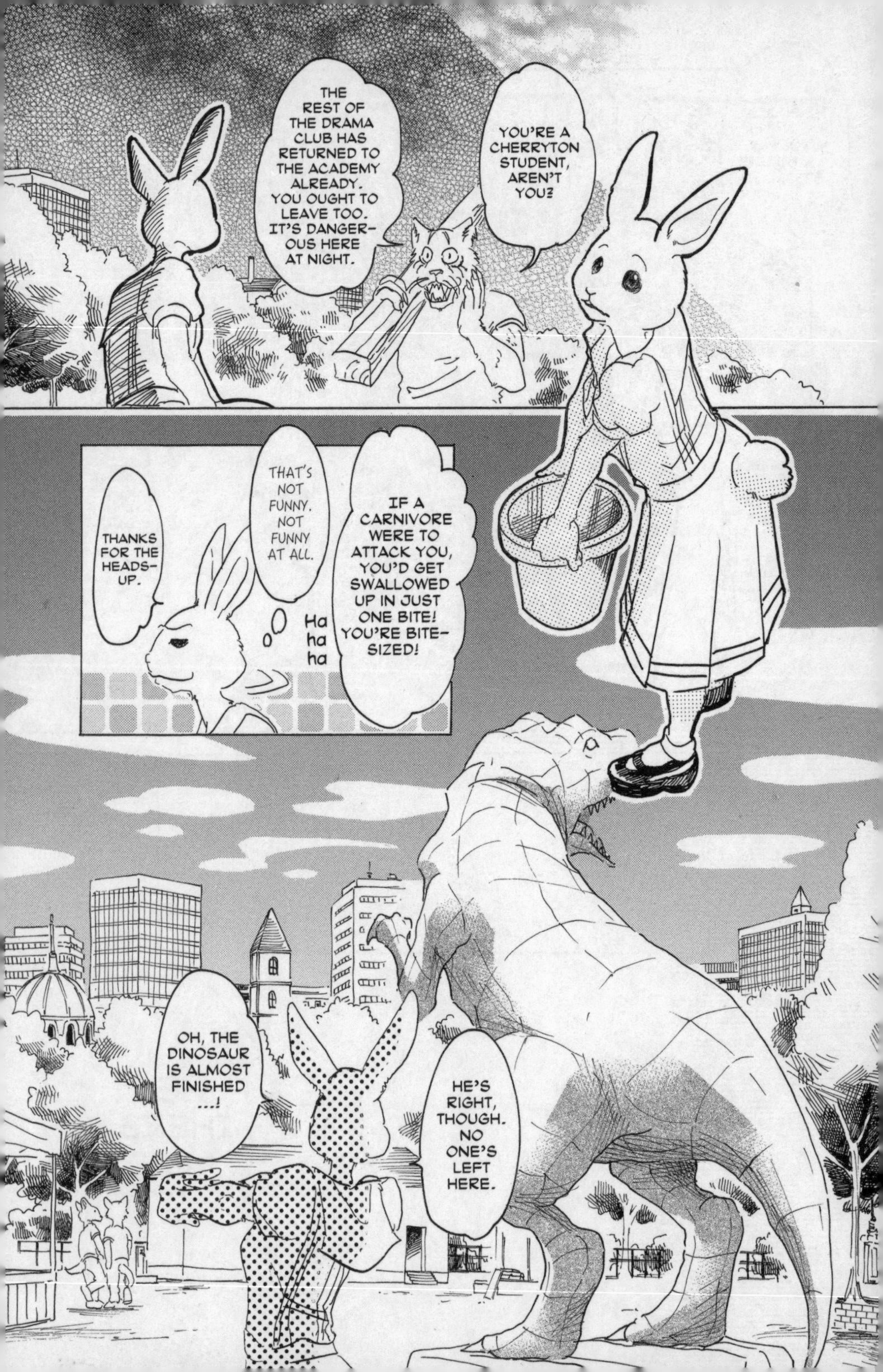
YOU'RE A CHERRYTON STUDENT, AREN'T YOU?
THE REST OF THE DRAMA CLUB HAS RETURNED TO THE ACADEMY ALREADY. YOU OUGHT TO LEAVE TOO. IT'S DANGEROUS HERE AT NIGHT.
IF A CARNIVORE WERE TO ATTACK YOU, YOU'D GET SWALLOWED UP IN JUST ONE BITE! YOU'RE BITE-SIZED!
Ha ha ha
THAT'S NOT FUNNY. NOT FUNNY AT ALL.
THANKS FOR THE HEADS-UP.
HE'S RIGHT, THOUGH. NO ONE'S LEFT HERE.
OH, THE DINOSAUR IS ALMOST FINISHED ...!

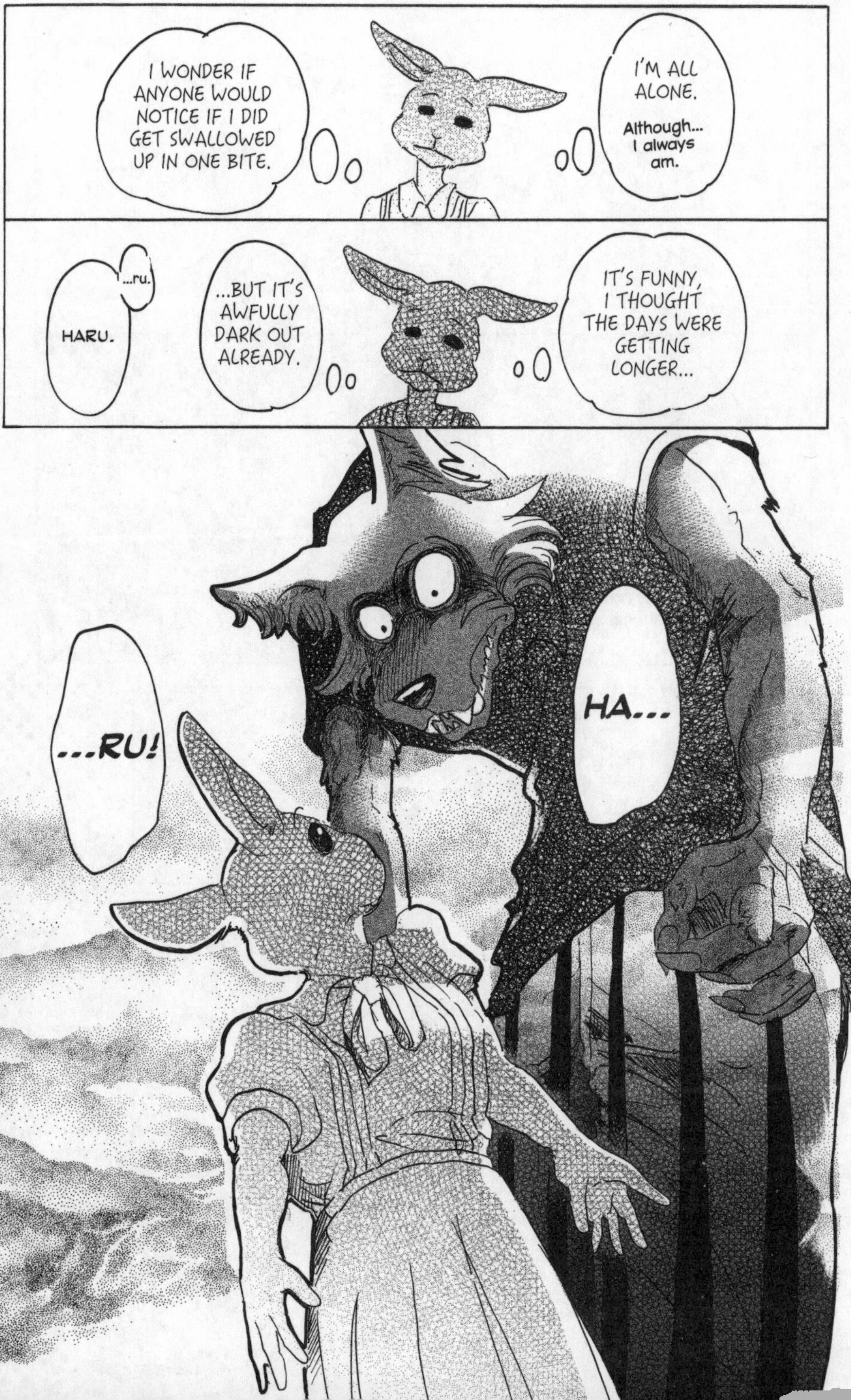
I'M ALL ALONE.
Although... I always am.
I WONDER IF ANYONE WOULD NOTICE IF I DID GET SWALLOWED UP IN ONE BITE.
IT'S FUNNY, I THOUGHT THE DAYS WERE GETTING LONGER...
...BUT IT'S AWFULLY DARK OUT ALREADY.
...ru.
HARU.
HA...
...RU!

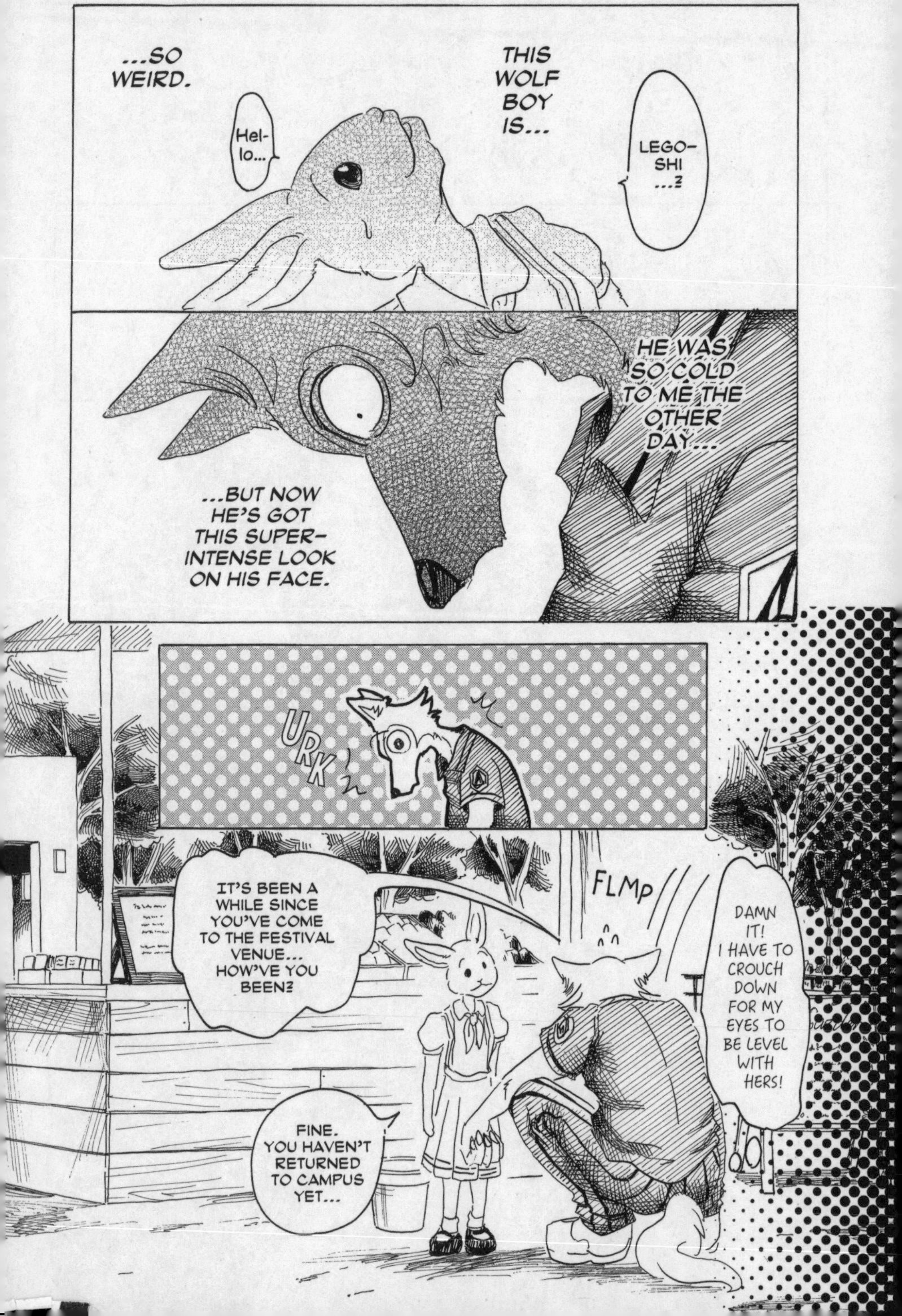
LEGO-SHI ...?
THIS WOLF BOY IS...
...SO WEIRD.
Hel-lo...
HE WAS SO COLD TO ME THE OTHER DAY...
...BUT NOW HE'S GOT THIS SUPER-INTENSE LOOK ON HIS FACE.
URK
DAMN IT! I HAVE TO CROUCH DOWN FOR MY EYES TO BE LEVEL WITH HERS!
FLMP
IT'S BEEN A WHILE SINCE YOU'VE COME TO THE FESTIVAL VENUE... HOW'VE YOU BEEN?
FINE. YOU HAVEN'T RETURNED TO CAMPUS YET...

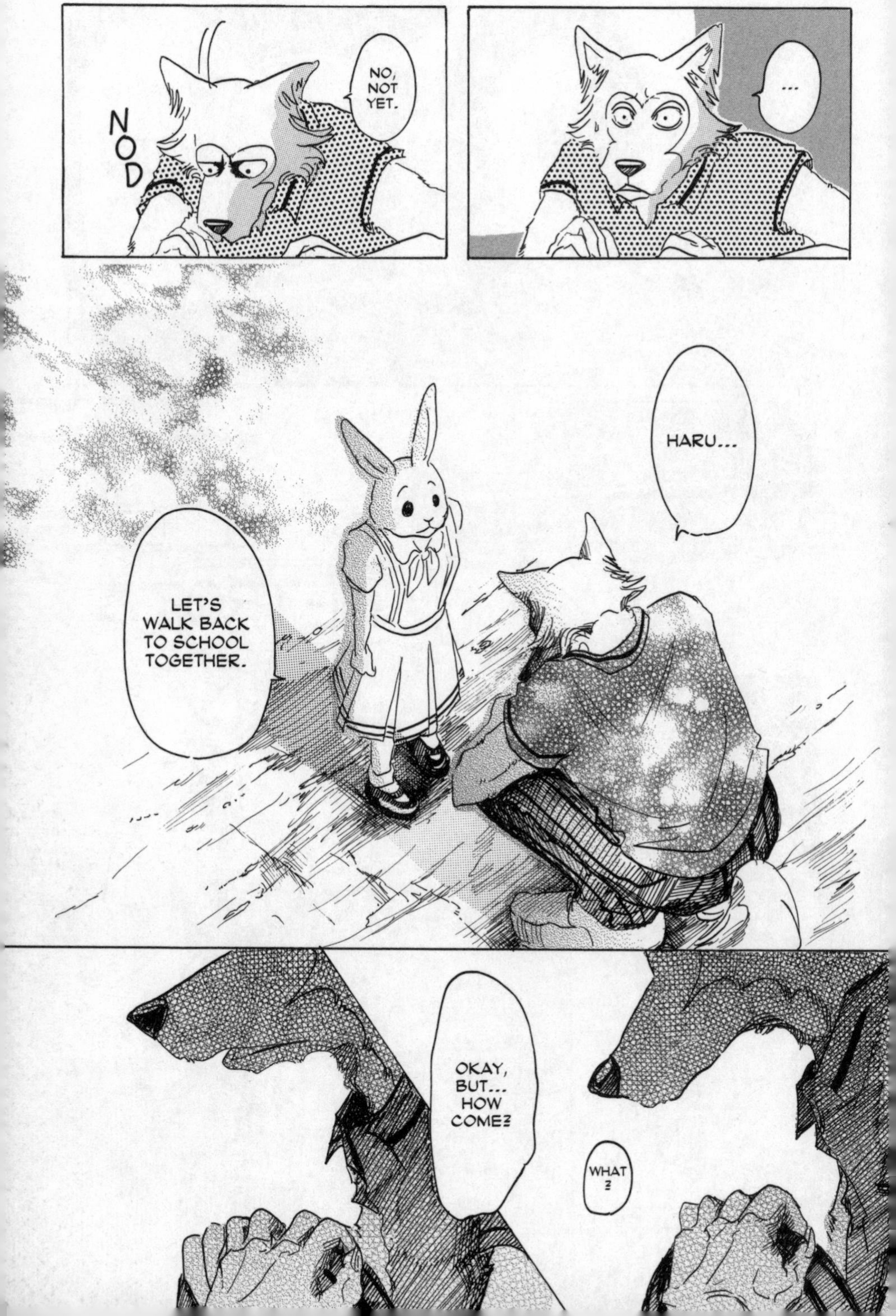
...
NO, NOT YET.
NOD
HARU...
LET'S WALK BACK TO SCHOOL TOGETHER.
WHAT?
OKAY, BUT... HOW COME?

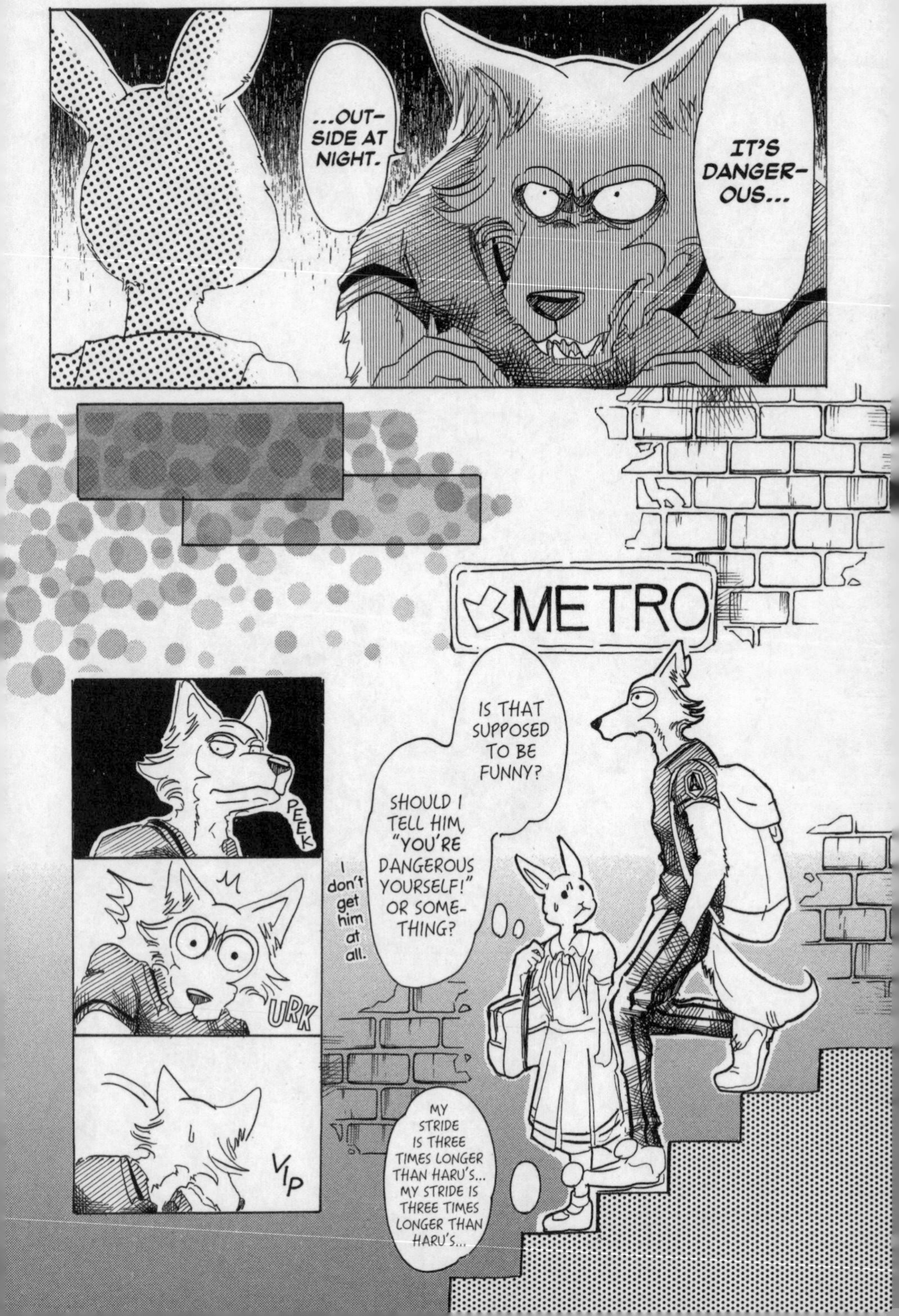
IT'S DANGER-OUS...
...OUT-SIDE AT NIGHT.
METRO
IS THAT SUPPOSED TO BE FUNNY?
SHOULD I TELL HIM, "YOU'RE DANGEROUS YOURSELF!" OR SOME-THING?
I don't get him at all.
MY STRIDE IS THREE TIMES LONGER THAN HARU'S... MY STRIDE IS THREE TIMES LONGER THAN HARU'S...
PEEK
URK
VIP

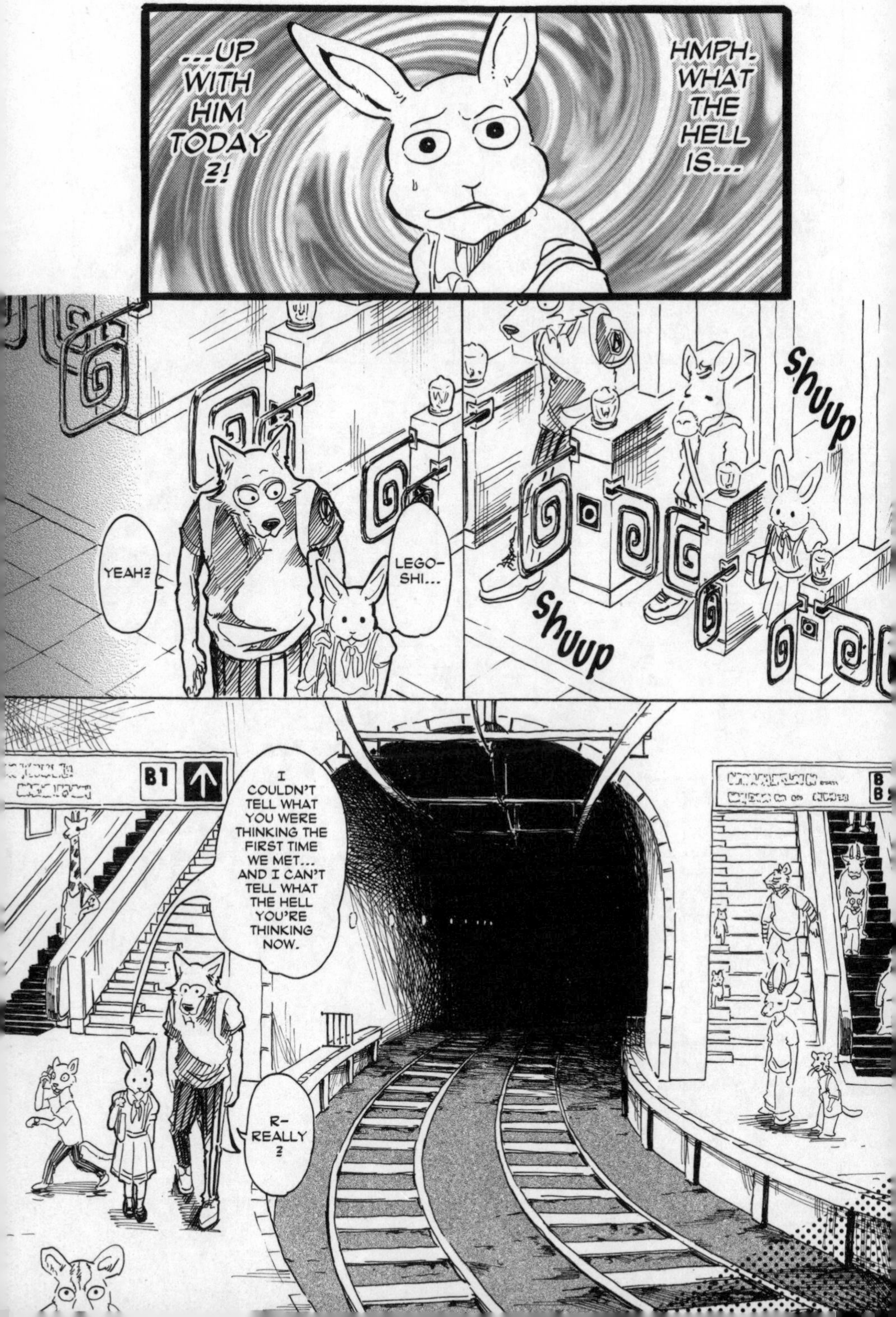
HMPH. WHAT THE HELL IS...
...UP WITH HIM TODAY?!
SHUUP
SHUUP
LEGO-SHI...
YEAH?
B1
I COULDN'T TELL WHAT YOU WERE THINKING THE FIRST TIME WE MET... AND I CAN'T TELL WHAT THE HELL YOU'RE THINKING NOW.
R-REALLY?

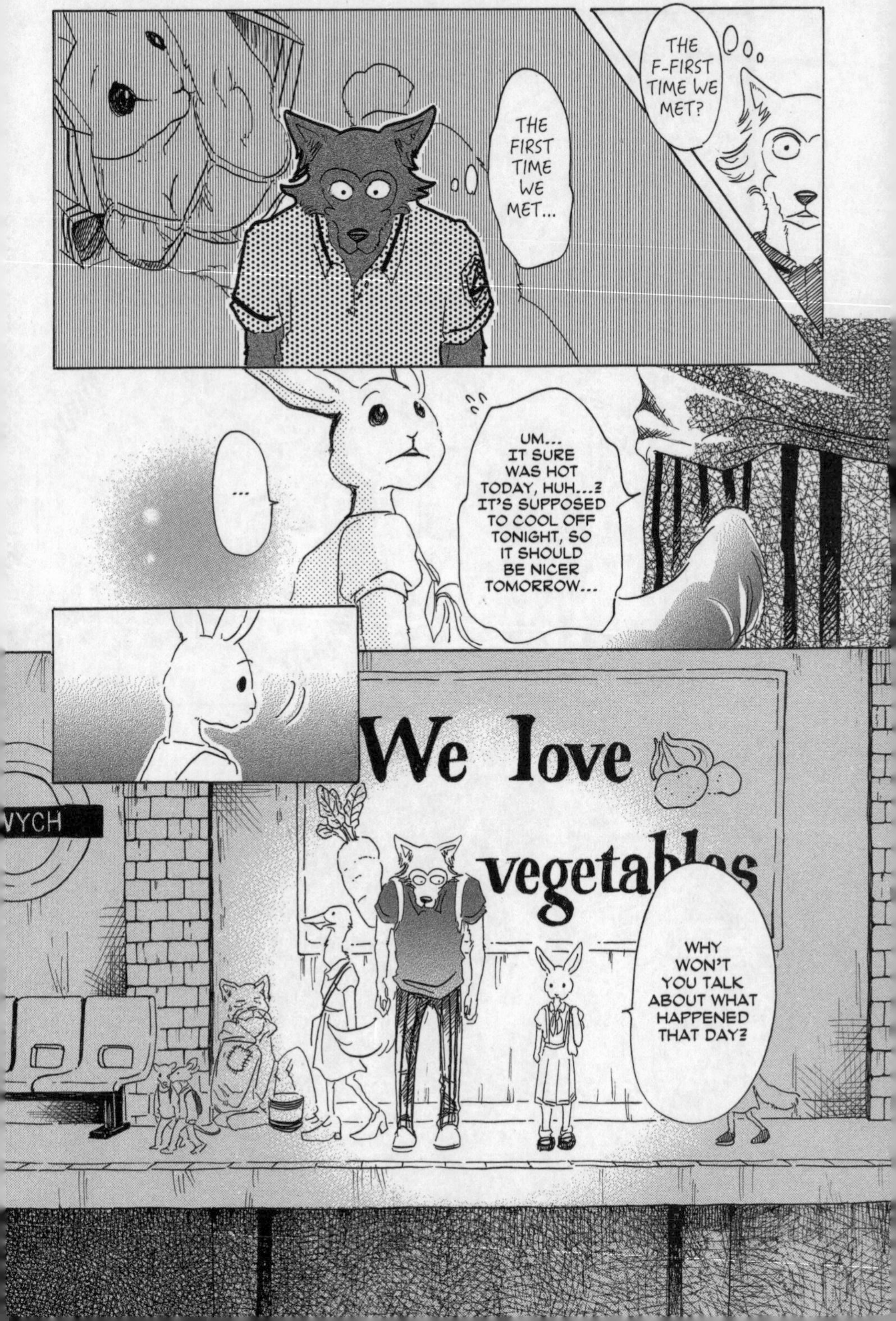

THE F-FIRST TIME WE MET?
THE FIRST TIME WE MET...
UM... IT SURE WAS HOT TODAY, HUH...? IT'S SUPPOSED TO COOL OFF TONIGHT, SO IT SHOULD BE NICER TOMORROW...
...
We love vegetab
VYCH
WHY WON'T YOU TALK ABOUT WHAT HAPPENED THAT DAY?

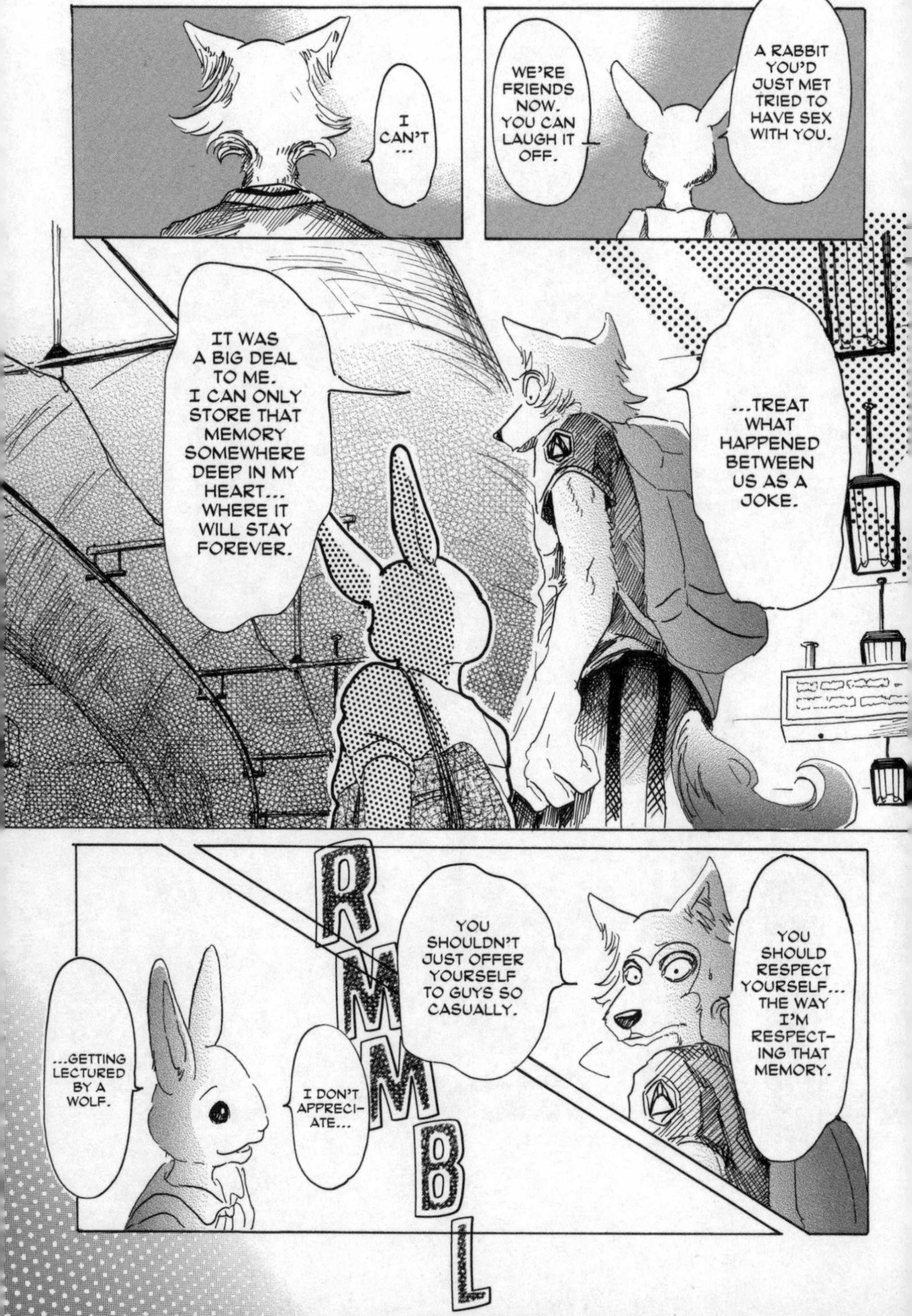
A RABBIT YOU'D JUST MET TRIED TO HAVE SEX WITH YOU.
WE'RE FRIENDS NOW. YOU CAN LAUGH IT OFF.
I CAN'T ...
...TREAT WHAT HAPPENED BETWEEN US AS A JOKE.
IT WAS A BIG DEAL TO ME. I CAN ONLY STORE THAT MEMORY SOMEWHERE DEEP IN MY HEART... WHERE IT WILL STAY FOREVER.
YOU SHOULD RESPECT YOURSELF... THE WAY I'M RESPECTING THAT MEMORY.
YOU SHOULDN'T JUST OFFER YOURSELF TO GUYS SO CASUALLY.
RMMMBL
I DON'T APPRECIATE...
...GETTING LECTURED BY A WOLF.

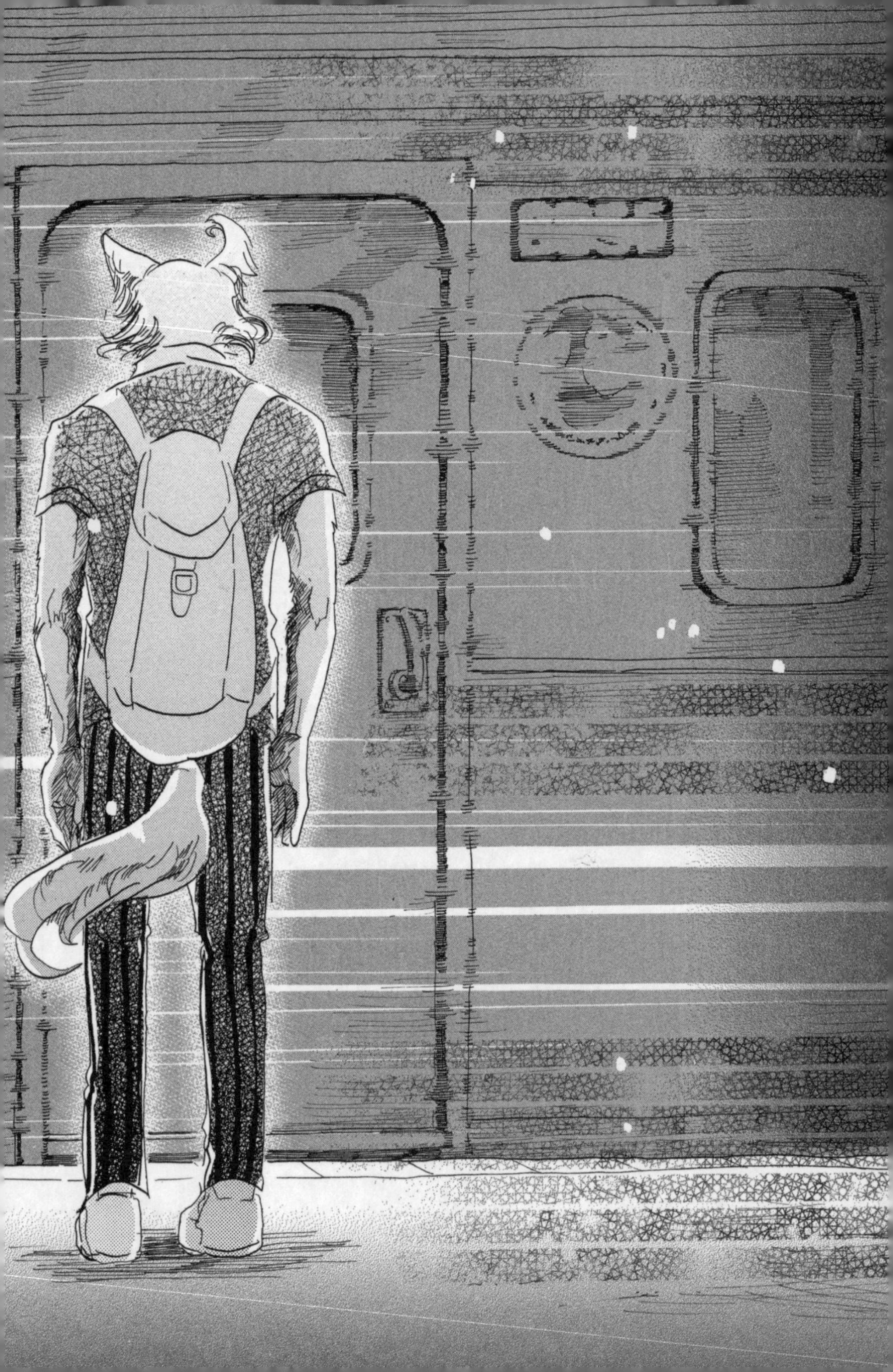

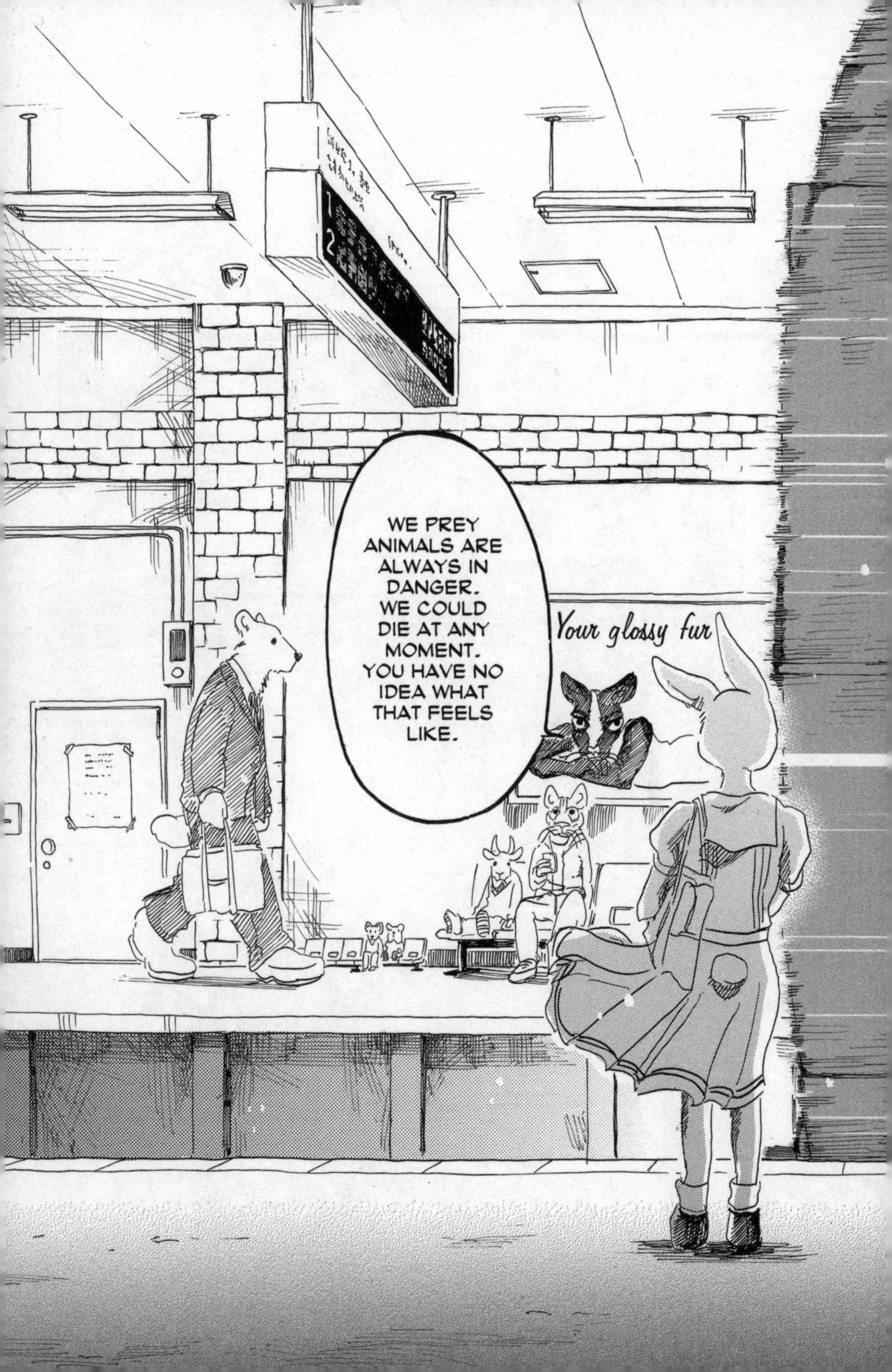
Your glossy fur
WE PREY ANIMALS ARE ALWAYS IN DANGER. WE COULD DIE AT ANY MOMENT. YOU HAVE NO IDEA WHAT THAT FEELS LIKE.

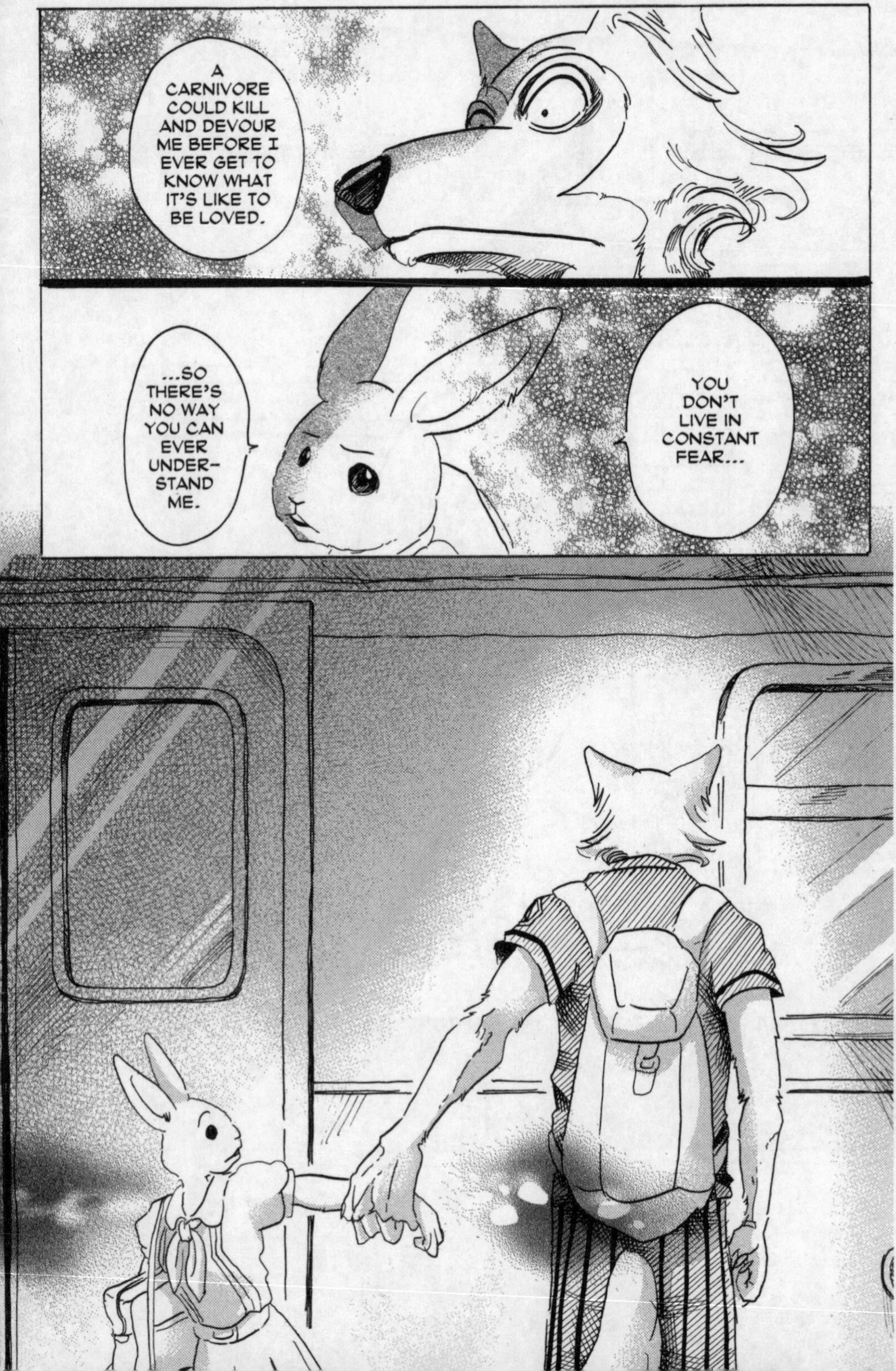
A CARNIVORE COULD KILL AND DEVOUR ME BEFORE I EVER GET TO KNOW WHAT IT'S LIKE TO BE LOVED.
YOU DON'T LIVE IN CONSTANT FEAR...
...SO THERE'S NO WAY YOU CAN EVER UNDER-STAND ME.

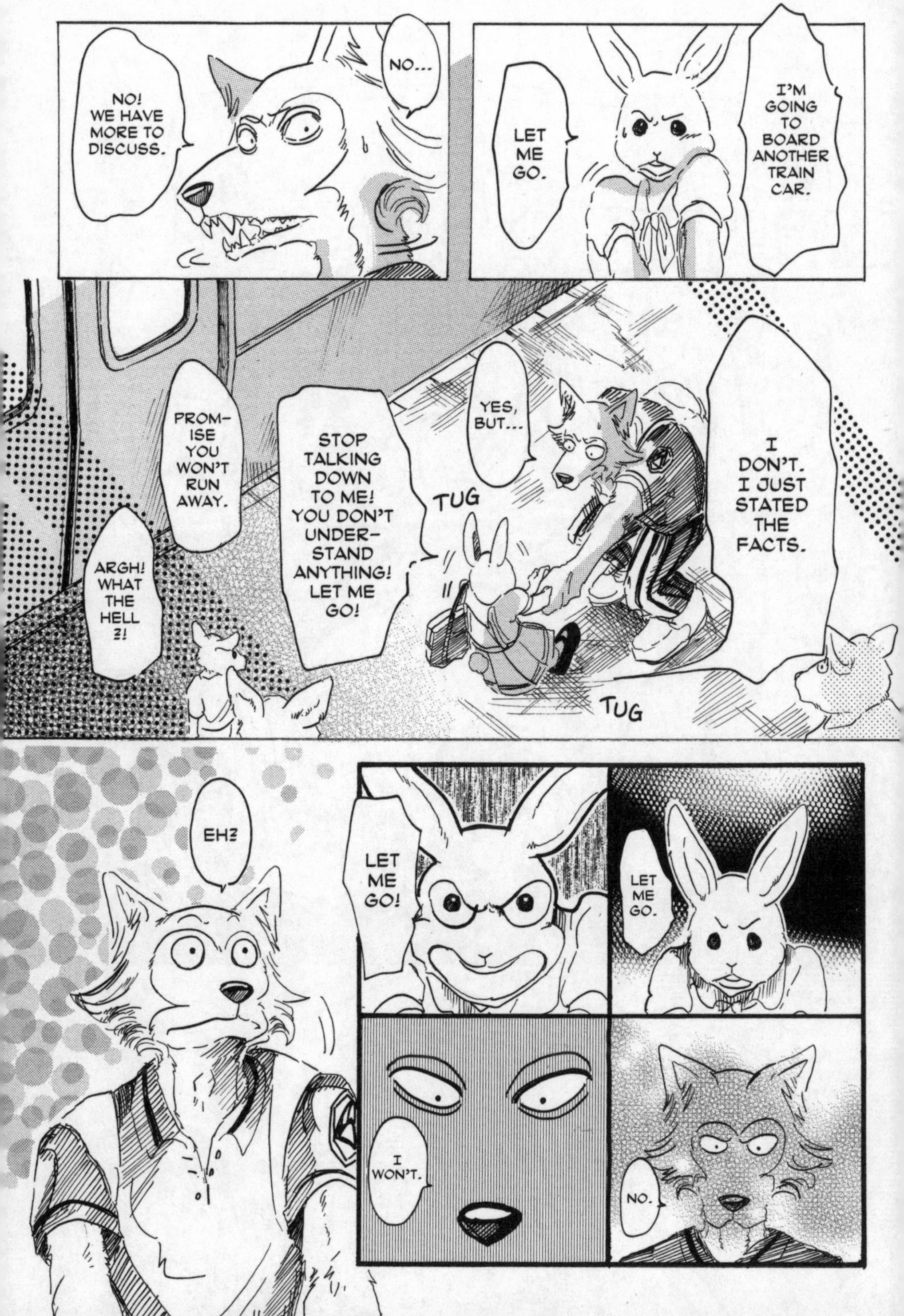
I'M GOING TO BOARD ANOTHER TRAIN CAR.
LET ME GO.
NO...
NO! WE HAVE MORE TO DISCUSS.
I DON'T. I JUST STATED THE FACTS.
YES, BUT...
TUG
STOP TALKING DOWN TO ME! YOU DON'T UNDERSTAND ANYTHING! LET ME GO!
PROMISE YOU WON'T RUN AWAY.
ARGH! WHAT THE HELL?!
TUG
LET ME GO.
LET ME GO!
NO.
I WON'T.
EH?

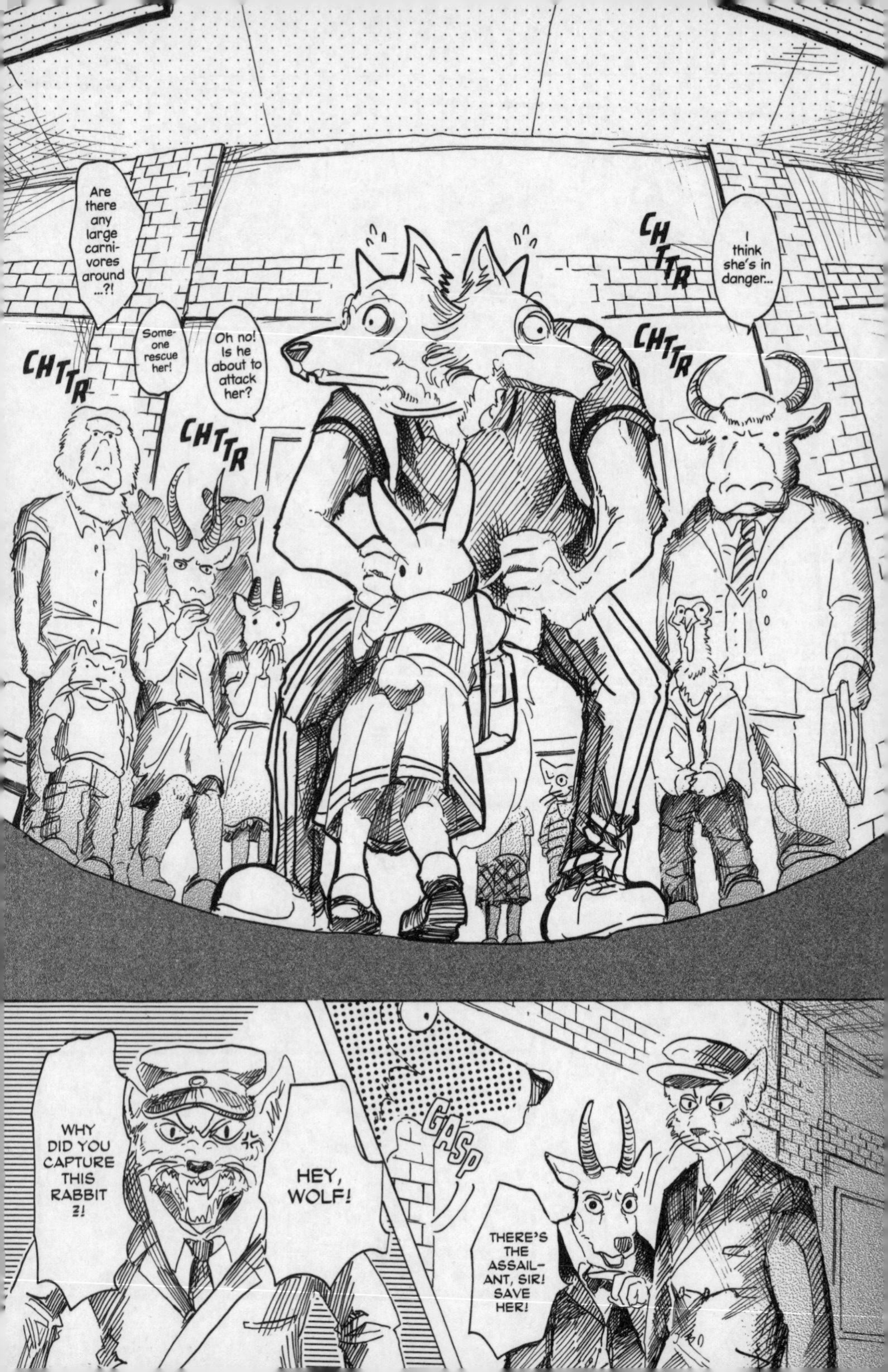
I think she's in danger...
CHTTR
CHTTR
Oh no! Is he about to attack her?
Some-one rescue her!
Are there any large carni-vores around ...?!
CHTTR
CHTTR
THERE'S THE ASSAIL-ANT, SIR! SAVE HER!
GASP
HEY, WOLF!
WHY DID YOU CAPTURE THIS RABBIT ?!

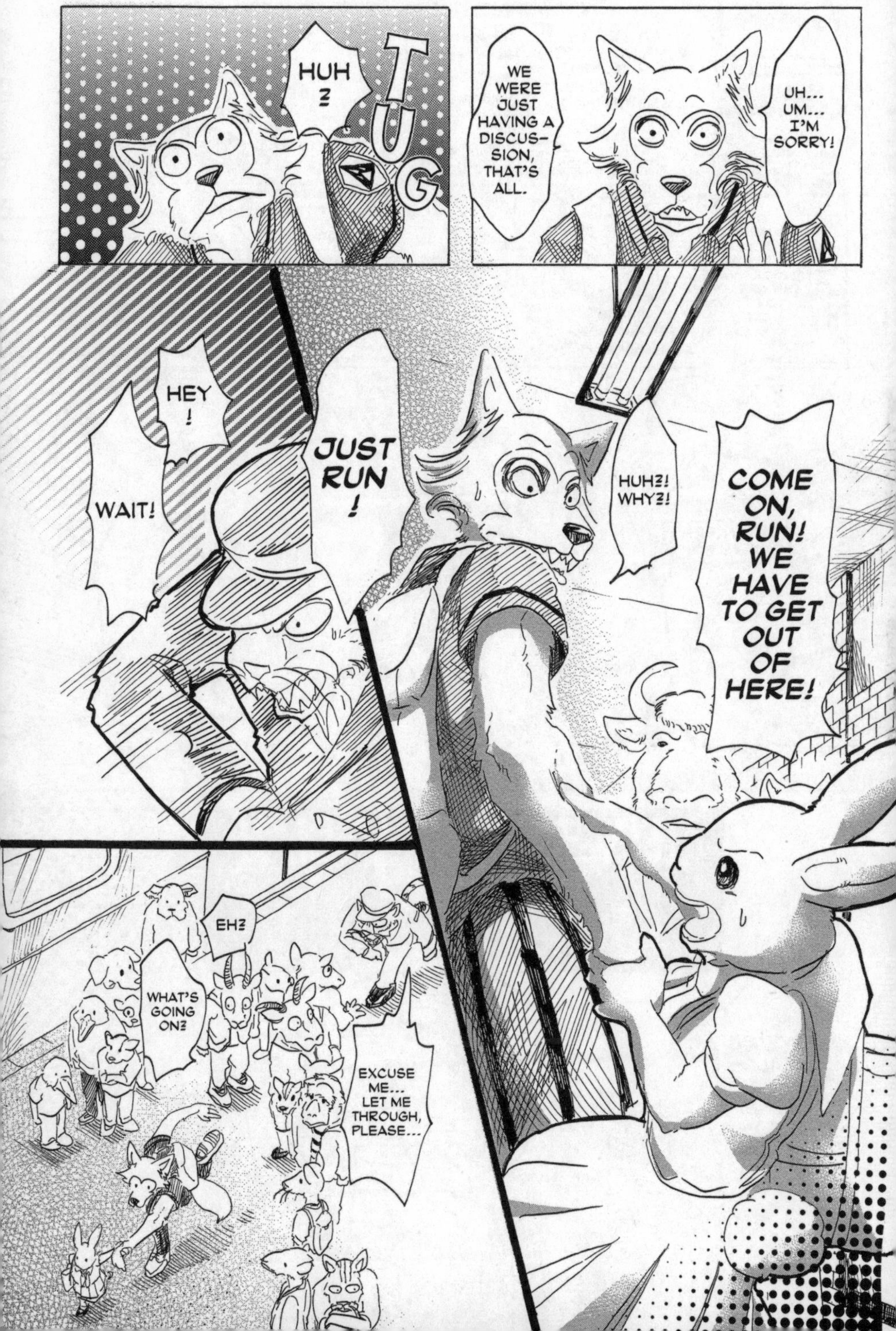
UH... UM... I'M SORRY!
WE WERE JUST HAVING A DISCUS-SION, THAT'S ALL.
TUG
HUH?
COME ON, RUN! WE HAVE TO GET OUT OF HERE!
HUH?! WHY?!
JUST RUN!
HEY!
WAIT!
EXCUSE ME... LET ME THROUGH, PLEASE...
EH?
WHAT'S GOING ON?

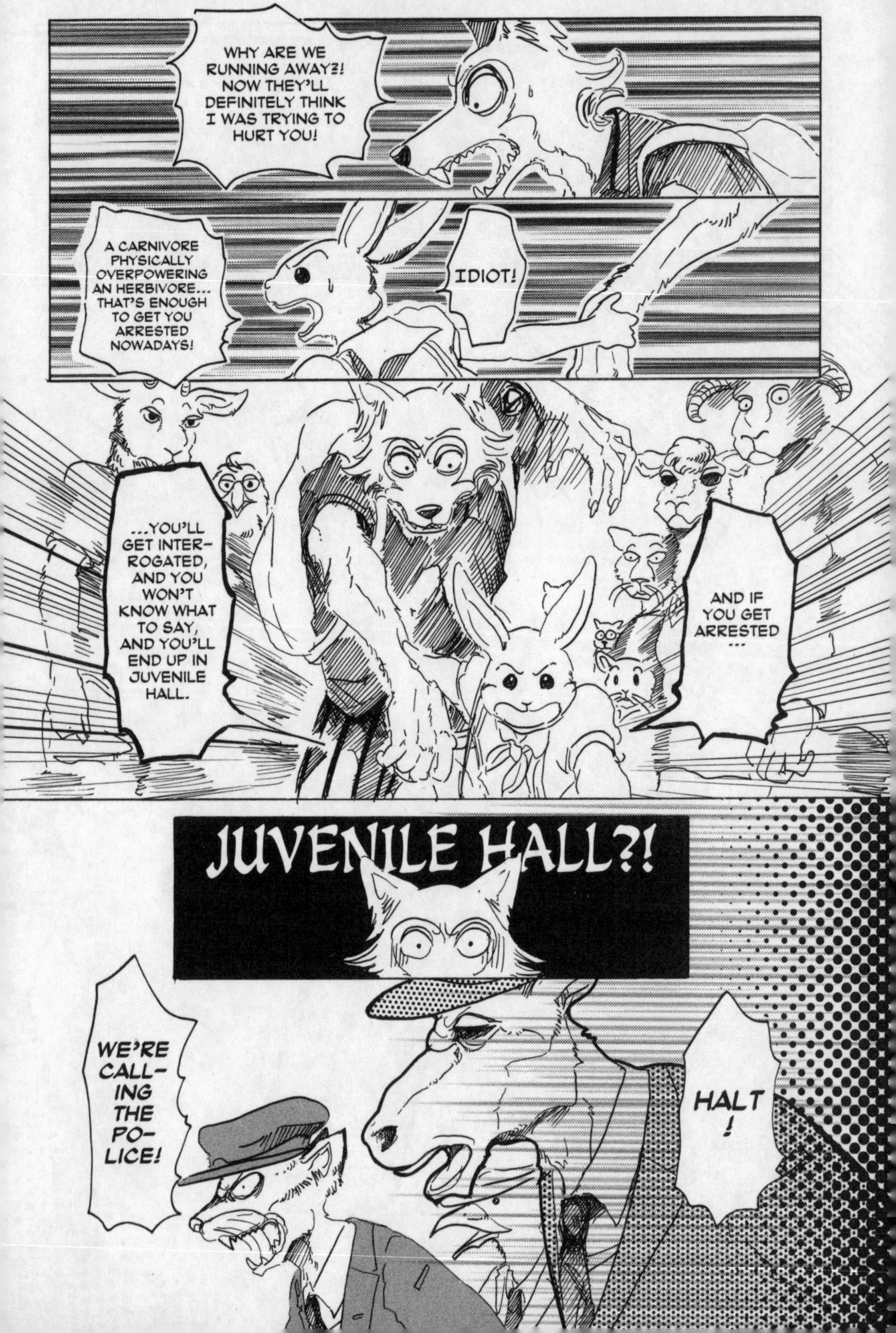
WHY ARE WE RUNNING AWAY?! NOW THEY'LL DEFINITELY THINK I WAS TRYING TO HURT YOU!
IDIOT!
A CARNIVORE PHYSICALLY OVERPOWERING AN HERBIVORE... THAT'S ENOUGH TO GET YOU ARRESTED NOWADAYS!
AND IF YOU GET ARRESTED...
...YOU'LL GET INTER-ROGATED, AND YOU WON'T KNOW WHAT TO SAY, AND YOU'LL END UP IN JUVENILE HALL.
JUVENILE HALL?!
HALT!
WE'RE CALL-ING THE PO-LICE!

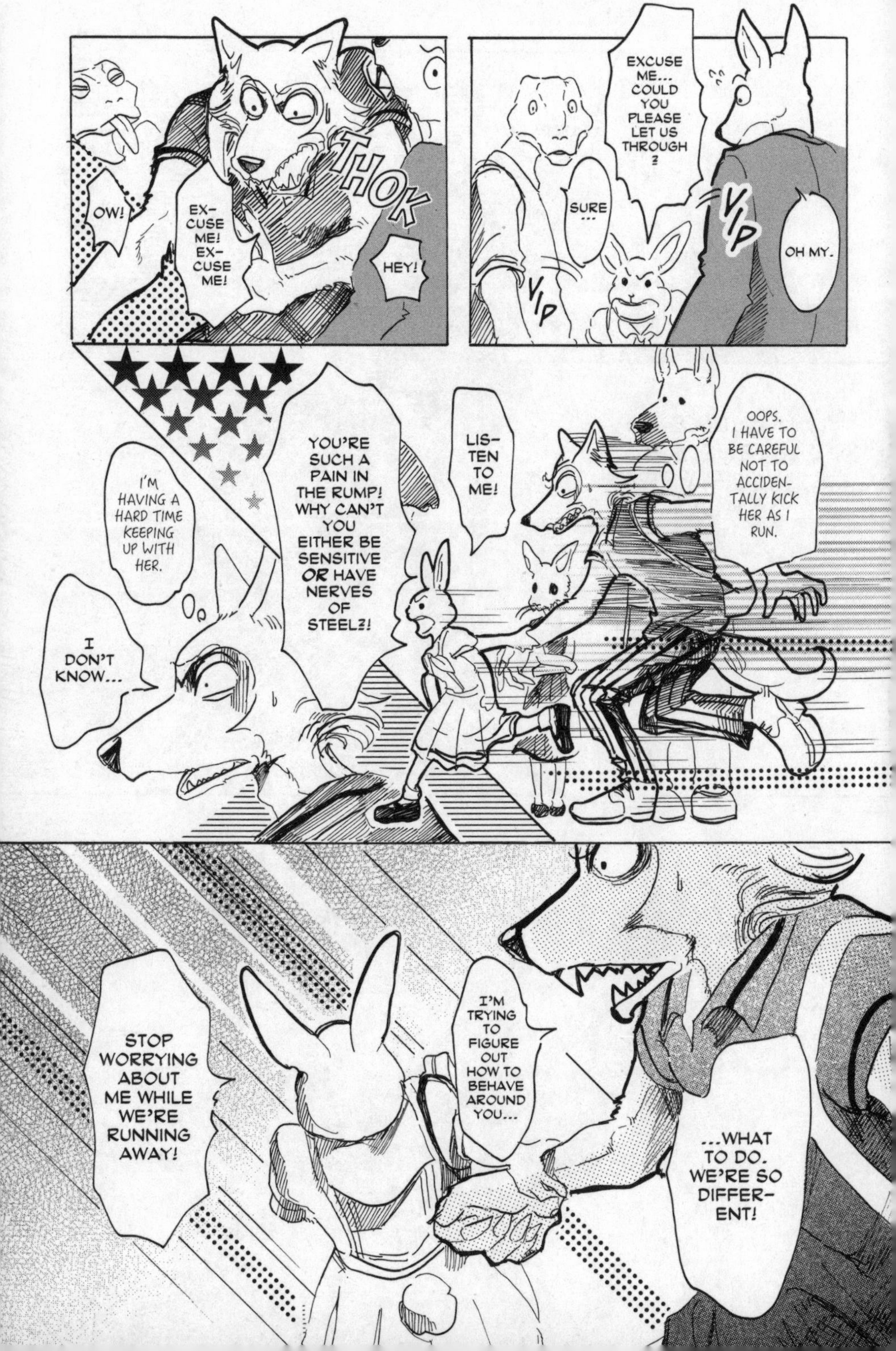
EXCUSE ME... COULD YOU PLEASE LET US THROUGH?
OH MY.
VIP
SURE...
VIP
THOK
HEY!
EX-CUSE ME! EX-CUSE ME!
OW!
OOPS. I HAVE TO BE CAREFUL NOT TO ACCIDEN-TALLY KICK HER AS I RUN.
LIS-TEN TO ME!
YOU'RE SUCH A PAIN IN THE RUMP! WHY CAN'T YOU EITHER BE SENSITIVE *OR* HAVE NERVES OF STEEL?!
I'M HAVING A HARD TIME KEEPING UP WITH HER.
I DON'T KNOW...
I'M TRYING TO FIGURE OUT HOW TO BEHAVE AROUND YOU...
...WHAT TO DO. WE'RE SO DIFFER-ENT!
STOP WORRYING ABOUT ME WHILE WE'RE RUNNING AWAY!

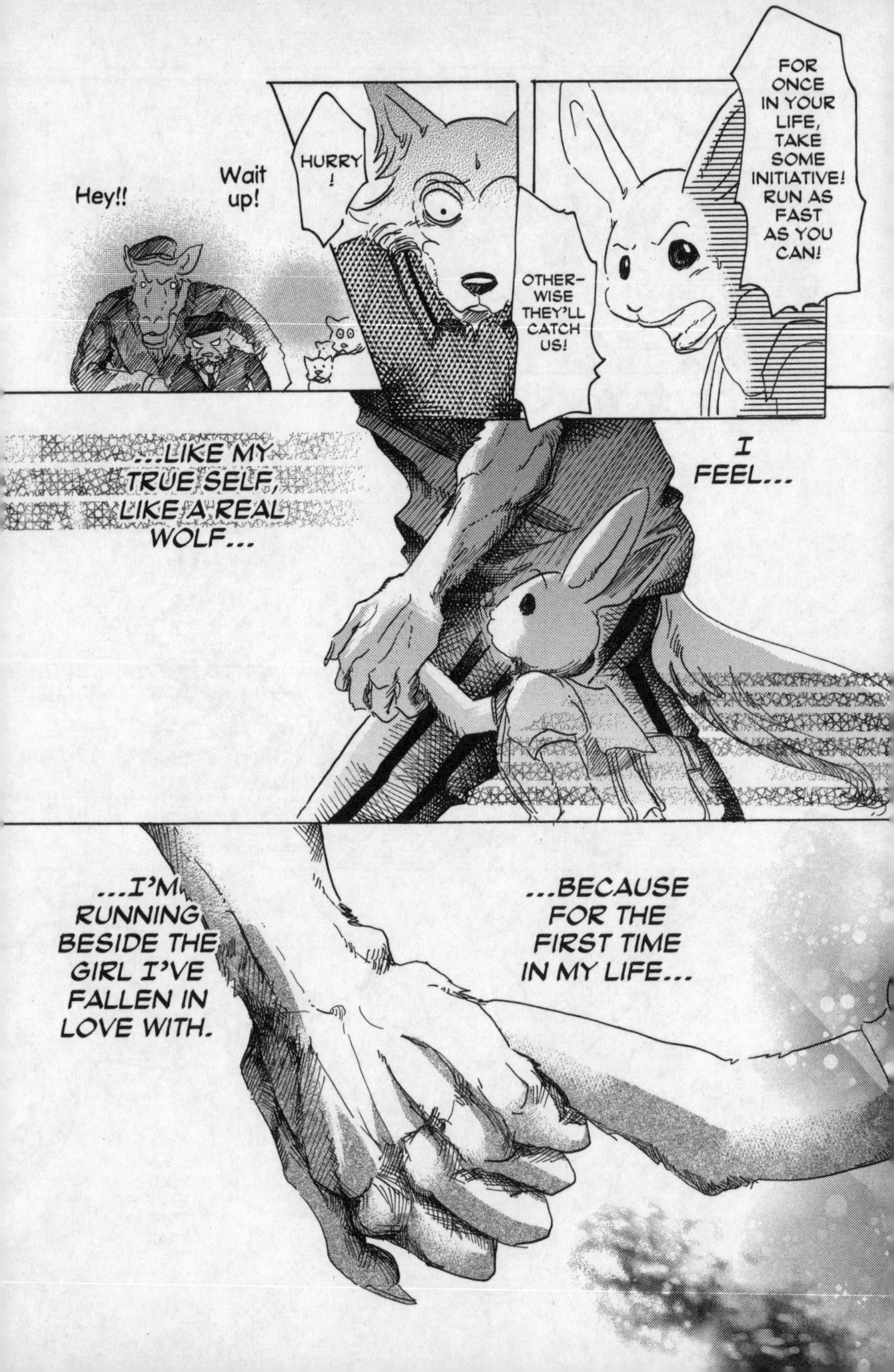
FOR ONCE IN YOUR LIFE, TAKE SOME INITIATIVE! RUN AS FAST AS YOU CAN!
OTHER-WISE THEY'LL CATCH US!
HURRY!
Wait up!
Hey!!
I FEEL...
...LIKE MY TRUE SELF, LIKE A REAL WOLF...
...BECAUSE FOR THE FIRST TIME IN MY LIFE...
...I'M RUNNING BESIDE THE GIRL I'VE FALLEN IN LOVE WITH.

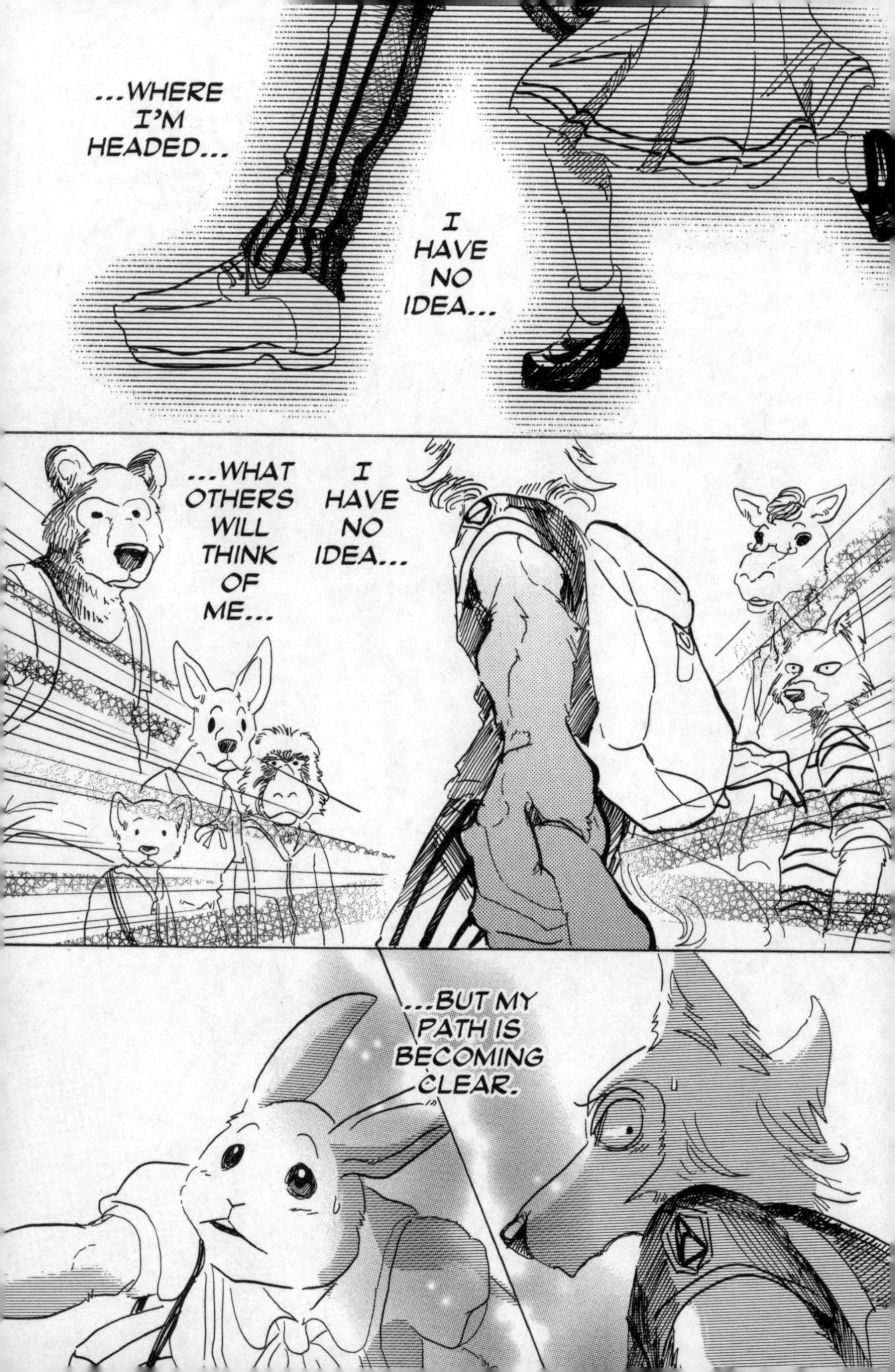
I HAVE NO IDEA...
...WHERE I'M HEADED...
I HAVE NO IDEA...
...WHAT OTHERS WILL THINK OF ME...
...BUT MY PATH IS BECOMING CLEAR.

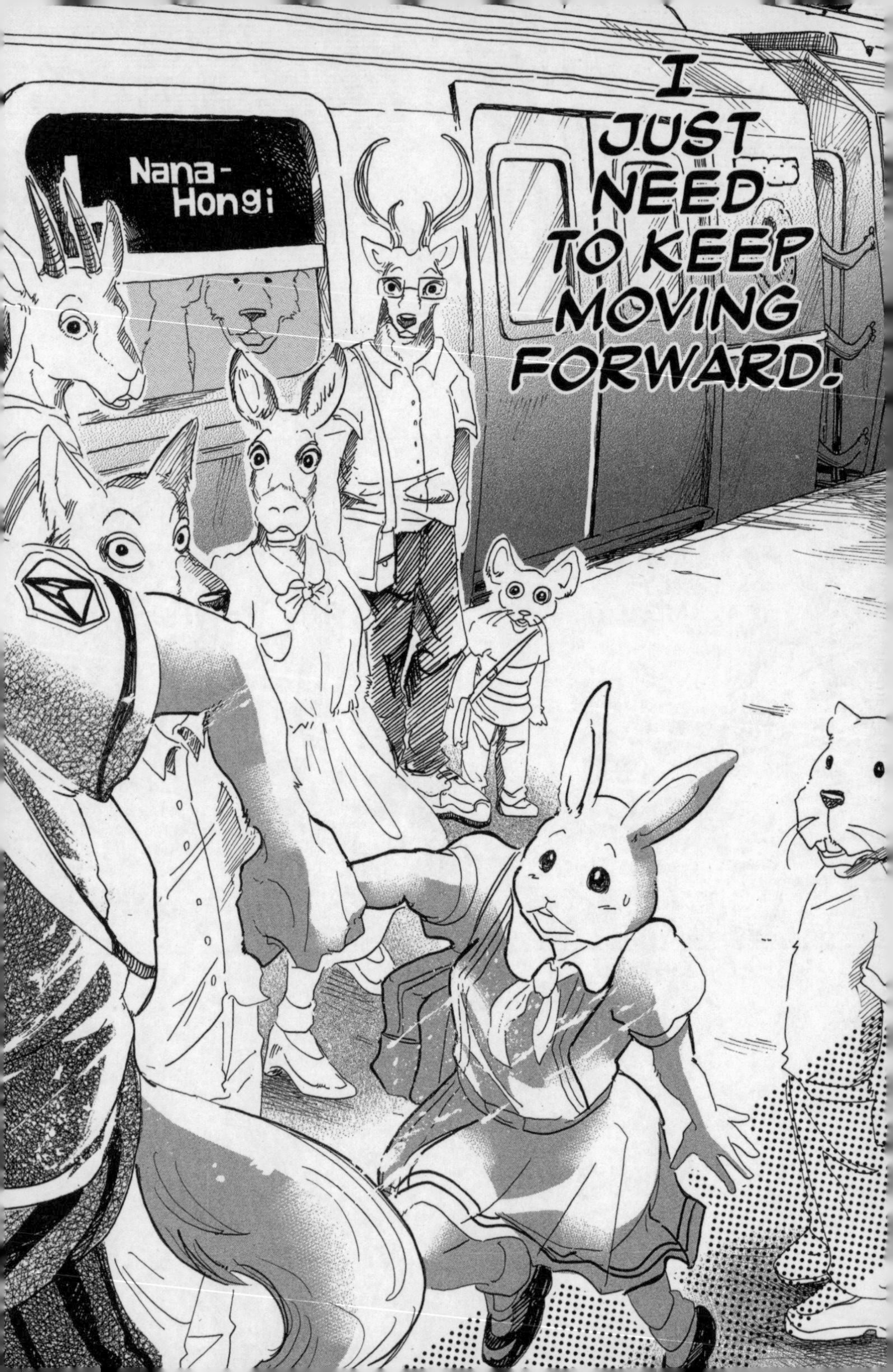
Nana-
Hongi
I JUST NEED TO KEEP MOVING FORWARD!

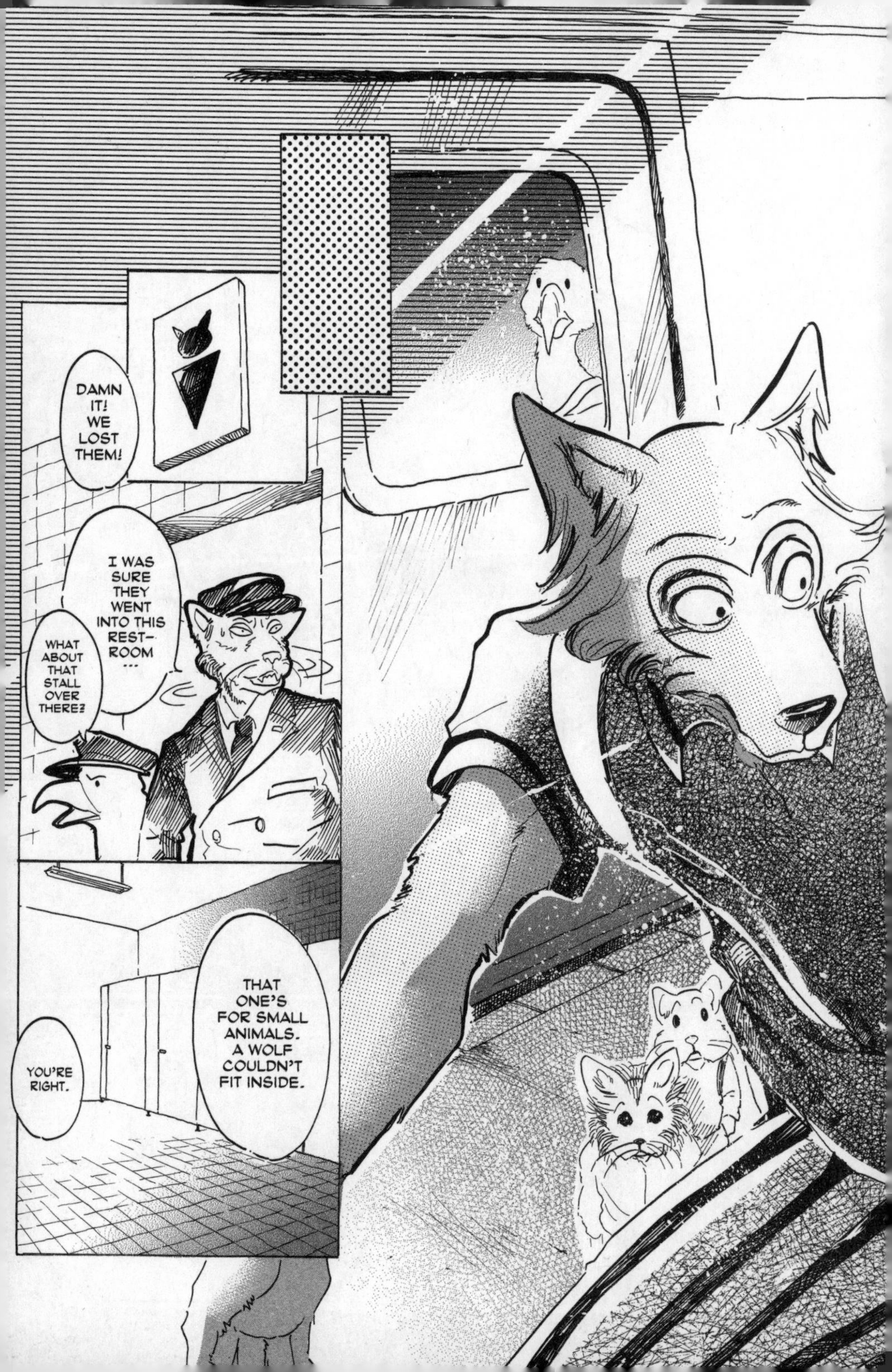
DAMN IT! WE LOST THEM!
I WAS SURE THEY WENT INTO THIS REST-ROOM...
WHAT ABOUT THAT STALL OVER THERE?
THAT ONE'S FOR SMALL ANIMALS. A WOLF COULDN'T FIT INSIDE.
YOU'RE RIGHT.

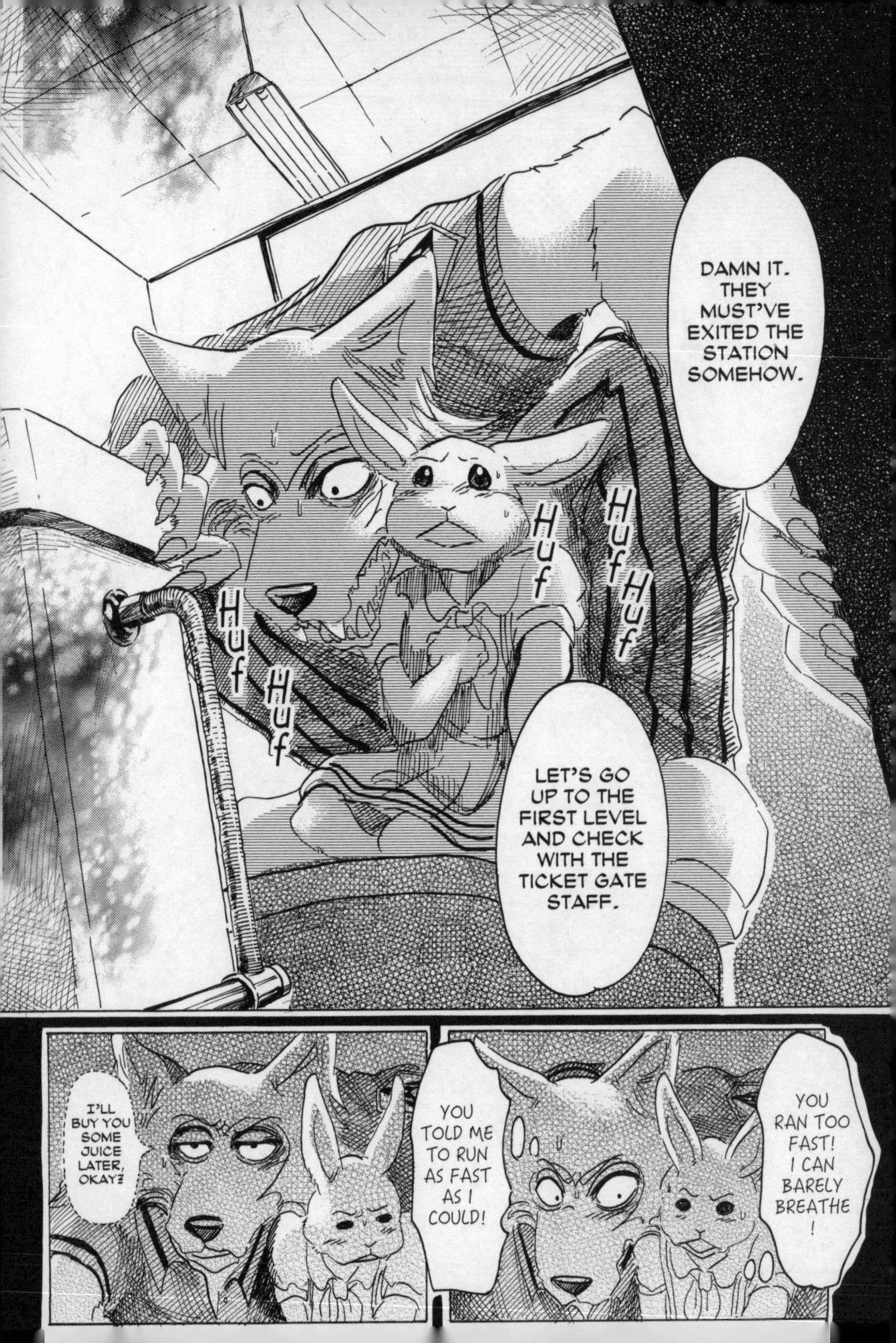
DAMN IT. THEY MUST'VE EXITED THE STATION SOMEHOW.
Huf Huf
Huf Huf
LET'S GO UP TO THE FIRST LEVEL AND CHECK WITH THE TICKET GATE STAFF.
YOU RAN TOO FAST! I CAN BARELY BREATHE!
YOU TOLD ME TO RUN AS FAST AS I COULD!
I'LL BUY YOU SOME JUICE LATER, OKAY?

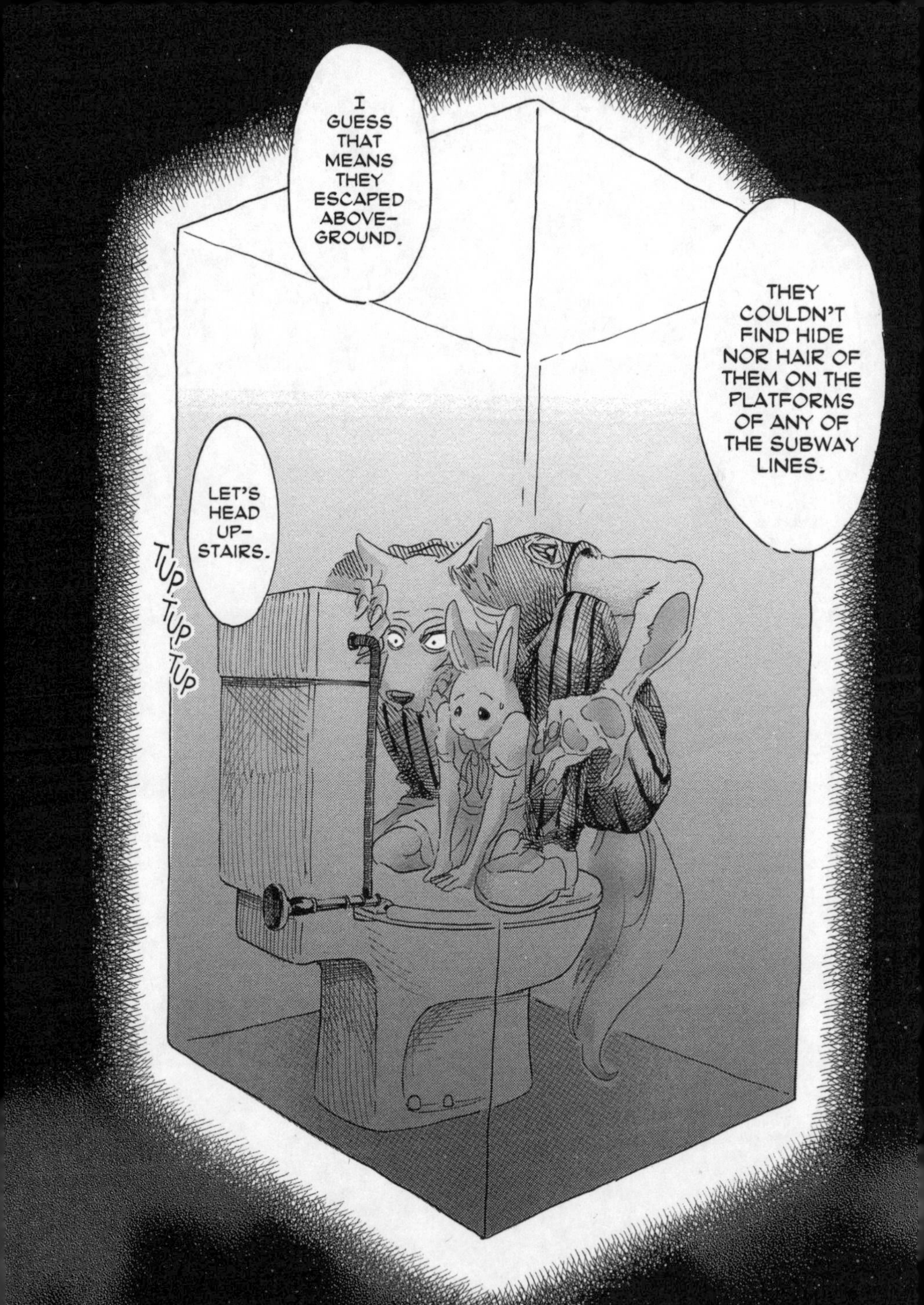
THEY COULDN'T FIND HIDE NOR HAIR OF THEM ON THE PLATFORMS OF ANY OF THE SUBWAY LINES.
I GUESS THAT MEANS THEY ESCAPED ABOVE-GROUND.
LET'S HEAD UP-STAIRS.
TUP TUP TUP TUP

Chapter 30: The Iron Tamer

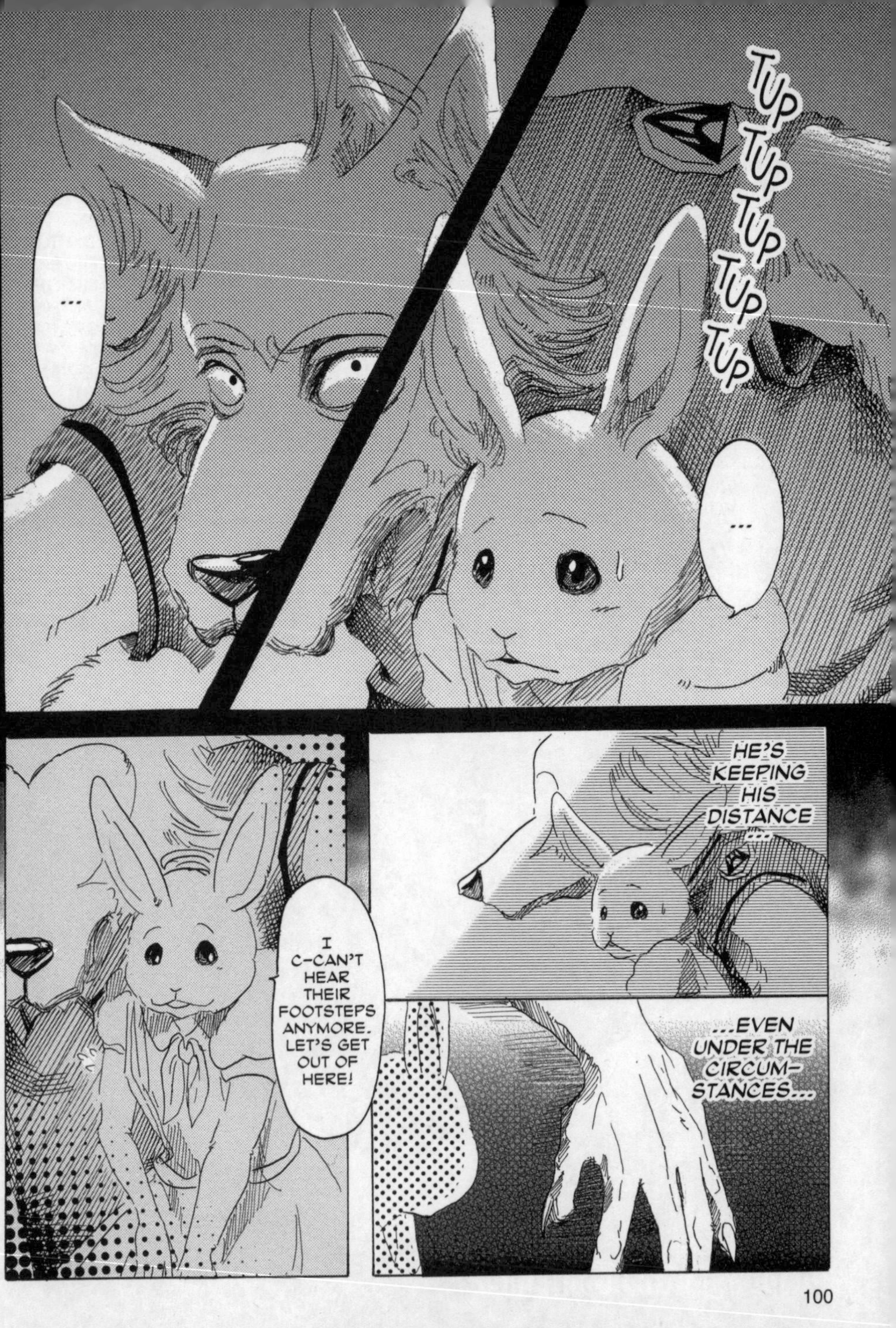
TUP TUP TUP TUP TUP TUP
...
...
HE'S KEEPING HIS DISTANCE...
...EVEN UNDER THE CIRCUMSTANCES...
I C-CAN'T HEAR THEIR FOOTSTEPS ANYMORE. LET'S GET OUT OF HERE!

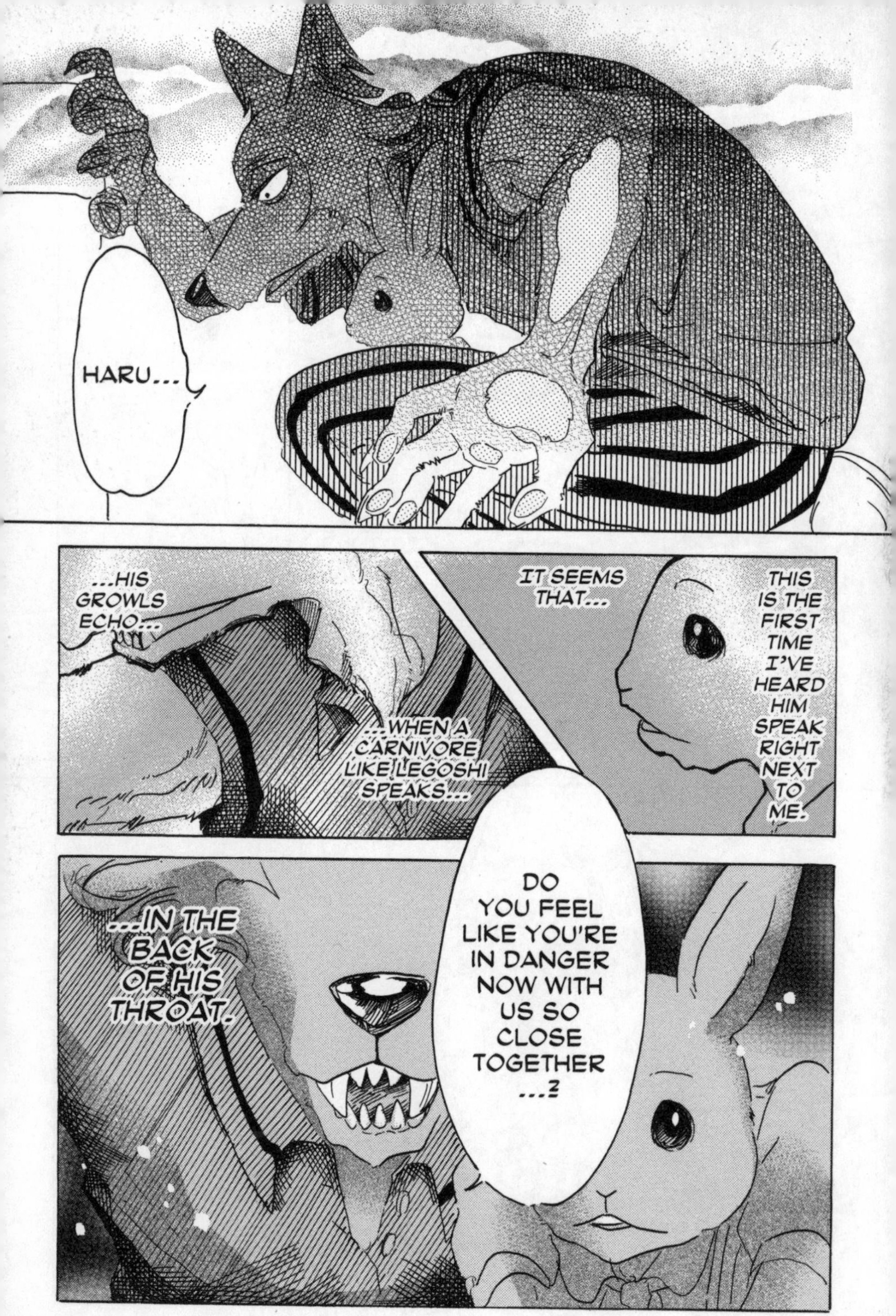
HARU...
THIS IS THE FIRST TIME I'VE HEARD HIM SPEAK RIGHT NEXT TO ME.
IT SEEMS THAT...
...HIS GROWLS ECHO...
...WHEN A CARNIVORE LIKE LEGOSHI SPEAKS...
DO YOU FEEL LIKE YOU'RE IN DANGER NOW WITH US SO CLOSE TOGETHER...?
...IN THE BACK OF HIS THROAT.

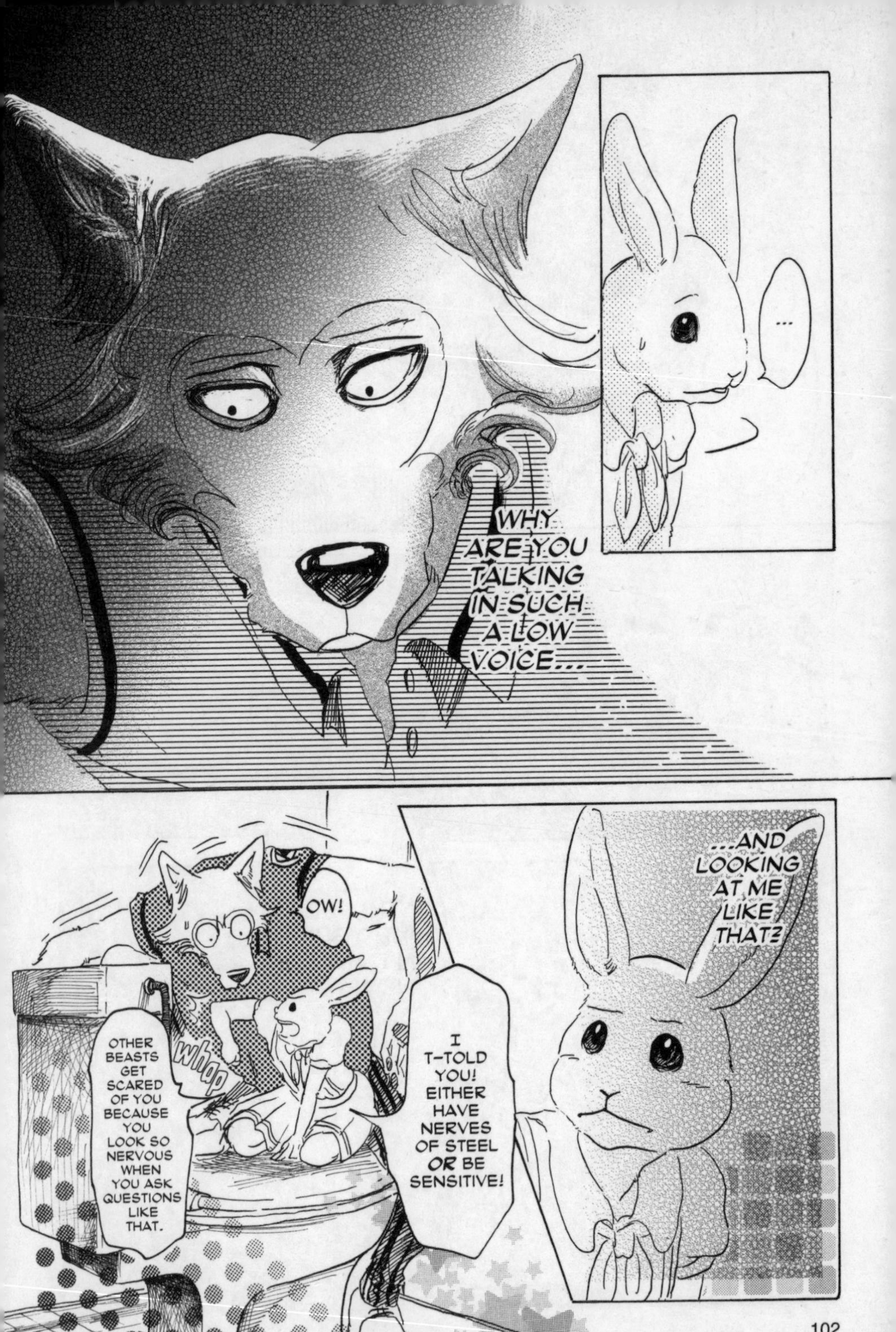
...
WHY ARE YOU TALKING IN SUCH A LOW VOICE...
...AND LOOKING AT ME LIKE THAT?
I T-TOLD YOU! EITHER HAVE NERVES OF STEEL **OR** BE SENSITIVE!
OW!
whap
OTHER BEASTS GET SCARED OF YOU BECAUSE YOU LOOK SO NERVOUS WHEN YOU ASK QUESTIONS LIKE THAT.

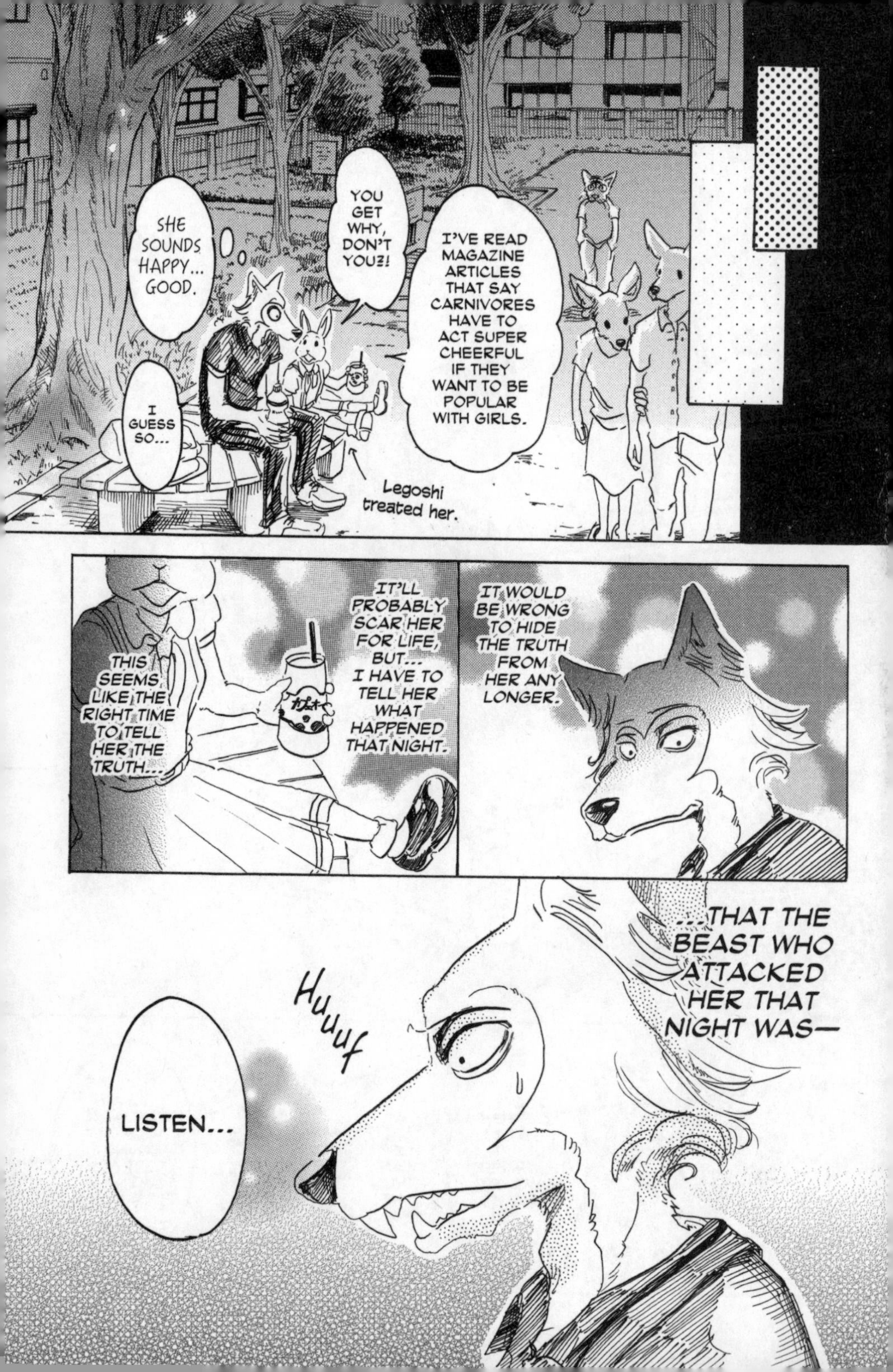
I'VE READ MAGAZINE ARTICLES THAT SAY CARNIVORES HAVE TO ACT SUPER CHEERFUL IF THEY WANT TO BE POPULAR WITH GIRLS.
YOU GET WHY, DON'T YOU?!
SHE SOUNDS HAPPY... GOOD.
I GUESS SO...
Legoshi treated her.
IT WOULD BE WRONG TO HIDE THE TRUTH FROM HER ANY LONGER.
IT'LL PROBABLY SCAR HER FOR LIFE, BUT... I HAVE TO TELL HER WHAT HAPPENED THAT NIGHT.
THIS SEEMS LIKE THE RIGHT TIME TO TELL HER THE TRUTH...
...THAT THE BEAST WHO ATTACKED HER THAT NIGHT WAS—
Huuuf
LISTEN...

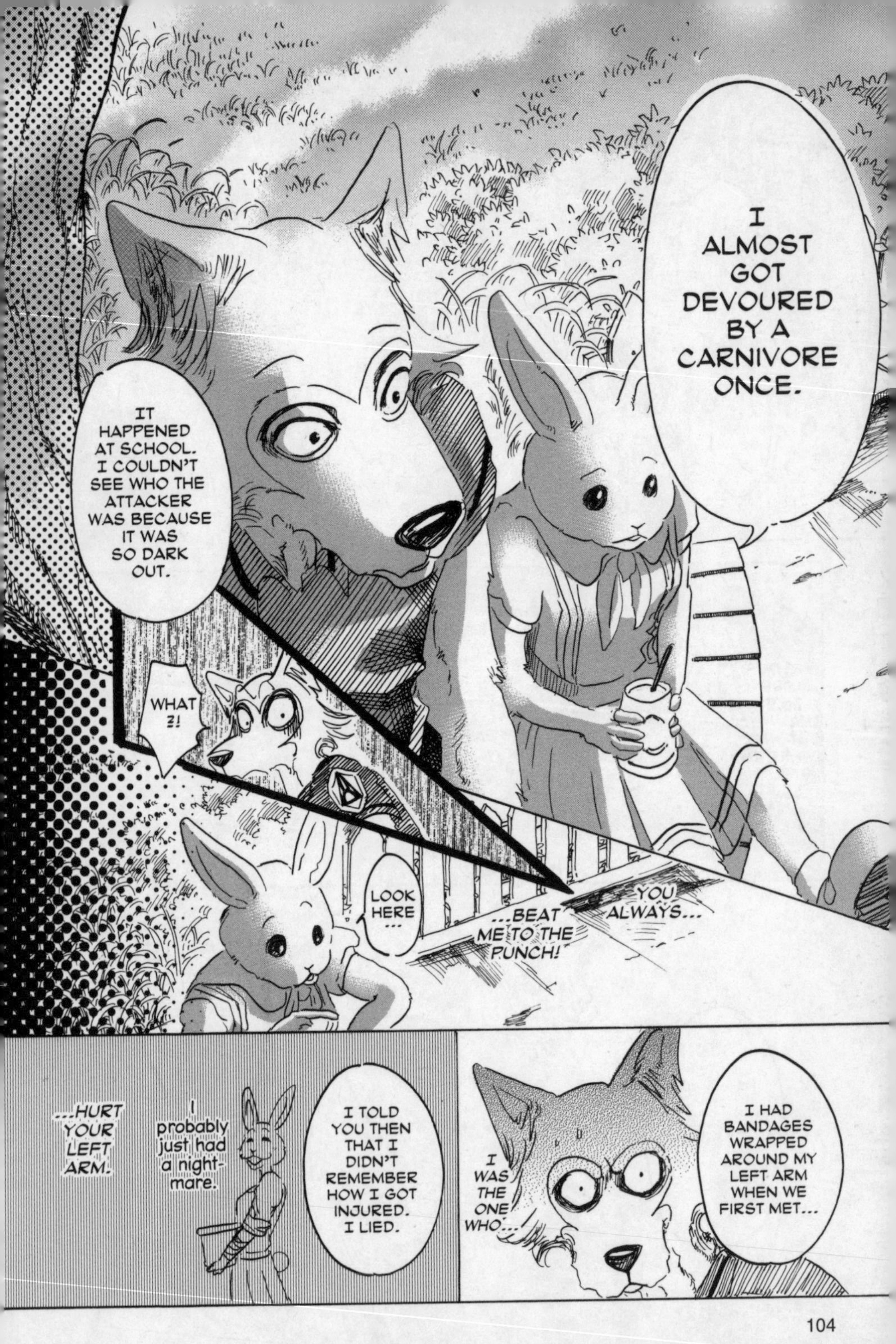
I ALMOST GOT DEVOURED BY A CARNIVORE ONCE.
IT HAPPENED AT SCHOOL. I COULDN'T SEE WHO THE ATTACKER WAS BECAUSE IT WAS SO DARK OUT.
WHAT?!
YOU ALWAYS...
...BEAT ME TO THE PUNCH!
LOOK HERE...
I HAD BANDAGES WRAPPED AROUND MY LEFT ARM WHEN WE FIRST MET...
I WAS THE ONE WHO...
I TOLD YOU THEN THAT I DIDN'T REMEMBER HOW I GOT INJURED. I LIED.
I probably just had a night-mare.
...HURT YOUR LEFT ARM.

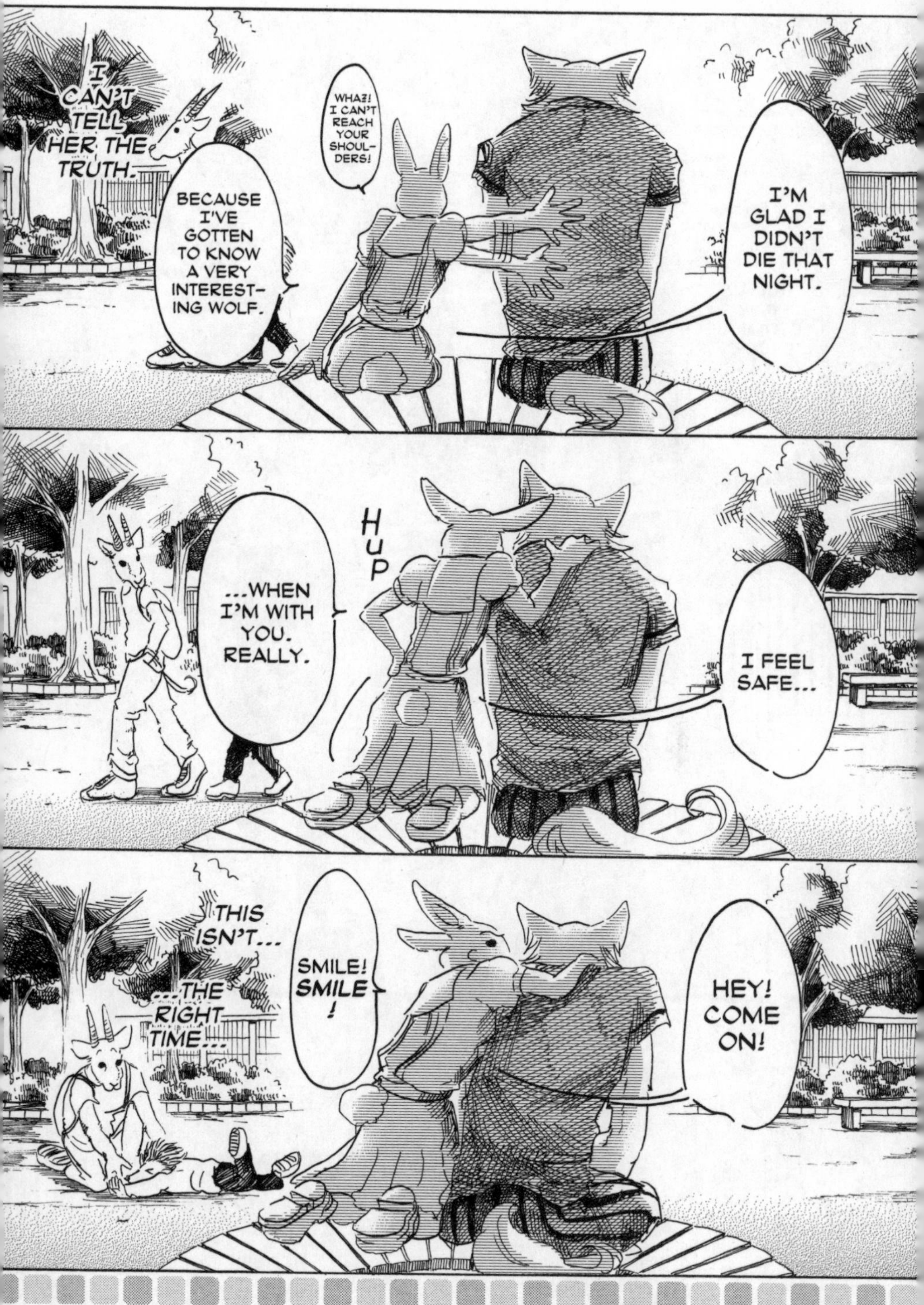
I'M GLAD I DIDN'T DIE THAT NIGHT.
WHA?! I CAN'T REACH YOUR SHOULDERS!
BECAUSE I'VE GOTTEN TO KNOW A VERY INTERESTING WOLF.
I CAN'T TELL HER THE TRUTH.
I FEEL SAFE...
HUP
...WHEN I'M WITH YOU. REALLY.
HEY! COME ON!
SMILE! SMILE!
THIS ISN'T...
...THE RIGHT TIME...

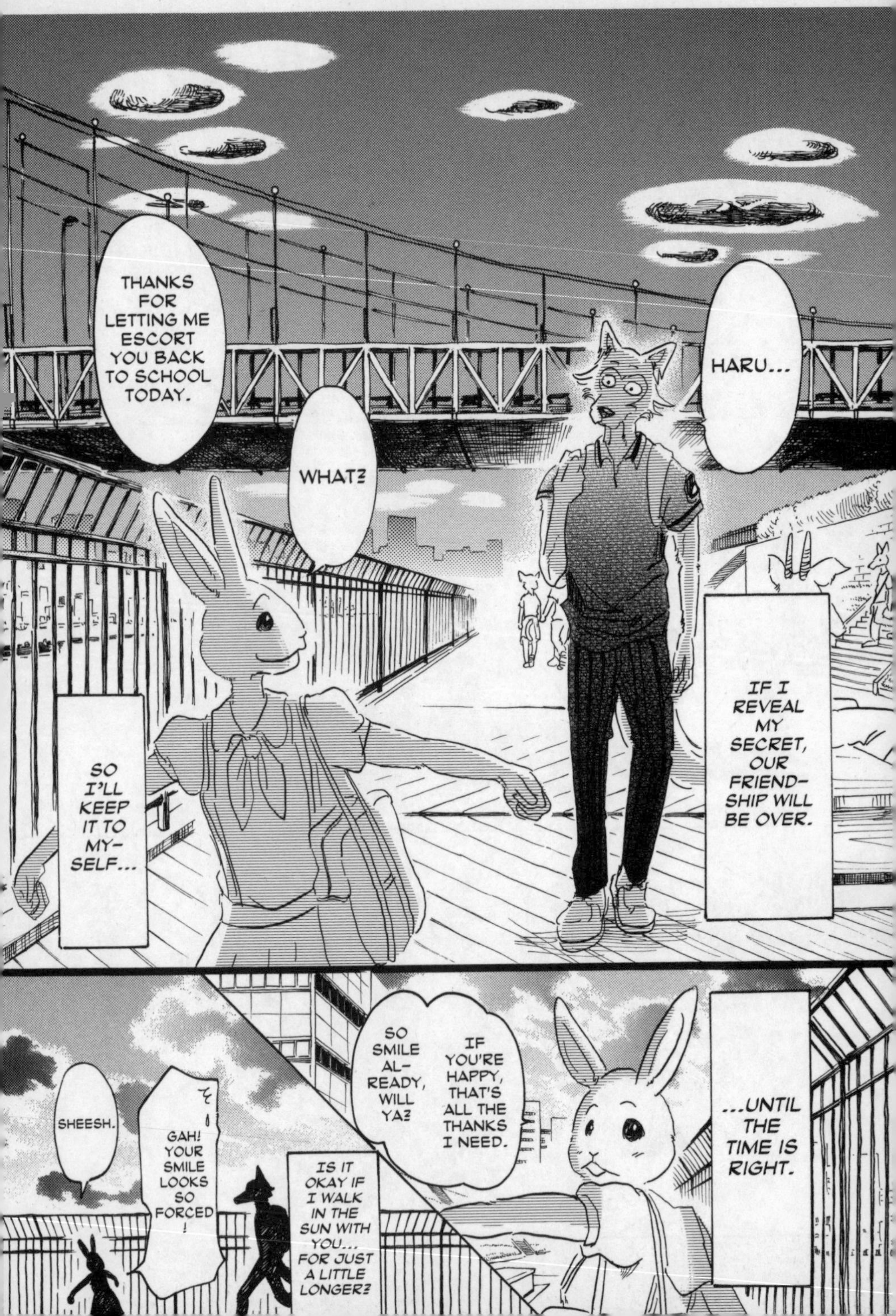
HARU...
THANKS FOR LETTING ME ESCORT YOU BACK TO SCHOOL TODAY.
WHAT?
IF I REVEAL MY SECRET, OUR FRIENDSHIP WILL BE OVER.
SO I'LL KEEP IT TO MYSELF...
...UNTIL THE TIME IS RIGHT.
IF YOU'RE HAPPY, THAT'S ALL THE THANKS I NEED.
SO SMILE ALREADY, WILL YA?
IS IT OKAY IF I WALK IN THE SUN WITH YOU... FOR JUST A LITTLE LONGER?
GAH! YOUR SMILE LOOKS SO FORCED!
SHEESH.

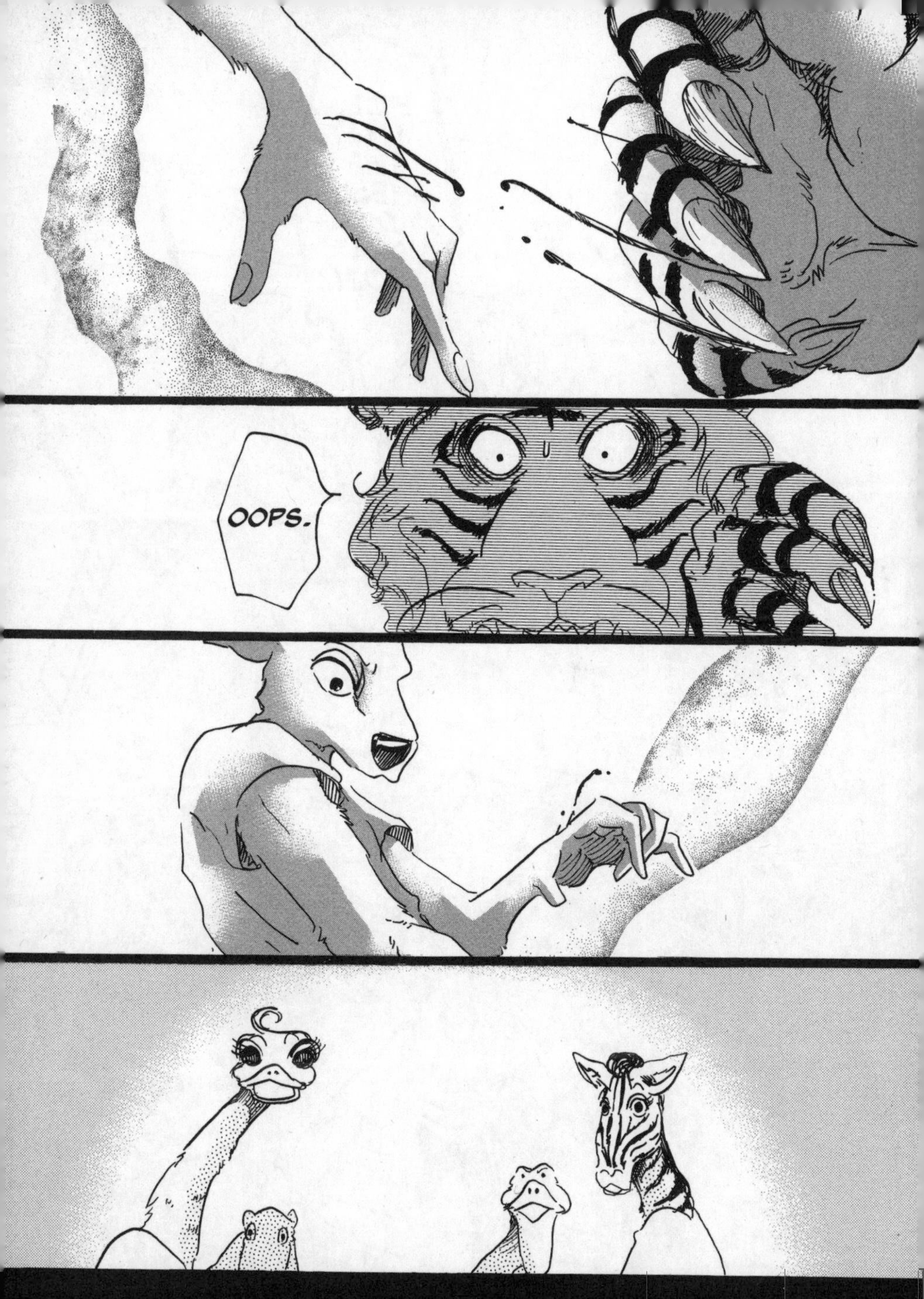
OOPS.

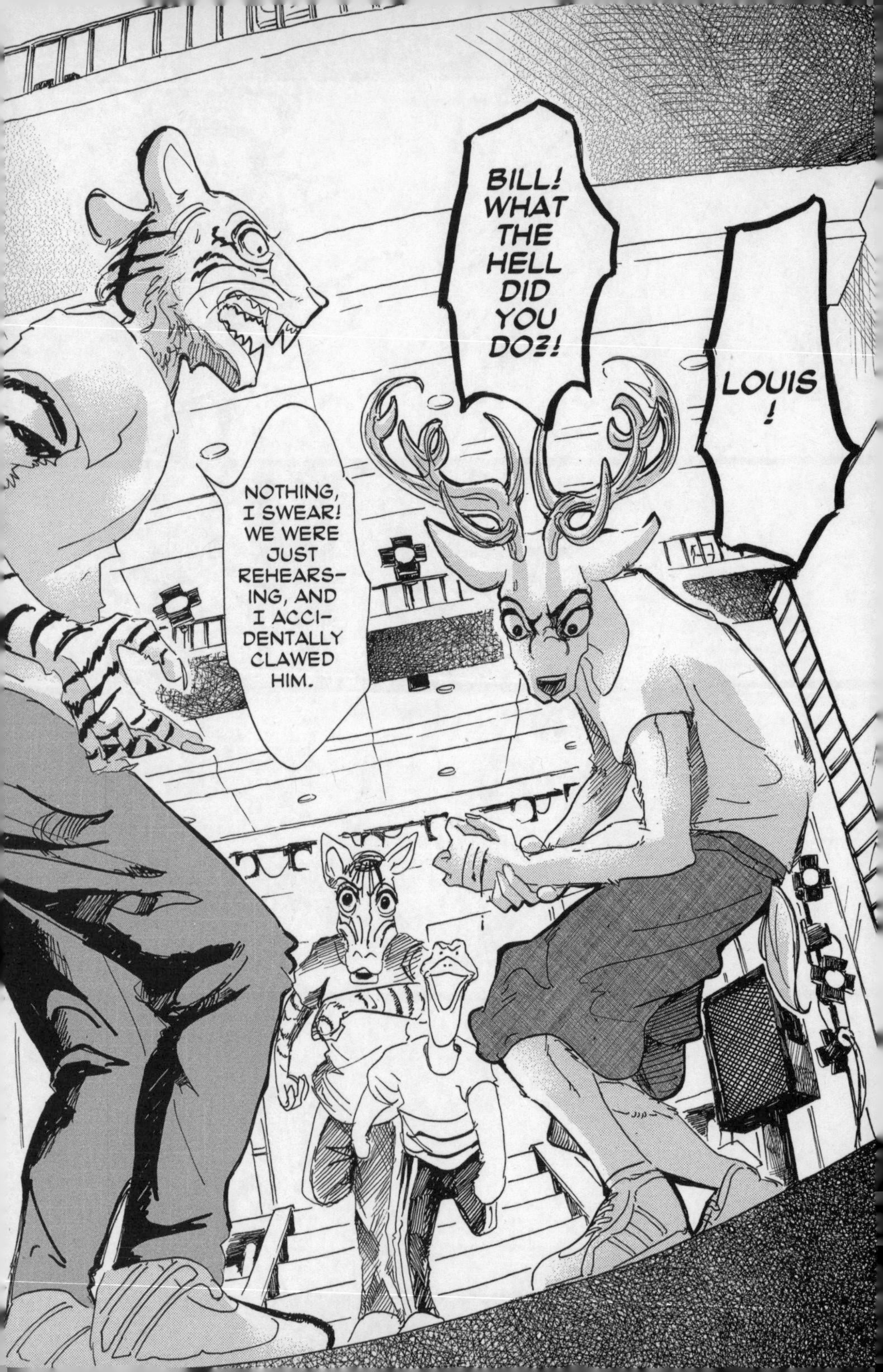
LOUIS!
BILL! WHAT THE HELL DID YOU DO?!
NOTHING, I SWEAR! WE WERE JUST REHEARSING, AND I ACCIDENTALLY CLAWED HIM.

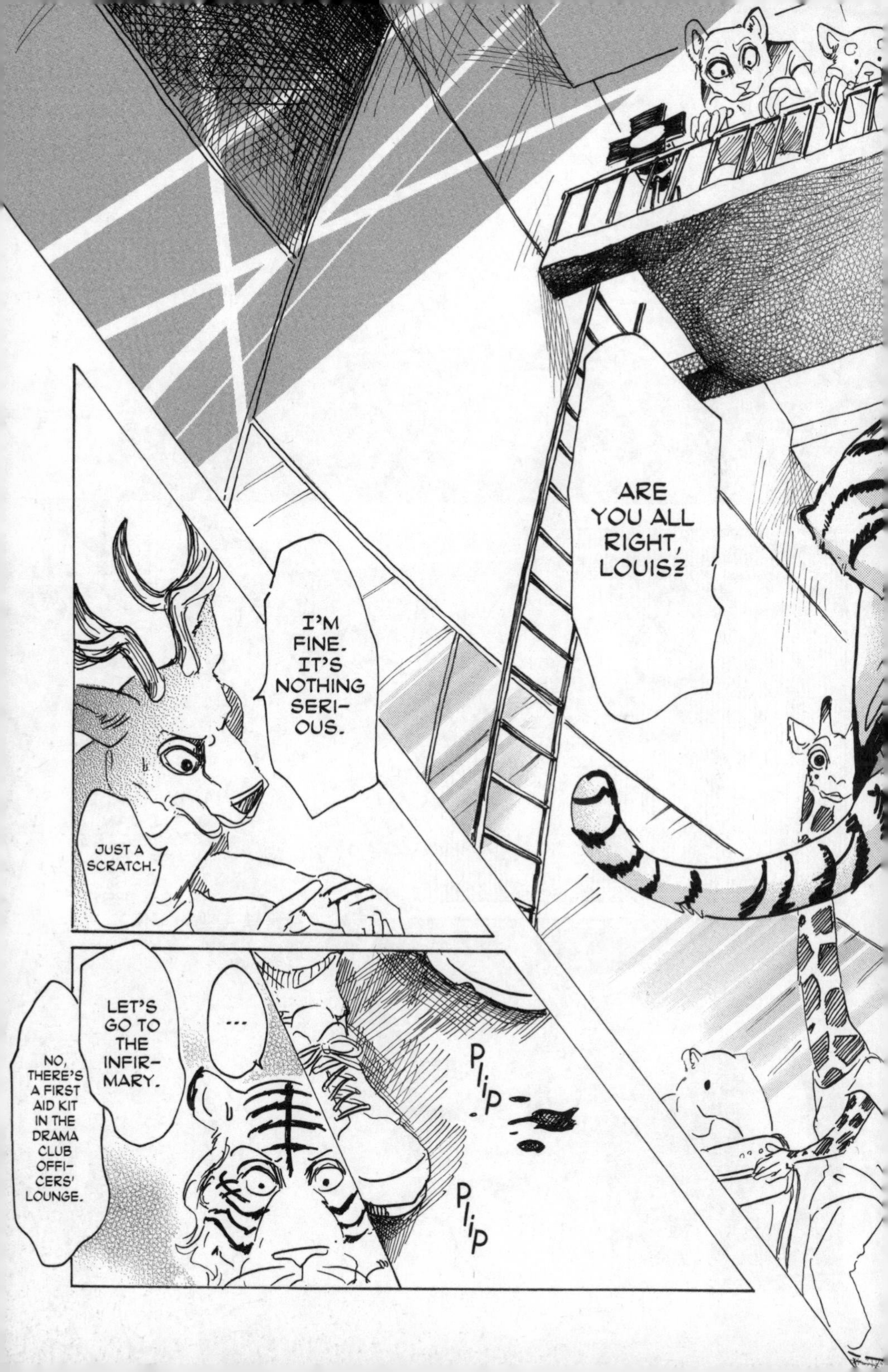

ARE YOU ALL RIGHT, LOUIS?
I'M FINE. IT'S NOTHING SERIOUS.
JUST A SCRATCH.
Plip
Plip
...
LET'S GO TO THE INFIRMARY.
NO, THERE'S A FIRST AID KIT IN THE DRAMA CLUB OFFICERS' LOUNGE.

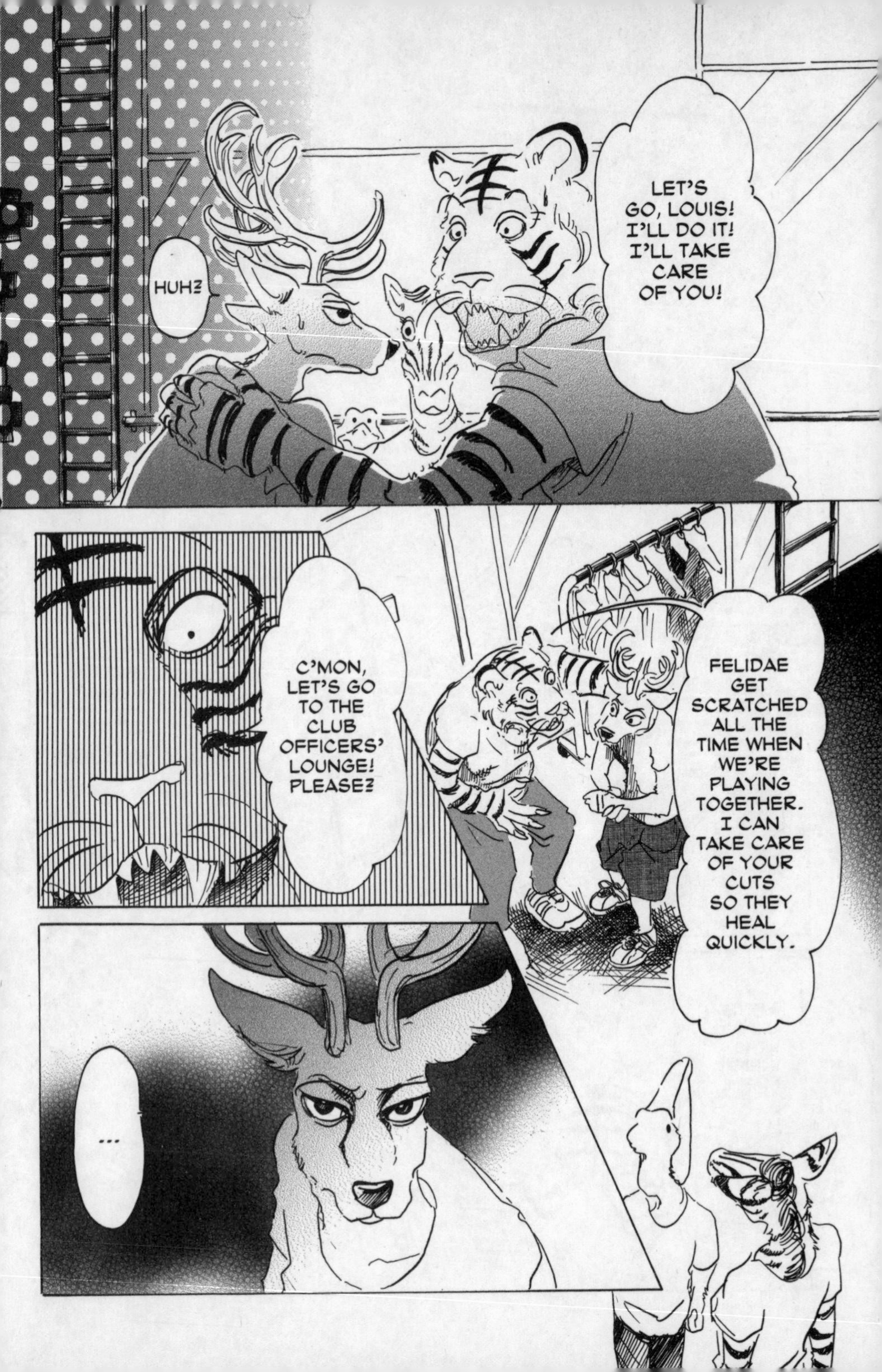
LET'S GO, LOUIS! I'LL DO IT! I'LL TAKE CARE OF YOU!
HUH?
FELIDAE GET SCRATCHED ALL THE TIME WHEN WE'RE PLAYING TOGETHER. I CAN TAKE CARE OF YOUR CUTS SO THEY HEAL QUICKLY.
C'MON, LET'S GO TO THE CLUB OFFICERS' LOUNGE! PLEASE?
...

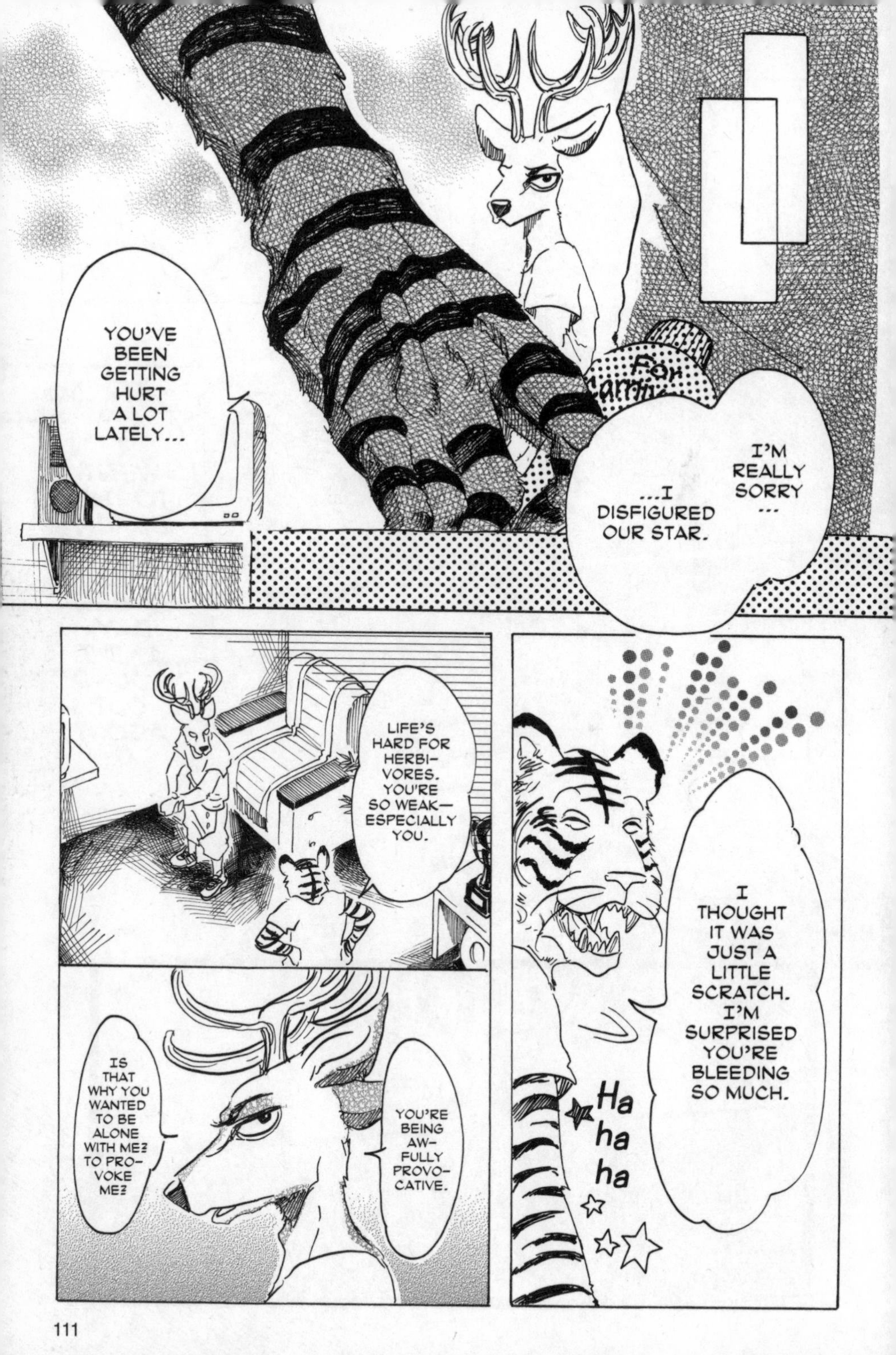
I'M REALLY SORRY... ...I DISFIGURED OUR STAR.
YOU'VE BEEN GETTING HURT A LOT LATELY...
I THOUGHT IT WAS JUST A LITTLE SCRATCH. I'M SURPRISED YOU'RE BLEEDING SO MUCH.
Ha ha ha
LIFE'S HARD FOR HERBIVORES. YOU'RE SO WEAK—ESPECIALLY YOU.
YOU'RE BEING AWFULLY PROVOCATIVE.
IS THAT WHY YOU WANTED TO BE ALONE WITH ME? TO PROVOKE ME?

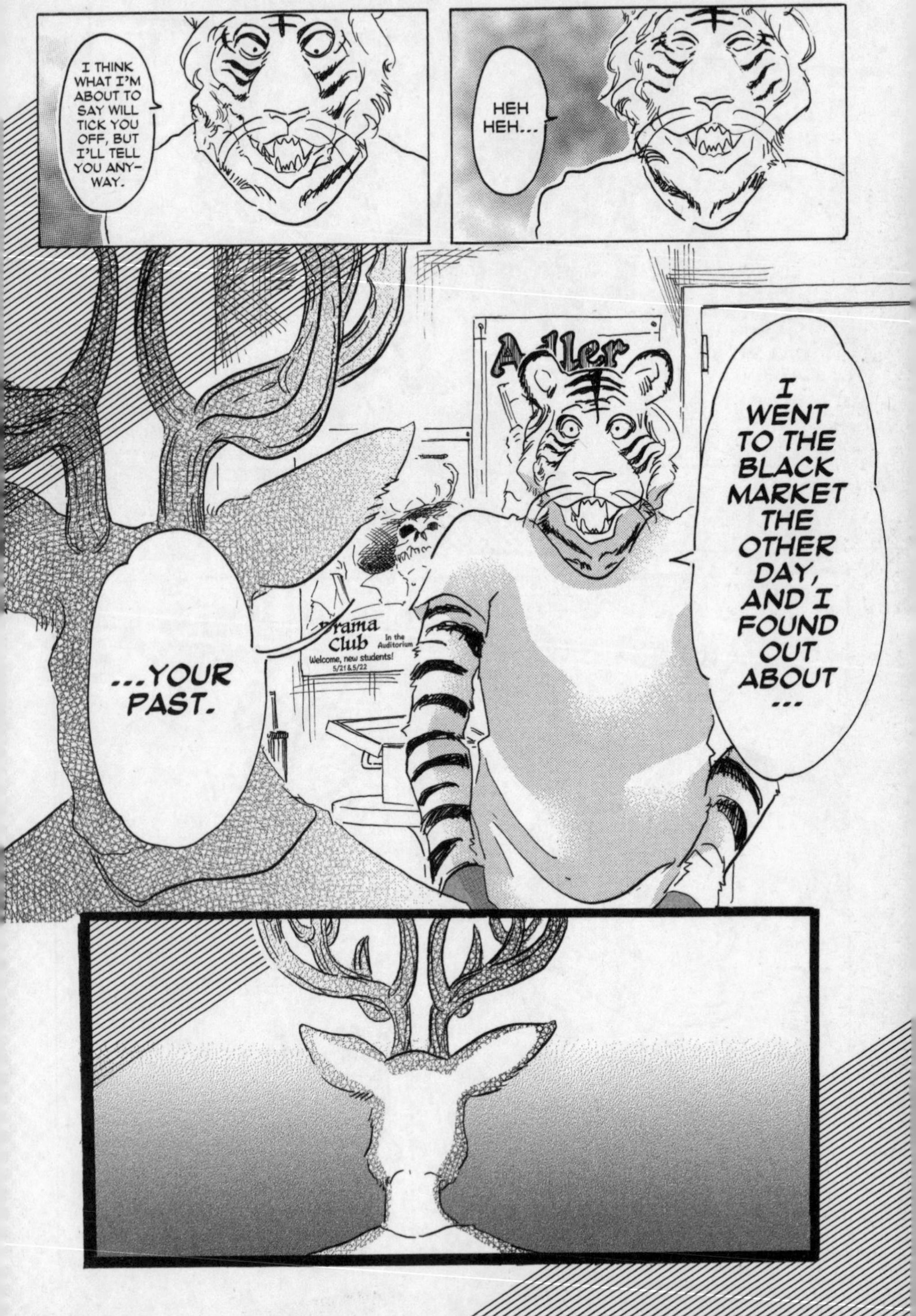
HEH HEH...
I THINK WHAT I'M ABOUT TO SAY WILL TICK YOU OFF, BUT I'LL TELL YOU ANYWAY.
Adler
I WENT TO THE BLACK MARKET THE OTHER DAY, AND I FOUND OUT ABOUT...
rama Club
In the Auditorium
Welcome, new students!
5/21 & 5/22
...YOUR PAST.

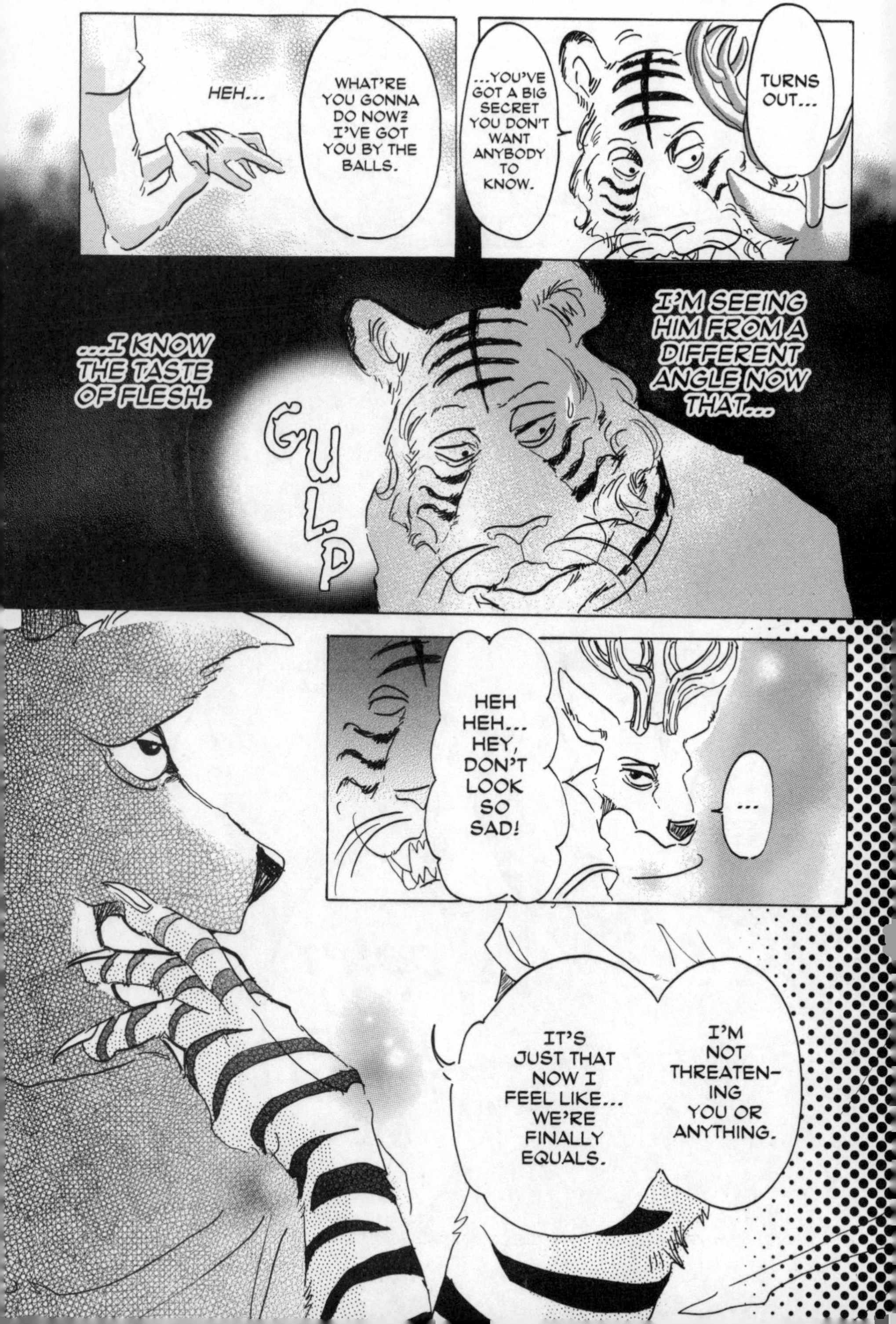

TURNS OUT...
...YOU'VE GOT A BIG SECRET YOU DON'T WANT ANYBODY TO KNOW.
WHAT'RE YOU GONNA DO NOW? I'VE GOT YOU BY THE BALLS.
HEH...
I'M SEEING HIM FROM A DIFFERENT ANGLE NOW THAT...
...I KNOW THE TASTE OF FLESH.
GULP
...
HEH HEH... HEY, DON'T LOOK SO SAD!
I'M NOT THREATEN-ING YOU OR ANYTHING.
IT'S JUST THAT NOW I FEEL LIKE... WE'RE FINALLY EQUALS.

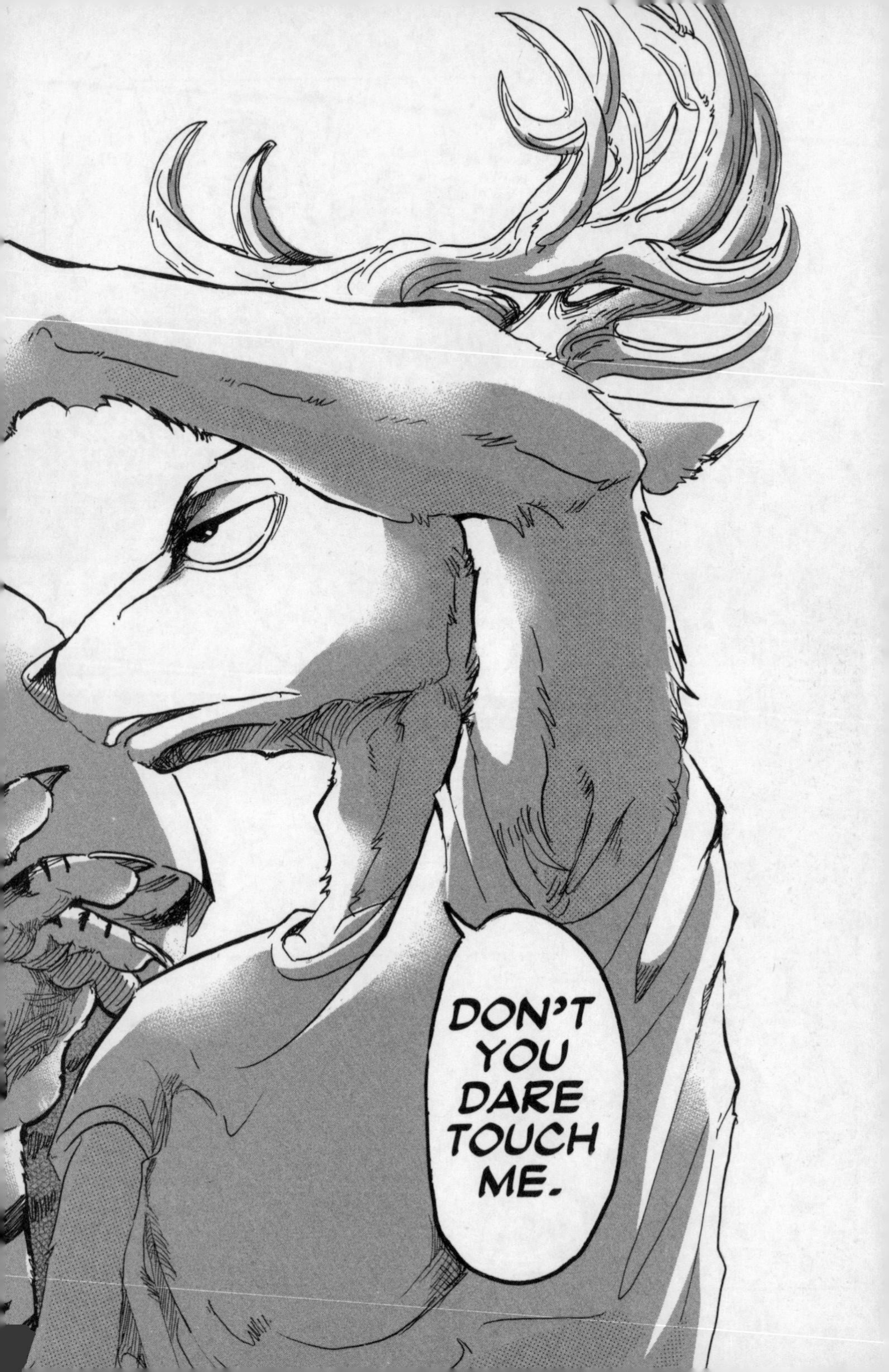
DON'T YOU DARE TOUCH ME.

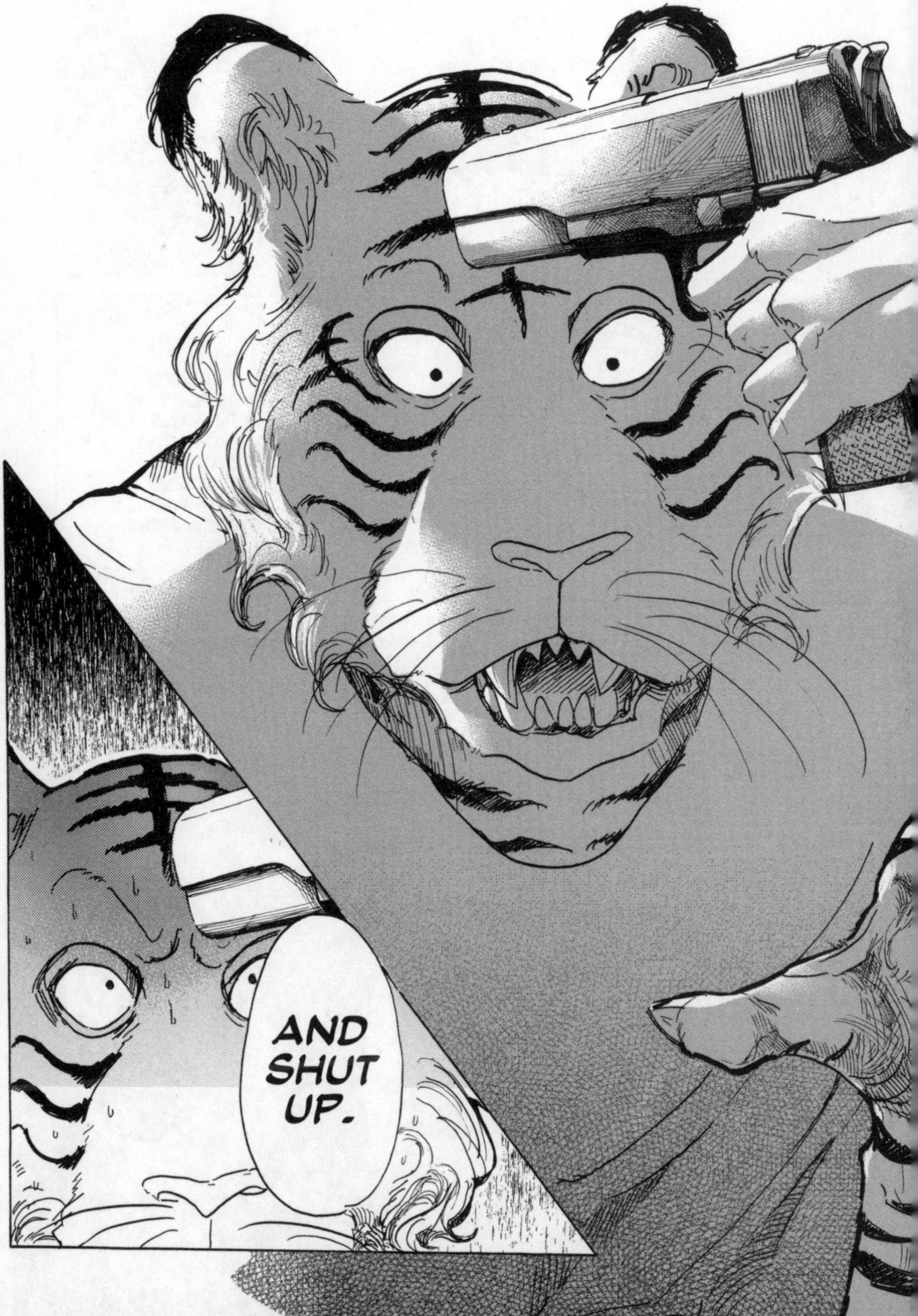
AND SHUT UP.

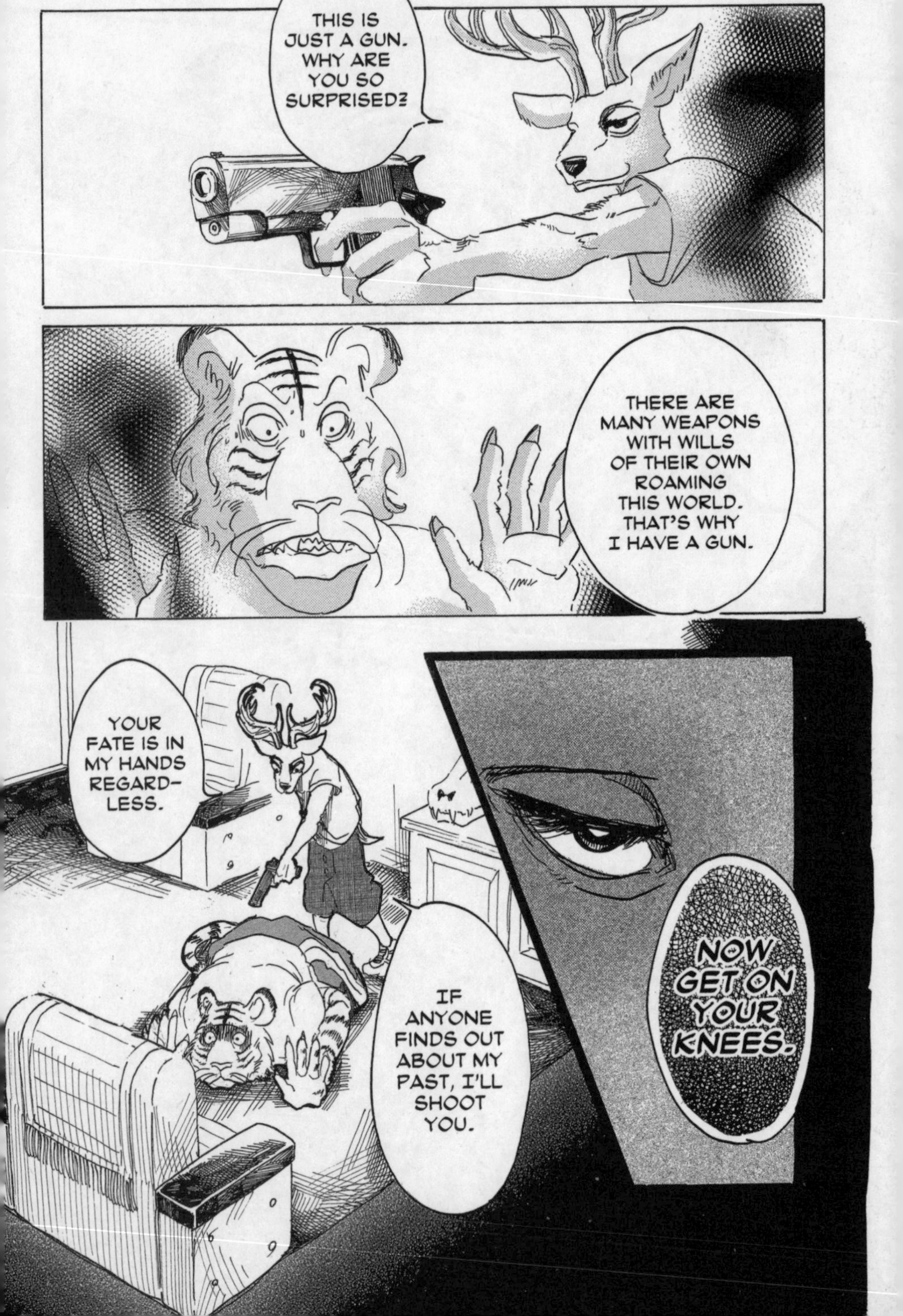
THIS IS JUST A GUN. WHY ARE YOU SO SURPRISED?
THERE ARE MANY WEAPONS WITH WILLS OF THEIR OWN ROAMING THIS WORLD. THAT'S WHY I HAVE A GUN.
NOW GET ON YOUR KNEES.
YOUR FATE IS IN MY HANDS REGARD-LESS.
IF ANYONE FINDS OUT ABOUT MY PAST, I'LL SHOOT YOU.

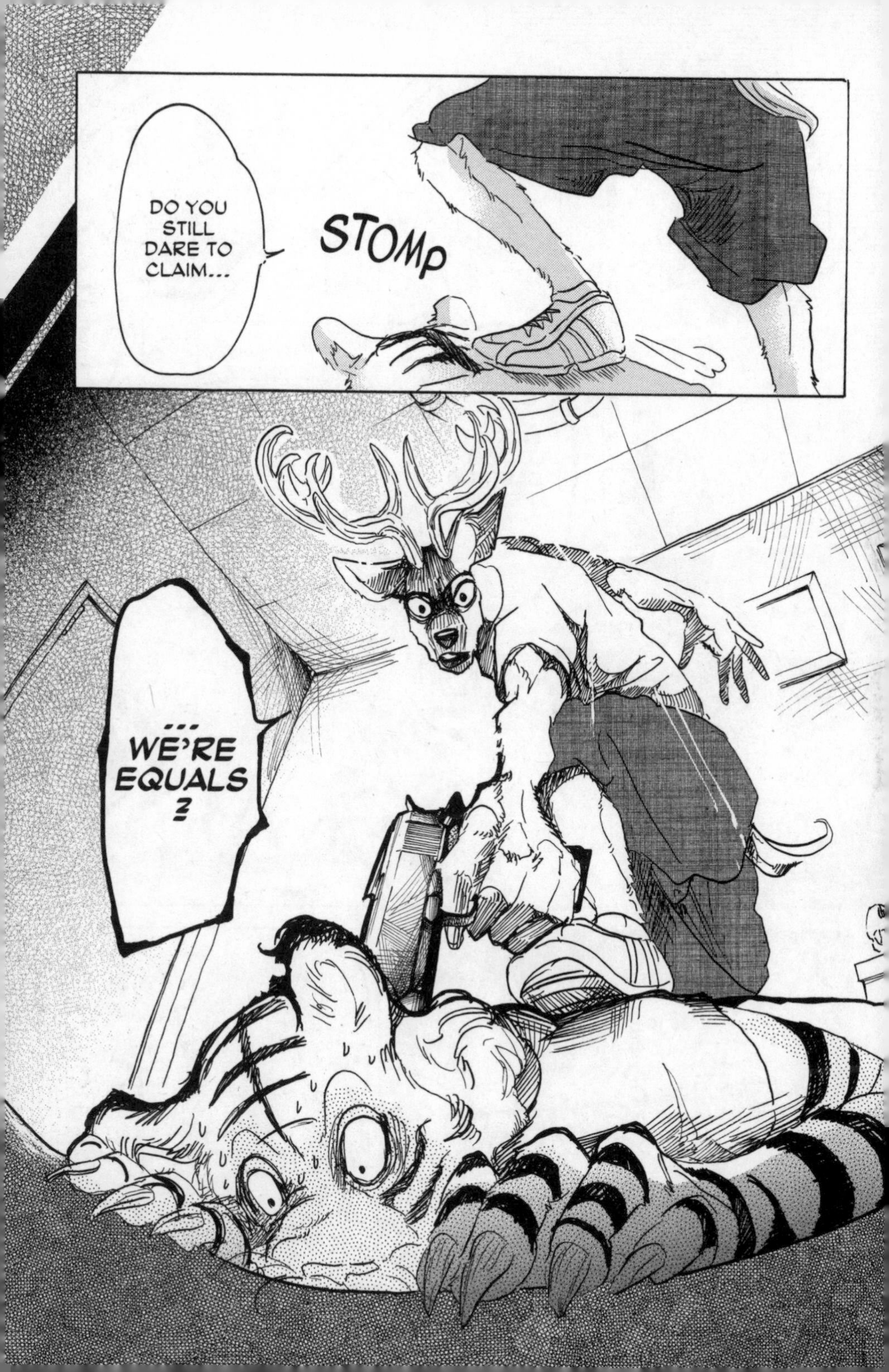
DO YOU STILL DARE TO CLAIM...
STOMP
...WE'RE EQUALS?

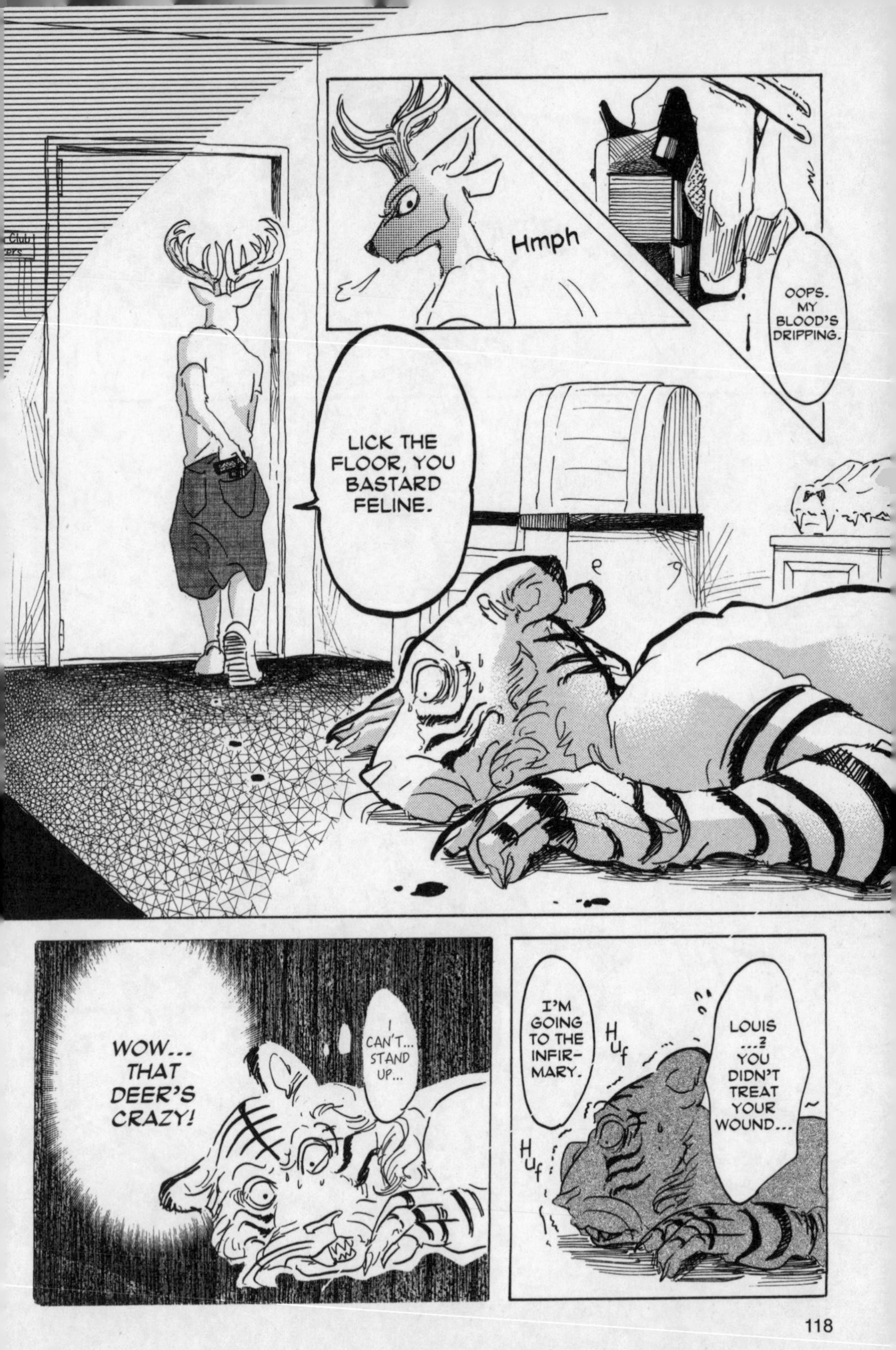
OOPS. MY BLOOD'S DRIPPING.
Hmph
LICK THE FLOOR, YOU BASTARD FELINE.
LOUIS...? YOU DIDN'T TREAT YOUR WOUND...
I'M GOING TO THE INFIRMARY.
Huf
Huf
I CAN'T... STAND UP...
WOW... THAT DEER'S CRAZY!

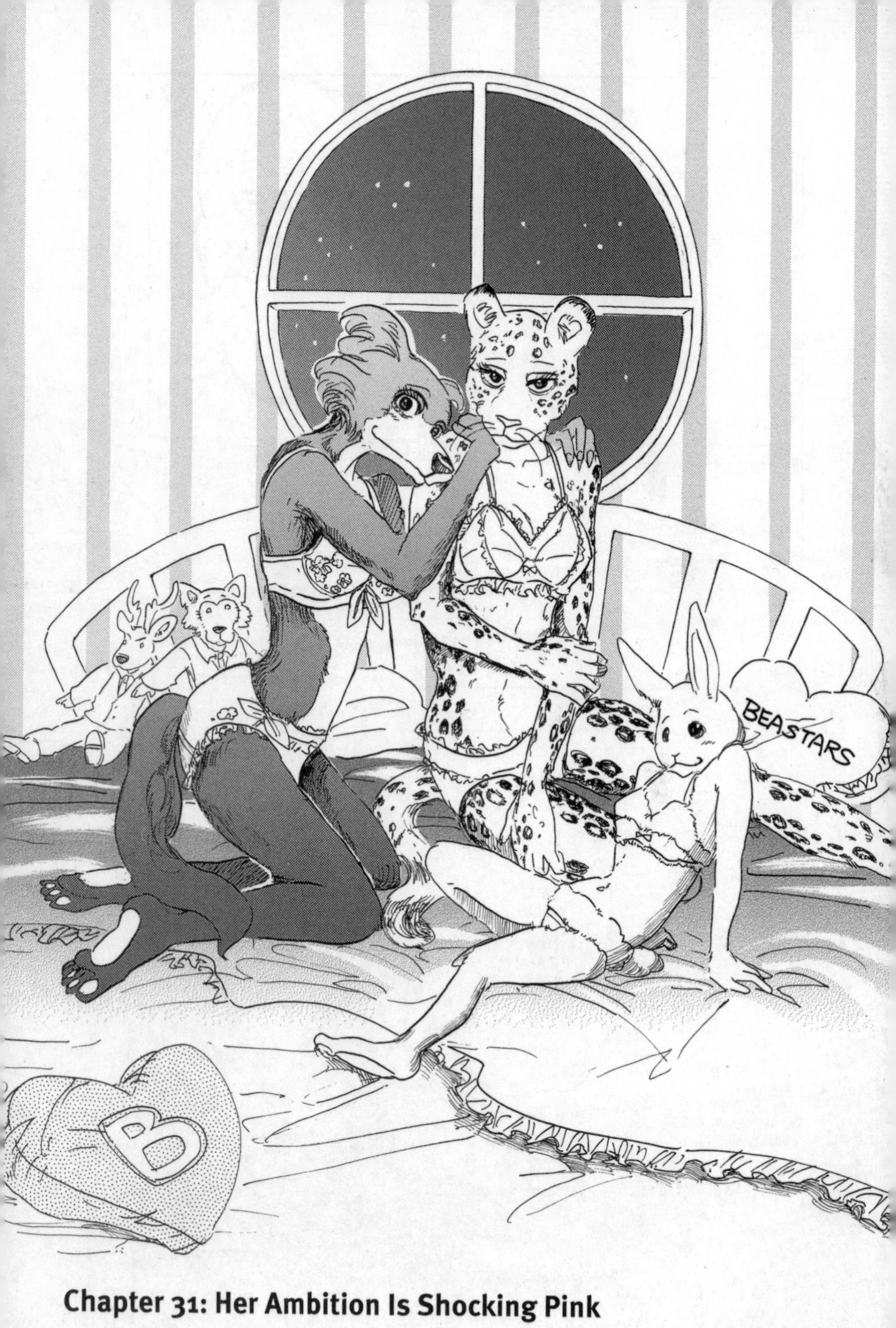
BEASTARS
B

Chapter 31: Her Ambition Is Shocking Pink

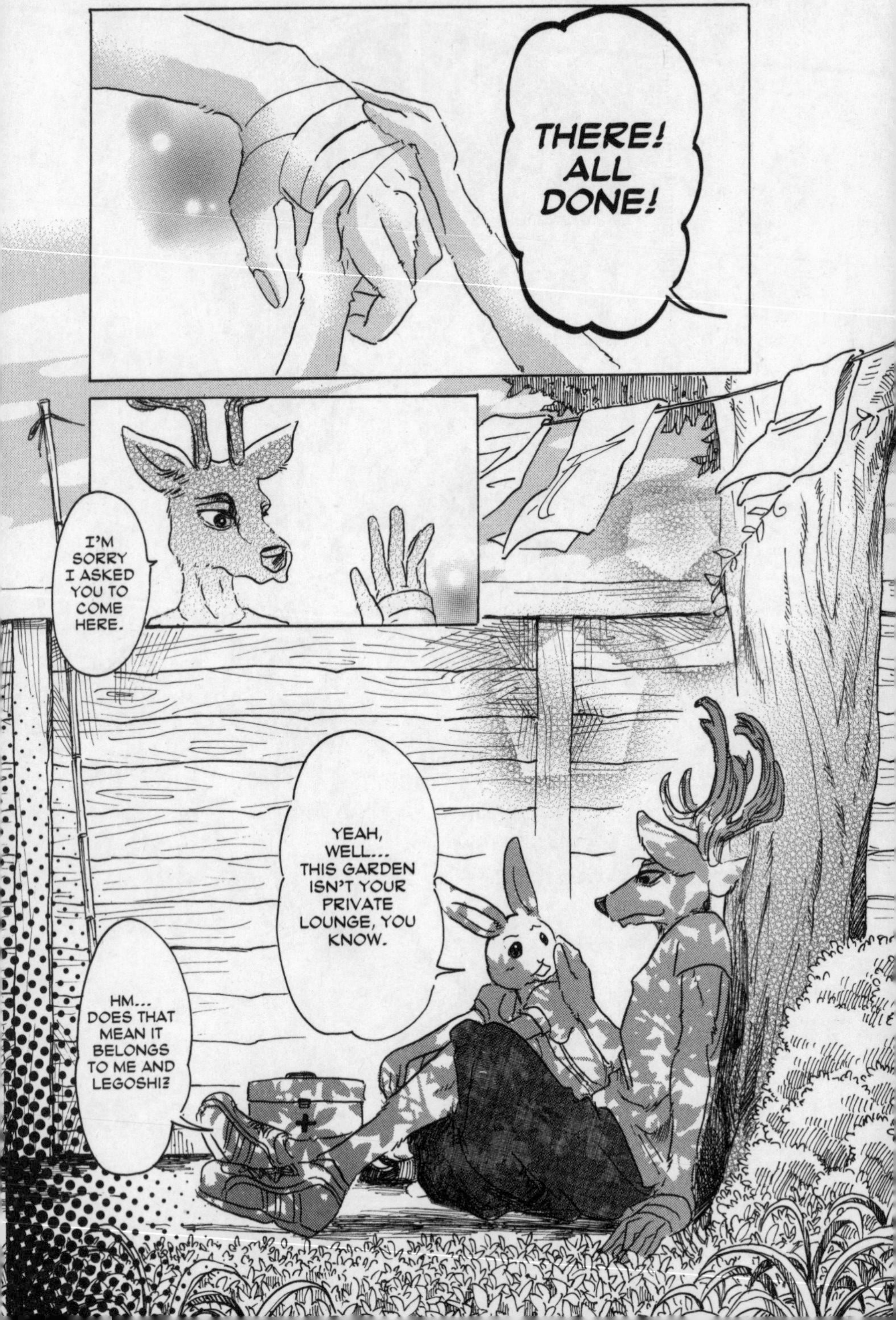
THERE! ALL DONE!
I'M SORRY I ASKED YOU TO COME HERE.
YEAH, WELL... THIS GARDEN ISN'T YOUR PRIVATE LOUNGE, YOU KNOW.
HM... DOES THAT MEAN IT BELONGS TO ME AND LEGOSHI?

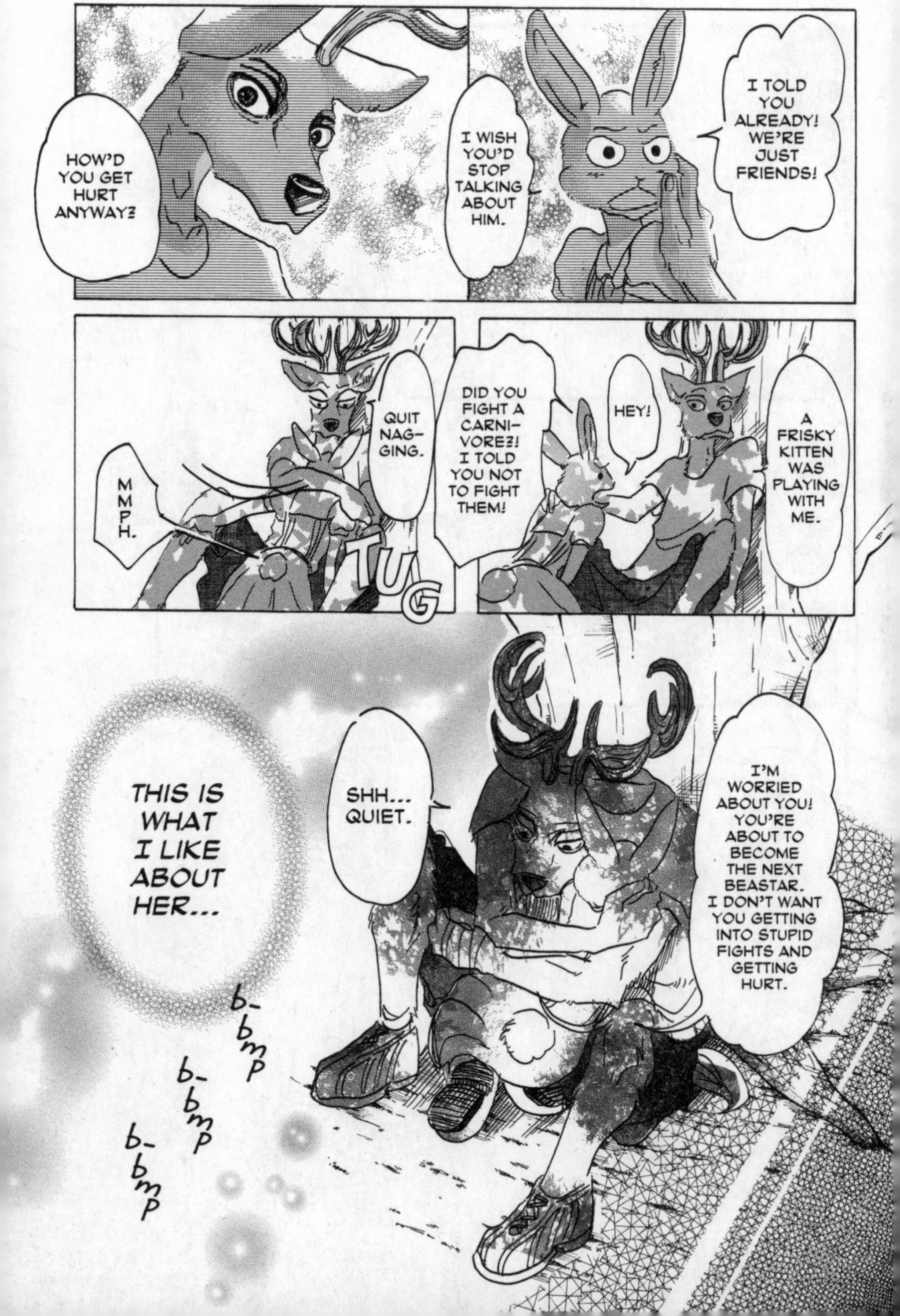
I TOLD YOU ALREADY! WE'RE JUST FRIENDS!
I WISH YOU'D STOP TALKING ABOUT HIM.
HOW'D YOU GET HURT ANYWAY?!
A FRISKY KITTEN WAS PLAYING WITH ME.
HEY!
DID YOU FIGHT A CARNIVORE?! I TOLD YOU NOT TO FIGHT THEM!
QUIT NAG-GING.
MMPH.
TUG
I'M WORRIED ABOUT YOU! YOU'RE ABOUT TO BECOME THE NEXT BEASTAR. I DON'T WANT YOU GETTING INTO STUPID FIGHTS AND GETTING HURT.
SHH... QUIET.
THIS IS WHAT I LIKE ABOUT HER...
b-bmp
b-bmp
b-bmp

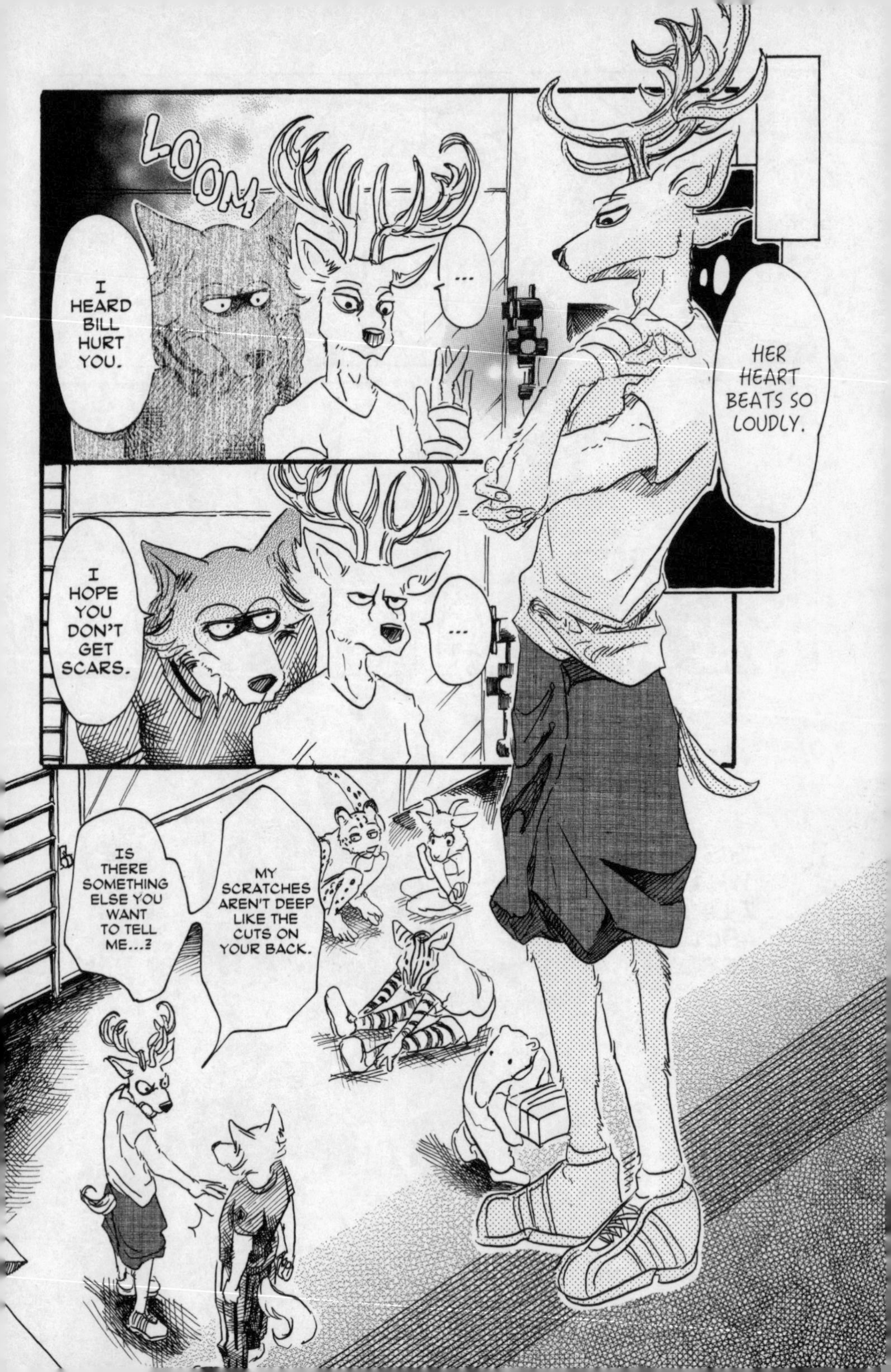
HER HEART BEATS SO LOUDLY.
LOOM
...
I HEARD BILL HURT YOU.
...
I HOPE YOU DON'T GET SCARS.
MY SCRATCHES AREN'T DEEP LIKE THE CUTS ON YOUR BACK.
IS THERE SOMETHING ELSE YOU WANT TO TELL ME...?

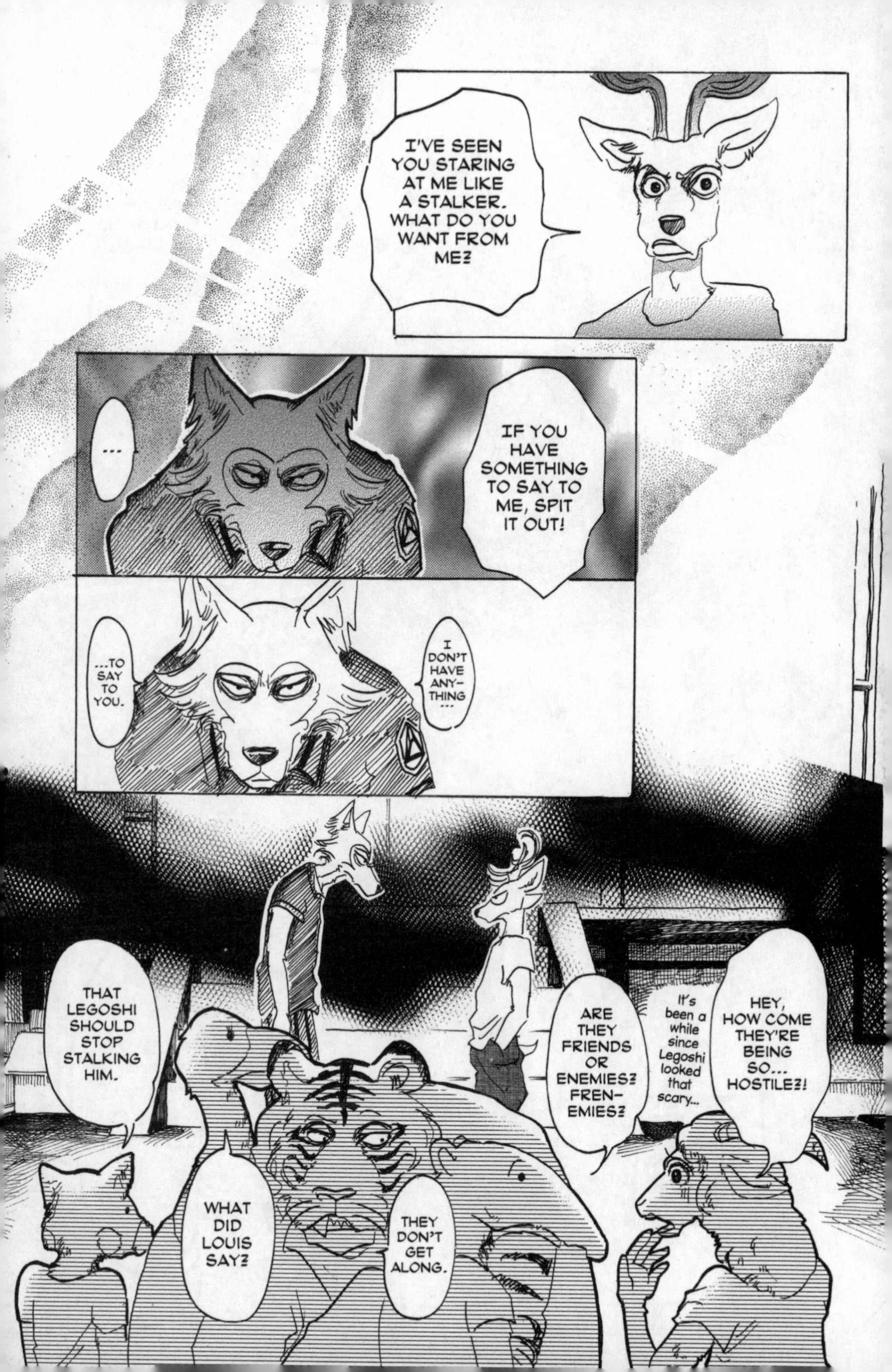
I'VE SEEN YOU STARING AT ME LIKE A STALKER. WHAT DO YOU WANT FROM ME?
IF YOU HAVE SOMETHING TO SAY TO ME, SPIT IT OUT!
...
I DON'T HAVE ANYTHING...
...TO SAY TO YOU.
HEY, HOW COME THEY'RE BEING SO... HOSTILE?!
It's been a while since Legoshi looked that scary...
ARE THEY FRIENDS OR ENEMIES? FRENEMIES?
THAT LEGOSHI SHOULD STOP STALKING HIM.
THEY DON'T GET ALONG.
WHAT DID LOUIS SAY?

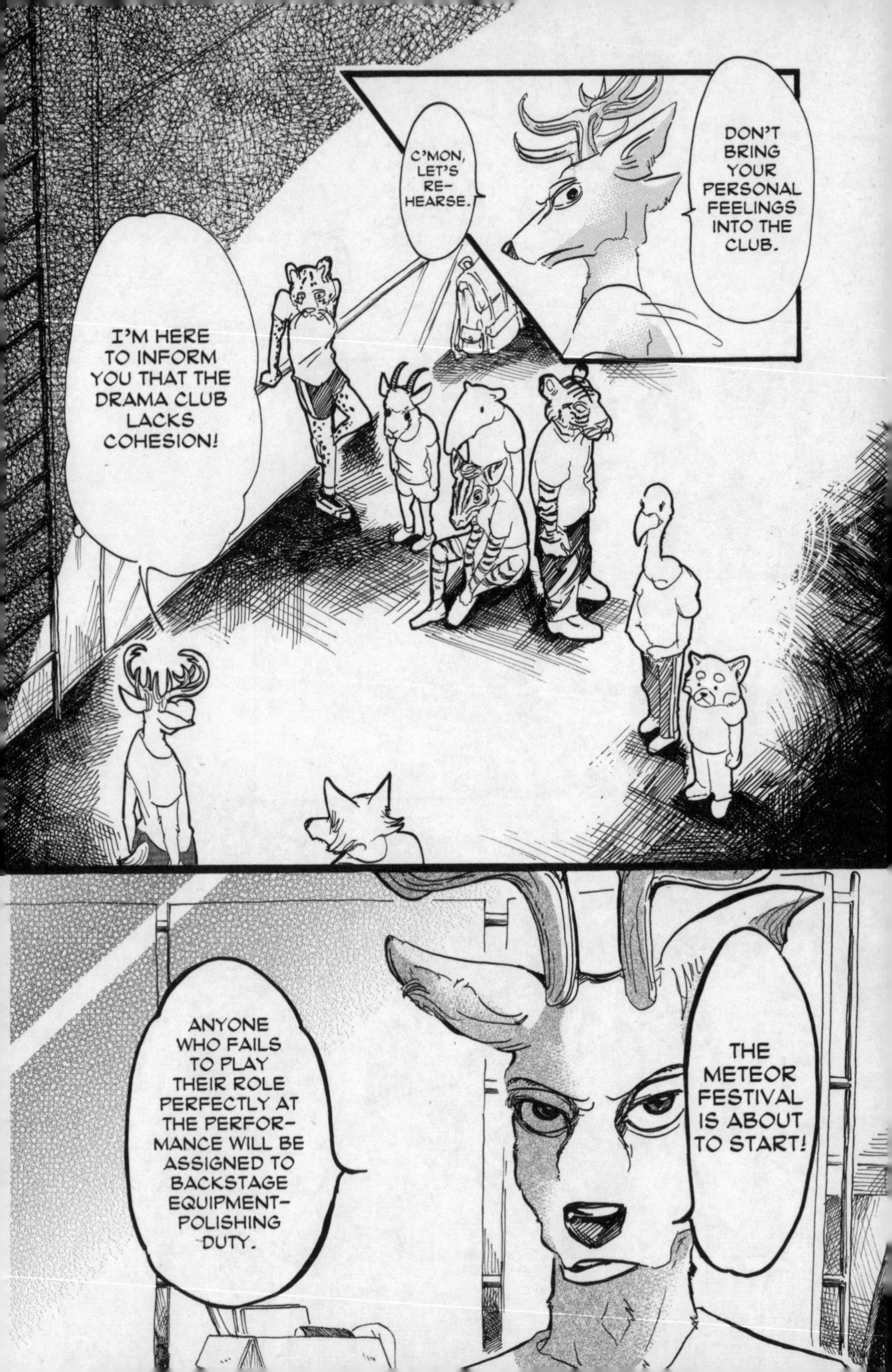
DON'T BRING YOUR PERSONAL FEELINGS INTO THE CLUB.
C'MON, LET'S RE-HEARSE.
I'M HERE TO INFORM YOU THAT THE DRAMA CLUB LACKS COHESION!
THE METEOR FESTIVAL IS ABOUT TO START!
ANYONE WHO FAILS TO PLAY THEIR ROLE PERFECTLY AT THE PERFOR-MANCE WILL BE ASSIGNED TO BACKSTAGE EQUIPMENT-POLISHING DUTY.

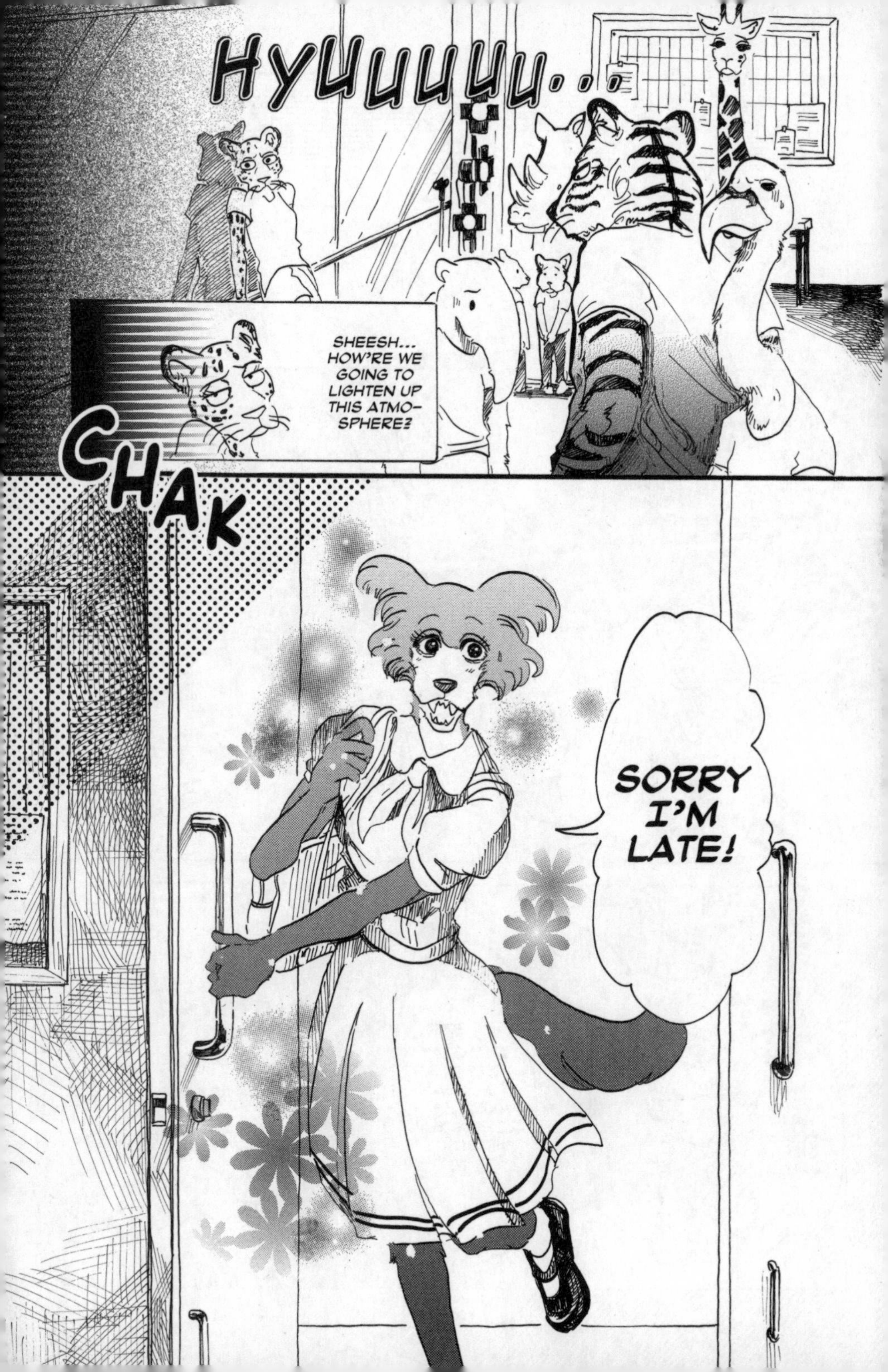
HYUUUUUU...
SHEESH... HOW'RE WE GOING TO LIGHTEN UP THIS ATMO-SPHERE?
CHAK
SORRY I'M LATE!

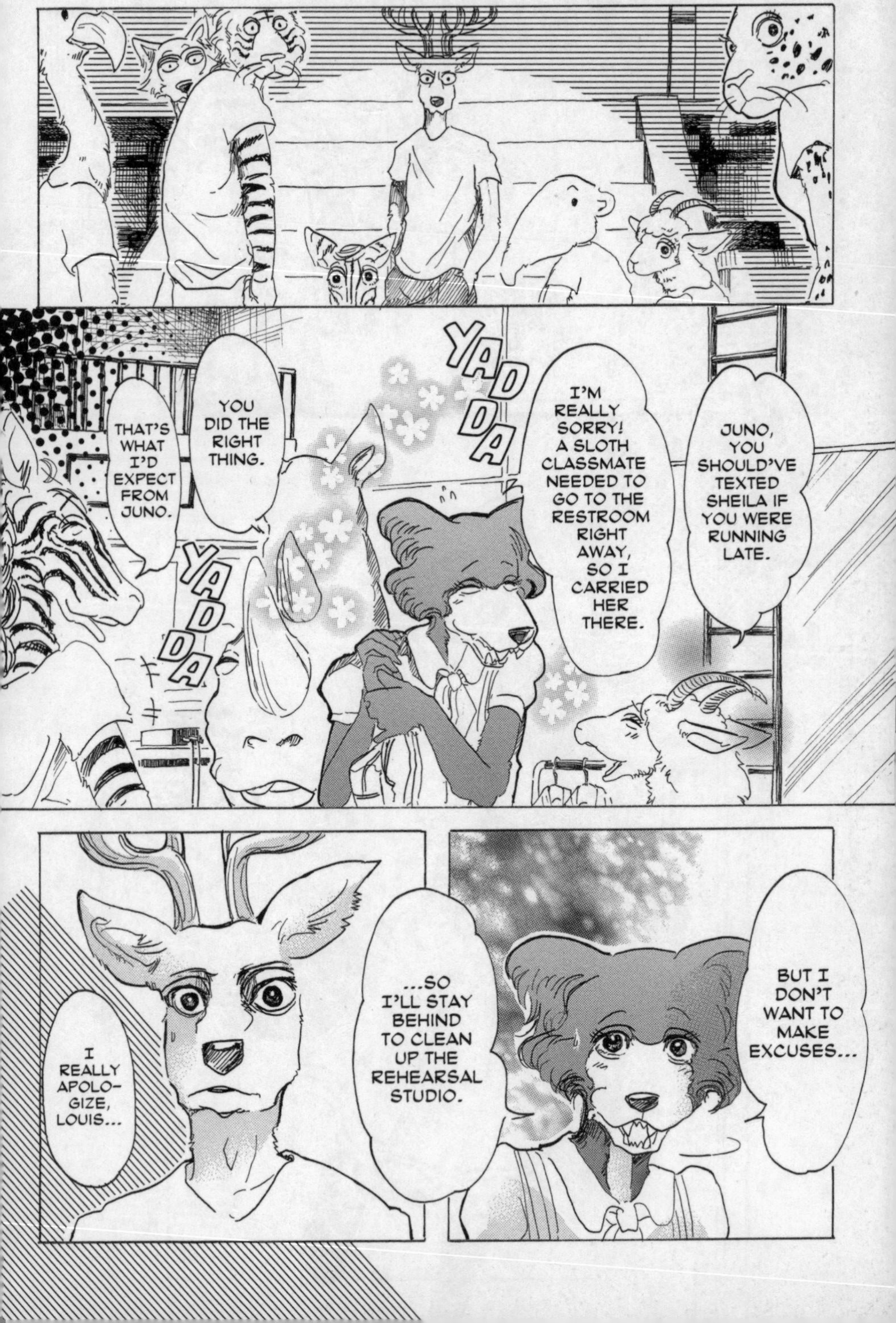
JUNO, YOU SHOULD'VE TEXTED SHEILA IF YOU WERE RUNNING LATE.
I'M REALLY SORRY! A SLOTH CLASSMATE NEEDED TO GO TO THE RESTROOM RIGHT AWAY, SO I CARRIED HER THERE.
YADDA
YADDA
YOU DID THE RIGHT THING.
THAT'S WHAT I'D EXPECT FROM JUNO.
BUT I DON'T WANT TO MAKE EXCUSES...
...SO I'LL STAY BEHIND TO CLEAN UP THE REHEARSAL STUDIO.
I REALLY APOLO-GIZE, LOUIS...

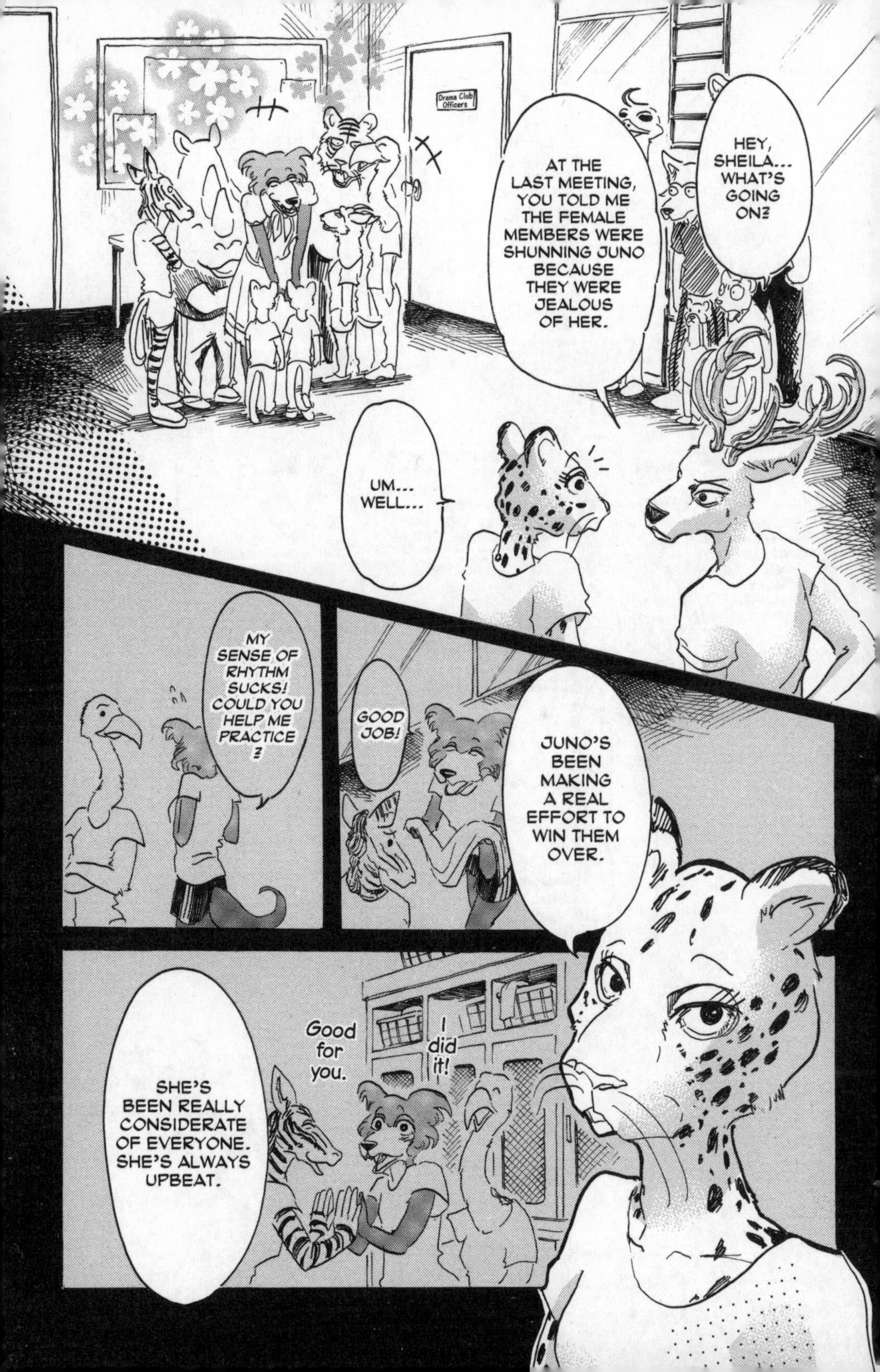
HEY, SHEILA... WHAT'S GOING ON?
AT THE LAST MEETING, YOU TOLD ME THE FEMALE MEMBERS WERE SHUNNING JUNO BECAUSE THEY WERE JEALOUS OF HER.
UM... WELL...
JUNO'S BEEN MAKING A REAL EFFORT TO WIN THEM OVER.
GOOD JOB!
MY SENSE OF RHYTHM SUCKS! COULD YOU HELP ME PRACTICE?
I did it!
Good for you.
SHE'S BEEN REALLY CONSIDERATE OF EVERYONE. SHE'S ALWAYS UPBEAT.

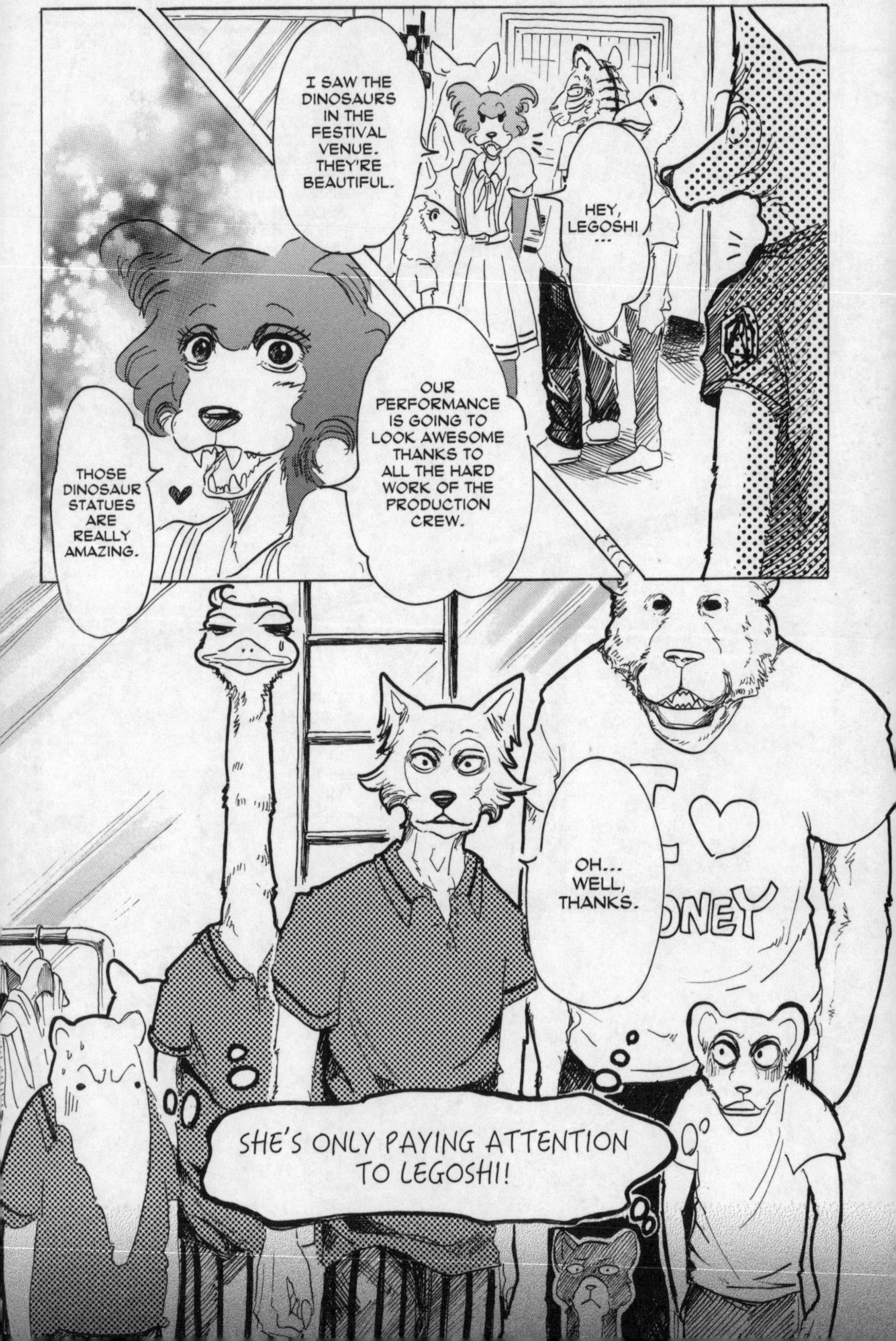
HEY, LEGOSHI...
I SAW THE DINOSAURS IN THE FESTIVAL VENUE. THEY'RE BEAUTIFUL.
OUR PERFORMANCE IS GOING TO LOOK AWESOME THANKS TO ALL THE HARD WORK OF THE PRODUCTION CREW.
THOSE DINOSAUR STATUES ARE REALLY AMAZING.
OH... WELL, THANKS.
SHE'S ONLY PAYING ATTENTION TO LEGOSHI!

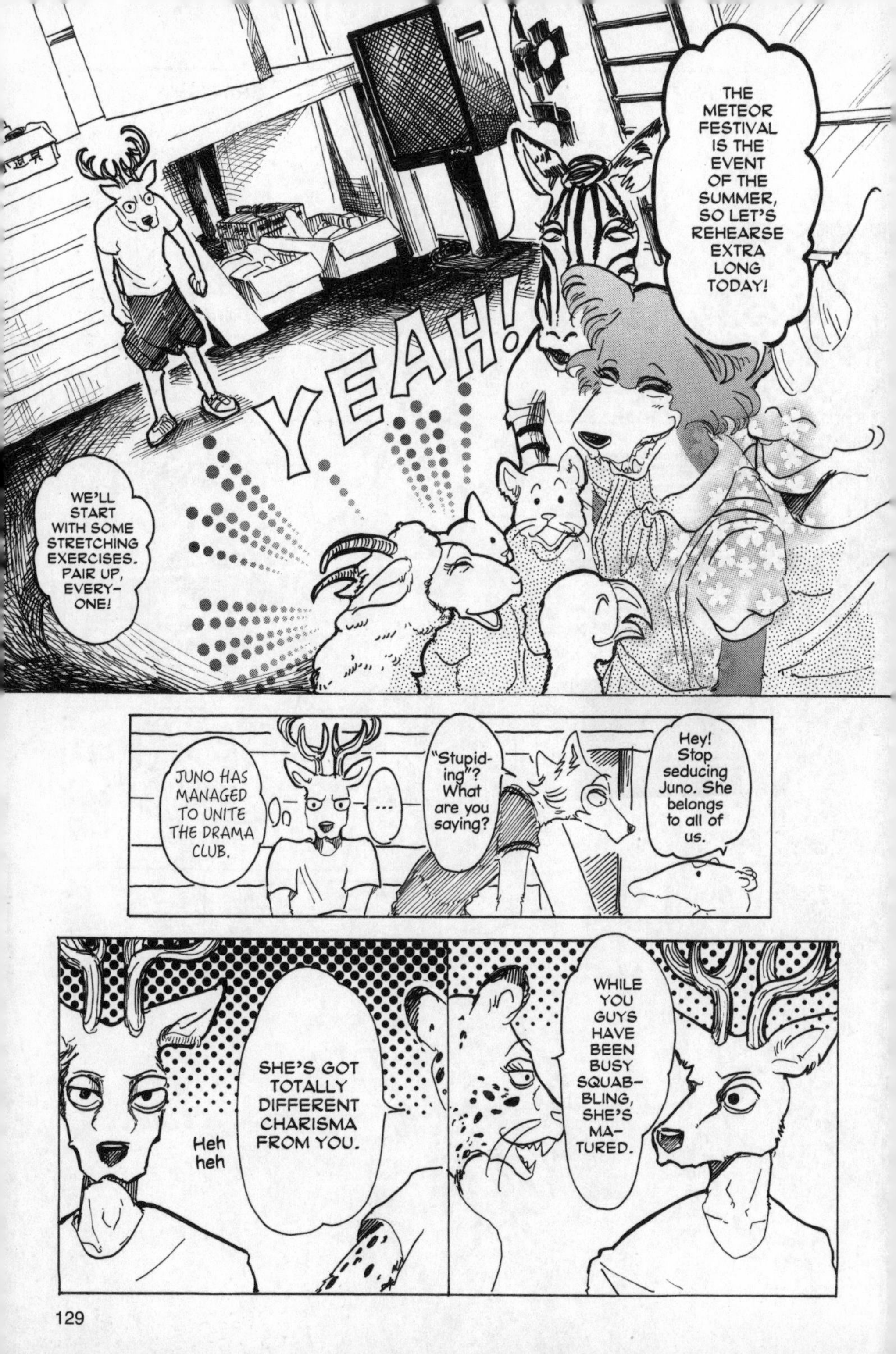
THE METEOR FESTIVAL IS THE EVENT OF THE SUMMER, SO LET'S REHEARSE EXTRA LONG TODAY!
YEAH!
WE'LL START WITH SOME STRETCHING EXERCISES. PAIR UP, EVERY-ONE!
Hey! Stop seducing Juno. She belongs to all of us.
"Stupid-ing"? What are you saying?
...
JUNO HAS MANAGED TO UNITE THE DRAMA CLUB.
WHILE YOU GUYS HAVE BEEN BUSY SQUAB-BLING, SHE'S MA-TURED.
SHE'S GOT TOTALLY DIFFERENT CHARISMA FROM YOU.
Heh heh

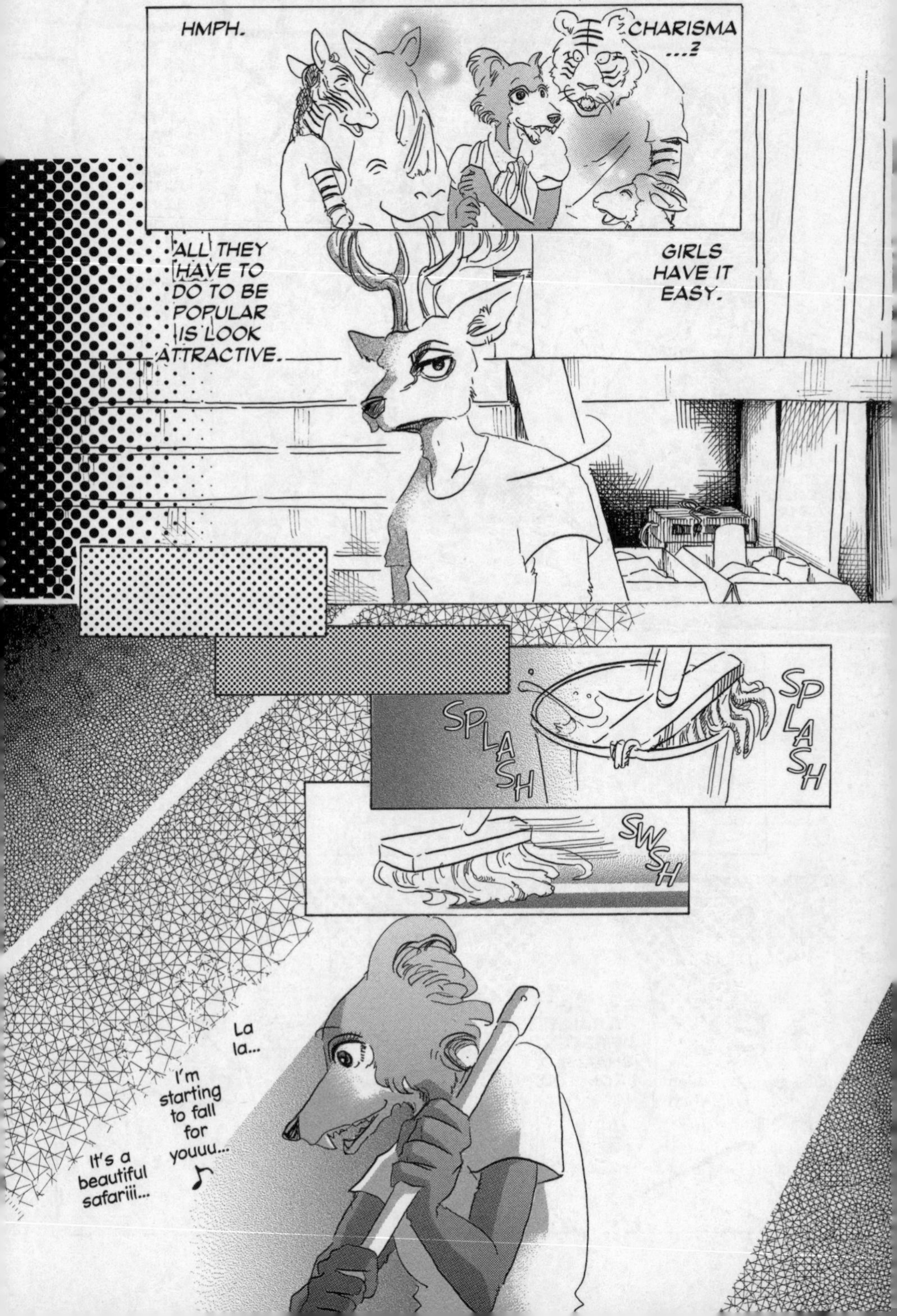
CHARISMA ...?
HMPH.
GIRLS HAVE IT EASY.
ALL THEY HAVE TO DO TO BE POPULAR IS LOOK ATTRACTIVE.
SPLASH
SPLASH
SWSH
La la...
I'm starting to fall for youuu... ♪
It's a beautiful safariii...

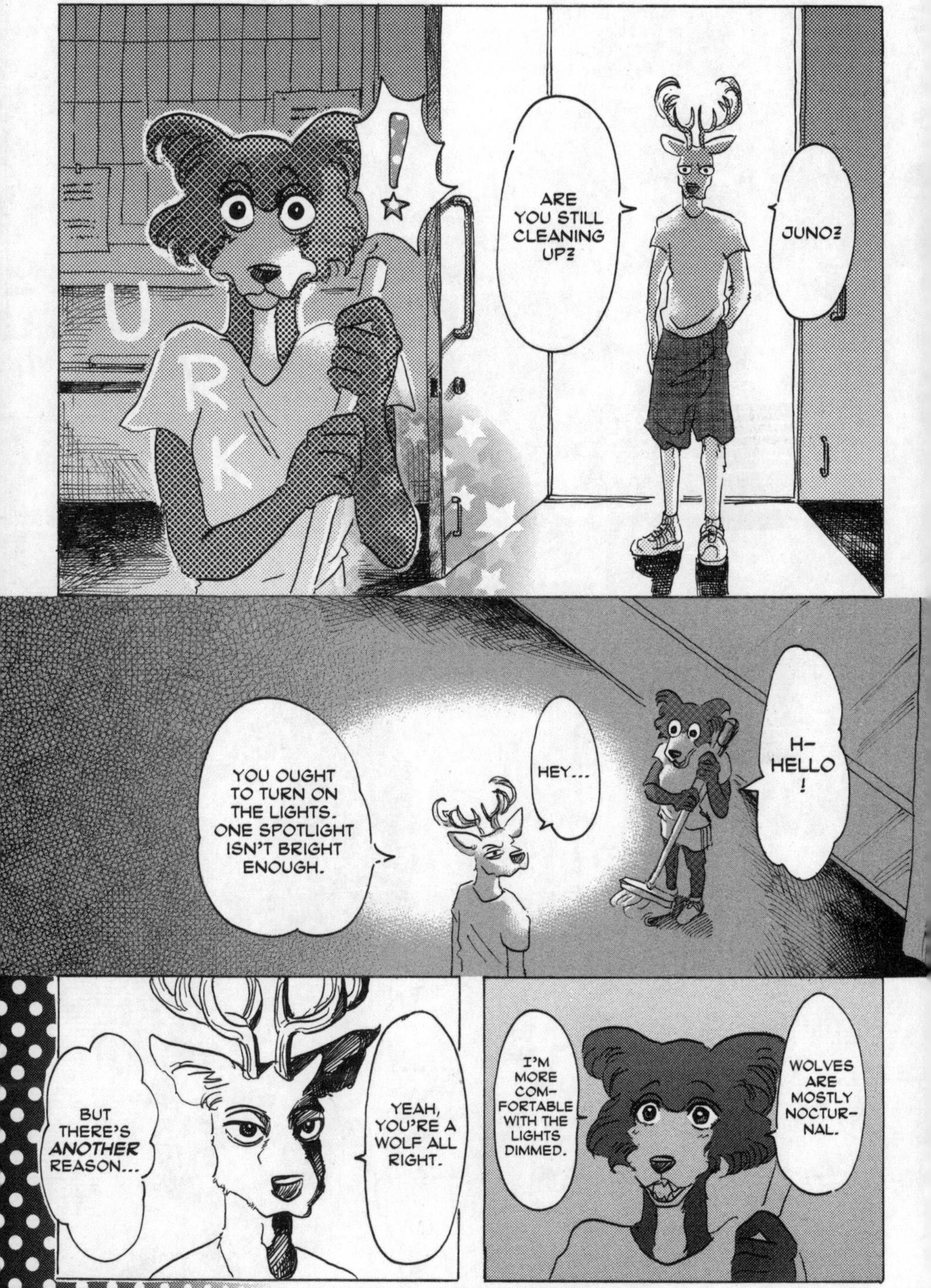
JUNO?
ARE YOU STILL CLEANING UP?
!
URK
H-HELLO!
HEY...
YOU OUGHT TO TURN ON THE LIGHTS. ONE SPOTLIGHT ISN'T BRIGHT ENOUGH.
WOLVES ARE MOSTLY NOCTUR-NAL.
I'M MORE COM-FORTABLE WITH THE LIGHTS DIMMED.
YEAH, YOU'RE A WOLF ALL RIGHT.
BUT THERE'S ***ANOTHER*** REASON...

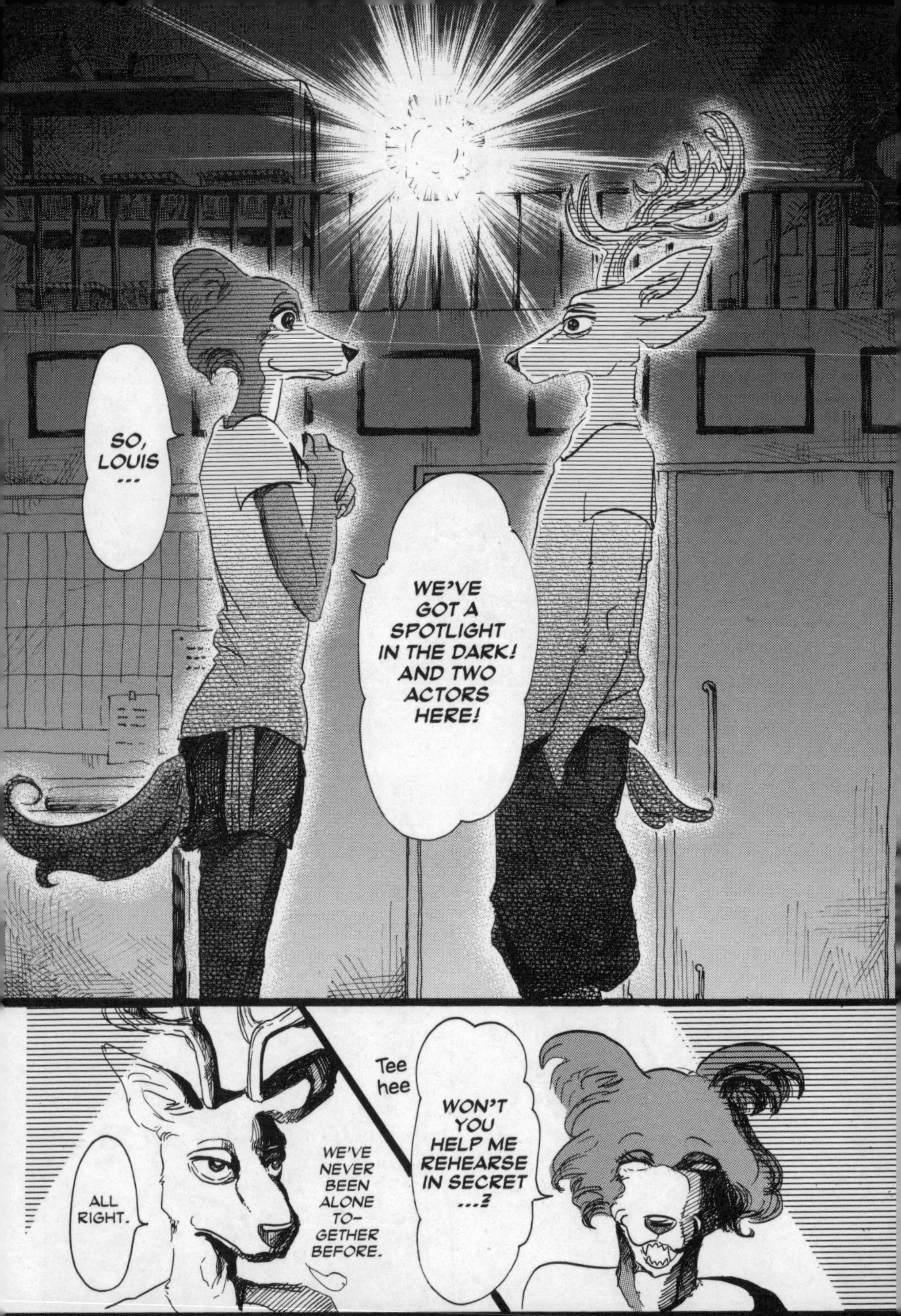
SO, LOUIS ...
WE'VE GOT A SPOTLIGHT IN THE DARK! AND TWO ACTORS HERE!
WON'T YOU HELP ME REHEARSE IN SECRET ...?
Tee hee
WE'VE NEVER BEEN ALONE TO-GETHER BEFORE.
ALL RIGHT.

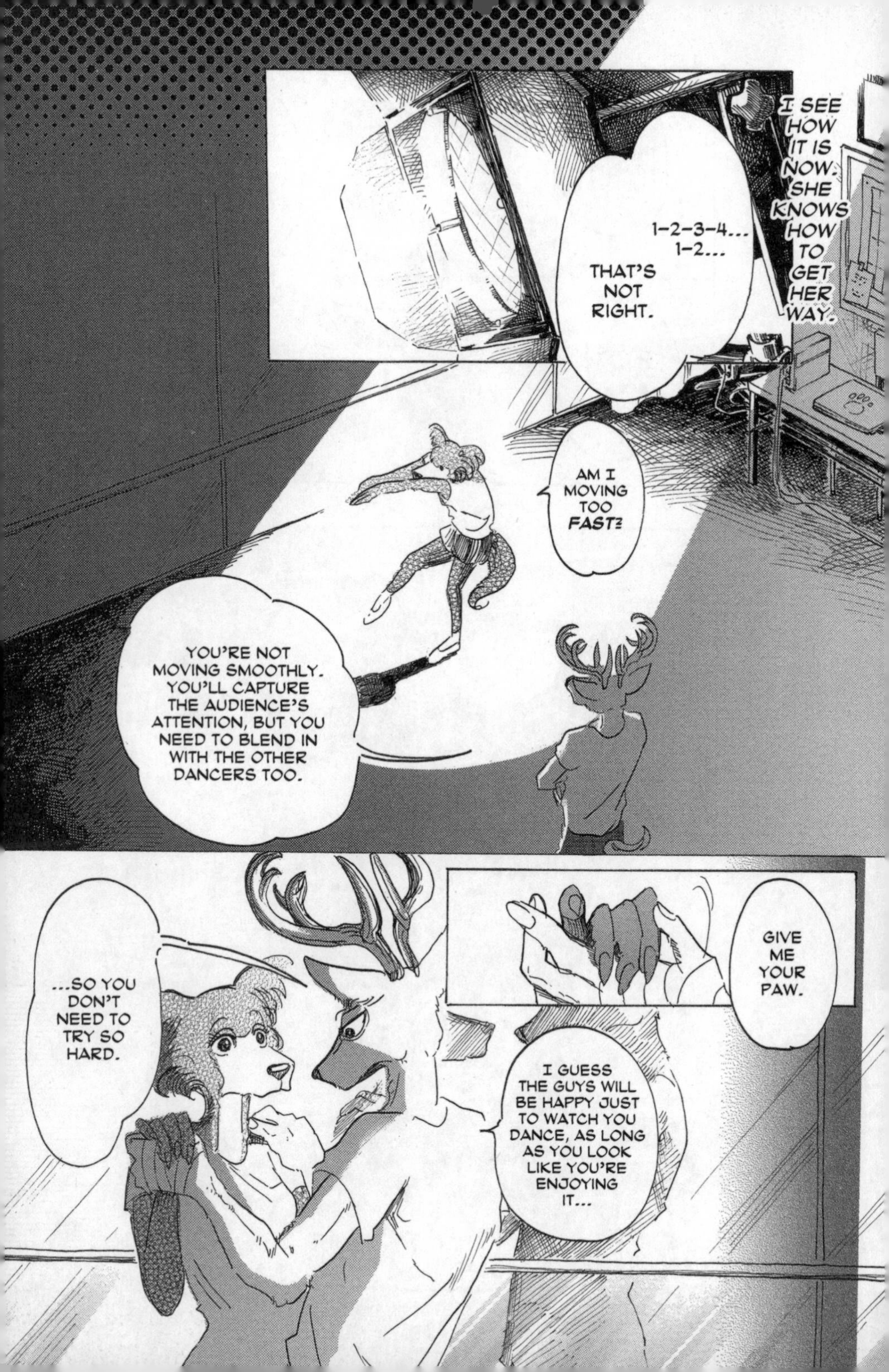
I SEE HOW IT IS NOW. SHE KNOWS HOW TO GET HER WAY.
1-2-3-4... 1-2... THAT'S NOT RIGHT.
AM I MOVING TOO FAST?
YOU'RE NOT MOVING SMOOTHLY. YOU'LL CAPTURE THE AUDIENCE'S ATTENTION, BUT YOU NEED TO BLEND IN WITH THE OTHER DANCERS TOO.
GIVE ME YOUR PAW.
I GUESS THE GUYS WILL BE HAPPY JUST TO WATCH YOU DANCE, AS LONG AS YOU LOOK LIKE YOU'RE ENJOYING IT...
...SO YOU DON'T NEED TO TRY SO HARD.

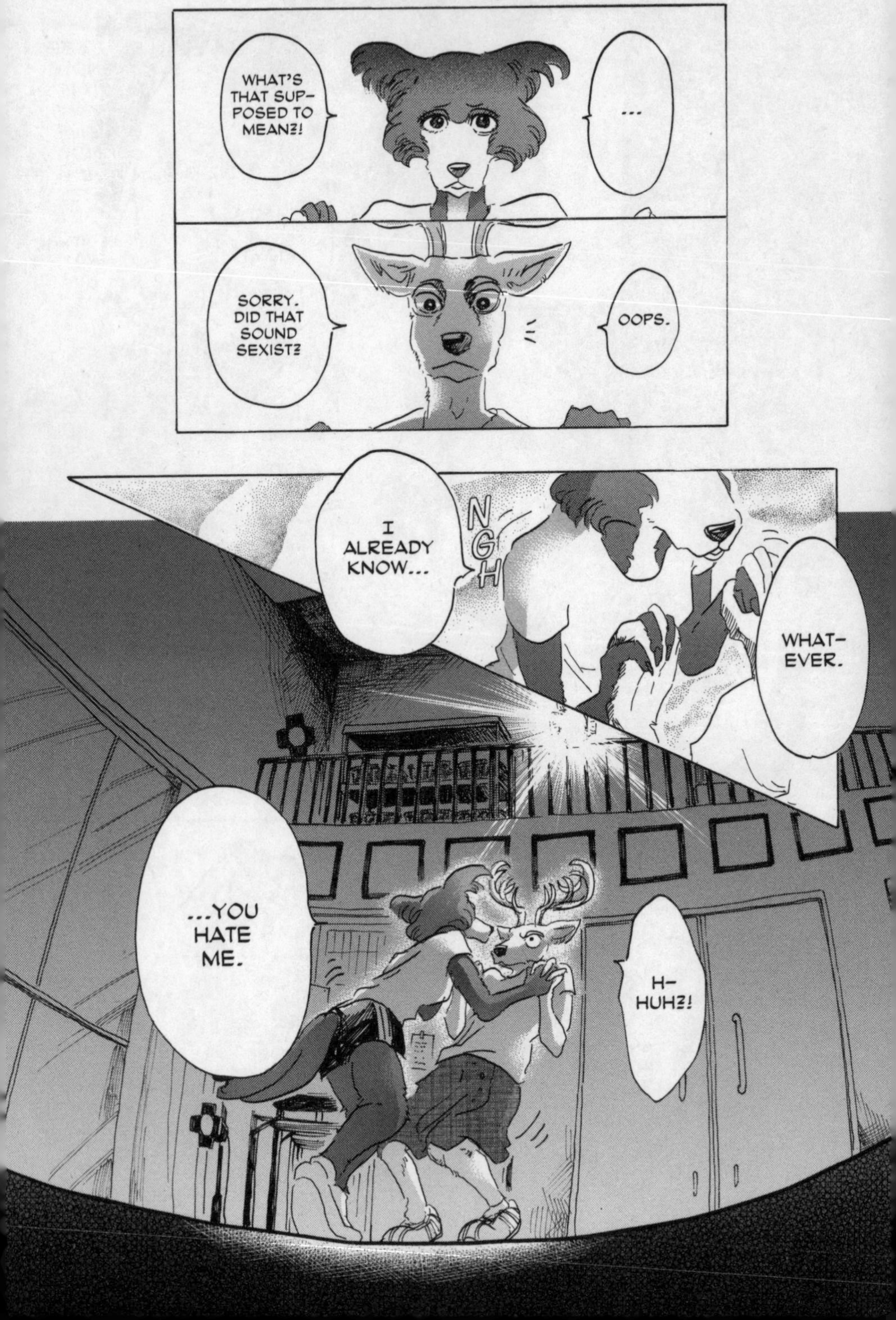
...
WHAT'S THAT SUP-POSED TO MEAN?!
OOPS.
SORRY. DID THAT SOUND SEXIST?
WHAT-EVER.
NGH
I ALREADY KNOW...
...YOU HATE ME.
H-HUH?!

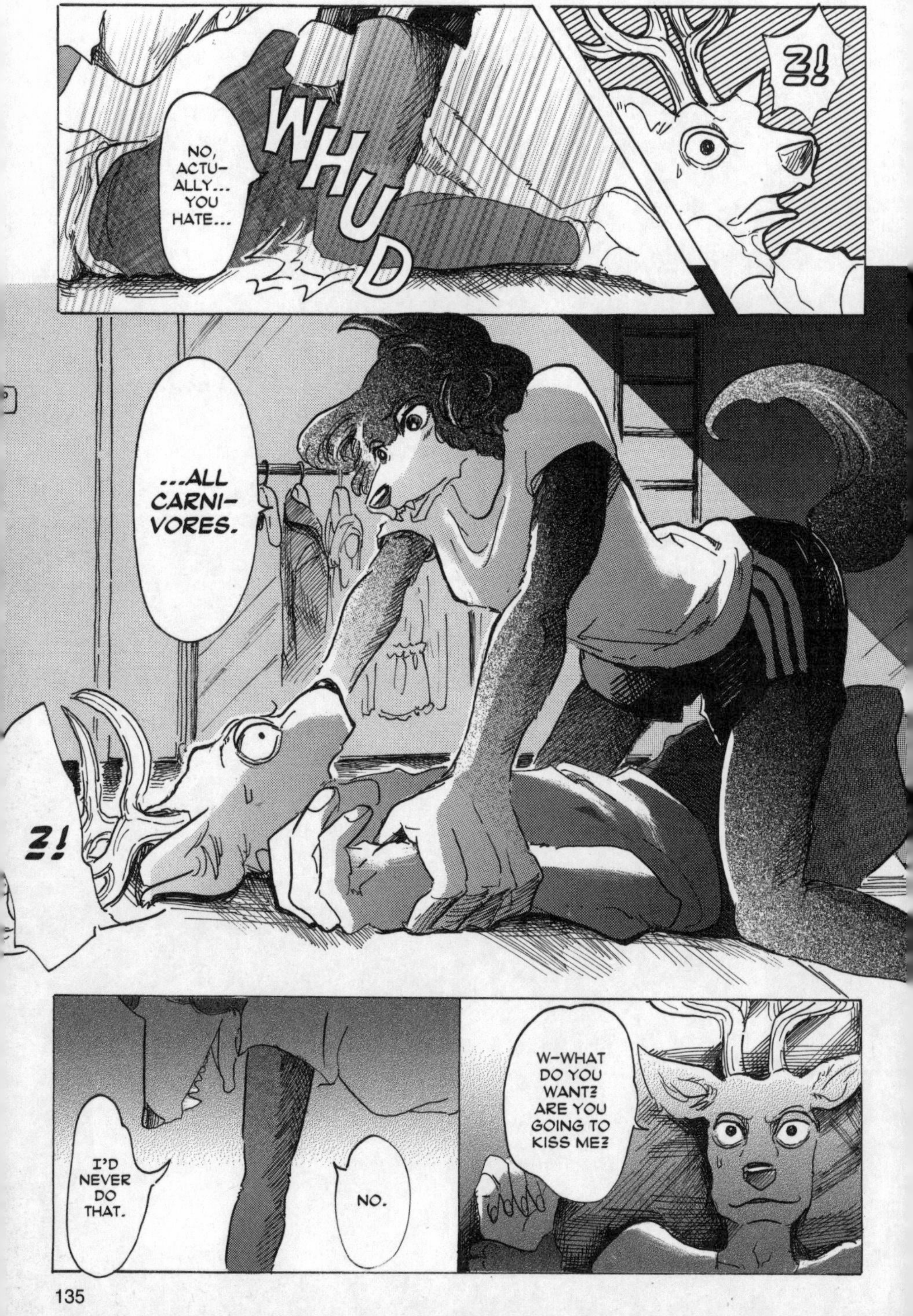
Z!
NO, ACTU- ALLY... YOU HATE...
WHUD
...ALL CARNI- VORES.
Z!
W-WHAT DO YOU WANT? ARE YOU GOING TO KISS ME?
NO.
I'D NEVER DO THAT.

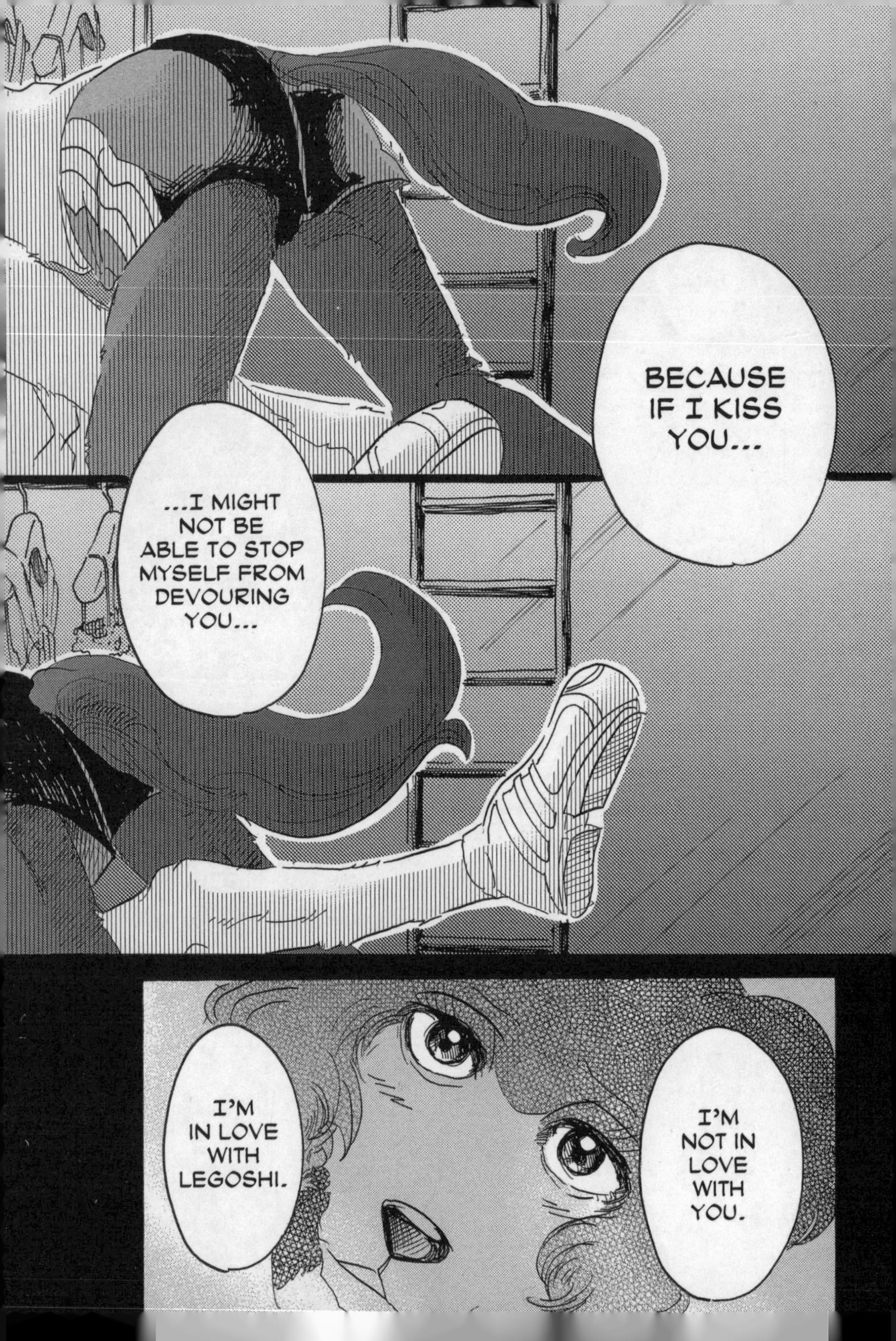
BECAUSE IF I KISS YOU...
...I MIGHT NOT BE ABLE TO STOP MYSELF FROM DEVOURING YOU...
I'M NOT IN LOVE WITH YOU.
I'M IN LOVE WITH LEGOSHI.

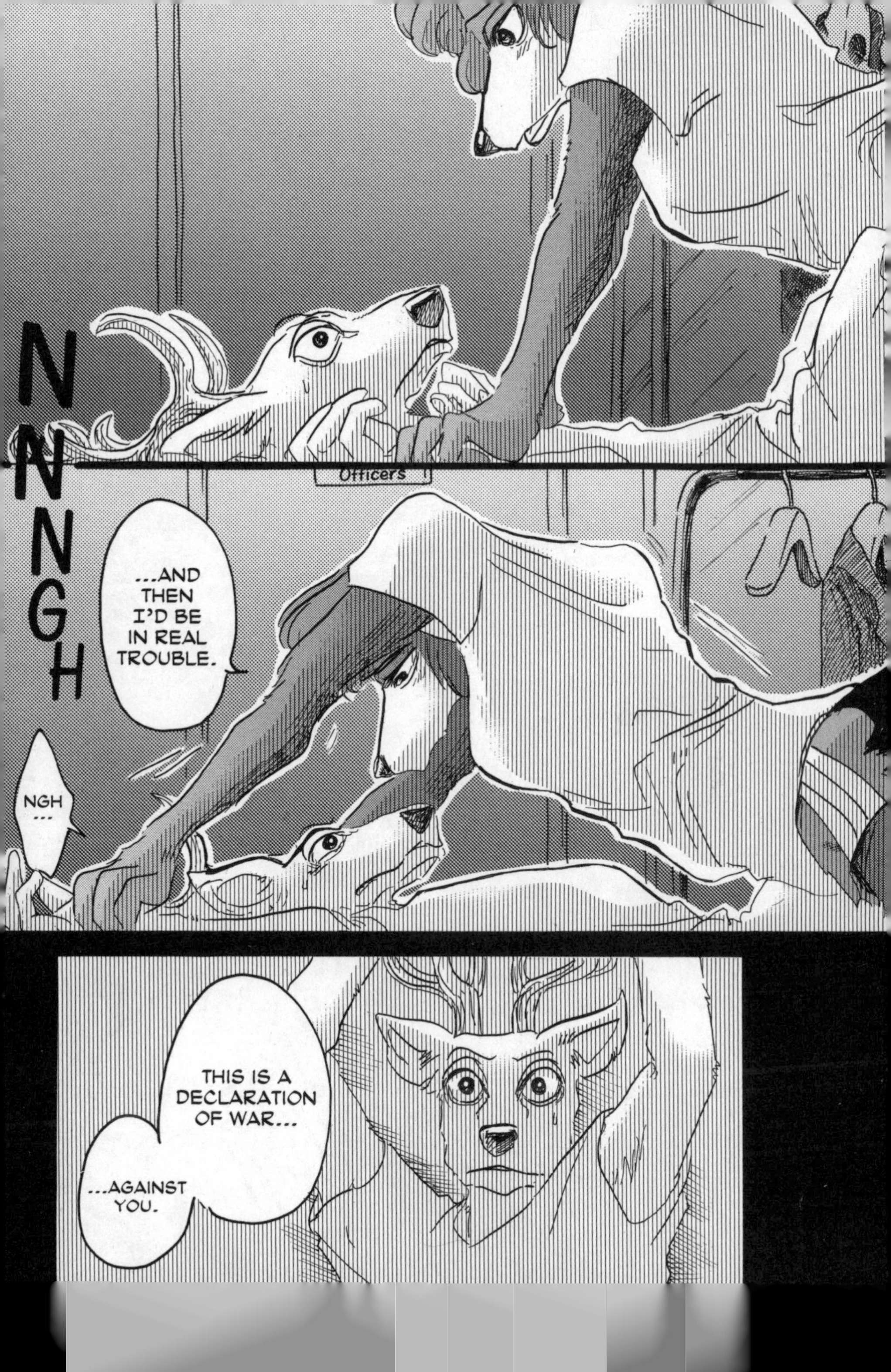
NNNGH
Officers
...AND THEN I'D BE IN REAL TROUBLE.
NGH...
THIS IS A DECLARATION OF WAR...
...AGAINST YOU.

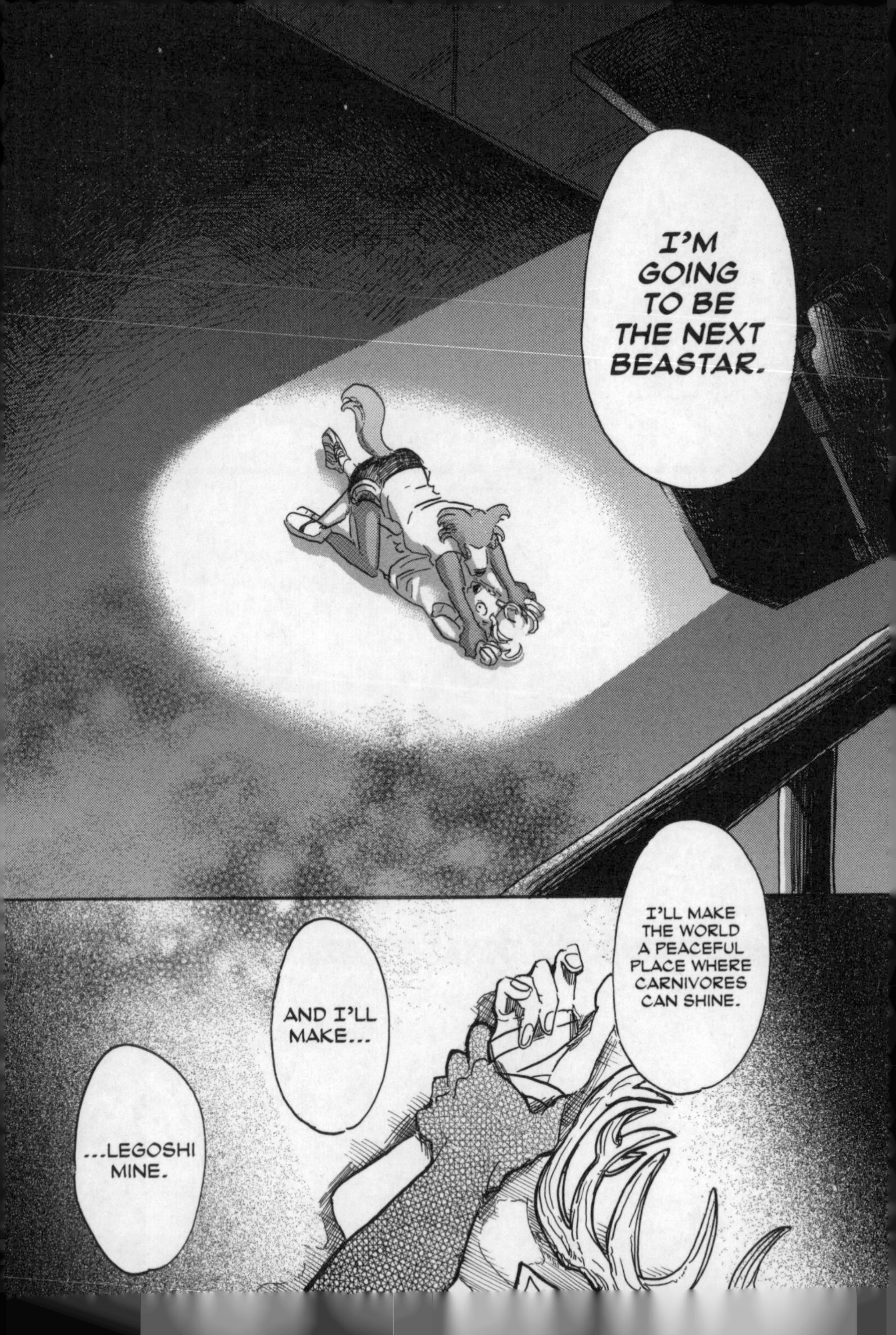
I'M GOING TO BE THE NEXT BEASTAR.
I'LL MAKE THE WORLD A PEACEFUL PLACE WHERE CARNIVORES CAN SHINE.
AND I'LL MAKE...
...LEGOSHI MINE.

Chapter 32: Then Will You Turn the Lights Off?

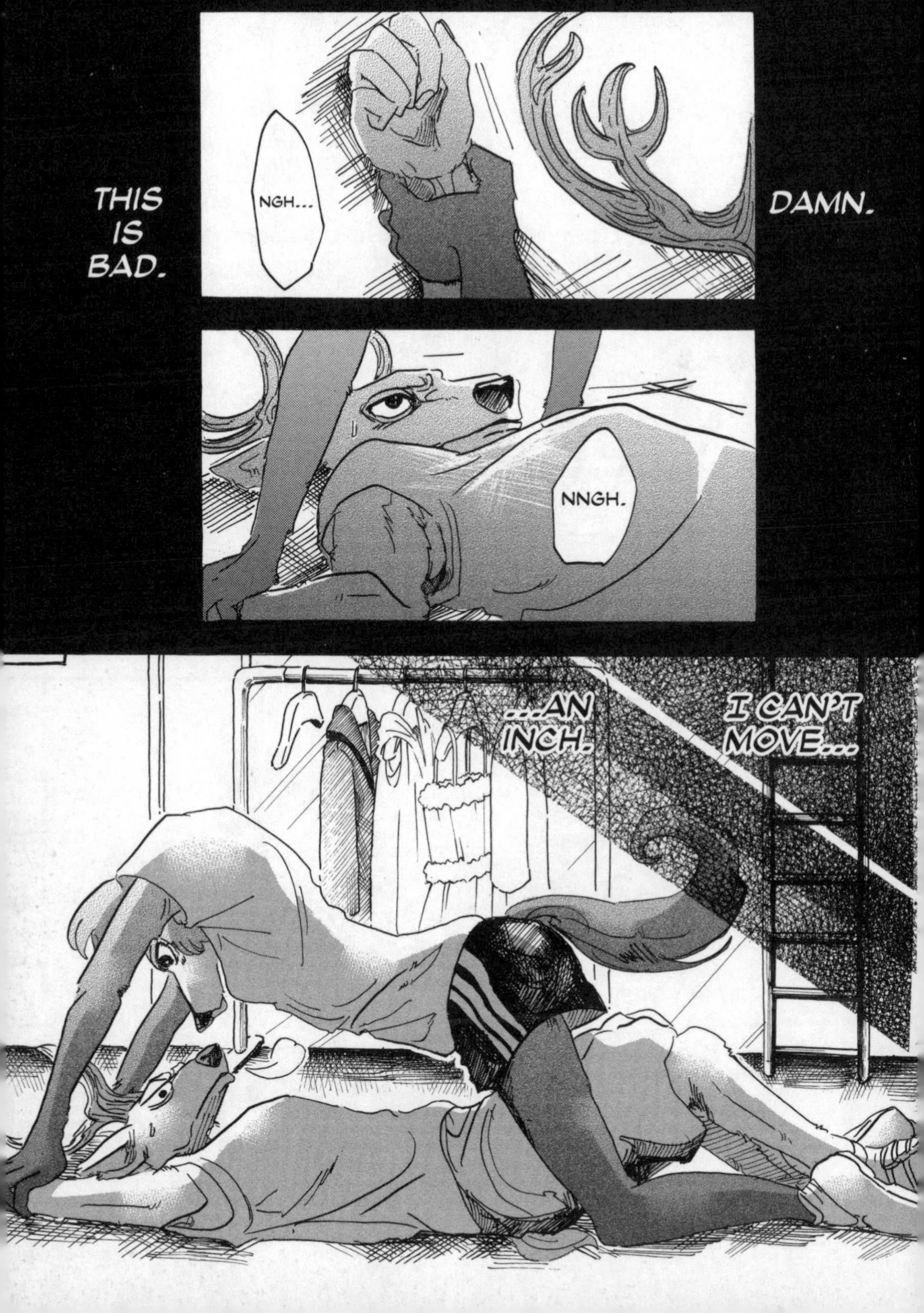

DAMN.
NGH...
THIS IS BAD.
NNGH.
I CAN'T MOVE...
...AN INCH.

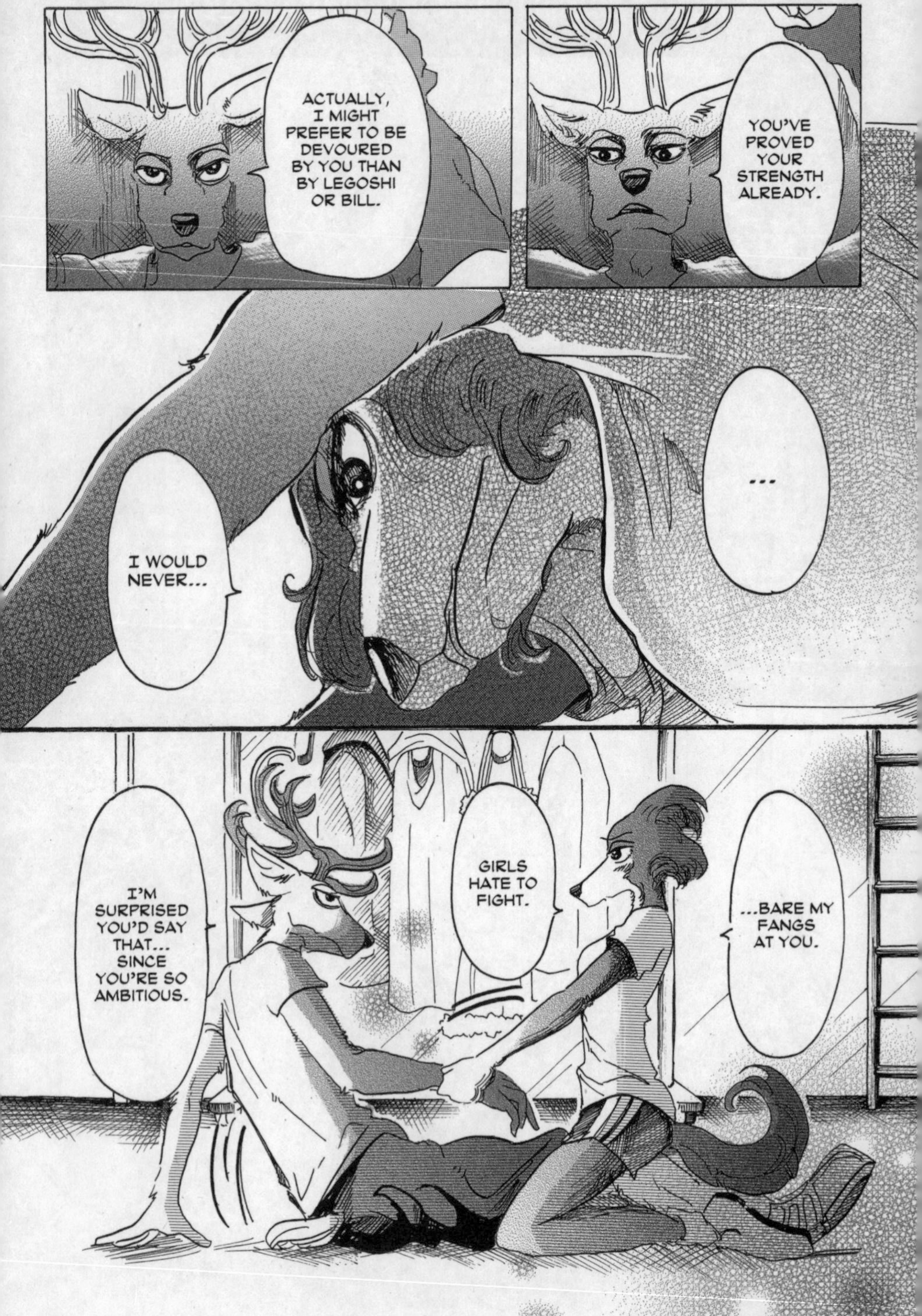
YOU'VE PROVED YOUR STRENGTH ALREADY.
ACTUALLY, I MIGHT PREFER TO BE DEVOURED BY YOU THAN BY LEGOSHI OR BILL.
...
I WOULD NEVER...
...BARE MY FANGS AT YOU.
GIRLS HATE TO FIGHT.
I'M SURPRISED YOU'D SAY THAT... SINCE YOU'RE SO AMBITIOUS.

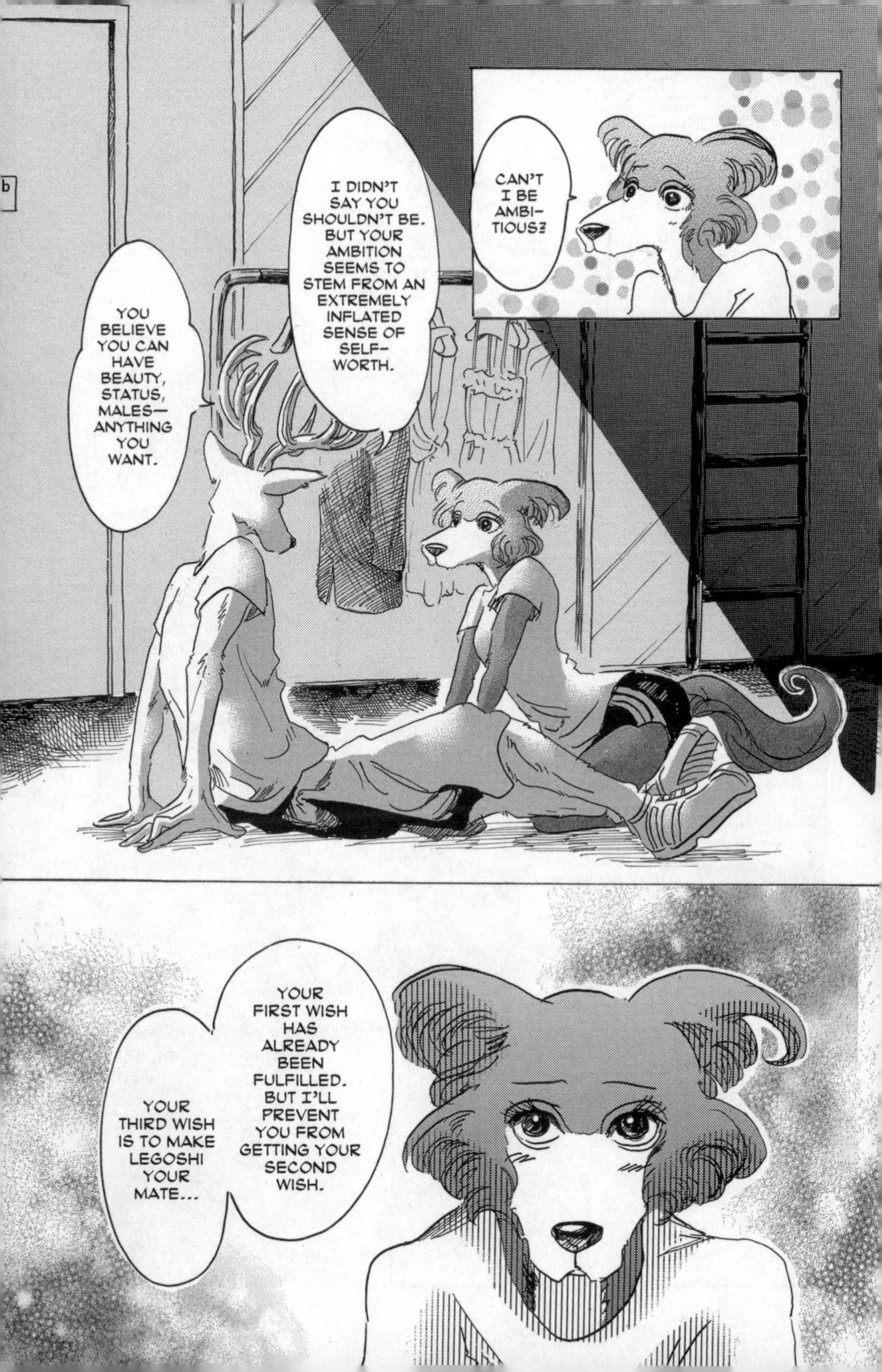
CAN'T I BE AMBITIOUS?
I DIDN'T SAY YOU SHOULDN'T BE. BUT YOUR AMBITION SEEMS TO STEM FROM AN EXTREMELY INFLATED SENSE OF SELF-WORTH.
YOU BELIEVE YOU CAN HAVE BEAUTY, STATUS, MALES—ANYTHING YOU WANT.
YOUR FIRST WISH HAS ALREADY BEEN FULFILLED. BUT I'LL PREVENT YOU FROM GETTING YOUR SECOND WISH.
YOUR THIRD WISH IS TO MAKE LEGOSHI YOUR MATE...

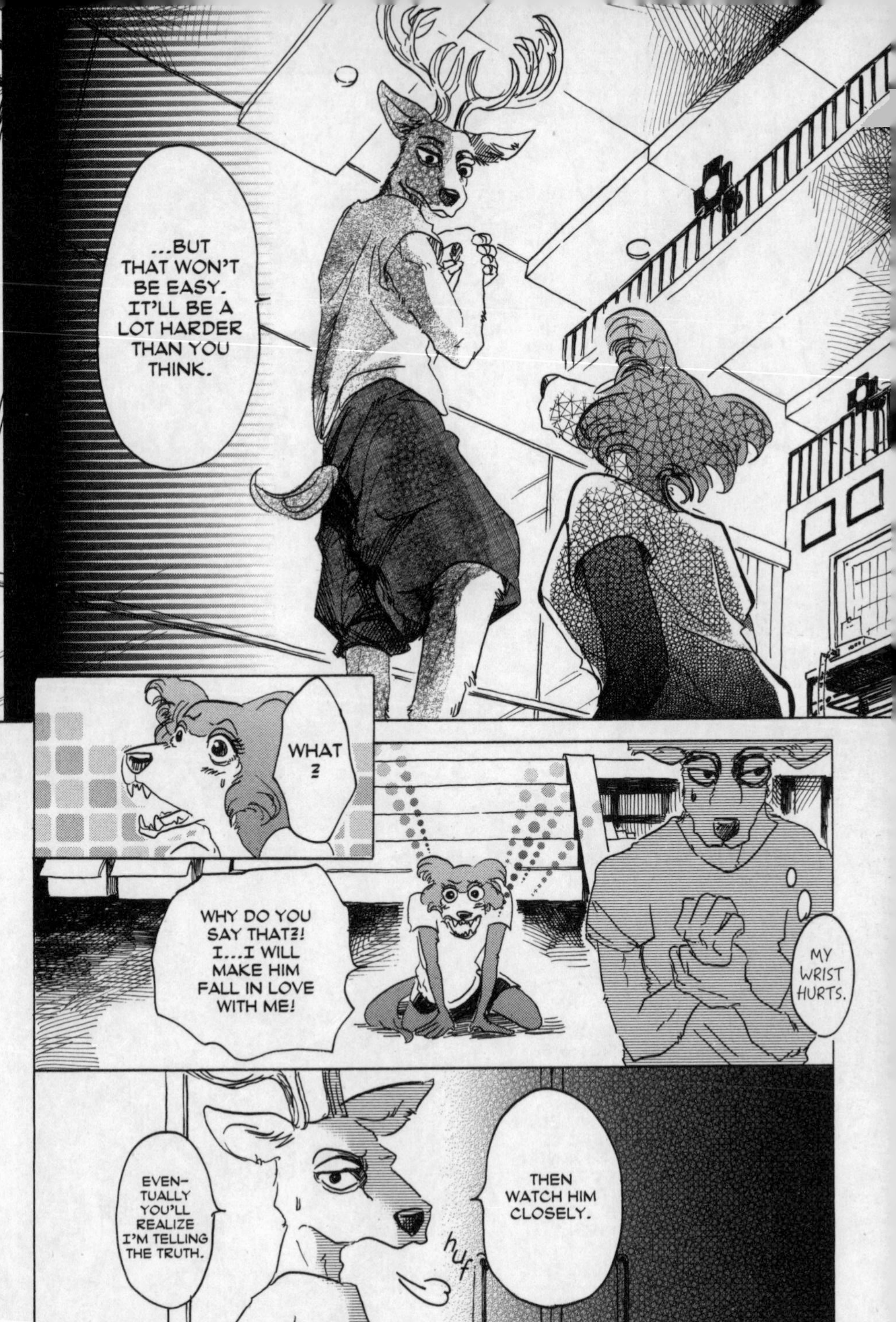
...BUT THAT WON'T BE EASY. IT'LL BE A LOT HARDER THAN YOU THINK.
WHAT?
WHY DO YOU SAY THAT?! I...I WILL MAKE HIM FALL IN LOVE WITH ME!
MY WRIST HURTS.
THEN WATCH HIM CLOSELY.
huf
EVEN-TUALLY YOU'LL REALIZE I'M TELLING THE TRUTH.

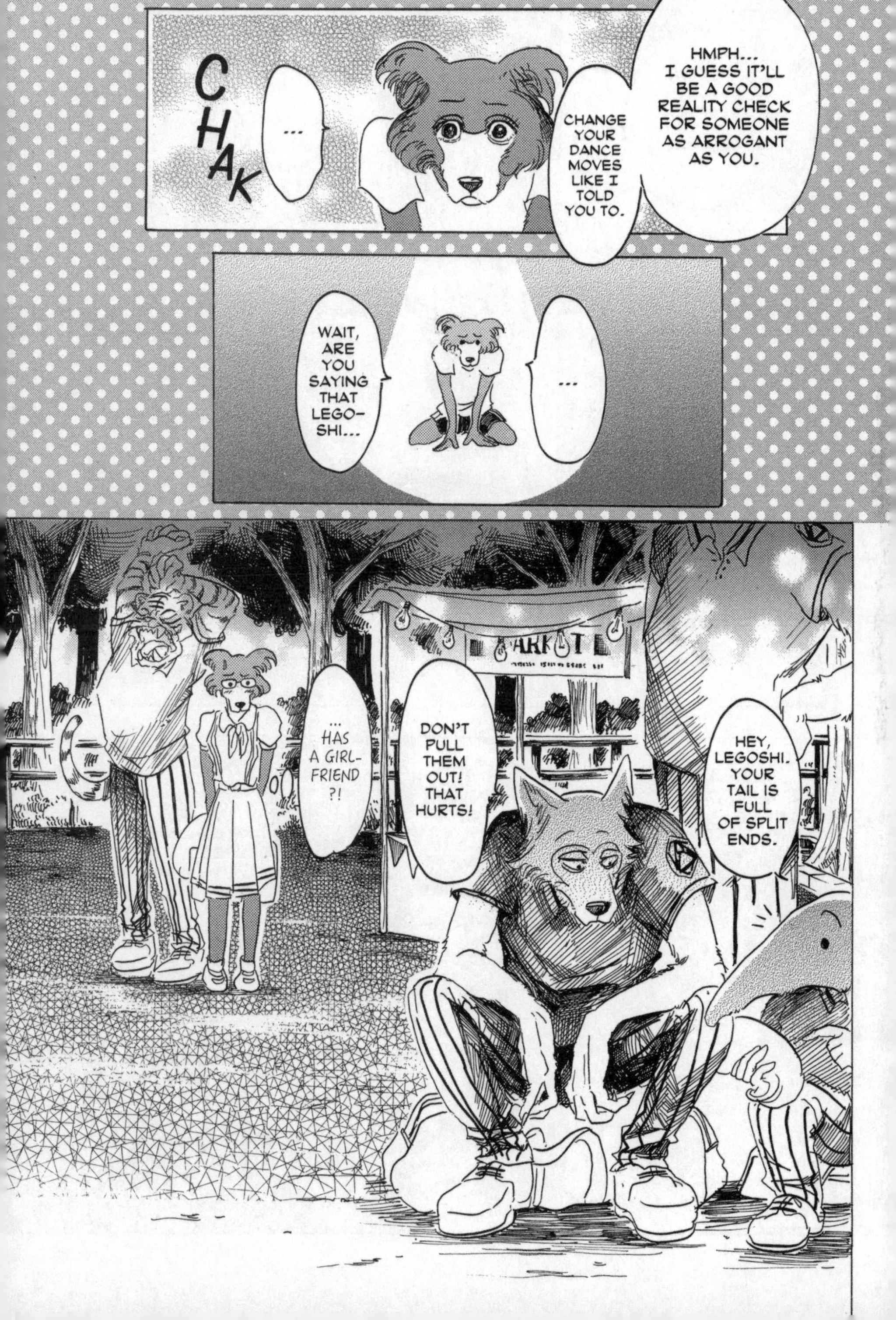
HMPH... I GUESS IT'LL BE A GOOD REALITY CHECK FOR SOMEONE AS ARROGANT AS YOU.
CHANGE YOUR DANCE MOVES LIKE I TOLD YOU TO.
...
CHAK
...
WAIT, ARE YOU SAYING THAT LEGO-SHI...
HEY, LEGOSHI. YOUR TAIL IS FULL OF SPLIT ENDS.
DON'T PULL THEM OUT! THAT HURTS!
... HAS A GIRL-FRIEND ?!

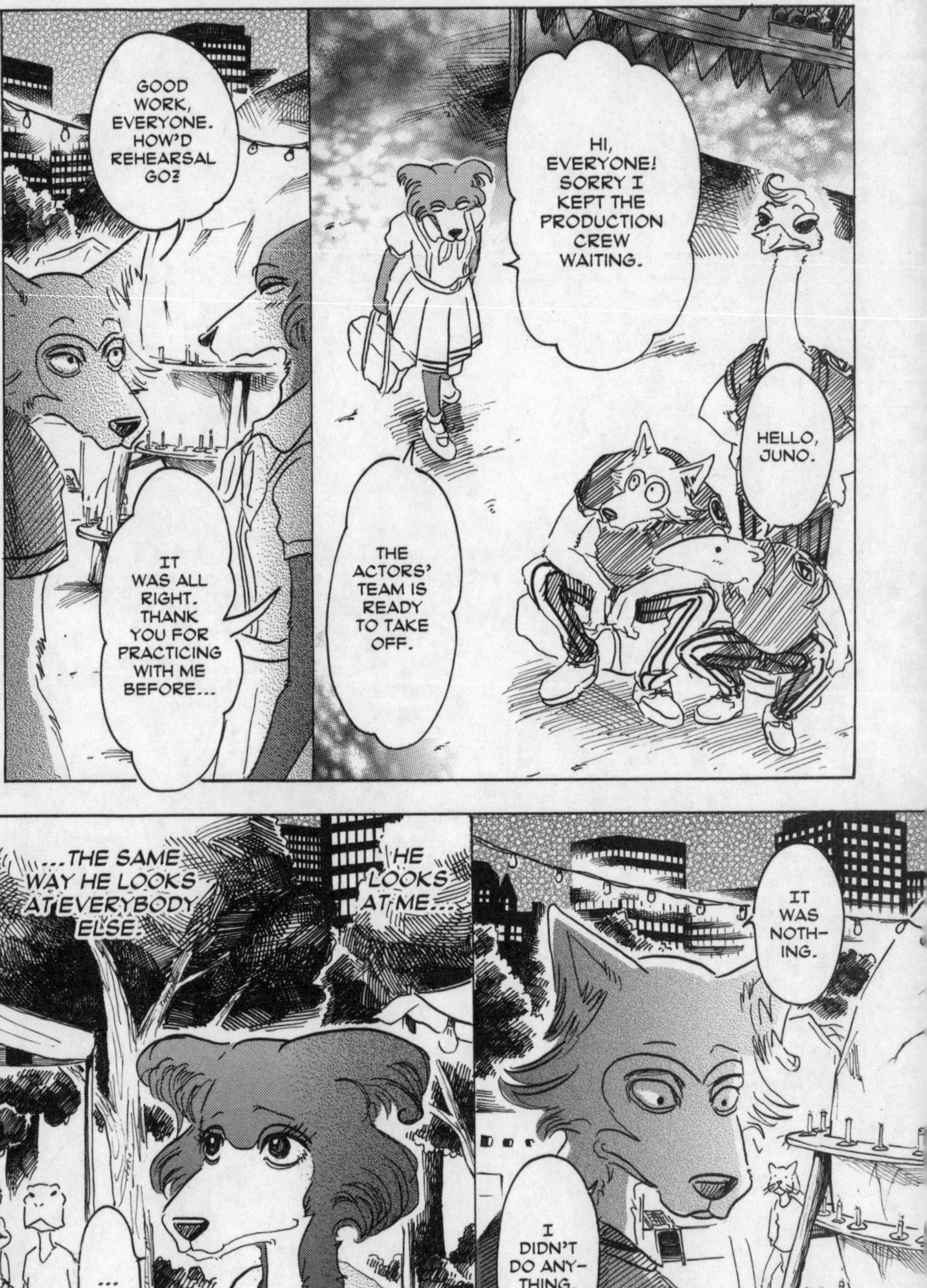
HI, EVERYONE! SORRY I KEPT THE PRODUCTION CREW WAITING.
HELLO, JUNO.
THE ACTORS' TEAM IS READY TO TAKE OFF.
GOOD WORK, EVERYONE. HOW'D REHEARSAL GO?
IT WAS ALL RIGHT. THANK YOU FOR PRACTICING WITH ME BEFORE...
IT WAS NOTHING.
I DIDN'T DO ANYTHING.
HE LOOKS AT ME...
...THE SAME WAY HE LOOKS AT EVERYBODY ELSE.
...

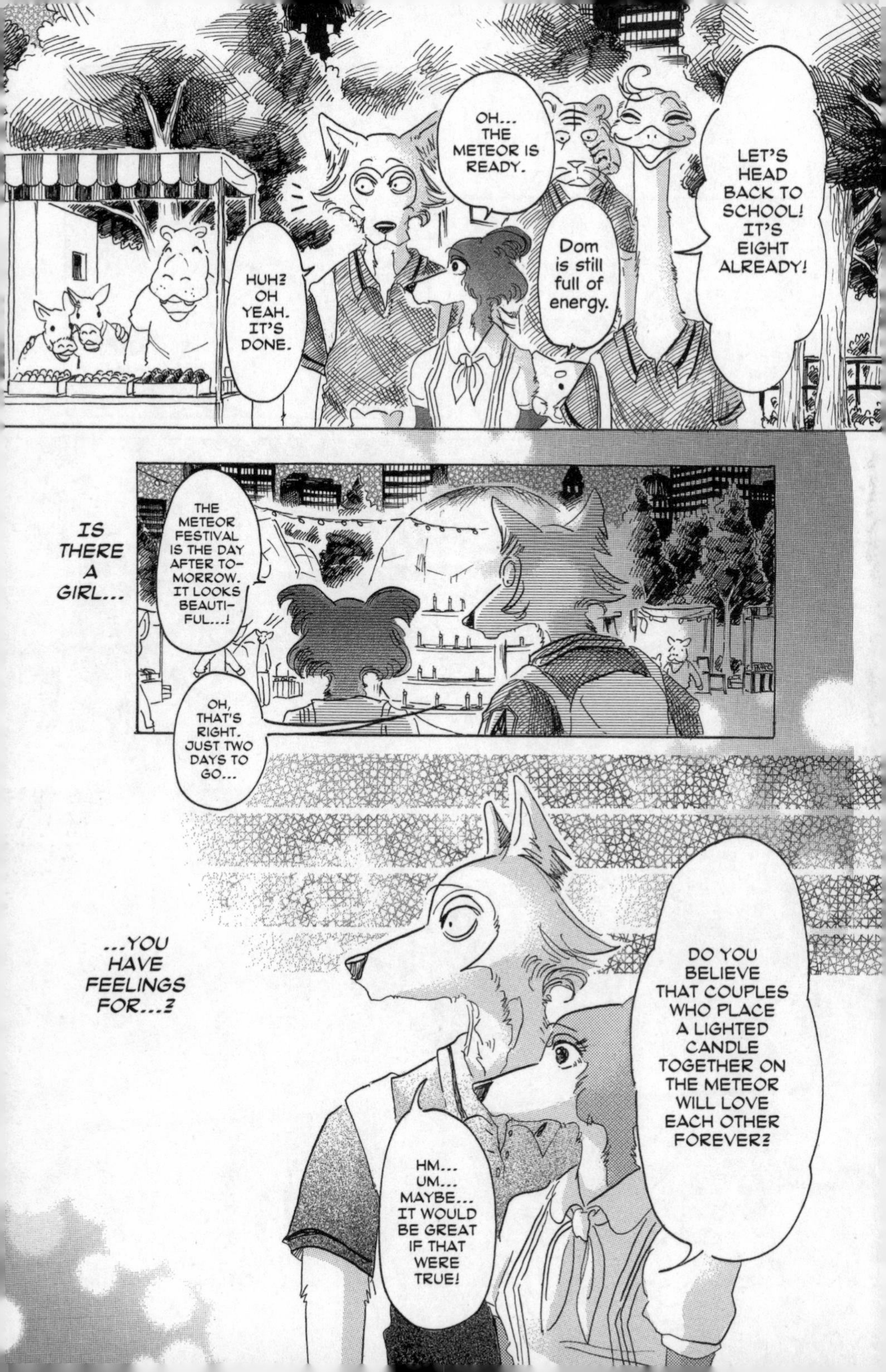
LET'S HEAD BACK TO SCHOOL! IT'S EIGHT ALREADY!
OH... THE METEOR IS READY.
Dom is still full of energy.
HUH? OH YEAH. IT'S DONE.
THE METEOR FESTIVAL IS THE DAY AFTER TO-MORROW. IT LOOKS BEAUTI-FUL...!
OH, THAT'S RIGHT. JUST TWO DAYS TO GO...
IS THERE A GIRL...
DO YOU BELIEVE THAT COUPLES WHO PLACE A LIGHTED CANDLE TOGETHER ON THE METEOR WILL LOVE EACH OTHER FOREVER?
HM... UM... MAYBE... IT WOULD BE GREAT IF THAT WERE TRUE!
...YOU HAVE FEELINGS FOR...?

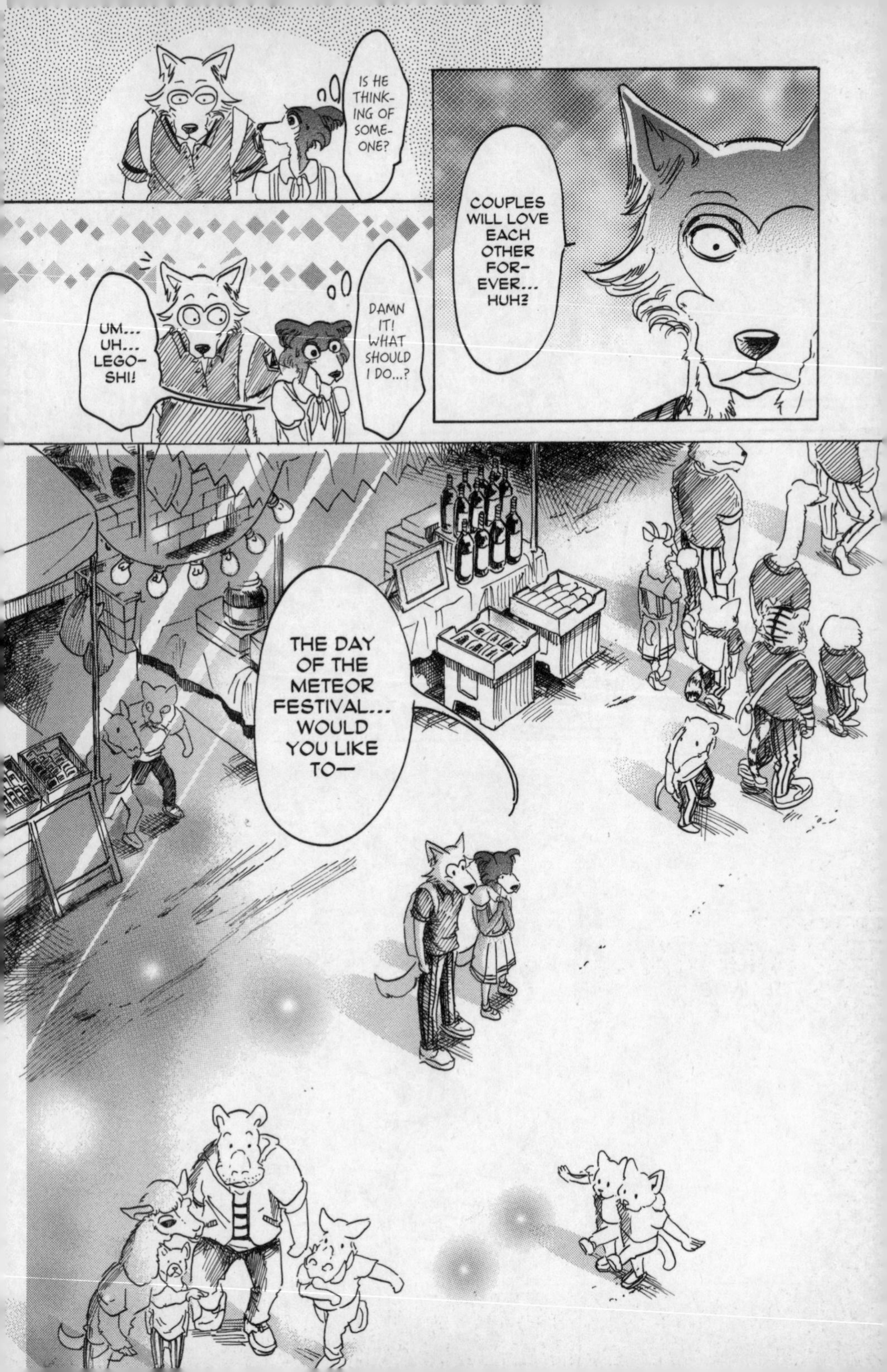
COUPLES WILL LOVE EACH OTHER FOR-EVER... HUH?
IS HE THINK-ING OF SOME-ONE?
DAMN IT! WHAT SHOULD I DO...?
UM... UH... LEGO-SHI!
THE DAY OF THE METEOR FESTIVAL... WOULD YOU LIKE TO—

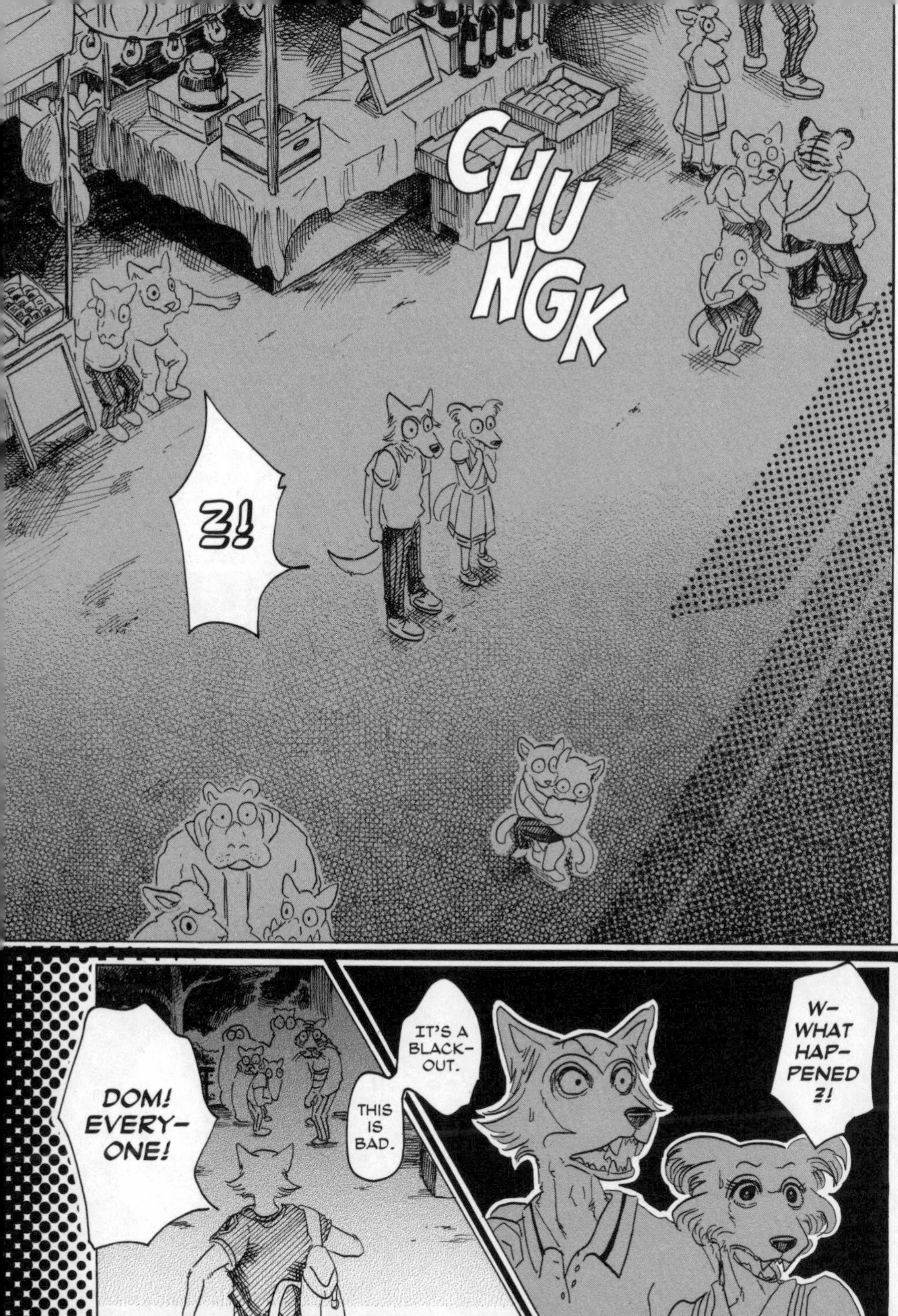
CHUNGK
?!
W-WHAT HAPPENED?!
IT'S A BLACKOUT.
THIS IS BAD.
DOM! EVERYONE!

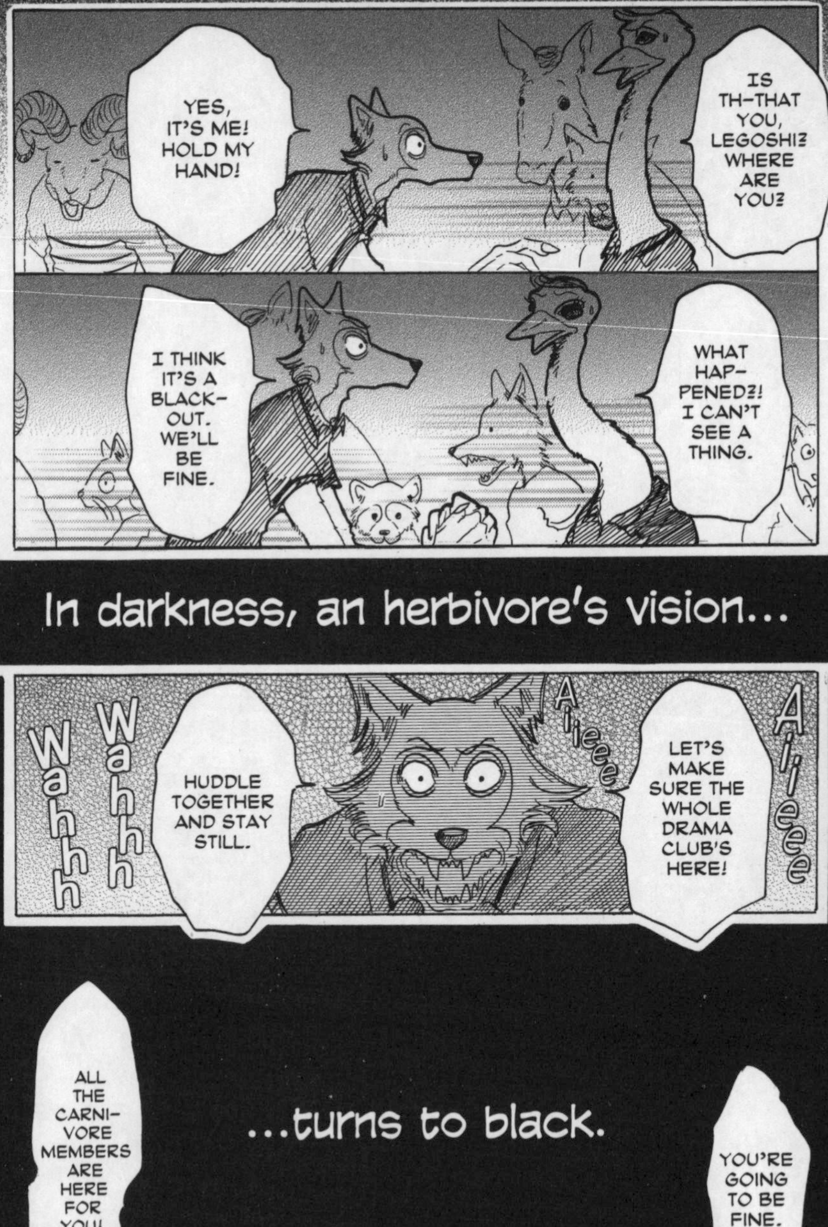
IS TH-THAT YOU, LEGOSHI? WHERE ARE YOU?
YES, IT'S ME! HOLD MY HAND!
WHAT HAPPENED?! I CAN'T SEE A THING.
I THINK IT'S A BLACKOUT. WE'LL BE FINE.
In darkness, an herbivore's vision...
Aiieee
Aiieee
LET'S MAKE SURE THE WHOLE DRAMA CLUB'S HERE!
HUDDLE TOGETHER AND STAY STILL.
Wahhh
Wahhh
YOU'RE GOING TO BE FINE.
...turns to black.
ALL THE CARNIVORE MEMBERS ARE HERE FOR YOU!

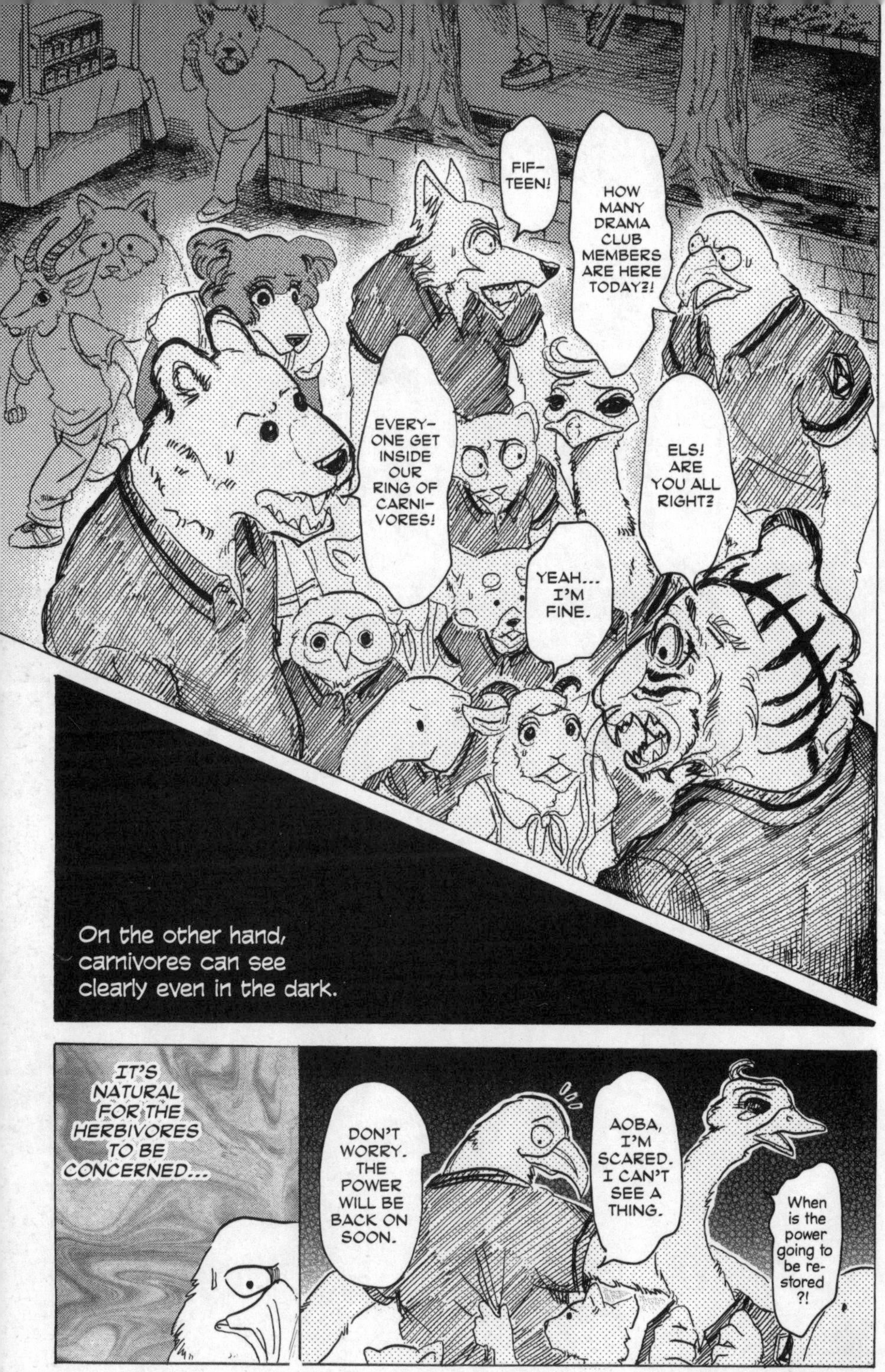
HOW MANY DRAMA CLUB MEMBERS ARE HERE TODAY?!
FIF-TEEN!
ELS! ARE YOU ALL RIGHT?
EVERY-ONE GET INSIDE OUR RING OF CARNI-VORES!
YEAH... I'M FINE.
On the other hand, carnivores can see clearly even in the dark.
When is the power going to be re-stored?!
AOBA, I'M SCARED. I CAN'T SEE A THING.
DON'T WORRY. THE POWER WILL BE BACK ON SOON.
IT'S NATURAL FOR THE HERBIVORES TO BE CONCERNED...

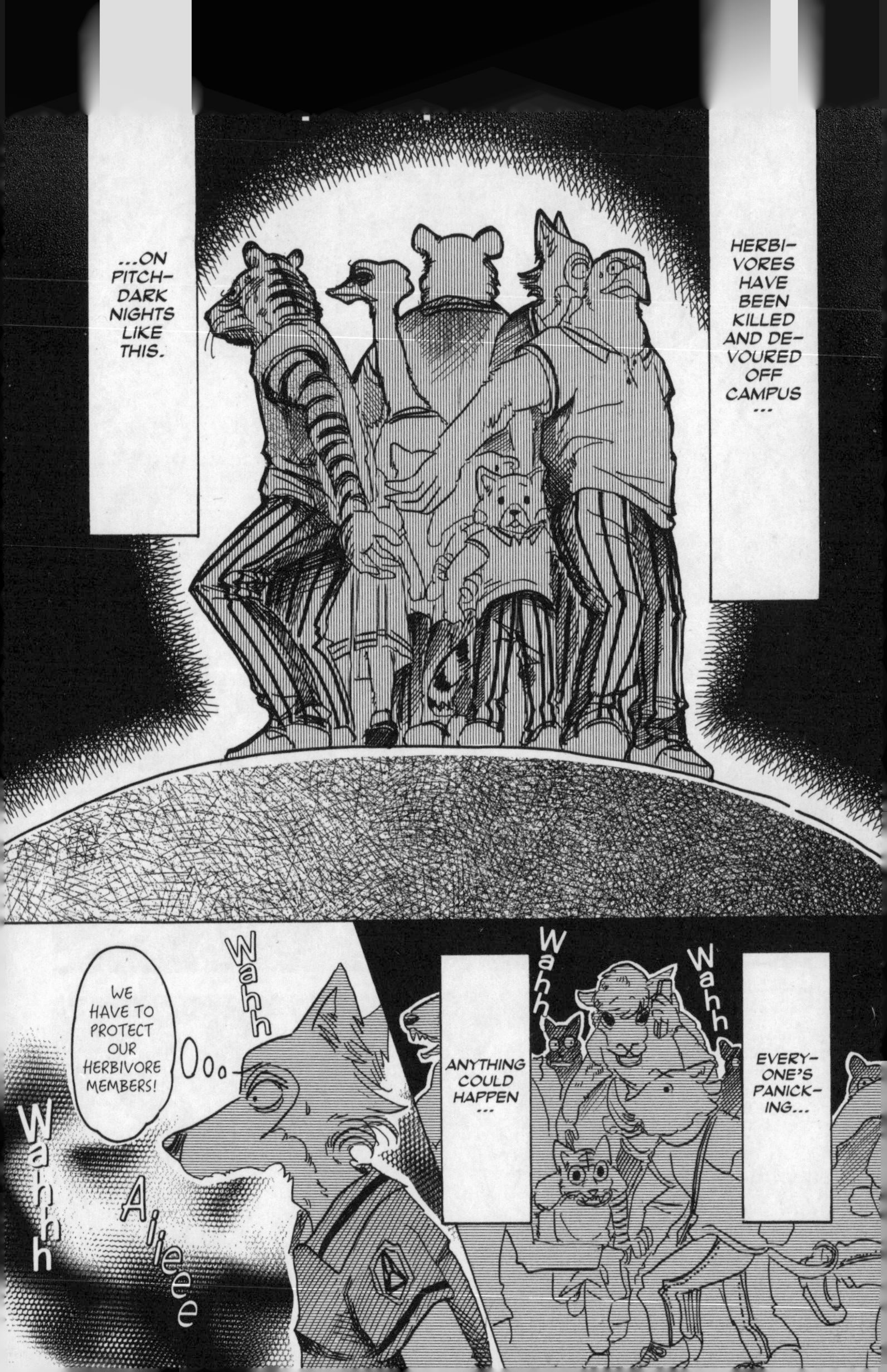
HERBI-VORES HAVE BEEN KILLED AND DE-VOURED OFF CAMPUS...
...ON PITCH-DARK NIGHTS LIKE THIS.
EVERY-ONE'S PANICK-ING...
Wahh
ANYTHING COULD HAPPEN...
Wahh
Wahh
WE HAVE TO PROTECT OUR HERBIVORE MEMBERS!
Ooo
Wahhh
Aiieee

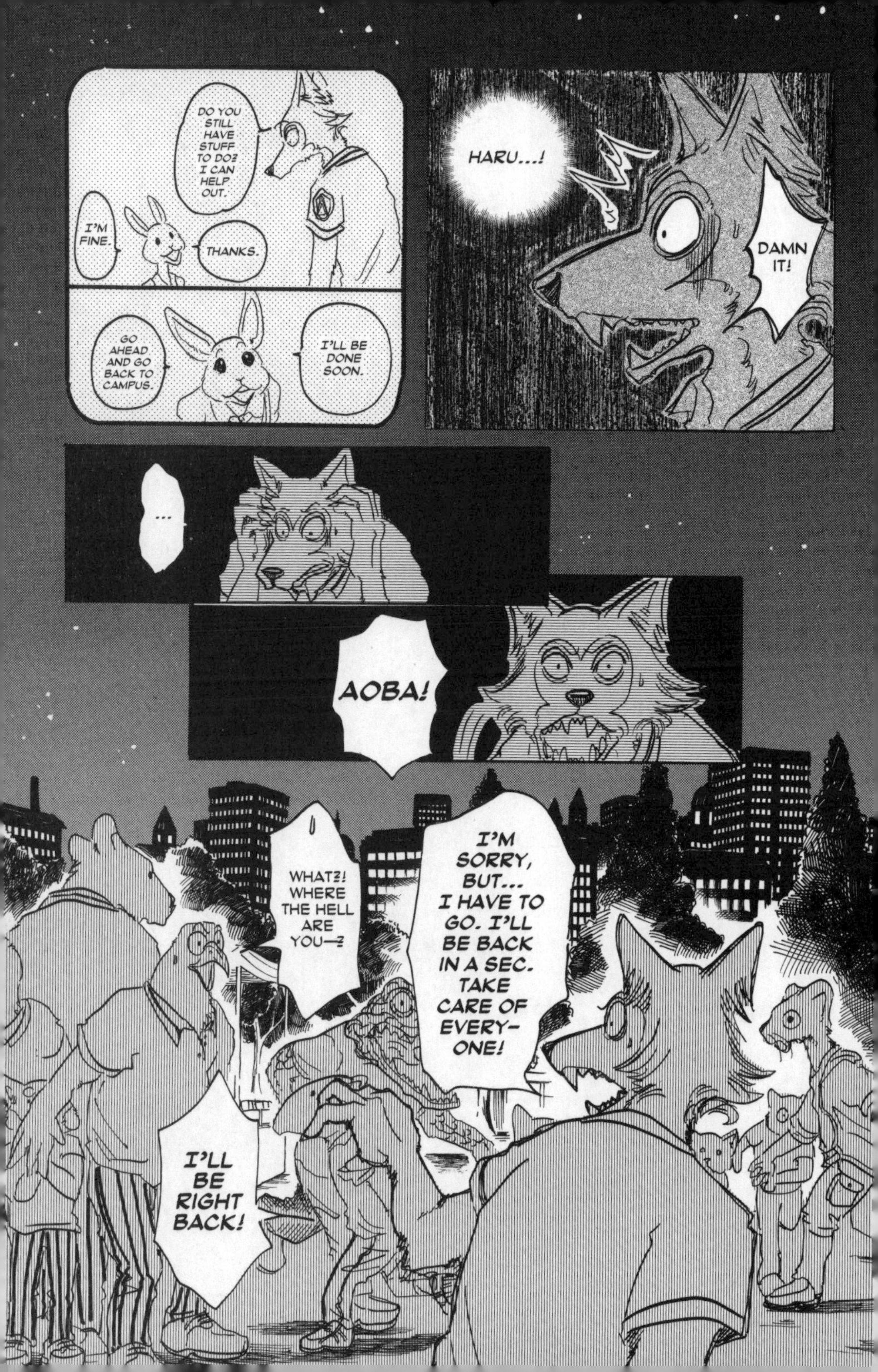
HARU...!
DAMN IT!
DO YOU STILL HAVE STUFF TO DO? I CAN HELP OUT.
I'M FINE.
THANKS.
I'LL BE DONE SOON.
GO AHEAD AND GO BACK TO CAMPUS.
...
AOBA!
I'M SORRY, BUT... I HAVE TO GO. I'LL BE BACK IN A SEC. TAKE CARE OF EVERY-ONE!
WHAT?! WHERE THE HELL ARE YOU—?
I'LL BE RIGHT BACK!

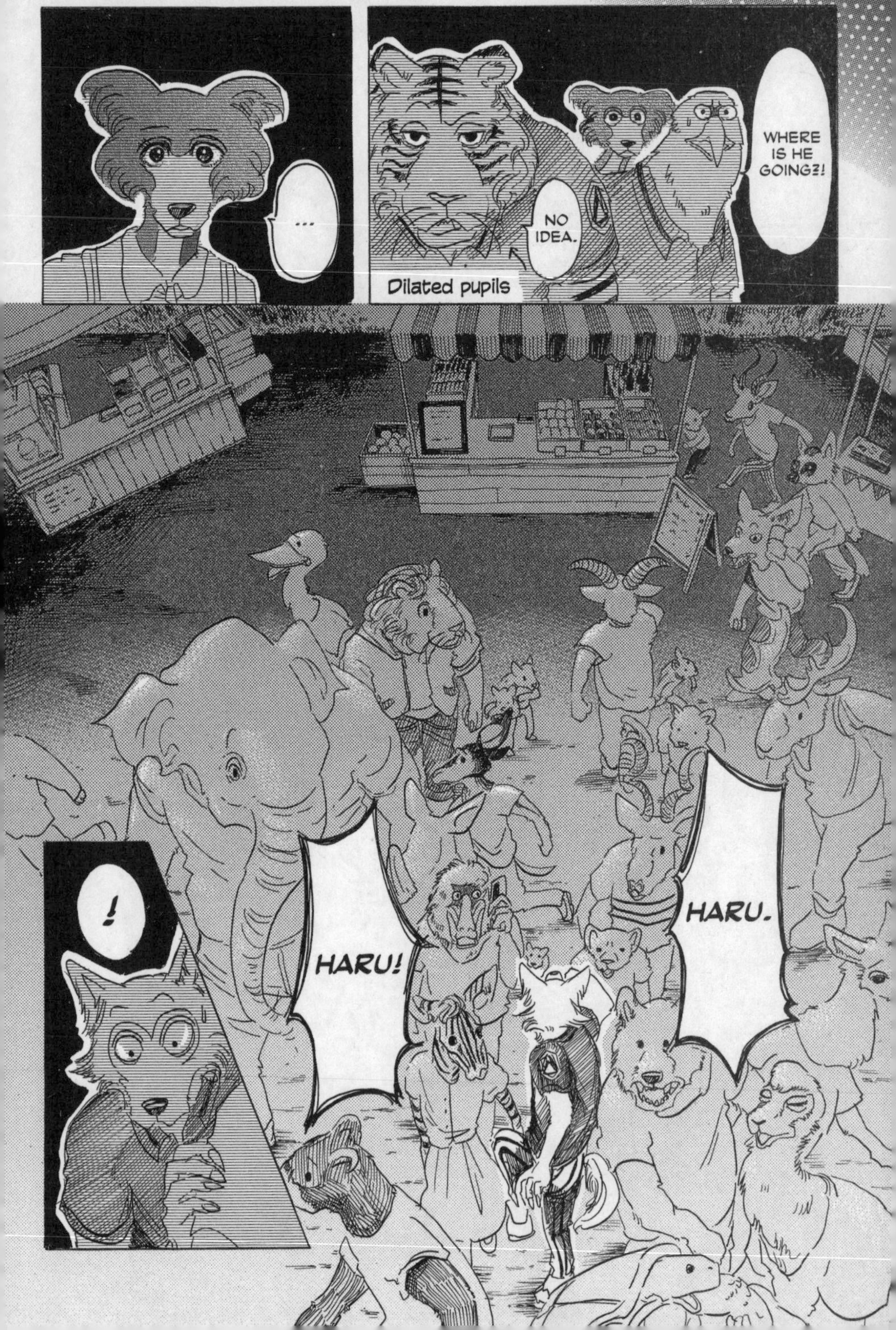
WHERE IS HE GOING?!
NO IDEA.
Dilated pupils
...
HARU.
HARU!
!

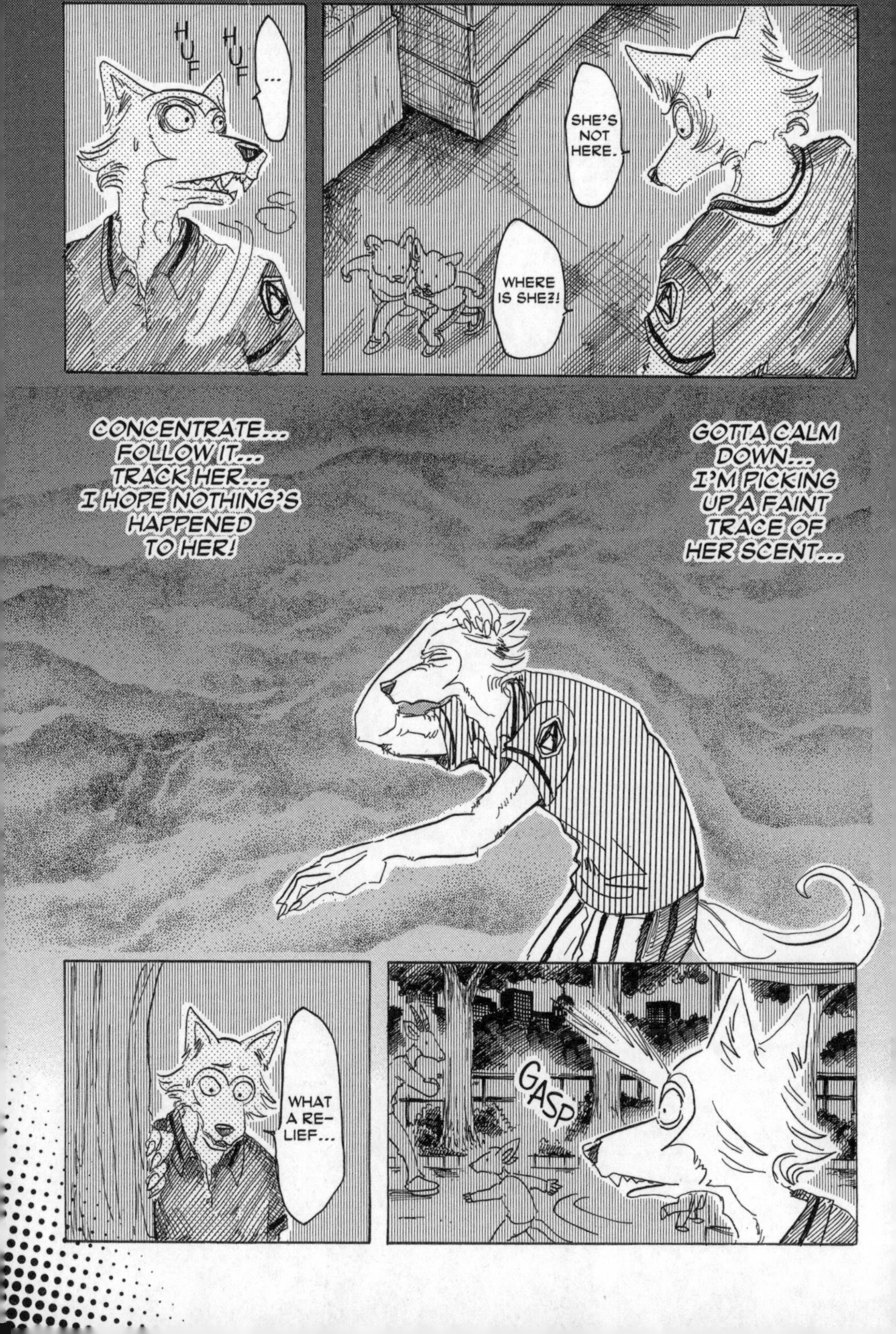
SHE'S NOT HERE...
WHERE IS SHE?!
HUF HUF
...
GOTTA CALM DOWN... I'M PICKING UP A FAINT TRACE OF HER SCENT...
CONCENTRATE... FOLLOW IT... TRACK HER... I HOPE NOTHING'S HAPPENED TO HER!
GASP
WHAT A RE-LIEF...

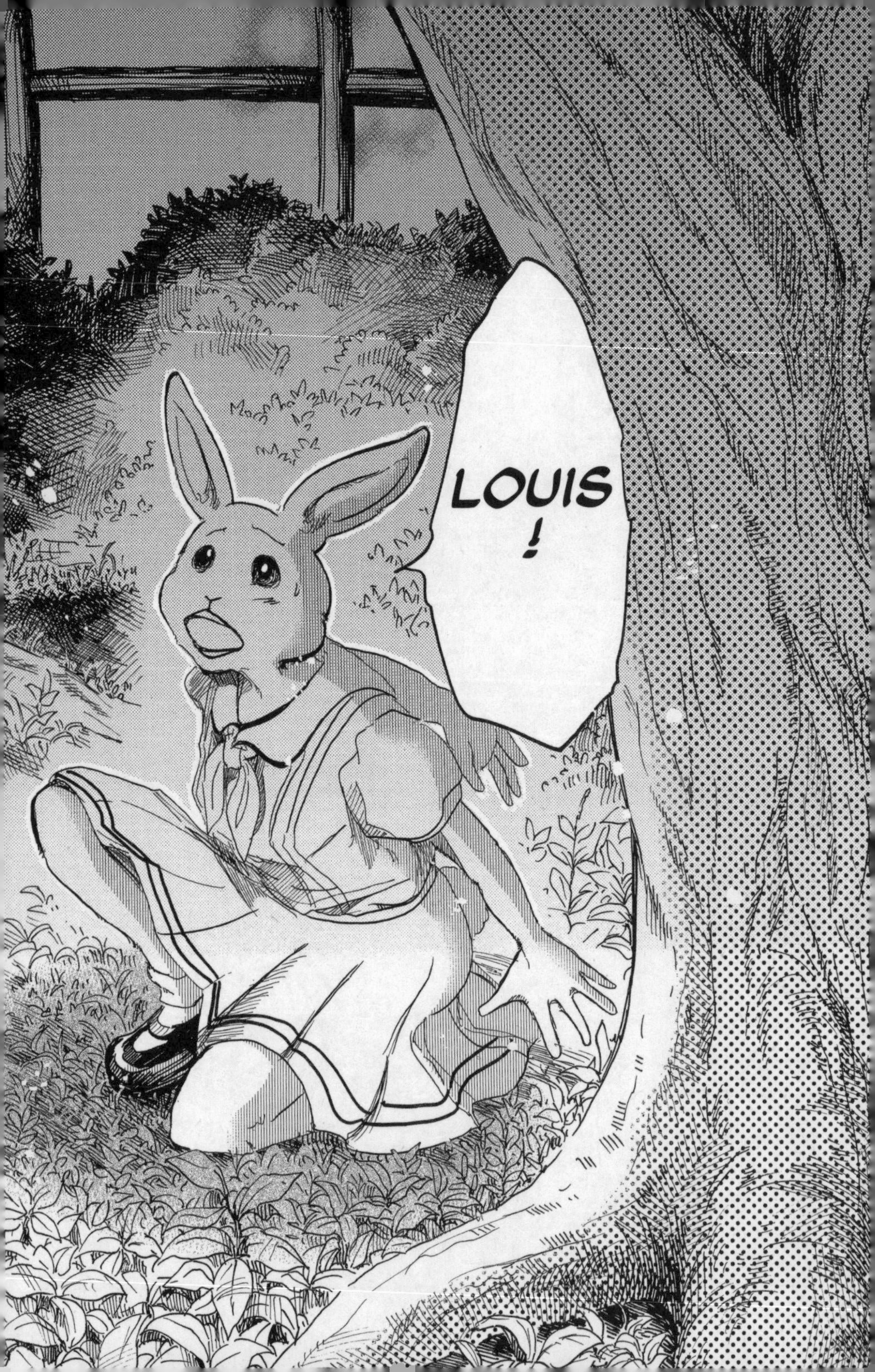
LOUIS
!

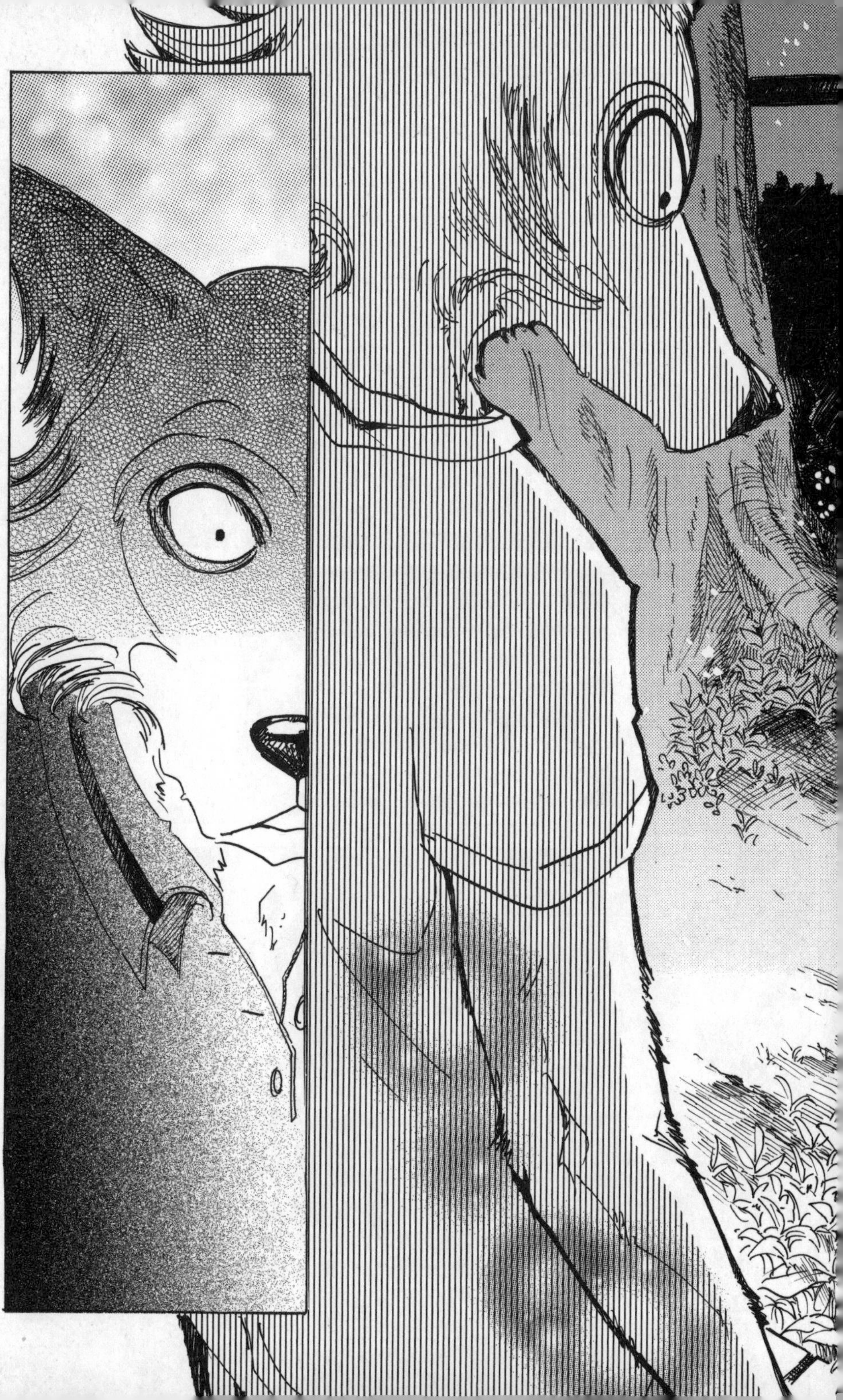

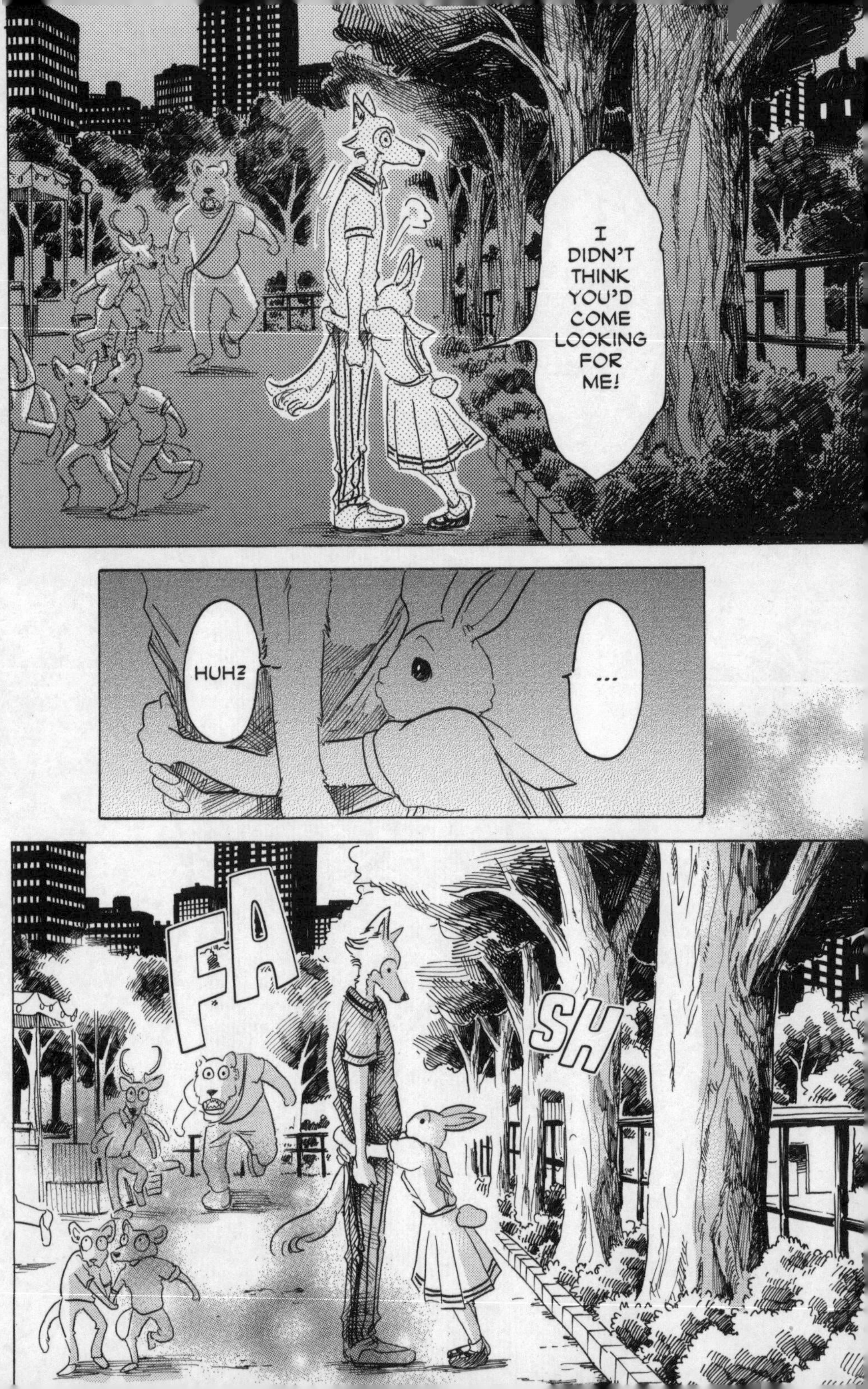
I DIDN'T THINK YOU'D COME LOOKING FOR ME!
...
HUH?
FASH

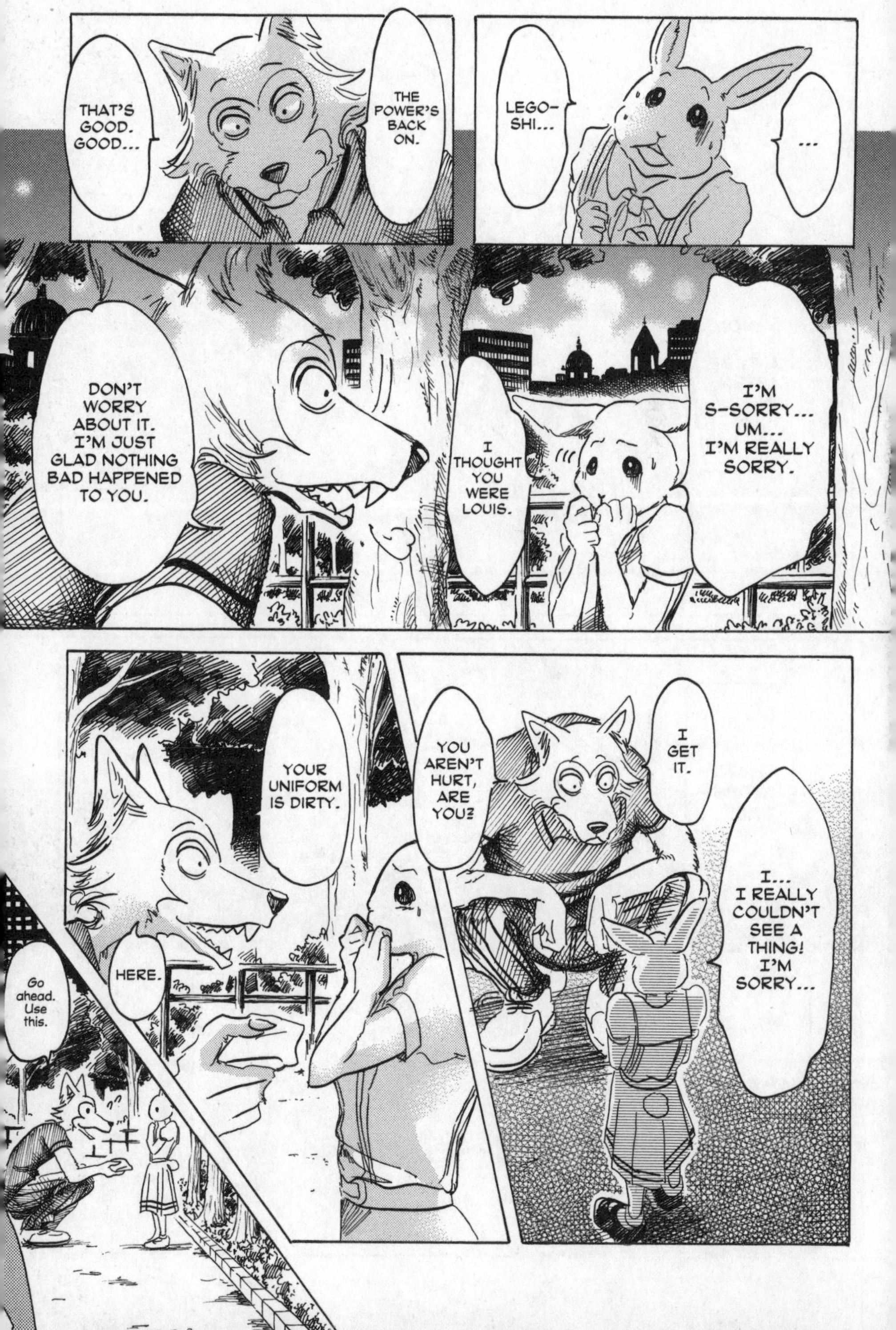
...
LEGO-SHI...
THE POWER'S BACK ON.
THAT'S GOOD. GOOD...
I'M S-SORRY... UM... I'M REALLY SORRY.
I THOUGHT YOU WERE LOUIS.
DON'T WORRY ABOUT IT. I'M JUST GLAD NOTHING BAD HAPPENED TO YOU.
I... I REALLY COULDN'T SEE A THING! I'M SORRY...
I GET IT.
YOU AREN'T HURT, ARE YOU?
YOUR UNIFORM IS DIRTY.
HERE.
Go ahead. Use this.

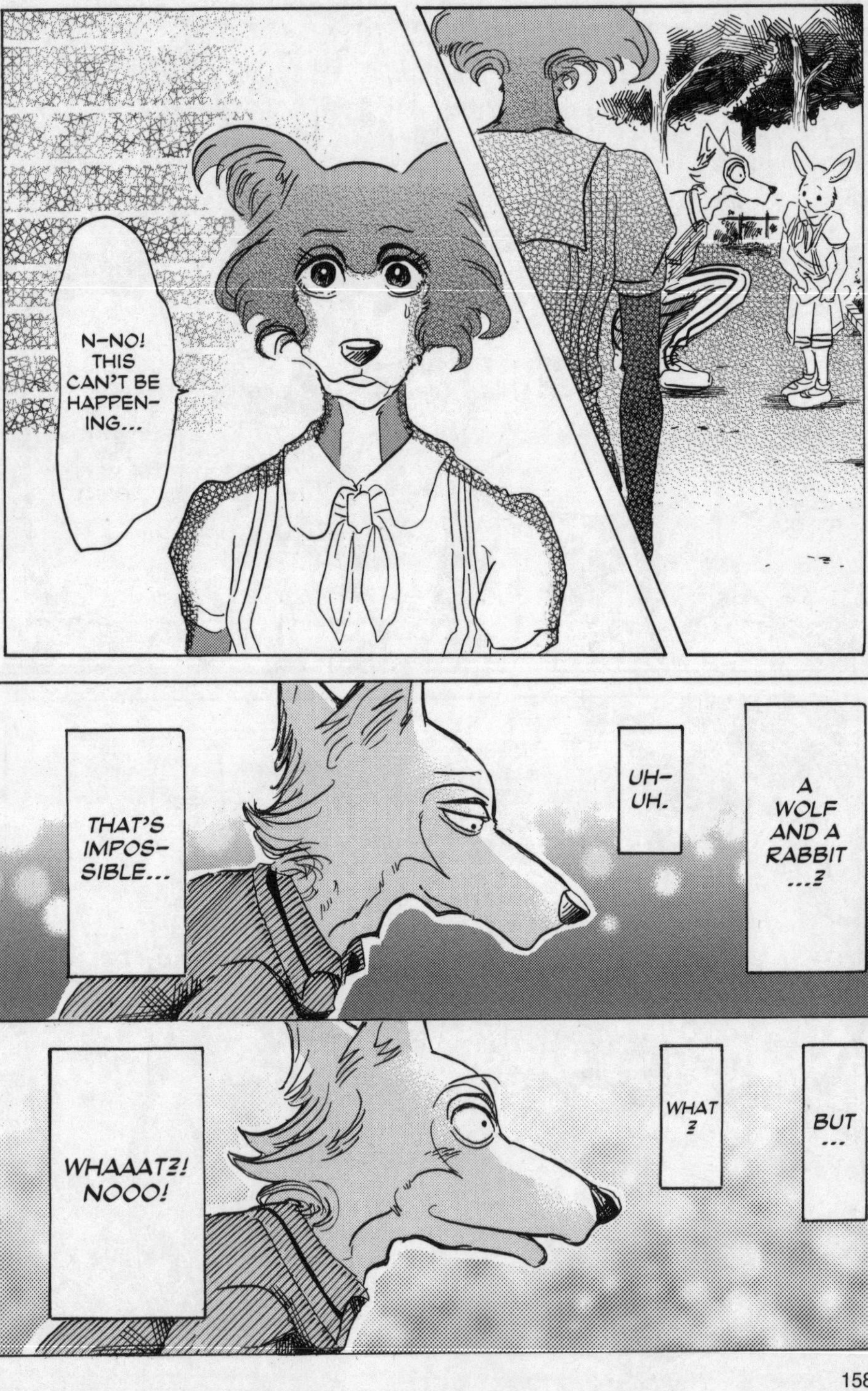
N-NO! THIS CAN'T BE HAPPENING...
A WOLF AND A RABBIT...?
UH-UH.
THAT'S IMPOSSIBLE...
BUT...
WHAT?
WHAAAT?! NOOO!

Chapter 33: I Swear I'll Rise Up

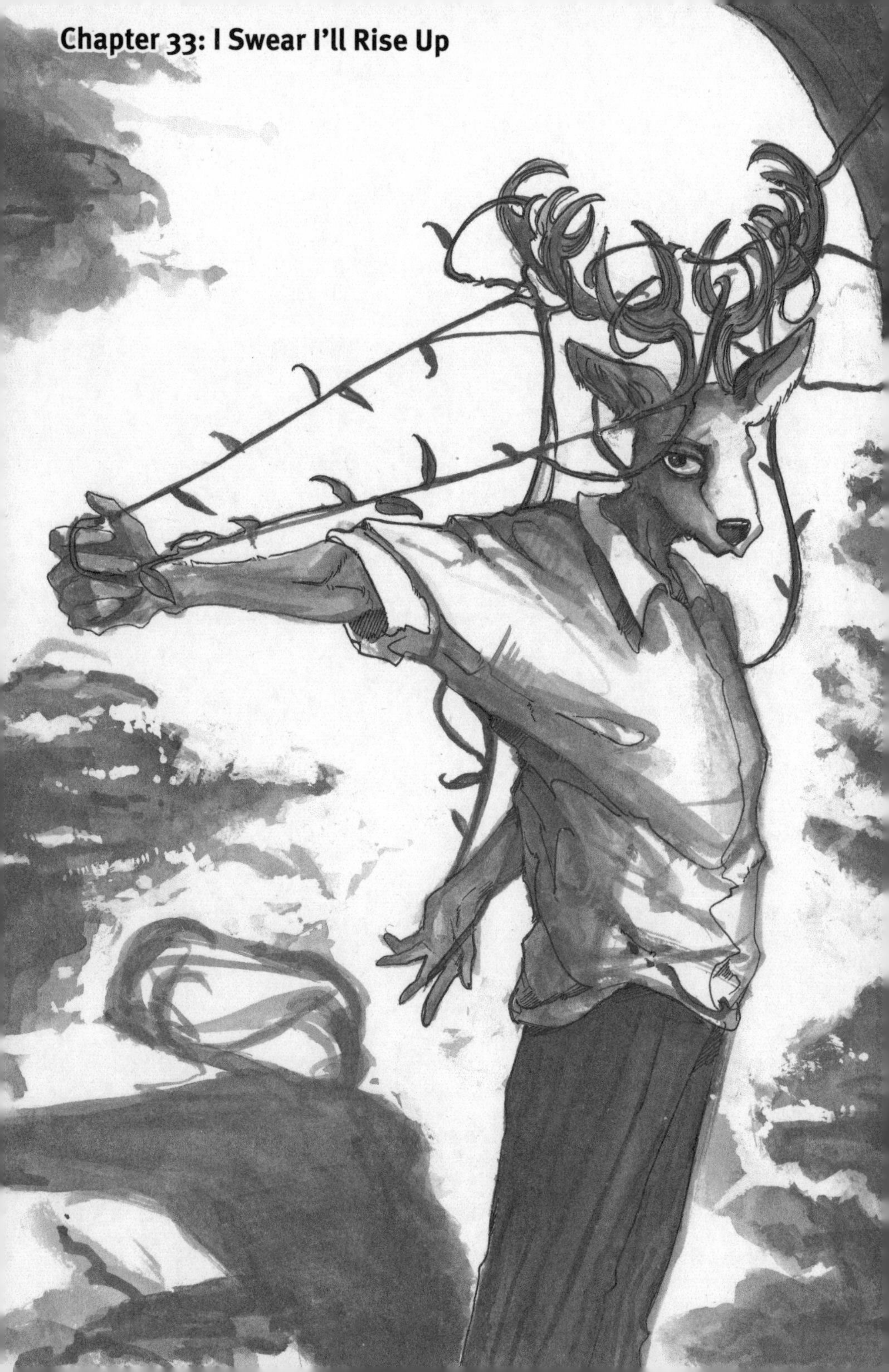

BEASTARS
Vol. 4

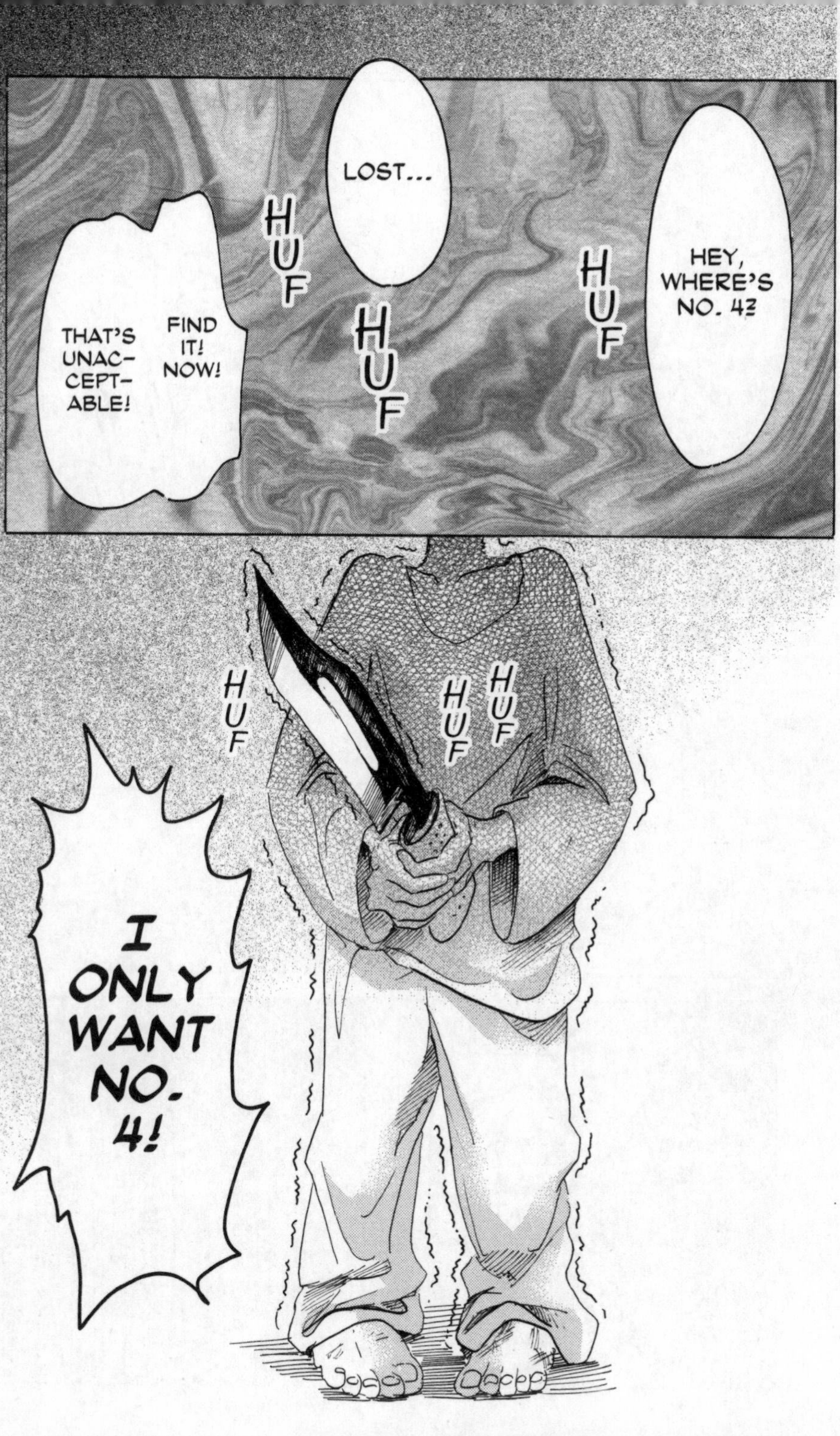
HEY, WHERE'S NO. 4?
HUF
LOST...
HUF
HUF
FIND IT! NOW!
THAT'S UNACCEPTABLE!
HUF
HUF
HUF
I ONLY WANT NO. 4!

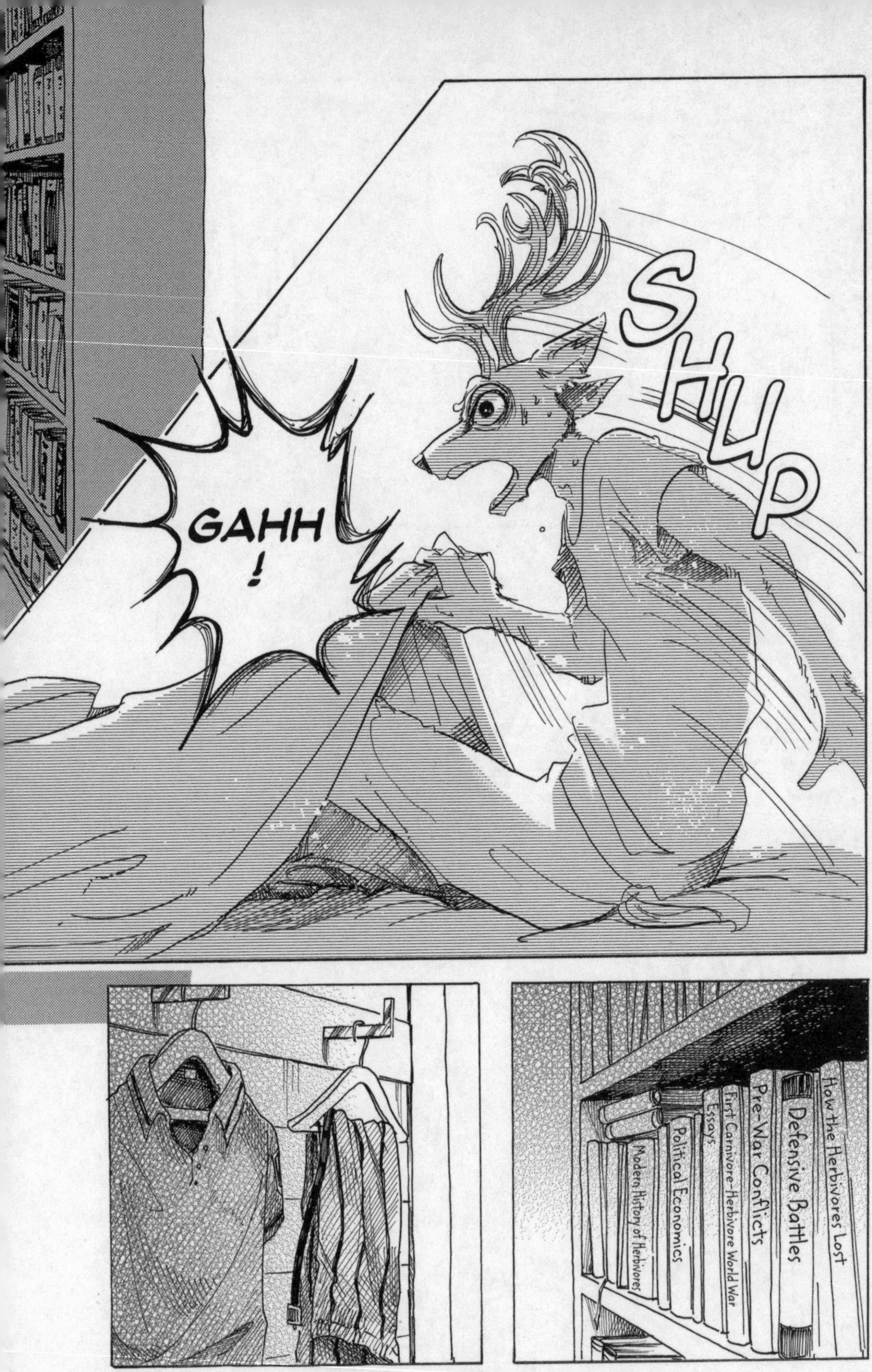
SHUP
GAHH!
How the Herbivores Lost
Defensive Battles
Pre-War Conflicts
First Carnivore-Herbivore World War Essays
Political Economics
Modern History of Herbivores

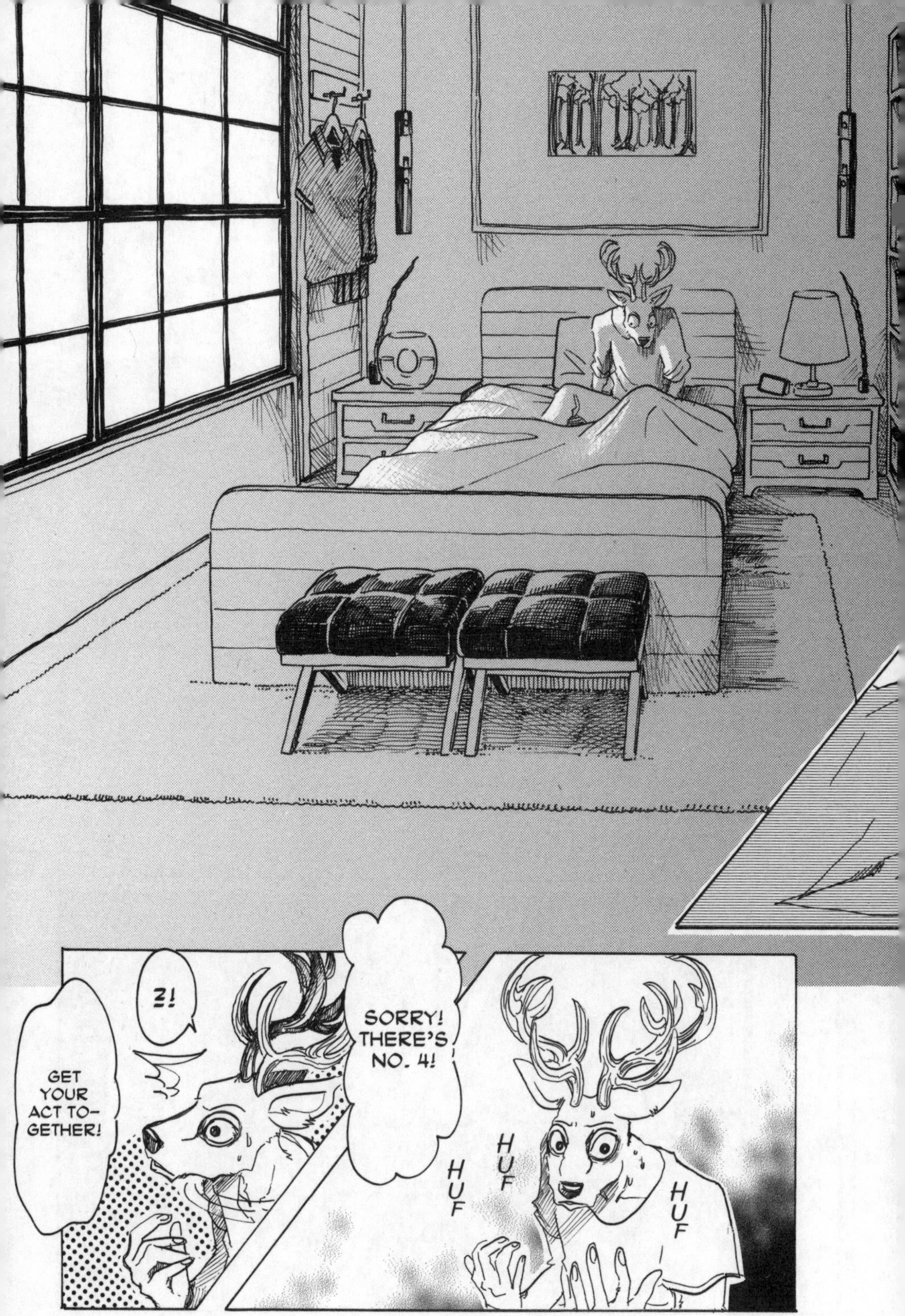
SORRY! THERE'S NO. 4!
HUF HUF HUF
?!
GET YOUR ACT TO-GETHER!

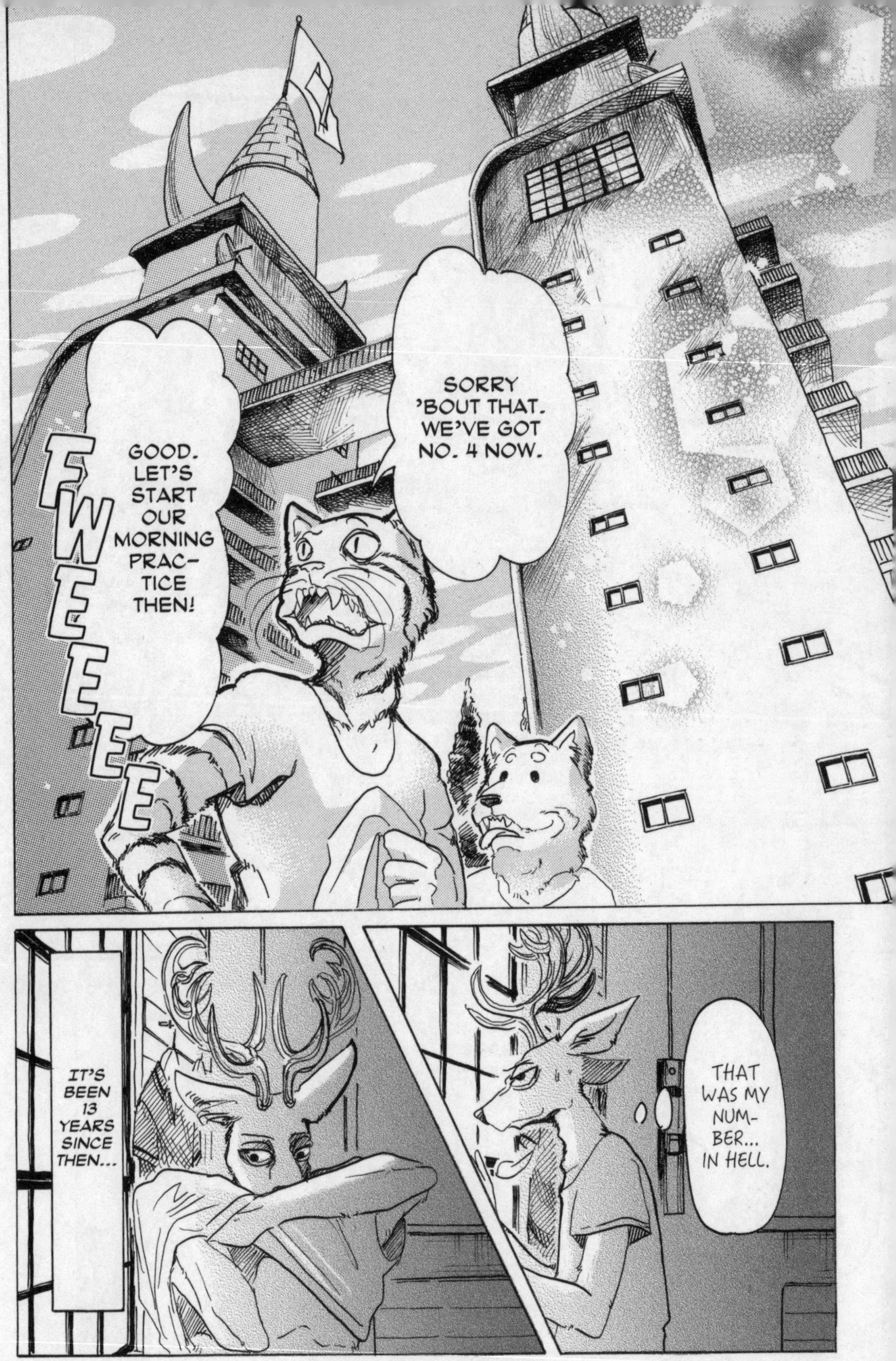
SORRY 'BOUT THAT. WE'VE GOT NO. 4 NOW.
GOOD. LET'S START OUR MORNING PRAC-TICE THEN!
FWEEEE
THAT WAS MY NUM-BER... IN HELL.
IT'S BEEN 13 YEARS SINCE THEN...

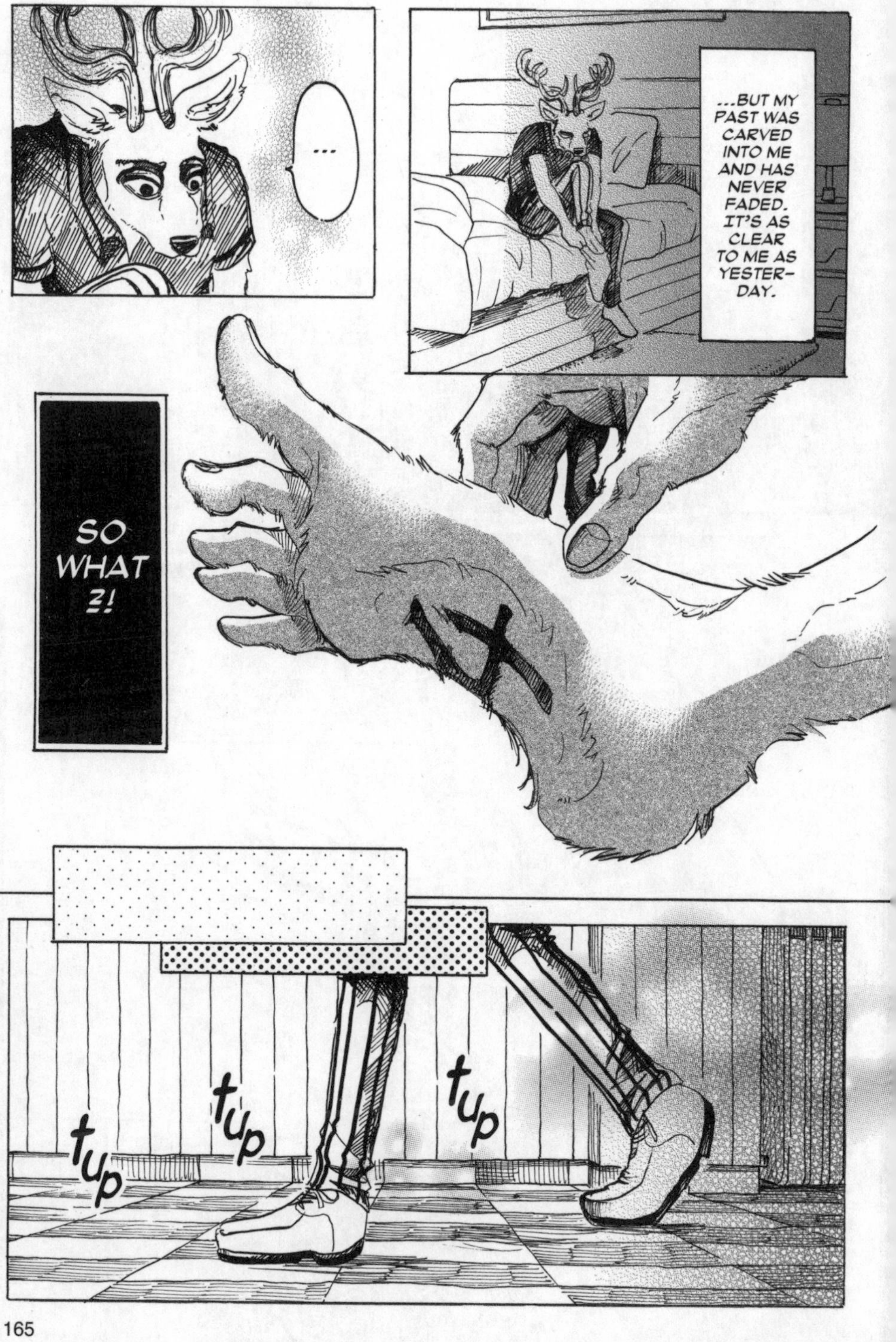
...BUT MY PAST WAS CARVED INTO ME AND HAS NEVER FADED. IT'S AS CLEAR TO ME AS YESTERDAY.
...
SO WHAT ?!
tup
tup
tup

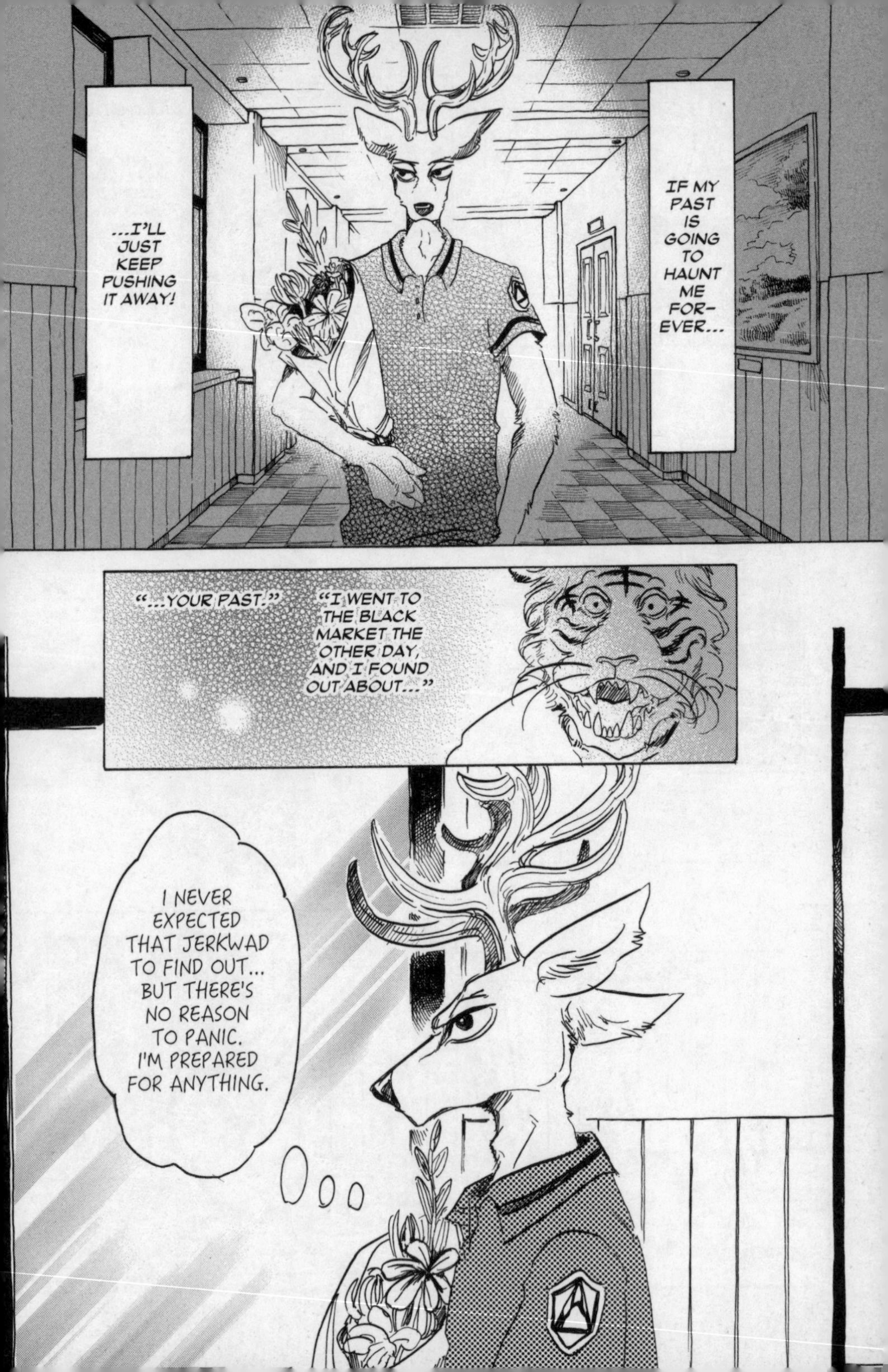
IF MY PAST IS GOING TO HAUNT ME FOR-EVER...
...I'LL JUST KEEP PUSHING IT AWAY!
"I WENT TO THE BLACK MARKET THE OTHER DAY, AND I FOUND OUT ABOUT..."
"...YOUR PAST."
I NEVER EXPECTED THAT JERKWAD TO FIND OUT... BUT THERE'S NO REASON TO PANIC. I'M PREPARED FOR ANYTHING.

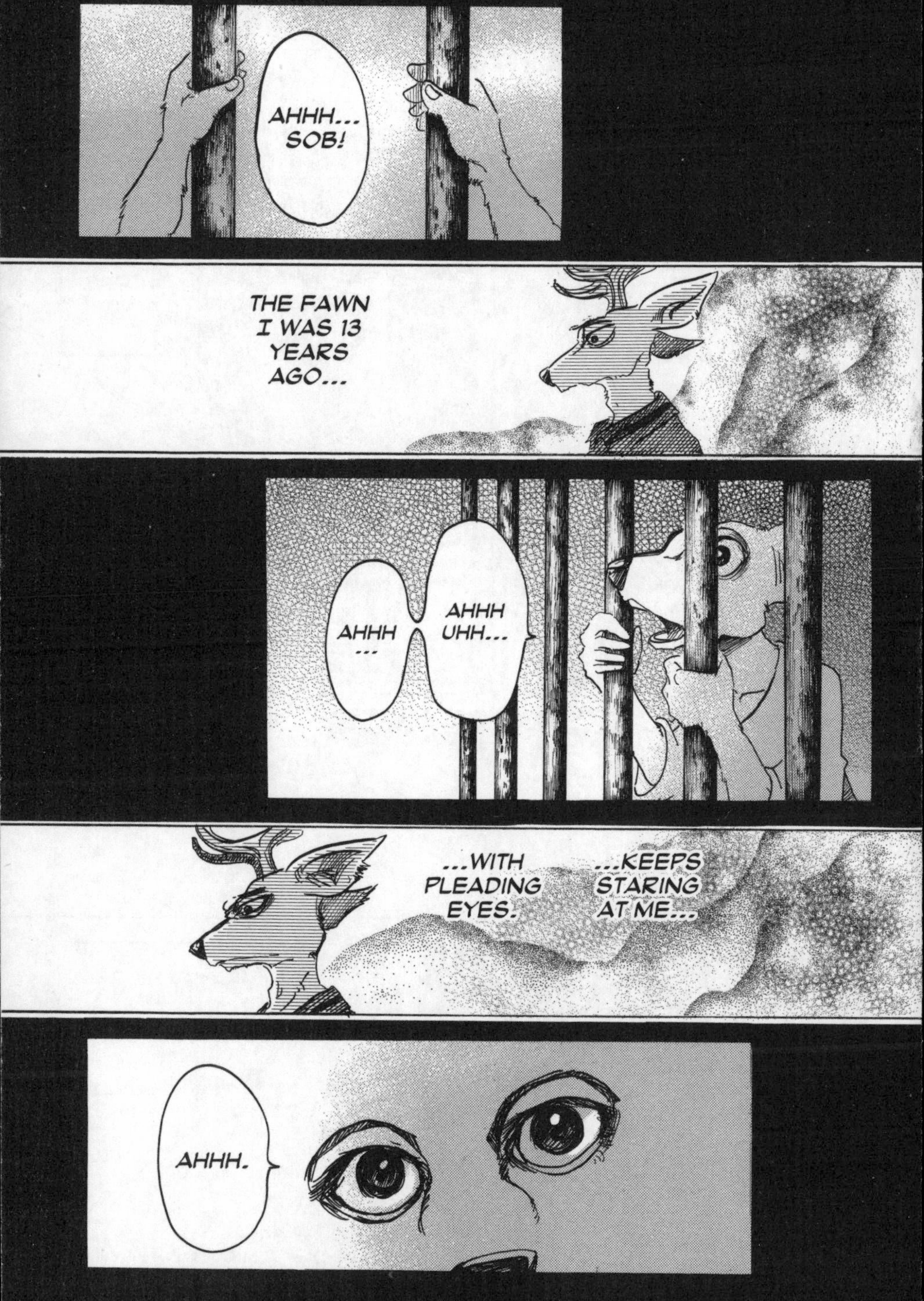
AHHH... SOB!
THE FAWN I WAS 13 YEARS AGO...
AHHH UHH...
AHHH ...
...KEEPS STARING AT ME...
...WITH PLEADING EYES.
AHHH.

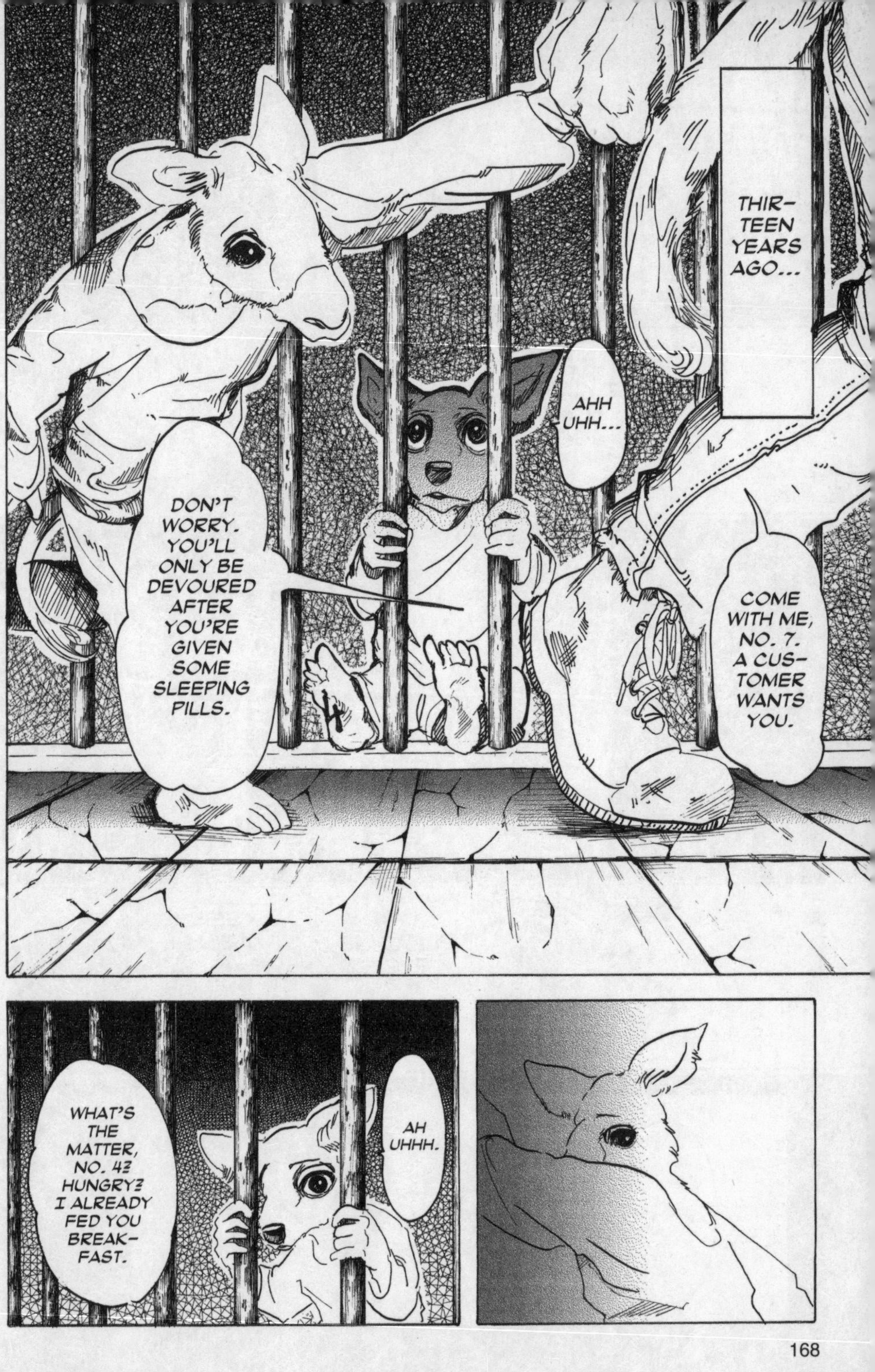
THIRTEEN YEARS AGO...
COME WITH ME, NO. 7. A CUSTOMER WANTS YOU.
AHH UHH...
DON'T WORRY. YOU'LL ONLY BE DEVOURED AFTER YOU'RE GIVEN SOME SLEEPING PILLS.
AH UHHH.
WHAT'S THE MATTER, NO. 4? HUNGRY? I ALREADY FED YOU BREAKFAST.

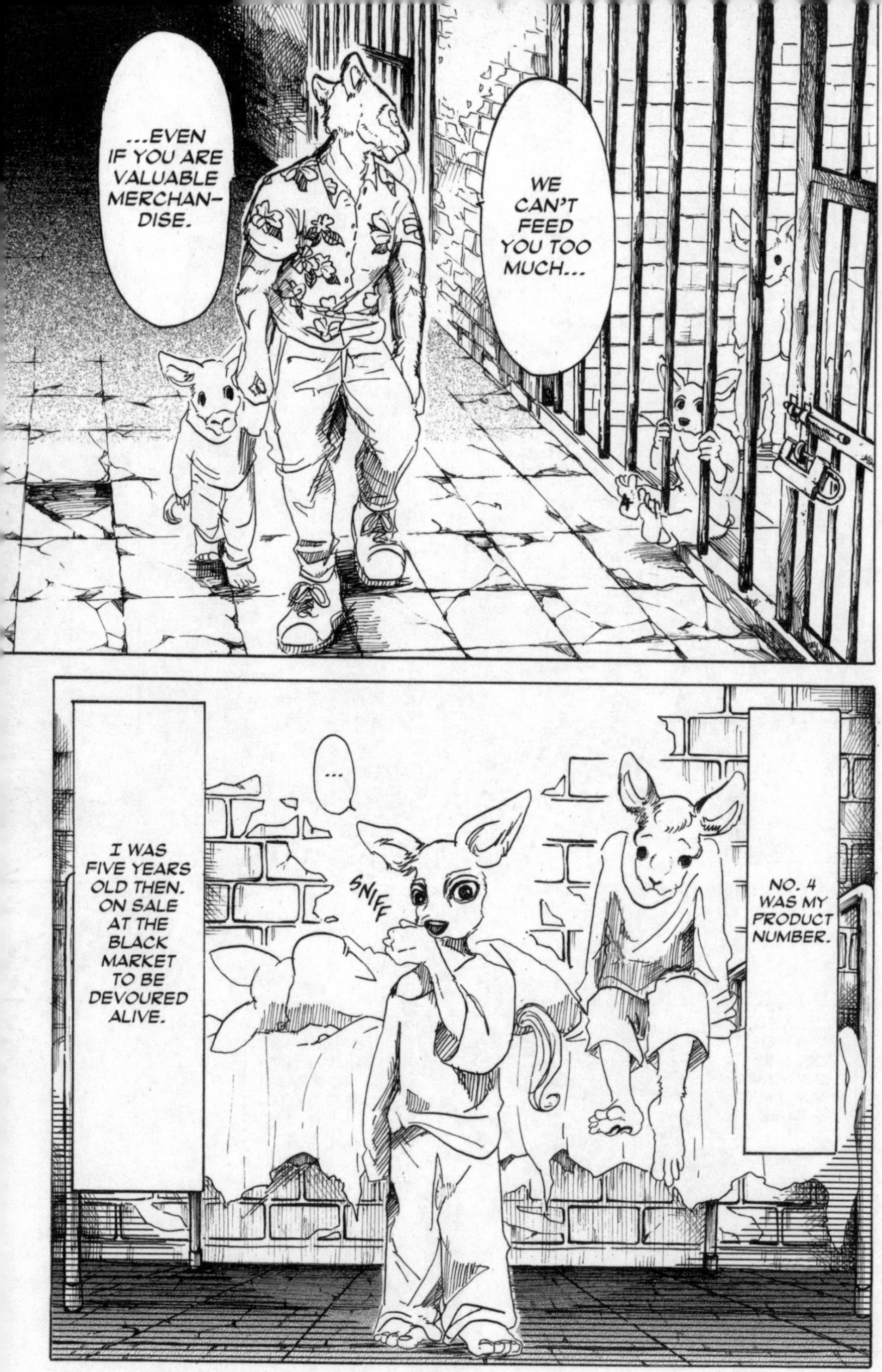
WE CAN'T FEED YOU TOO MUCH...
...EVEN IF YOU ARE VALUABLE MERCHANDISE.
NO. 4 WAS MY PRODUCT NUMBER.
...
SNIFF
I WAS FIVE YEARS OLD THEN. ON SALE AT THE BLACK MARKET TO BE DEVOURED ALIVE.

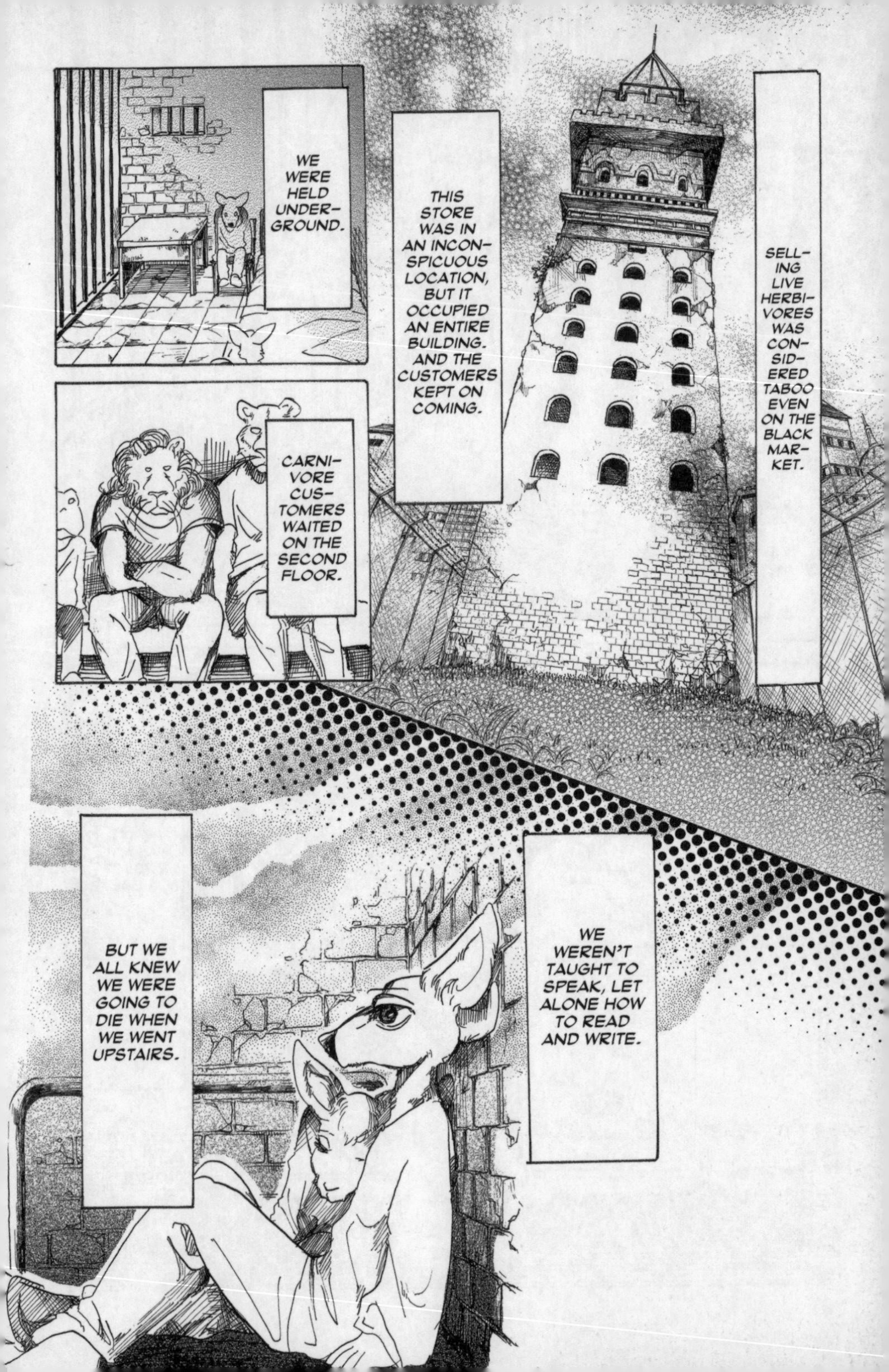
SELLING LIVE HERBIVORES WAS CONSIDERED TABOO EVEN ON THE BLACK MARKET.
THIS STORE WAS IN AN INCONSPICUOUS LOCATION, BUT IT OCCUPIED AN ENTIRE BUILDING. AND THE CUSTOMERS KEPT ON COMING.
WE WERE HELD UNDERGROUND.
CARNIVORE CUSTOMERS WAITED ON THE SECOND FLOOR.
WE WEREN'T TAUGHT TO SPEAK, LET ALONE HOW TO READ AND WRITE.
BUT WE ALL KNEW WE WERE GOING TO DIE WHEN WE WENT UPSTAIRS.

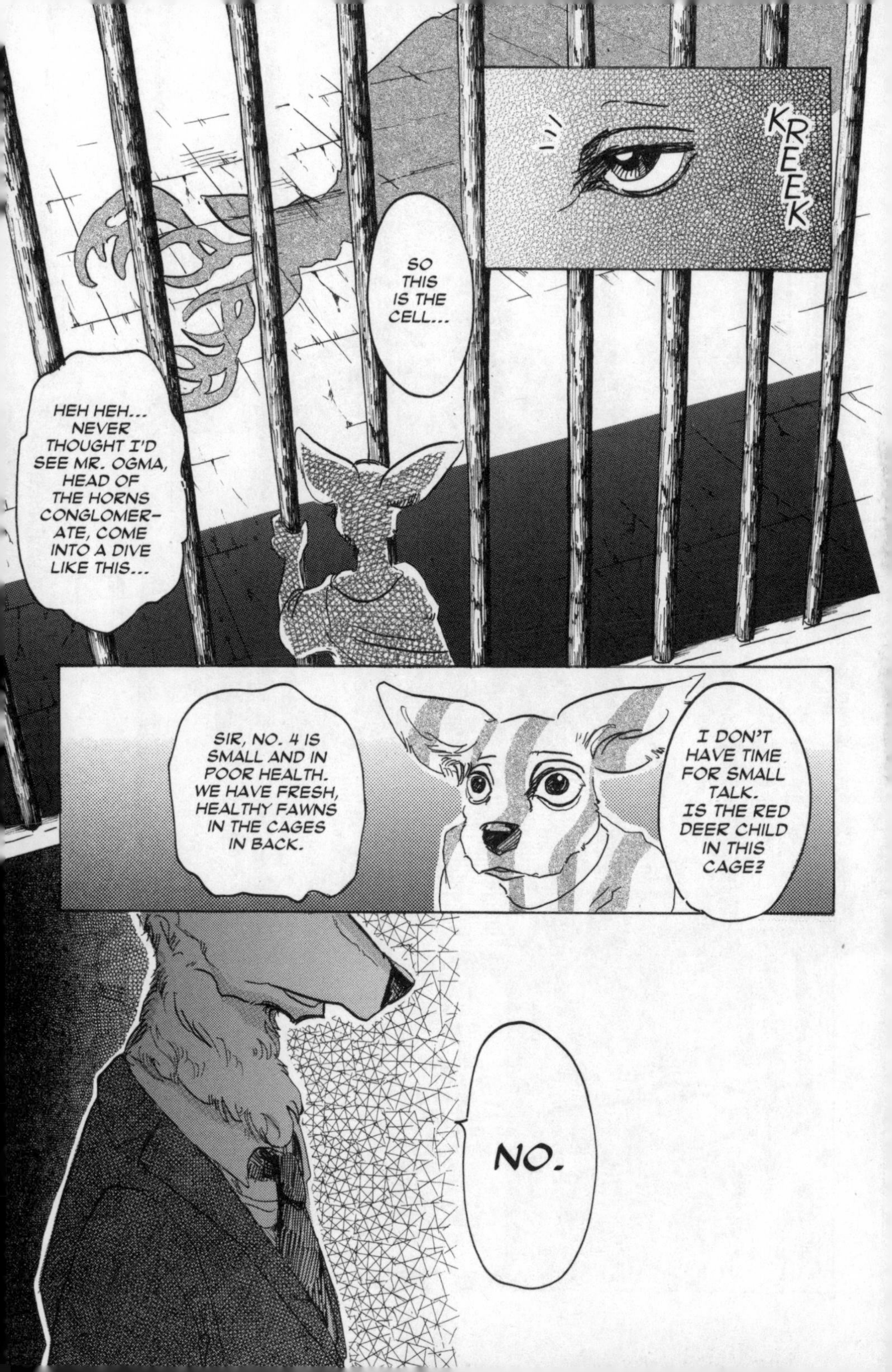
KREEK
SO THIS IS THE CELL...
HEH HEH... NEVER THOUGHT I'D SEE MR. OGMA, HEAD OF THE HORNS CONGLOMERATE, COME INTO A DIVE LIKE THIS...
I DON'T HAVE TIME FOR SMALL TALK. IS THE RED DEER CHILD IN THIS CAGE?
SIR, NO. 4 IS SMALL AND IN POOR HEALTH. WE HAVE FRESH, HEALTHY FAWNS IN THE CAGES IN BACK.
NO.

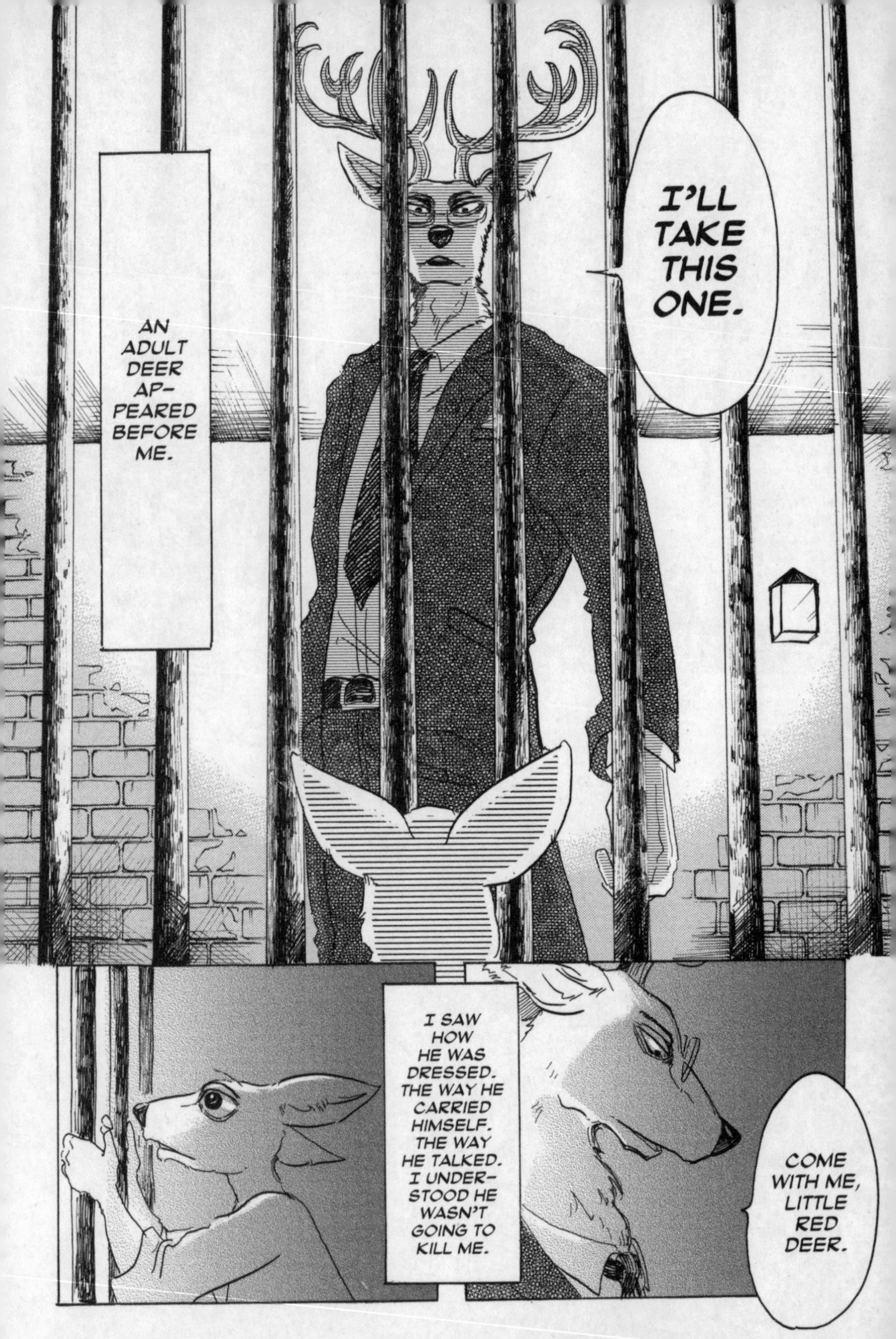
I'LL TAKE THIS ONE.
AN ADULT DEER APPEARED BEFORE ME.
COME WITH ME, LITTLE RED DEER.
I SAW HOW HE WAS DRESSED. THE WAY HE CARRIED HIMSELF. THE WAY HE TALKED. I UNDERSTOOD HE WASN'T GOING TO KILL ME.

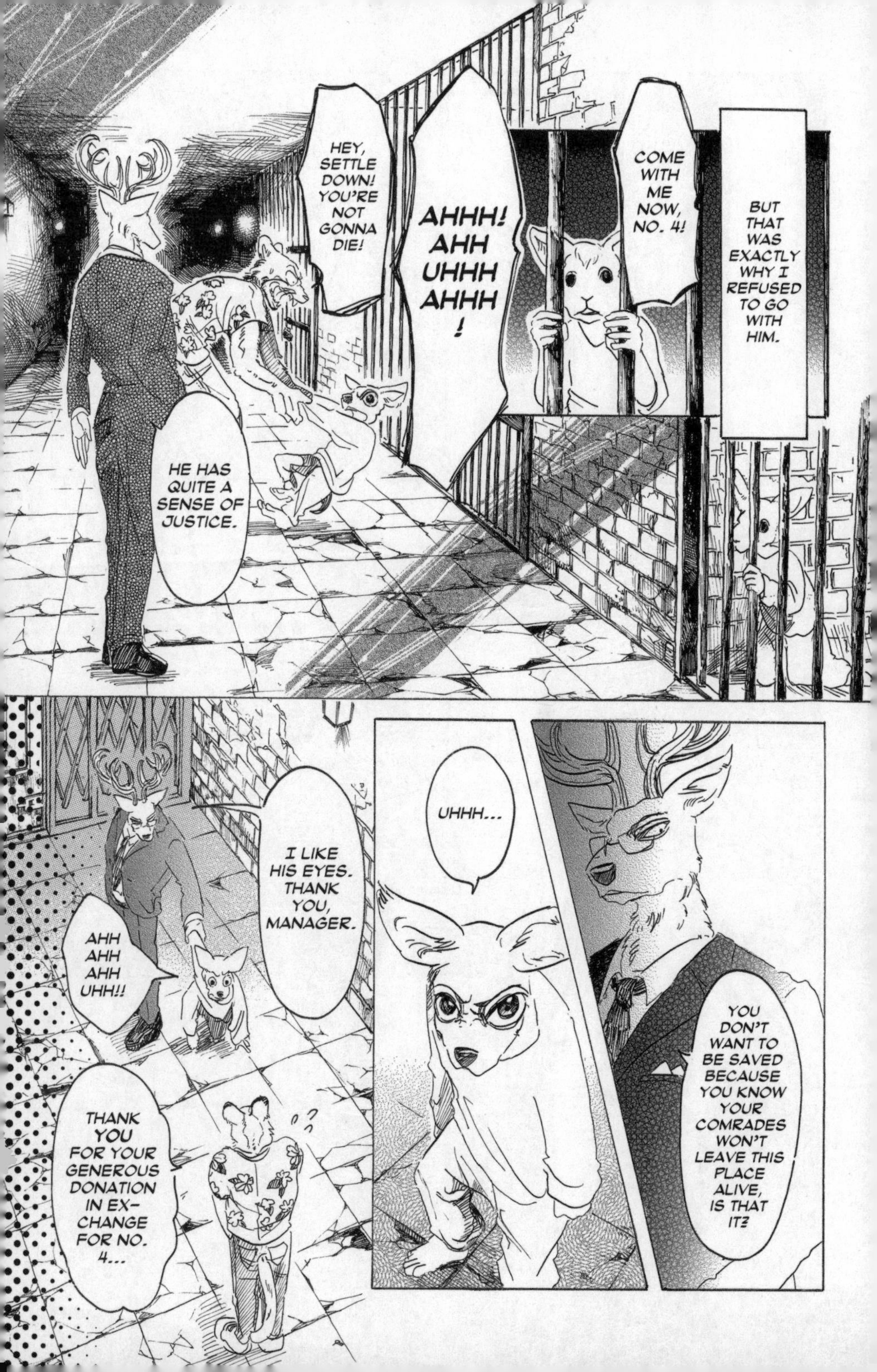
BUT THAT WAS EXACTLY WHY I REFUSED TO GO WITH HIM.
COME WITH ME NOW, NO. 4!
AHHH! AHH UHHH AHHH!
HEY, SETTLE DOWN! YOU'RE NOT GONNA DIE!
HE HAS QUITE A SENSE OF JUSTICE.
YOU DON'T WANT TO BE SAVED BECAUSE YOU KNOW YOUR COMRADES WON'T LEAVE THIS PLACE ALIVE, IS THAT IT?
UHHH...
I LIKE HIS EYES. THANK YOU, MANAGER.
AHH AHH AHH UHH!!
THANK YOU FOR YOUR GENEROUS DONATION IN EX-CHANGE FOR NO. 4...

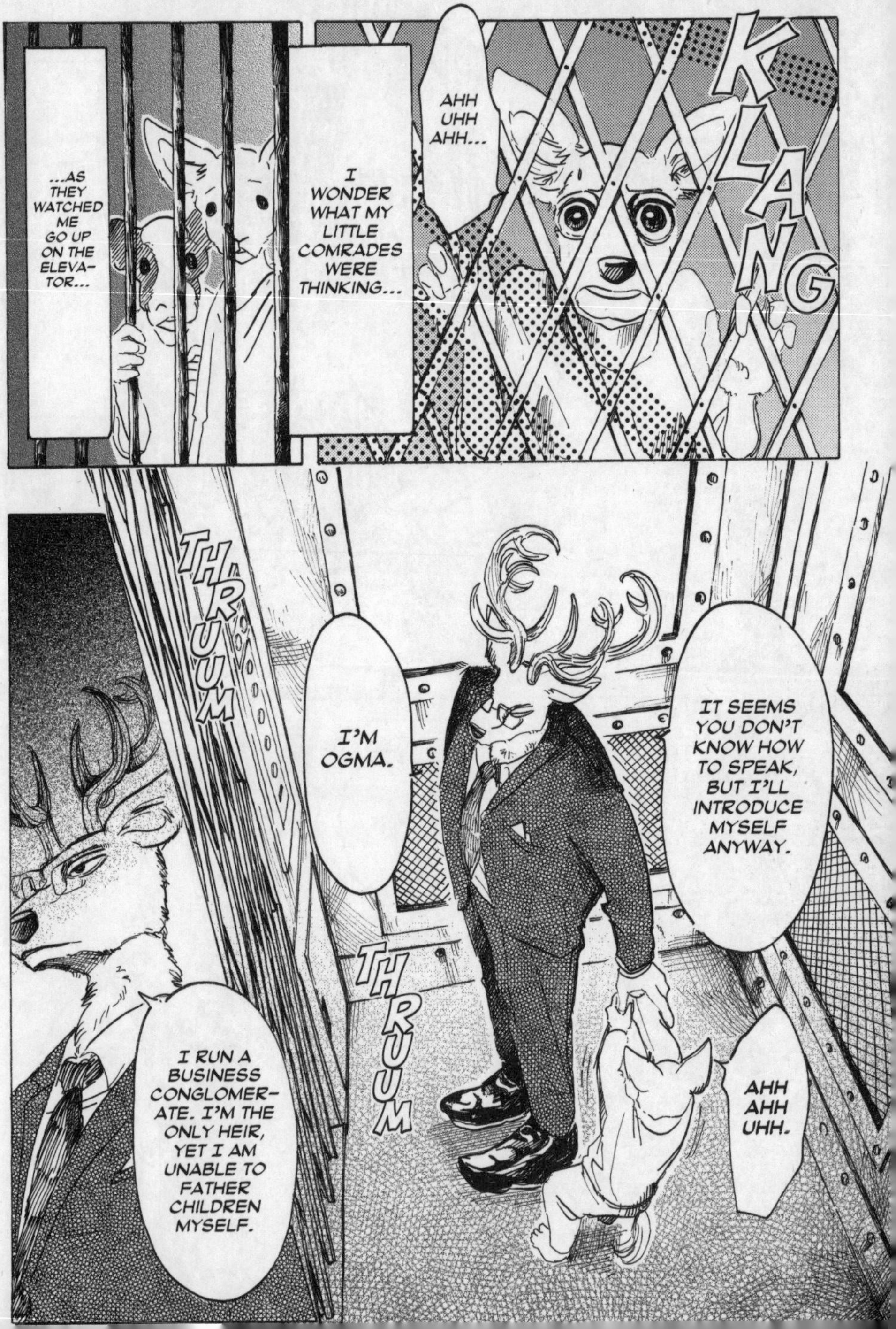
KLANG
AHH UHH AHH...
I WONDER WHAT MY LITTLE COMRADES WERE THINKING...
...AS THEY WATCHED ME GO UP ON THE ELEVATOR...
IT SEEMS YOU DON'T KNOW HOW TO SPEAK, BUT I'LL INTRODUCE MYSELF ANYWAY.
I'M OGMA.
THRUUM
THRUUM
AHH AHH UHH.
I RUN A BUSINESS CONGLOMERATE. I'M THE ONLY HEIR, YET I AM UNABLE TO FATHER CHILDREN MYSELF.

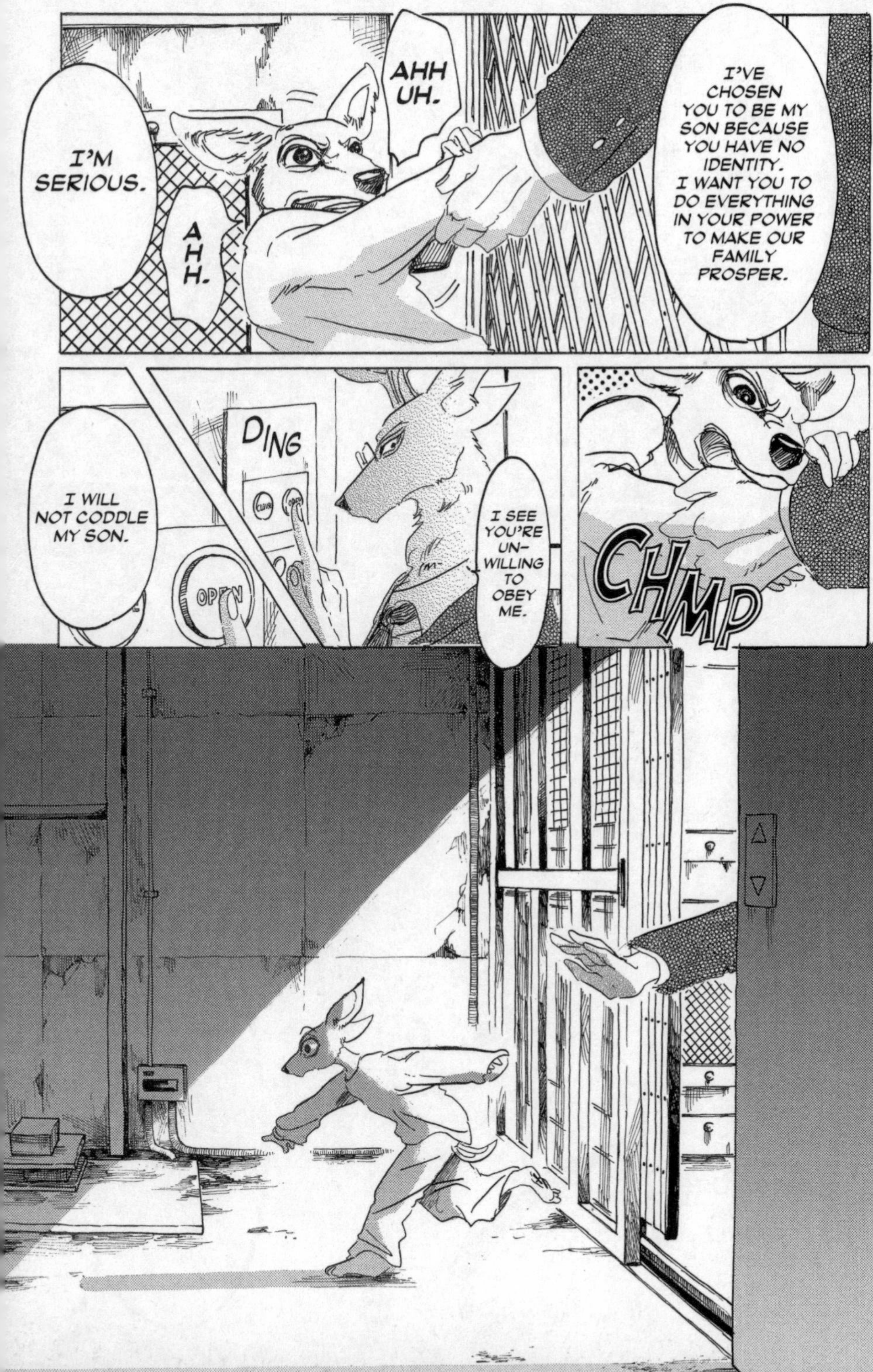
I'VE CHOSEN YOU TO BE MY SON BECAUSE YOU HAVE NO IDENTITY. I WANT YOU TO DO EVERYTHING IN YOUR POWER TO MAKE OUR FAMILY PROSPER.
AHH UH.
AHH.
I'M SERIOUS.
CHMP
I SEE YOU'RE UN-WILLING TO OBEY ME.
DING
OPEN
I WILL NOT CODDLE MY SON.

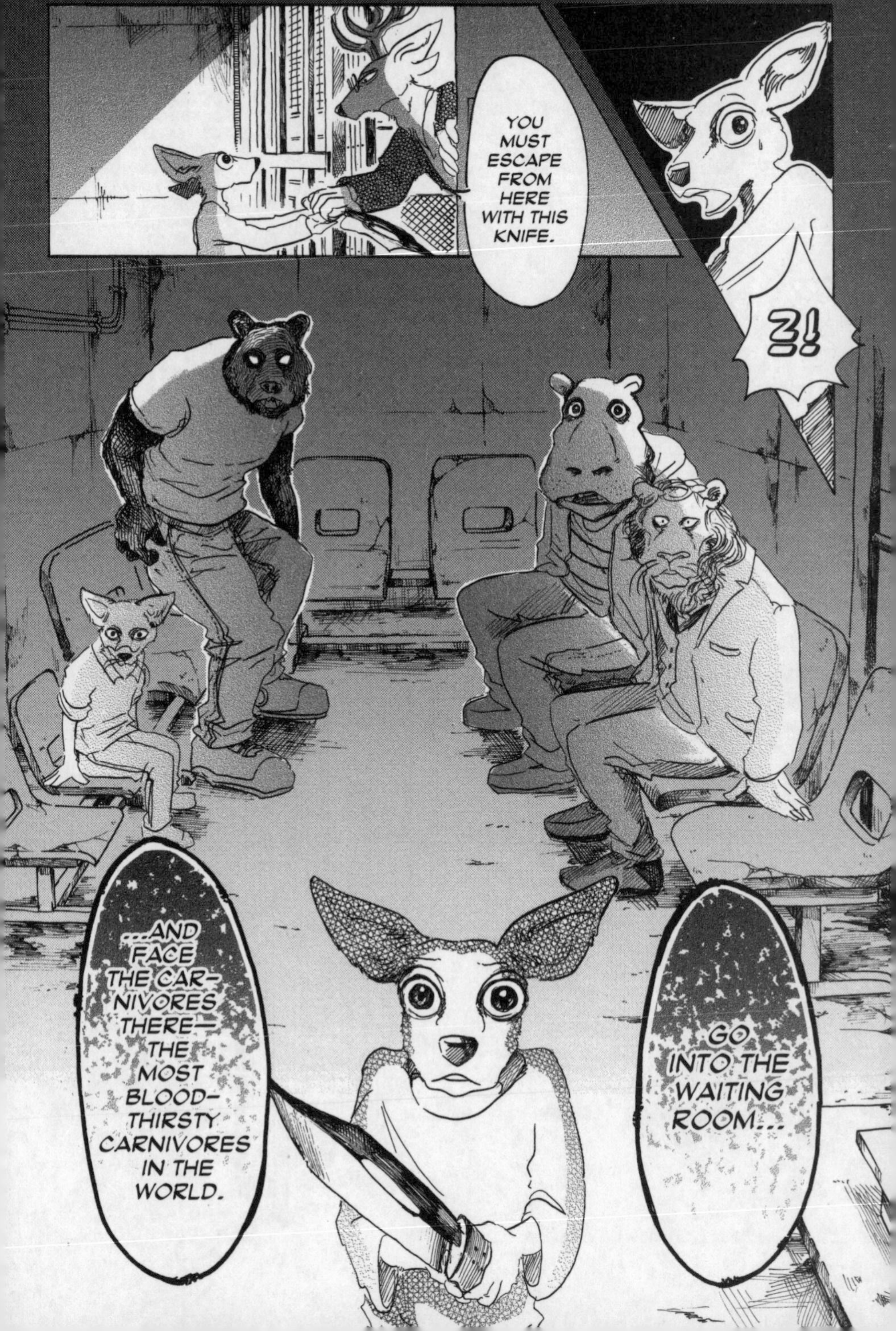
?!
YOU MUST ESCAPE FROM HERE WITH THIS KNIFE.
GO INTO THE WAITING ROOM...
...AND FACE THE CARNIVORES THERE—THE MOST BLOOD-THIRSTY CARNIVORES IN THE WORLD.

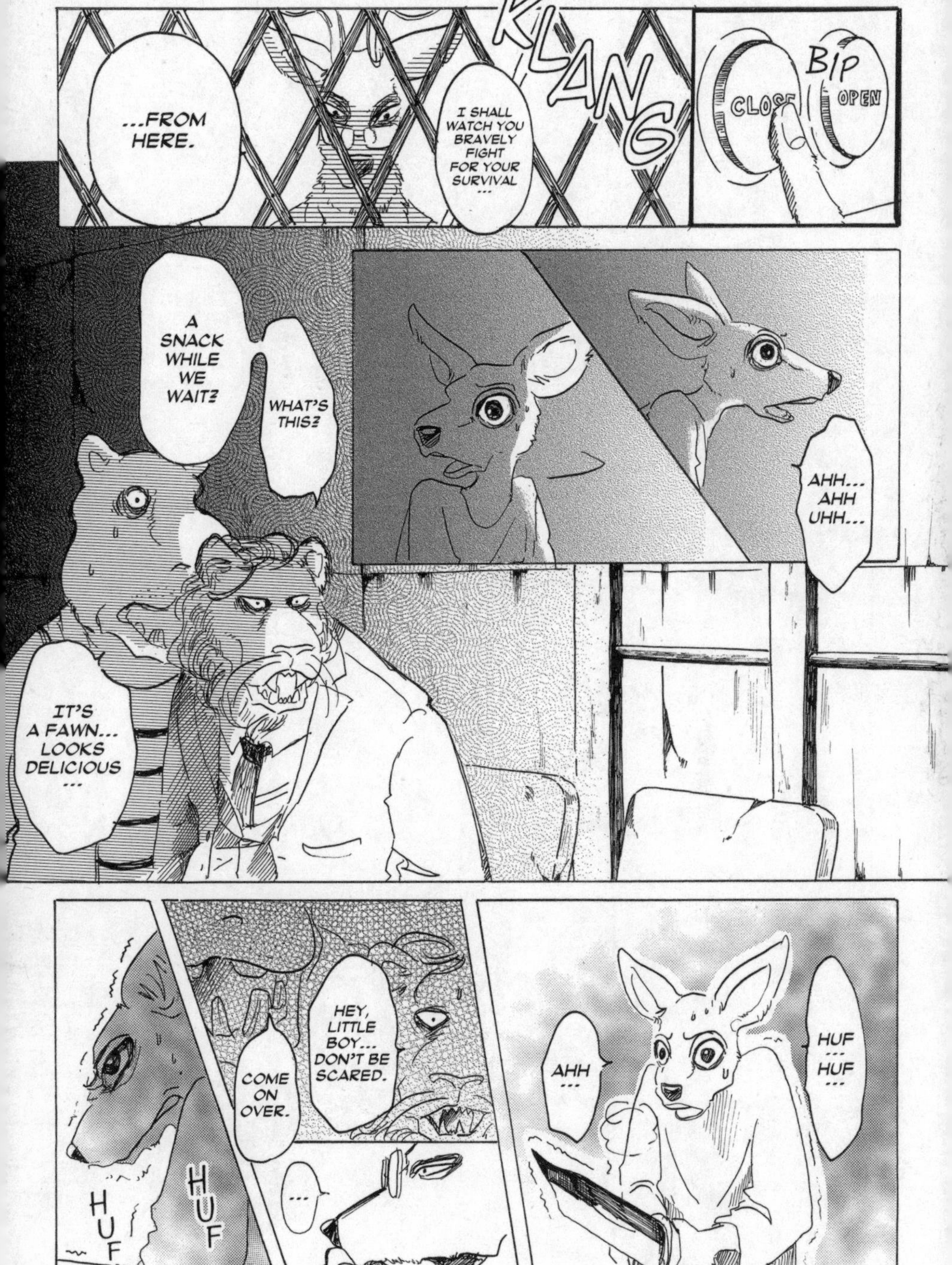
BIP
CLOSE
OPEN
KLANG
I SHALL WATCH YOU BRAVELY FIGHT FOR YOUR SURVIVAL...
...FROM HERE.
AHH... AHH UHH...
WHAT'S THIS?
A SNACK WHILE WE WAIT?
IT'S A FAWN... LOOKS DELICIOUS...
HUF... HUF...
AHH...
HEY, LITTLE BOY... DON'T BE SCARED.
COME ON OVER.
...
HUF
HUF

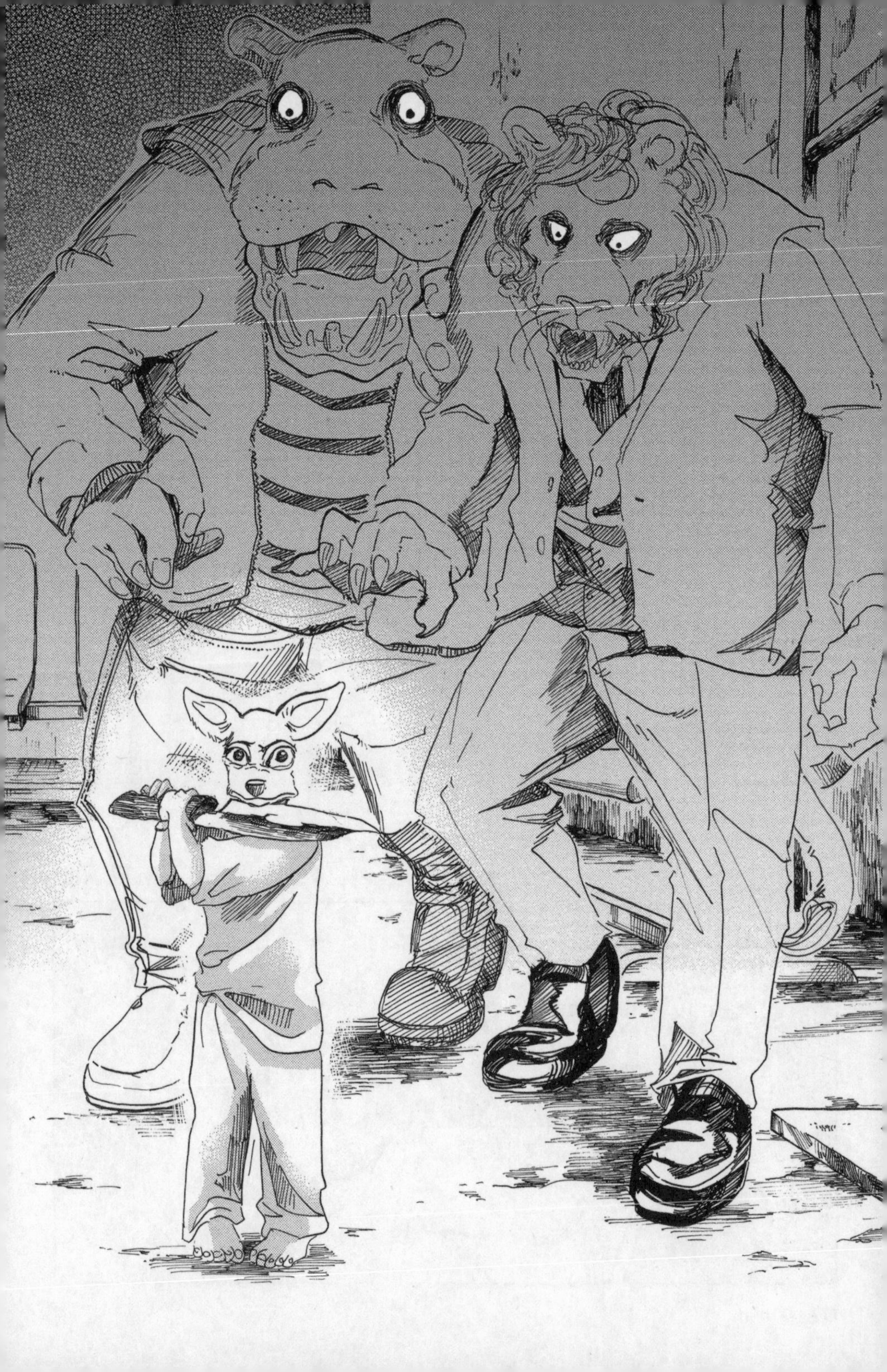

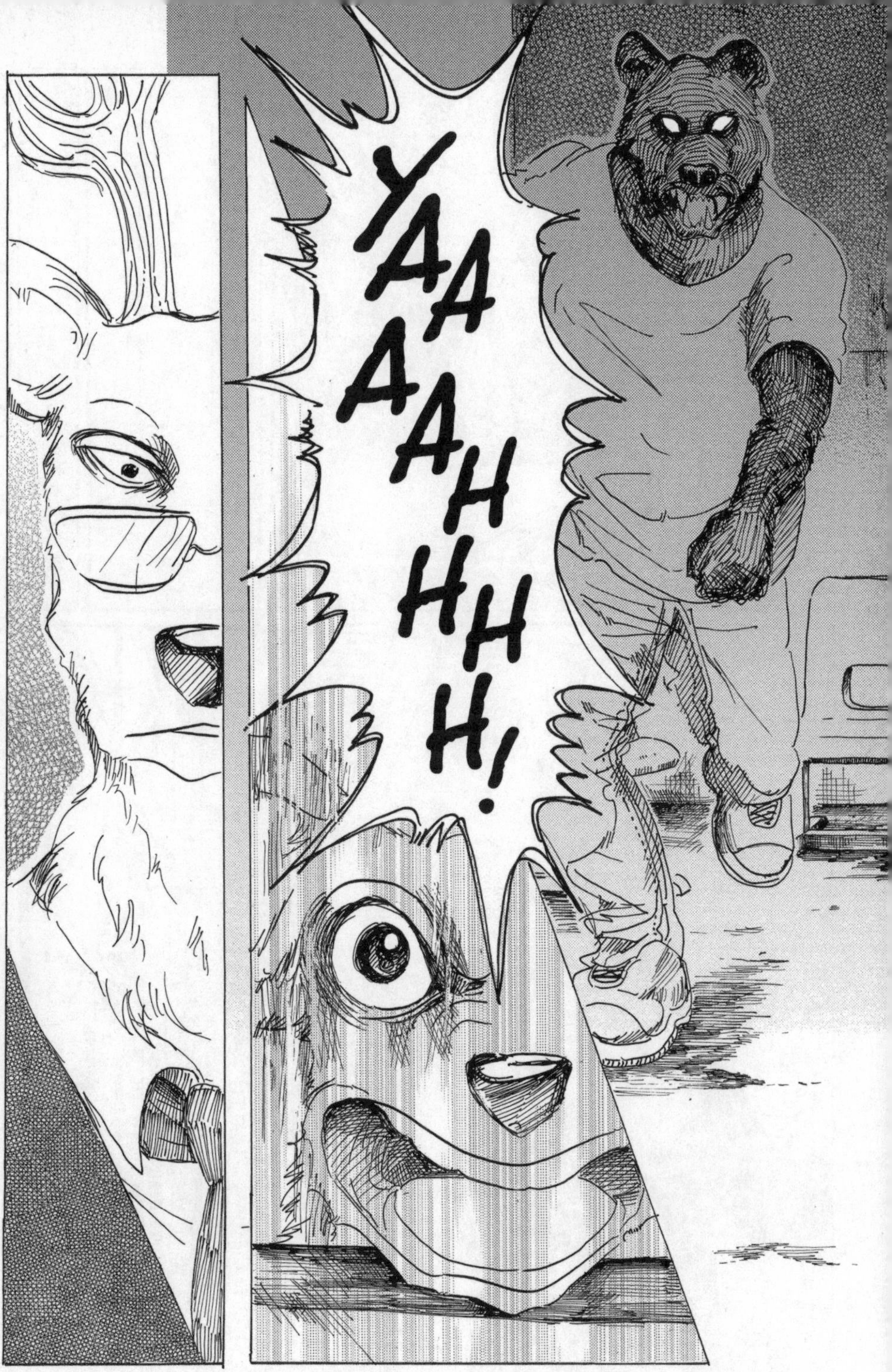
YAAAAHHHH!

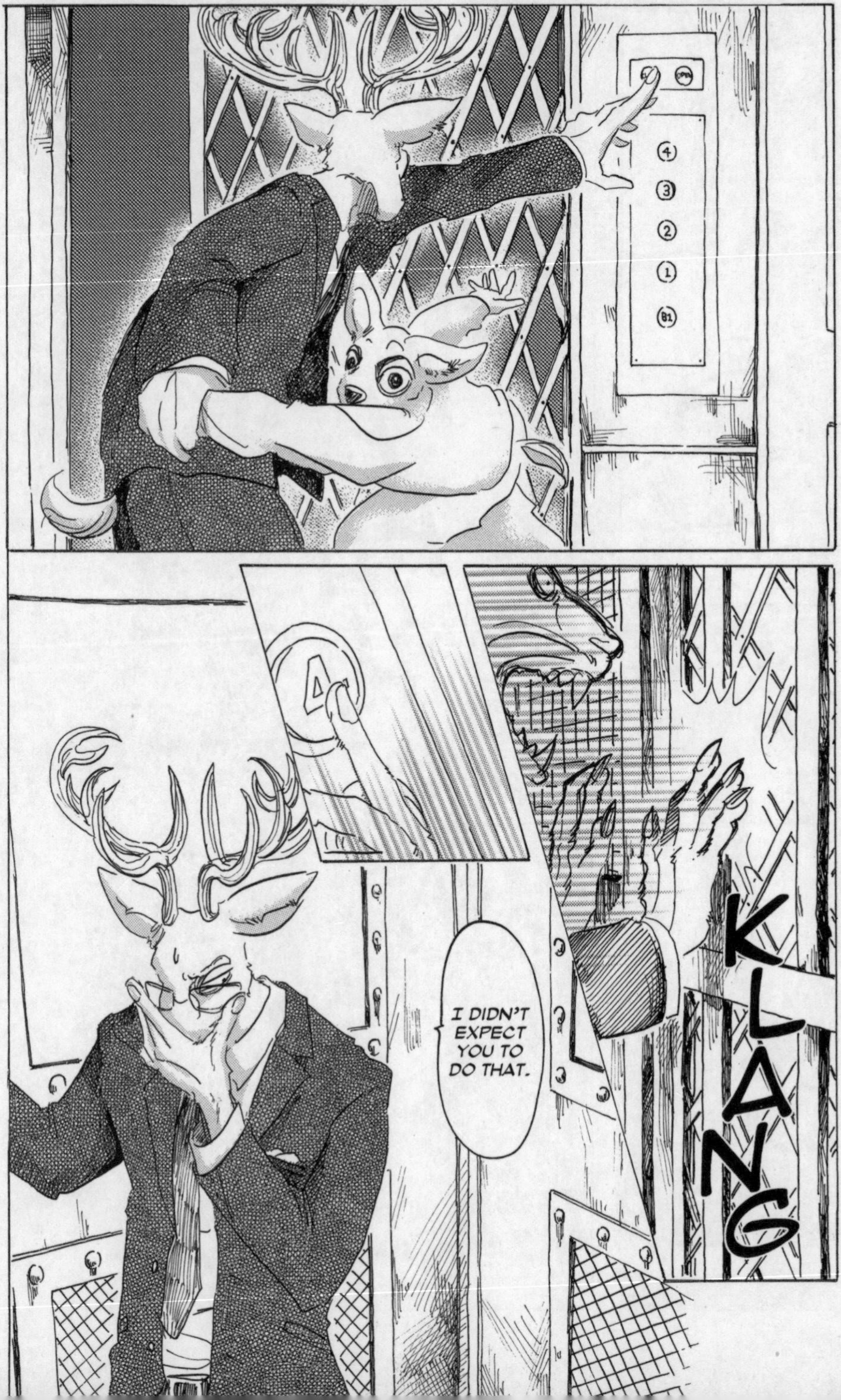
OPEN
4
3
2
1
B1
KLANG
I DIDN'T EXPECT YOU TO DO THAT.

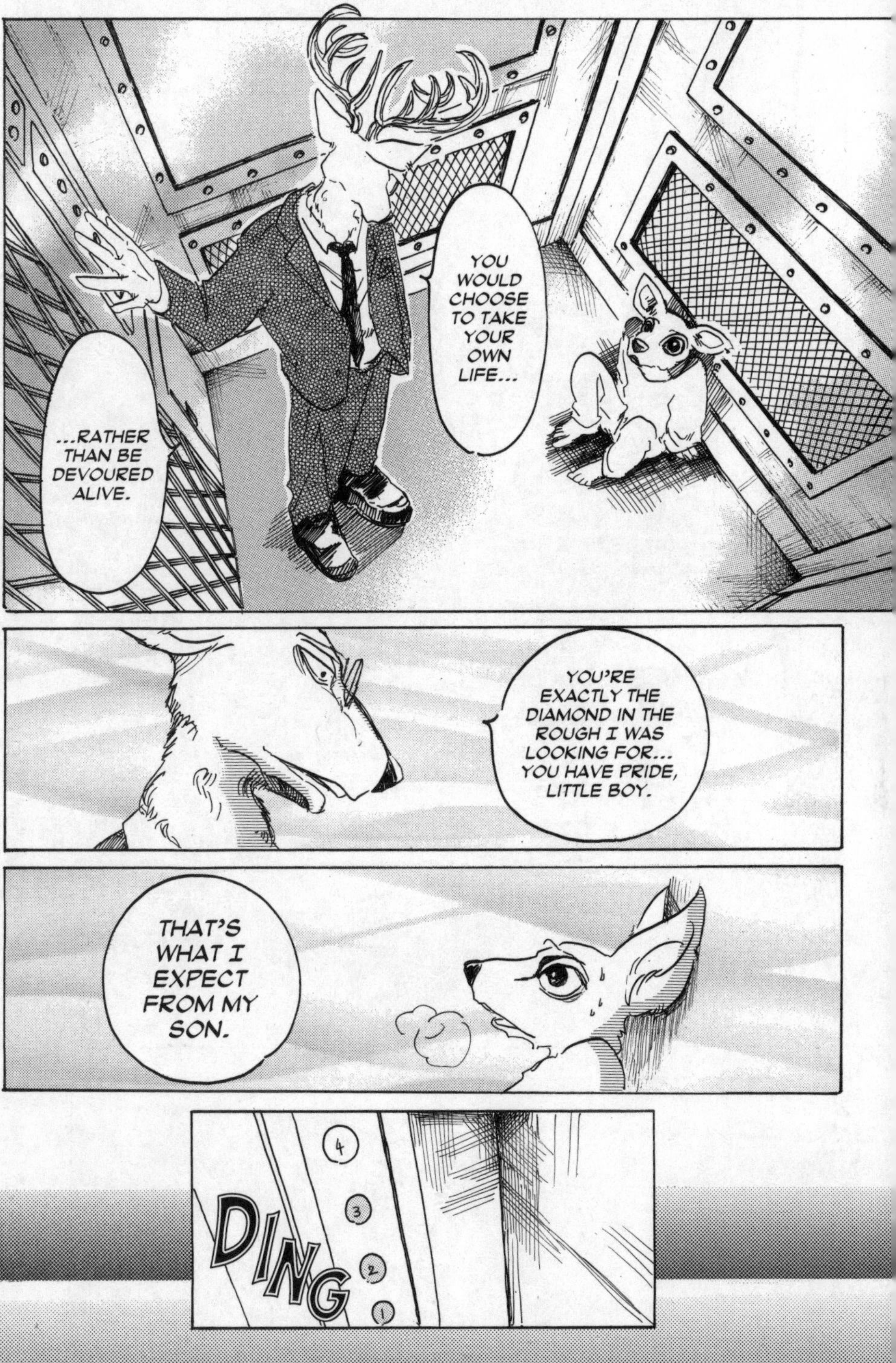
YOU WOULD CHOOSE TO TAKE YOUR OWN LIFE...
...RATHER THAN BE DEVOURED ALIVE.
YOU'RE EXACTLY THE DIAMOND IN THE ROUGH I WAS LOOKING FOR... YOU HAVE PRIDE, LITTLE BOY.
THAT'S WHAT I EXPECT FROM MY SON.
4
3
2
1
DING

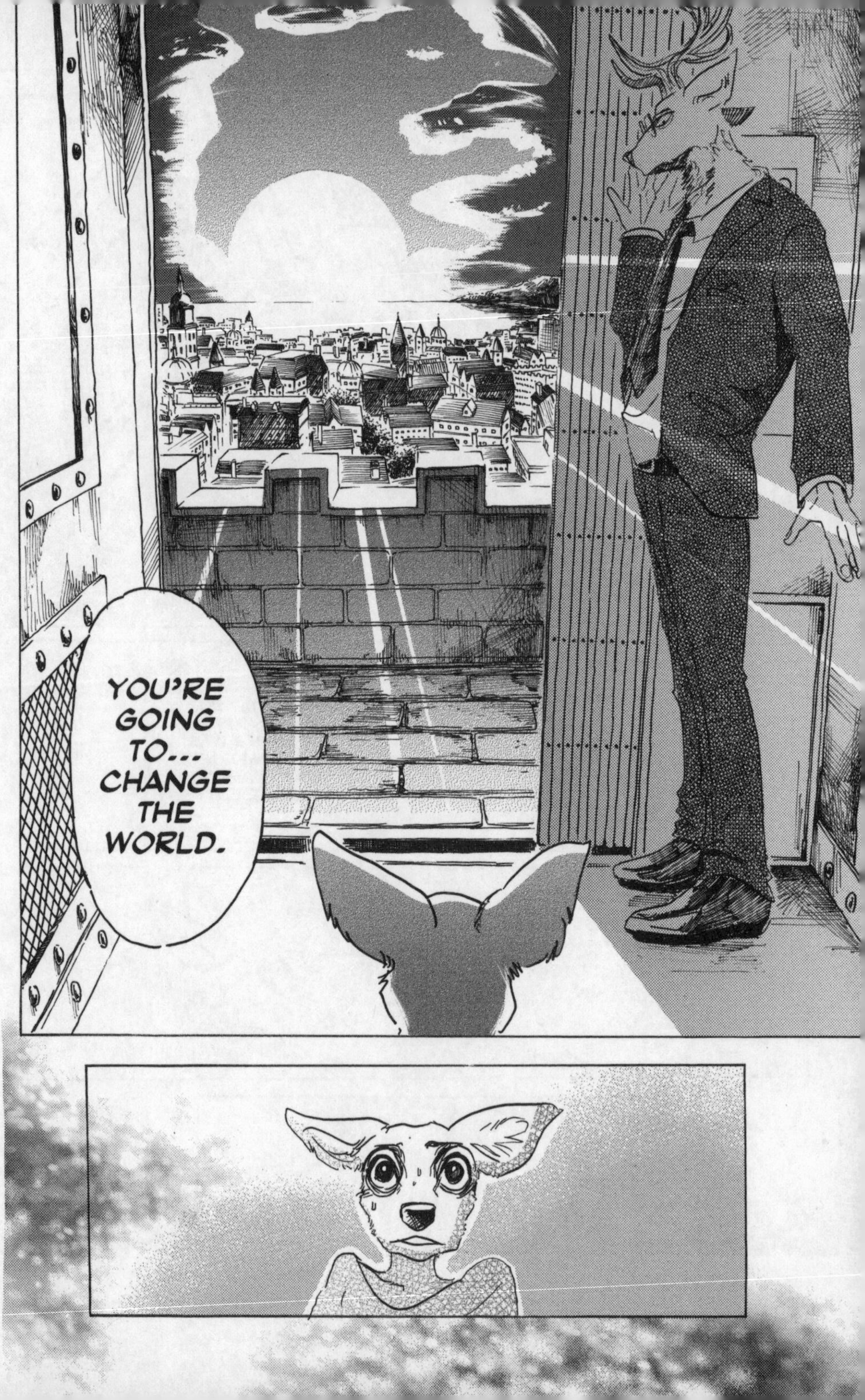
YOU'RE GOING TO... CHANGE THE WORLD.

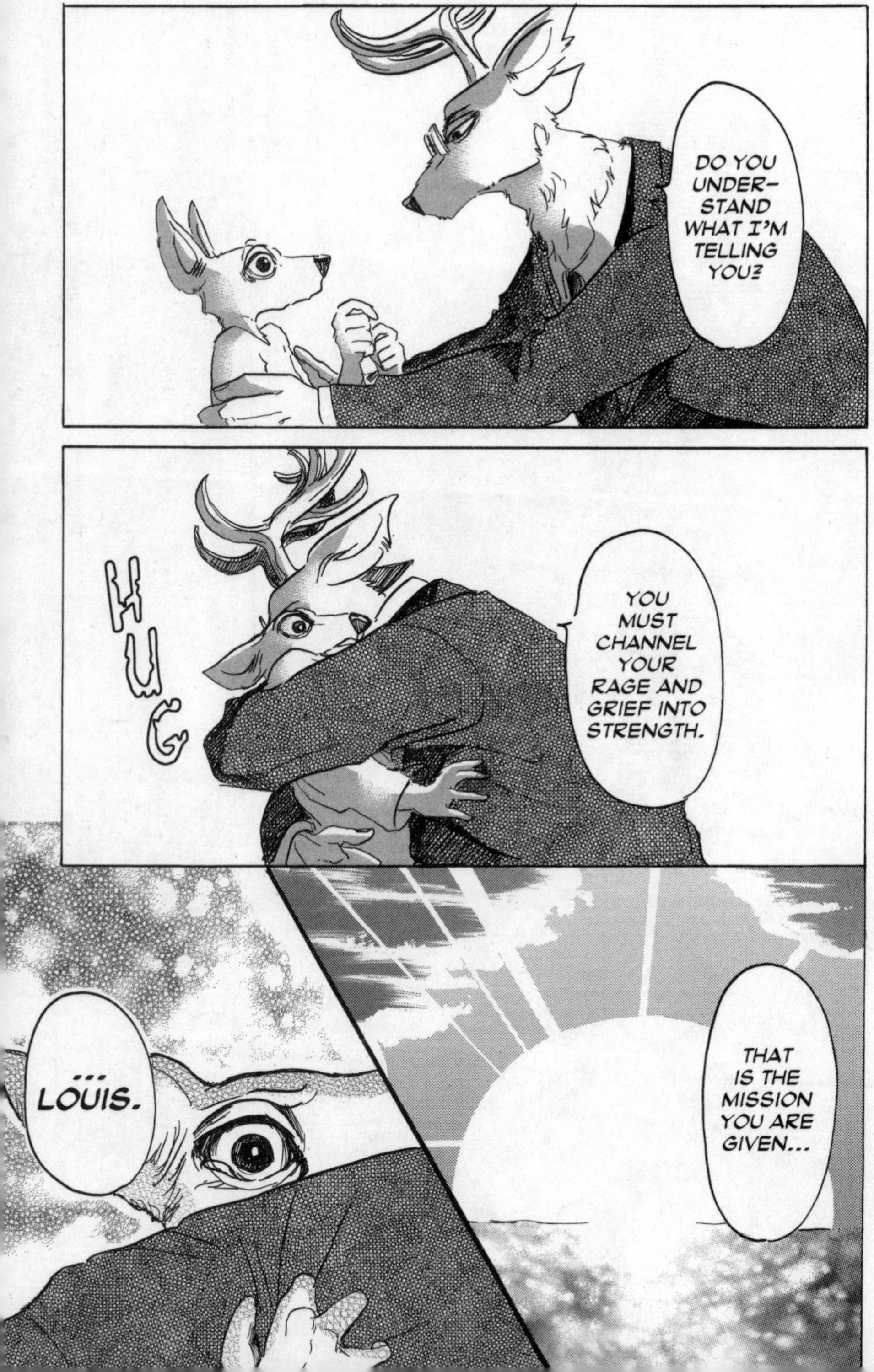

DO YOU UNDER-STAND WHAT I'M TELLING YOU?
YOU MUST CHANNEL YOUR RAGE AND GRIEF INTO STRENGTH.
HUG
THAT IS THE MISSION YOU ARE GIVEN...
...LOUIS.

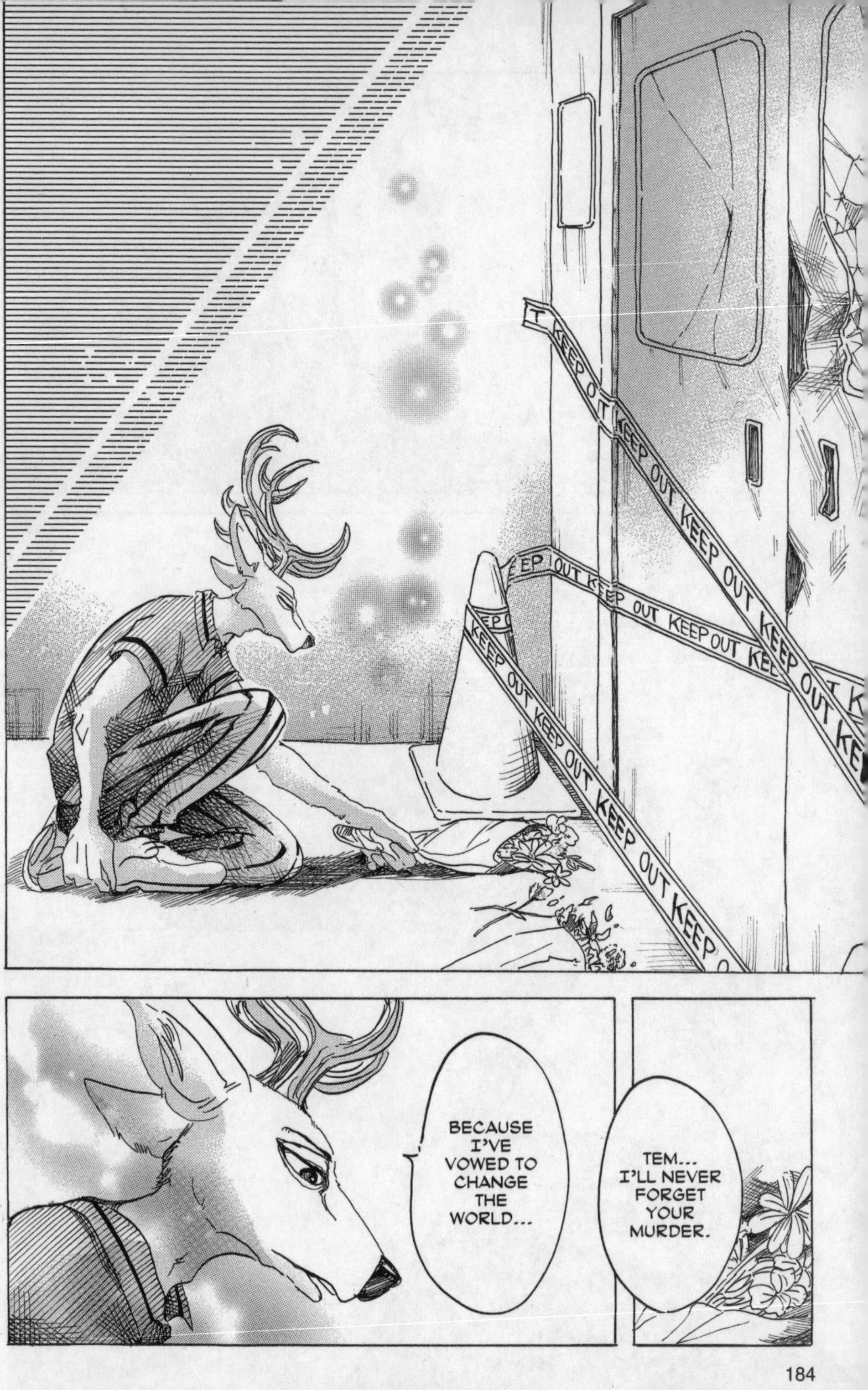
KEEP OUT
TEM... I'LL NEVER FORGET YOUR MURDER.
BECAUSE I'VE VOWED TO CHANGE THE WORLD...

Chapter 34: Secret Bodyguard

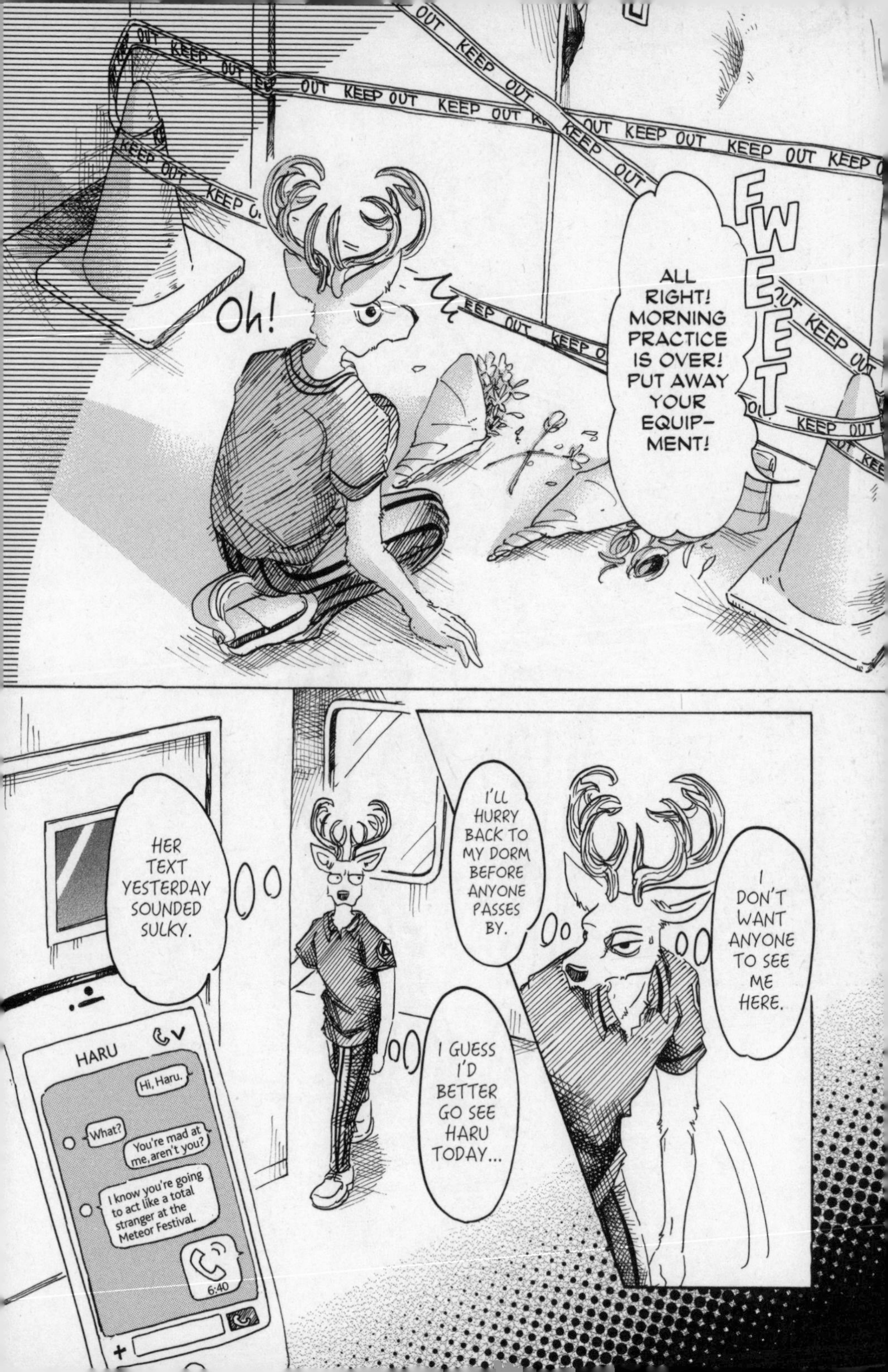
FWEET
ALL RIGHT! MORNING PRACTICE IS OVER! PUT AWAY YOUR EQUIPMENT!
Oh!
I DON'T WANT ANYONE TO SEE ME HERE.
I'LL HURRY BACK TO MY DORM BEFORE ANYONE PASSES BY.
I GUESS I'D BETTER GO SEE HARU TODAY...
HER TEXT YESTERDAY SOUNDED SULKY.
HARU
Hi, Haru.
What?
You're mad at me, aren't you?
I know you're going to act like a total stranger at the Meteor Festival.
6:40

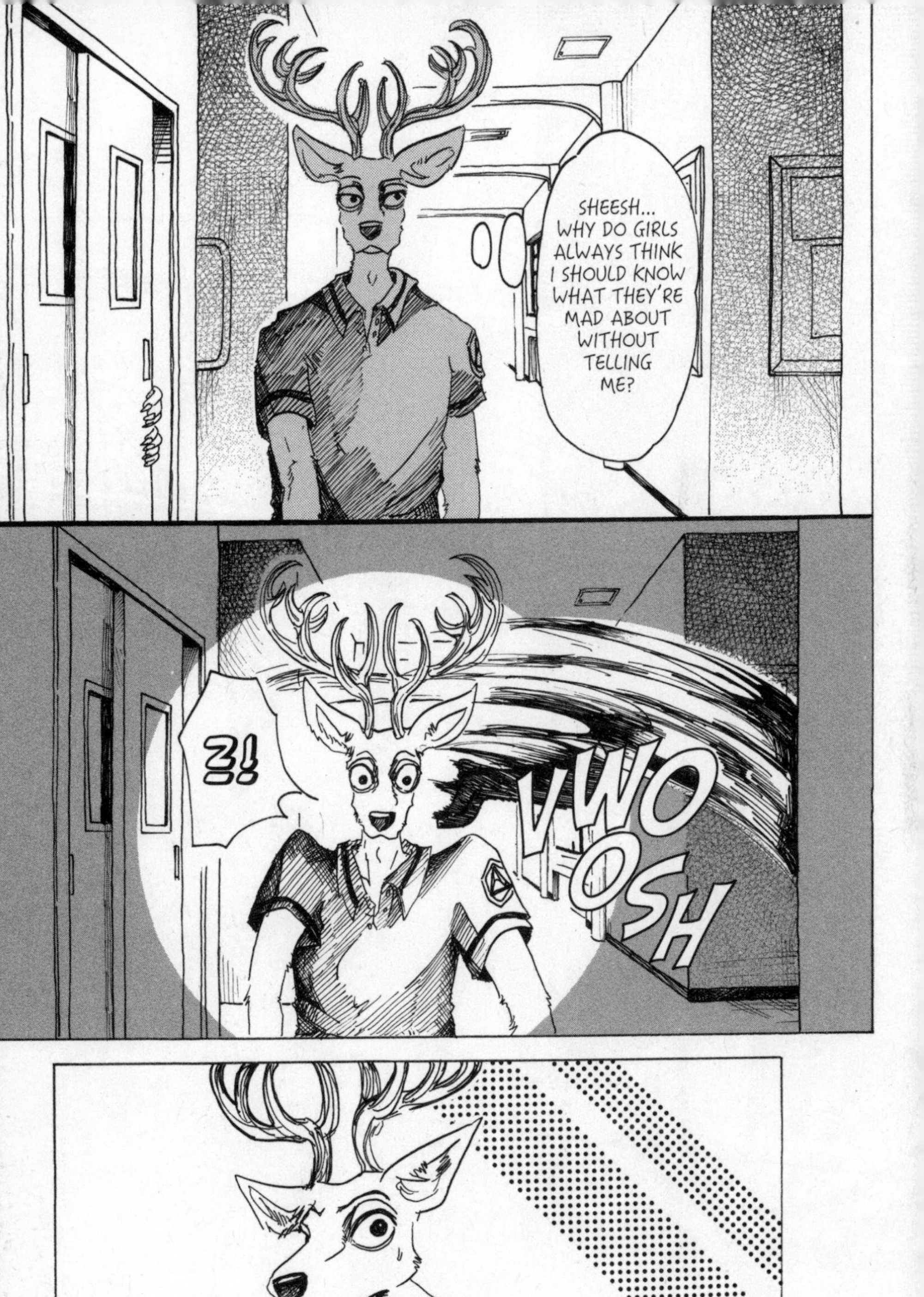
SHEESH... WHY DO GIRLS ALWAYS THINK I SHOULD KNOW WHAT THEY'RE MAD ABOUT WITHOUT TELLING ME?
VWOOSH
!!

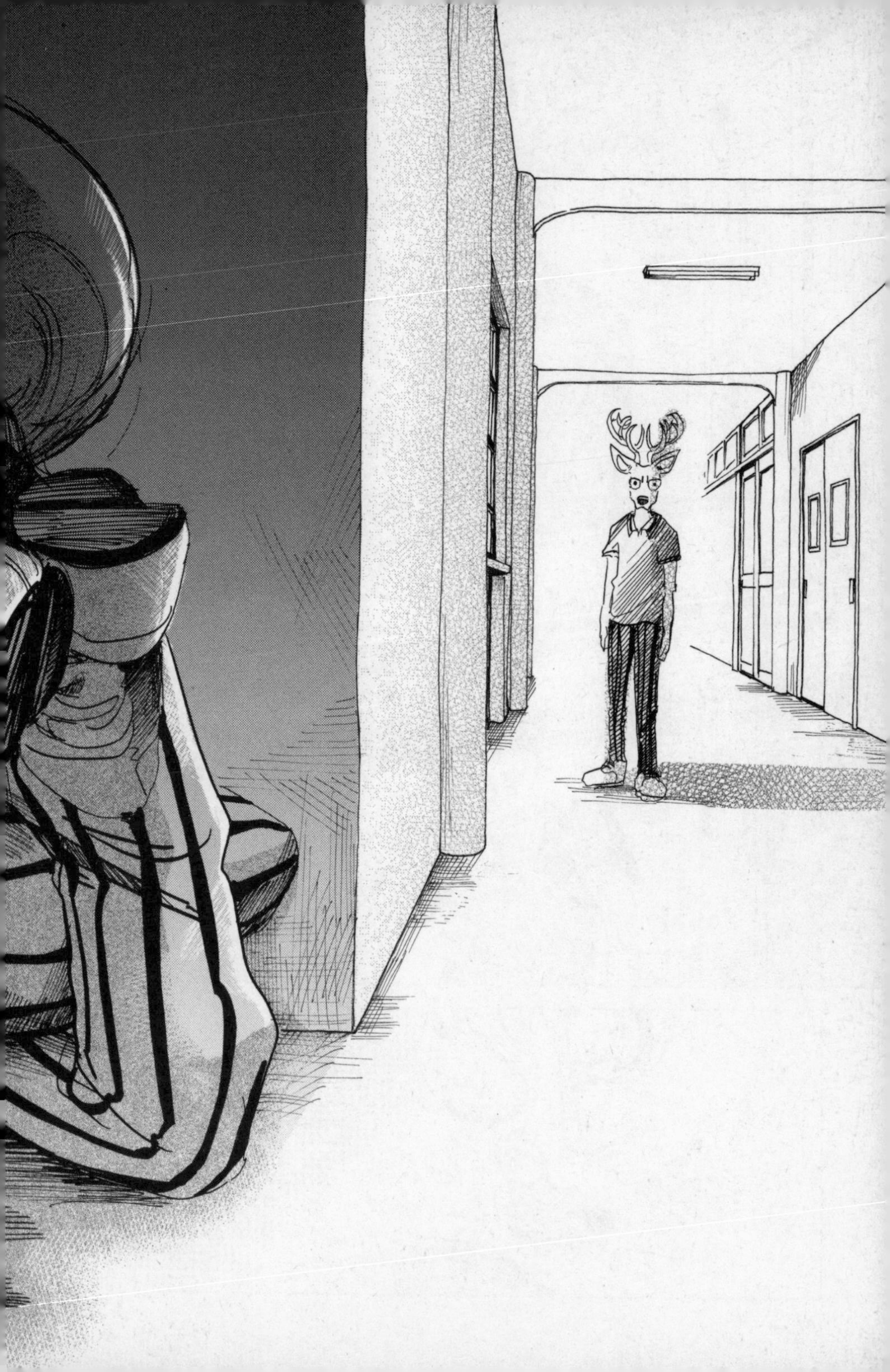

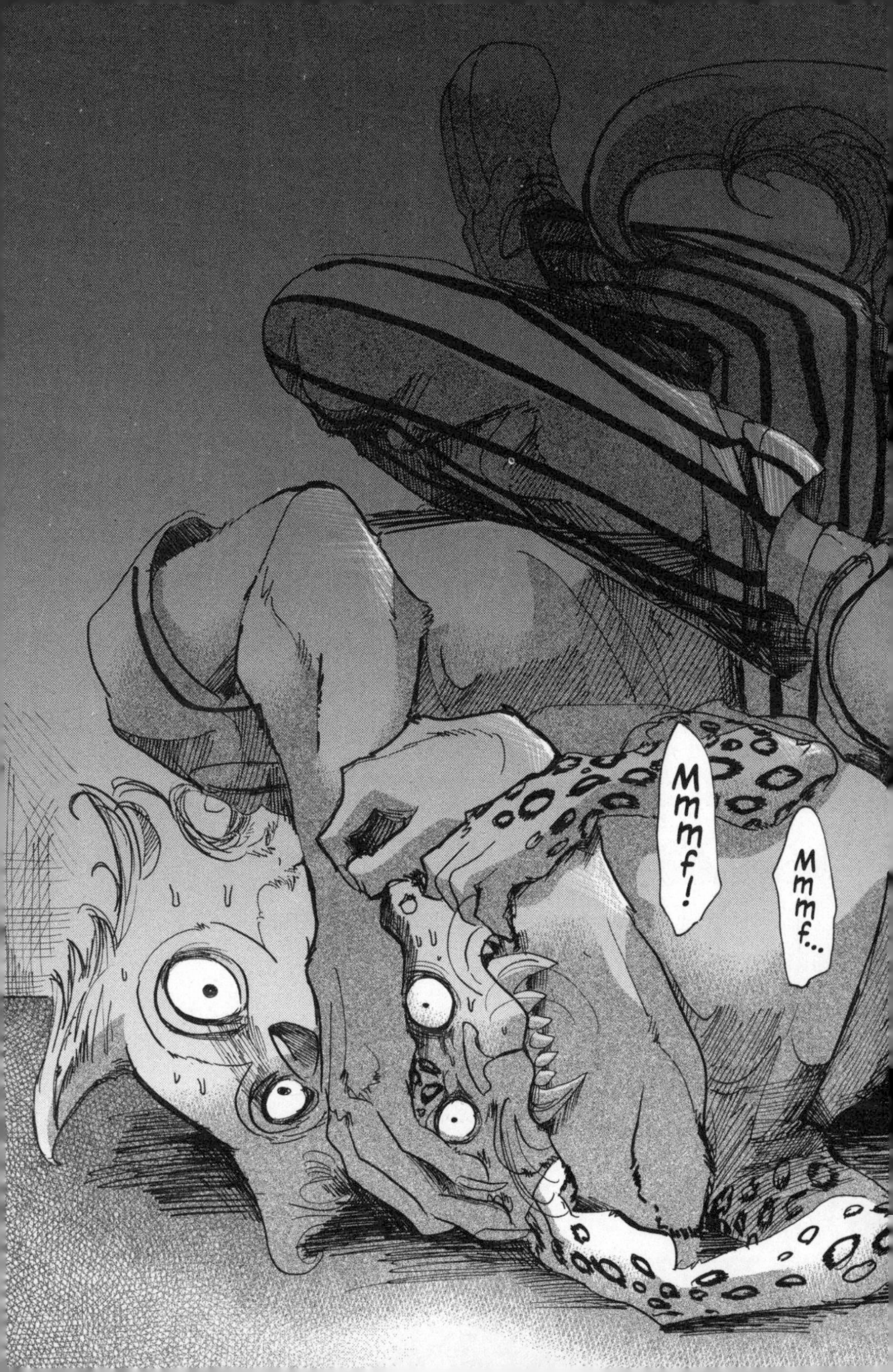
Mmmf!
Mmmf...

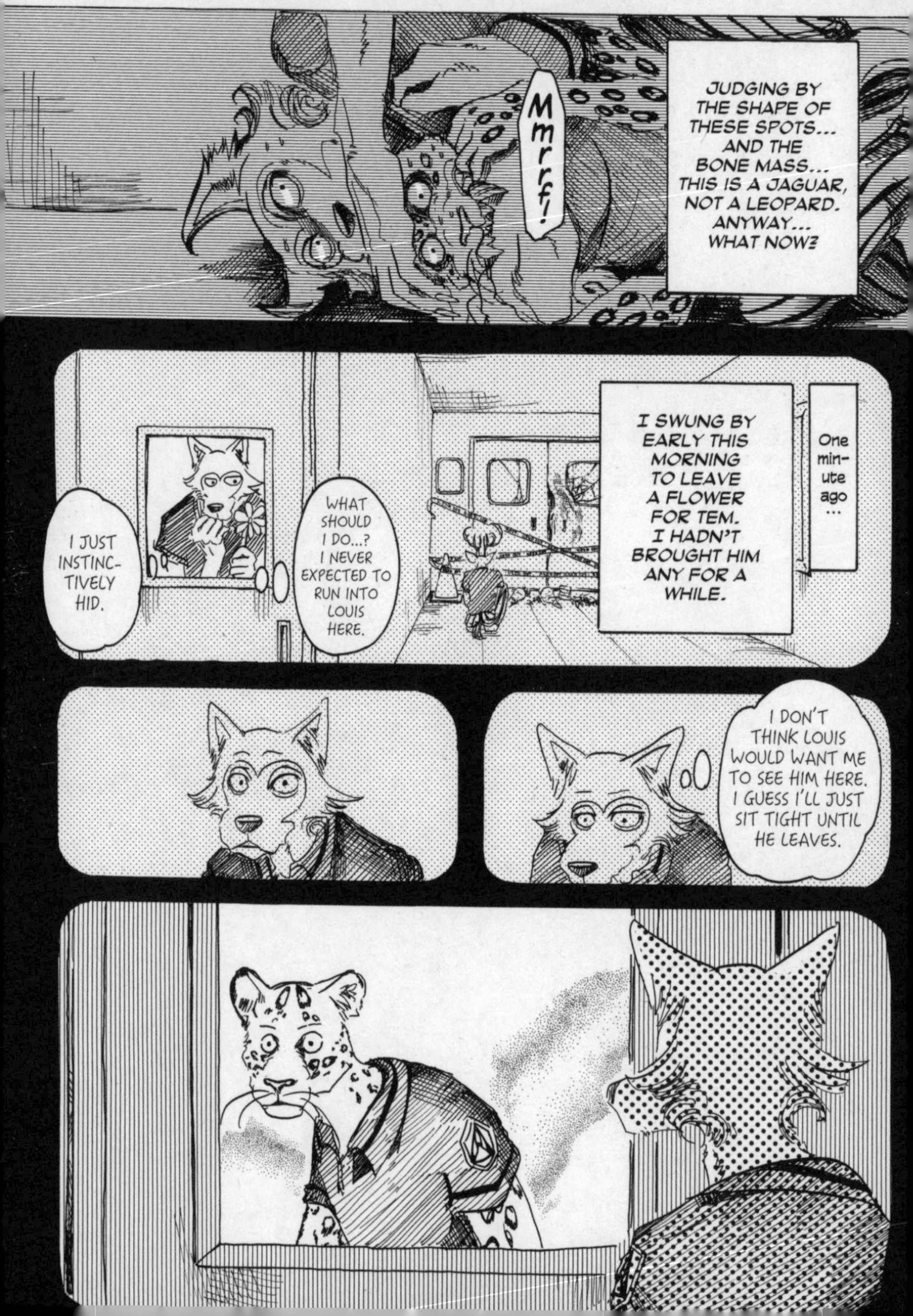
JUDGING BY THE SHAPE OF THESE SPOTS... AND THE BONE MASS... THIS IS A JAGUAR, NOT A LEOPARD. ANYWAY... WHAT NOW?
Mmrrf!
One min-ute ago...
I SWUNG BY EARLY THIS MORNING TO LEAVE A FLOWER FOR TEM. I HADN'T BROUGHT HIM ANY FOR A WHILE.
WHAT SHOULD I DO...? I NEVER EXPECTED TO RUN INTO LOUIS HERE.
I JUST INSTINC-TIVELY HID.
I DON'T THINK LOUIS WOULD WANT ME TO SEE HIM HERE. I GUESS I'LL JUST SIT TIGHT UNTIL HE LEAVES.

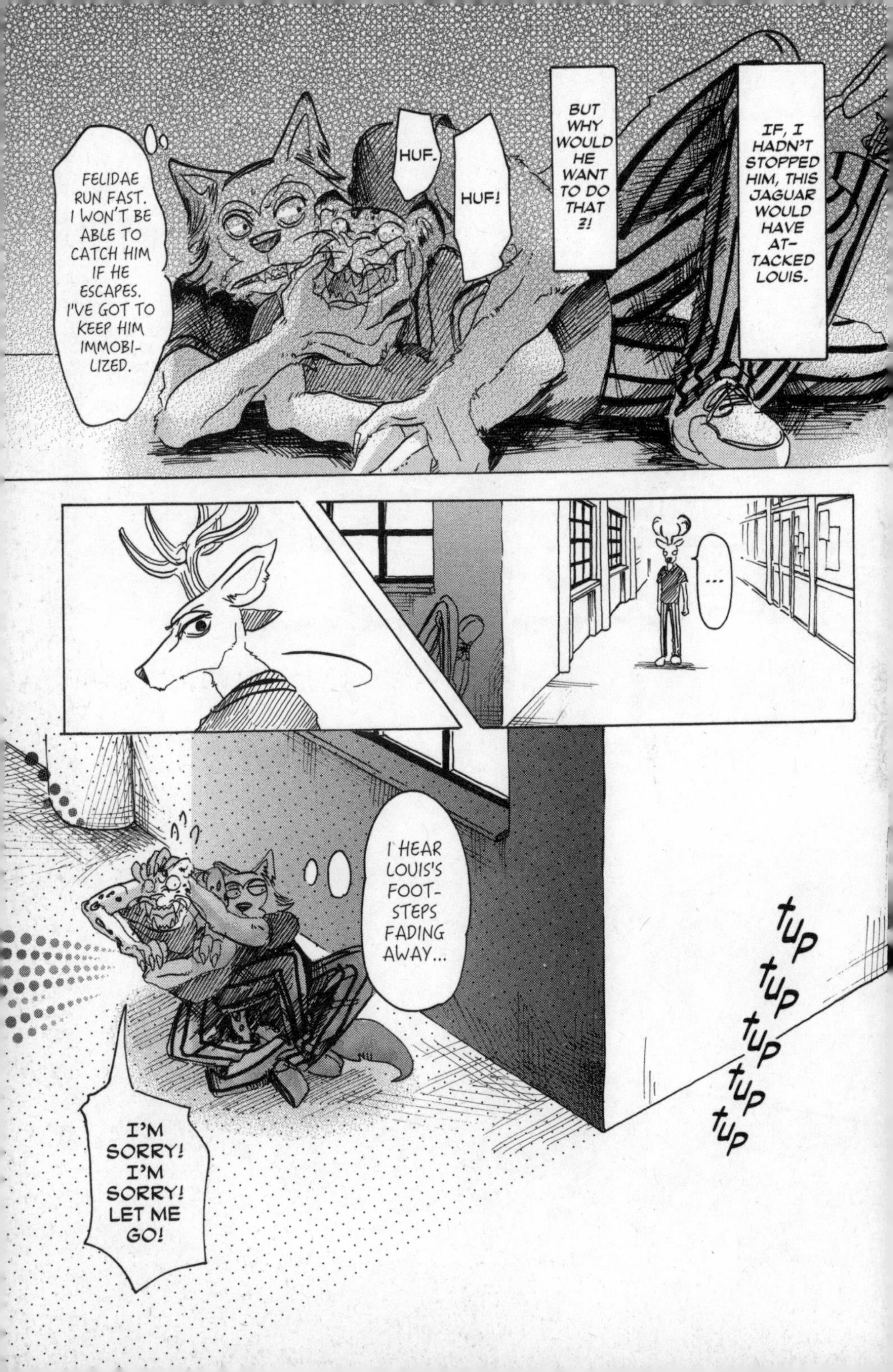
IF, I HADN'T STOPPED HIM, THIS JAGUAR WOULD HAVE AT-TACKED LOUIS.
BUT WHY WOULD HE WANT TO DO THAT ?!
HUF!
HUF.
FELIDAE RUN FAST. I WON'T BE ABLE TO CATCH HIM IF HE ESCAPES. I'VE GOT TO KEEP HIM IMMOBI-LIZED.
...
I HEAR LOUIS'S FOOT-STEPS FADING AWAY...
tup tup tup tup tup
I'M SORRY! I'M SORRY! LET ME GO!

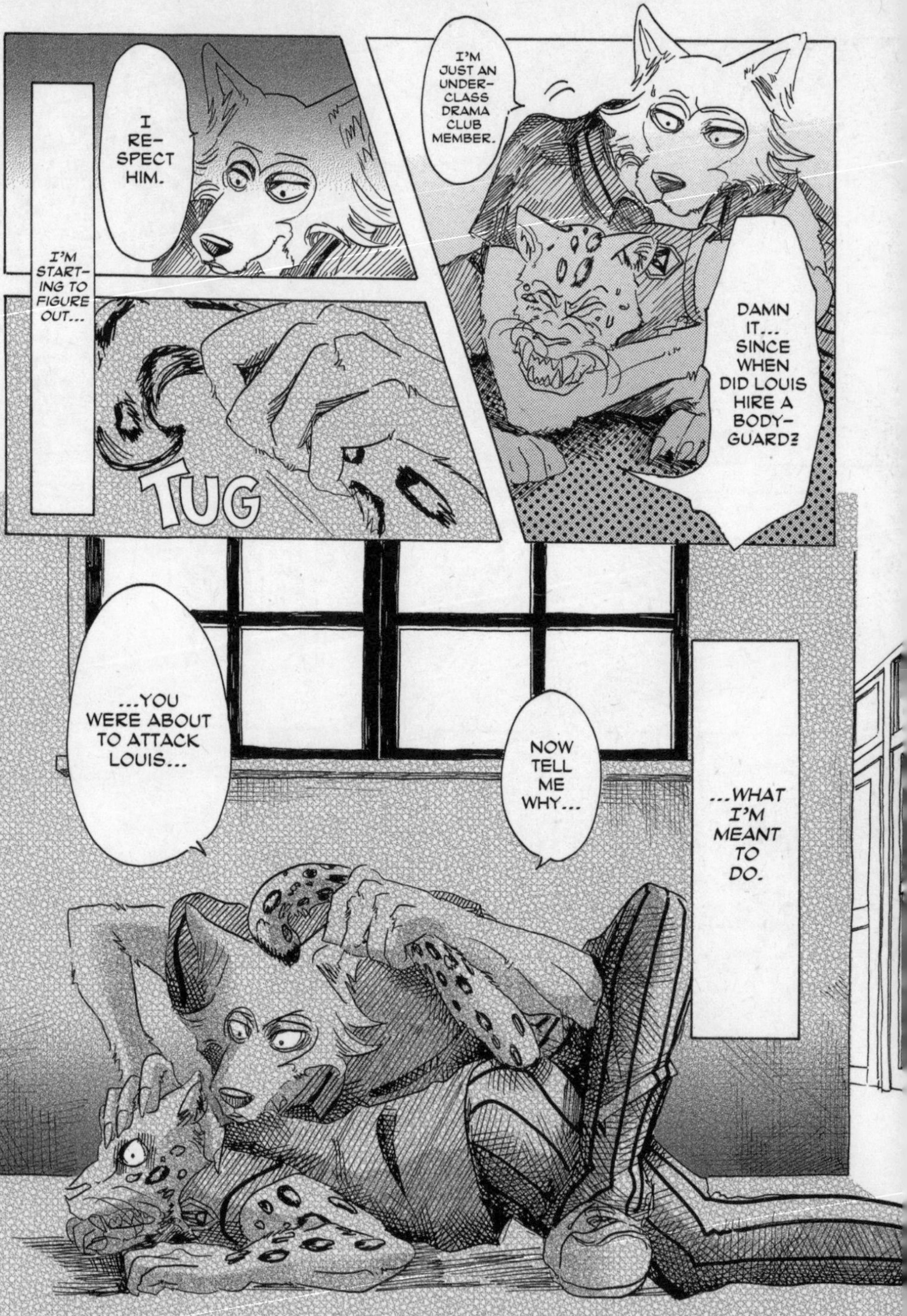
I'M JUST AN UNDER-CLASS DRAMA CLUB MEMBER.
DAMN IT... SINCE WHEN DID LOUIS HIRE A BODY-GUARD?
I RE-SPECT HIM.
I'M START-ING TO FIGURE OUT...
TUG
...WHAT I'M MEANT TO DO.
NOW TELL ME WHY...
...YOU WERE ABOUT TO ATTACK LOUIS...

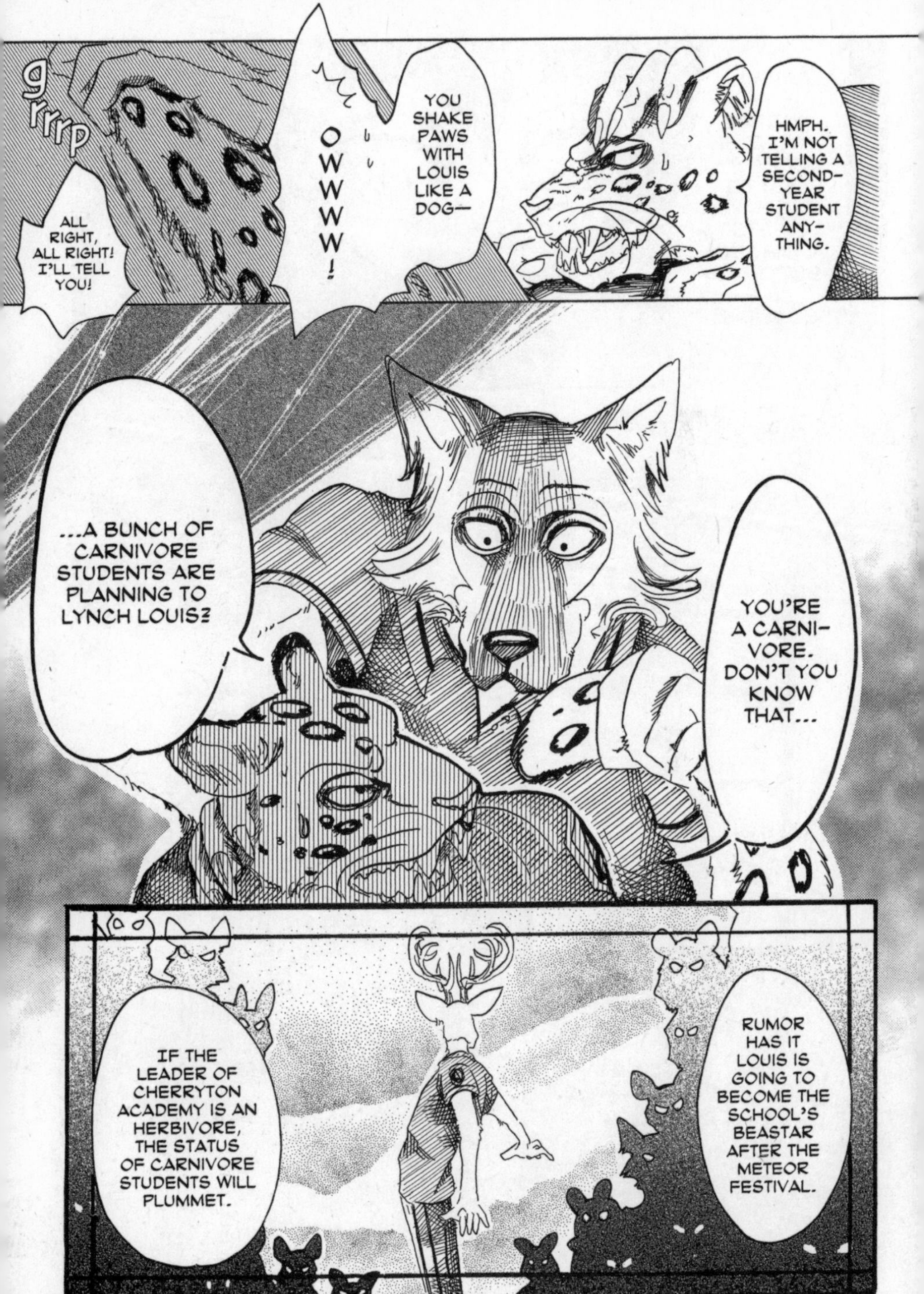
HMPH. I'M NOT TELLING A SECOND-YEAR STUDENT ANYTHING.
YOU SHAKE PAWS WITH LOUIS LIKE A DOG—
OWWWWW!
grrrp
ALL RIGHT, ALL RIGHT! I'LL TELL YOU!
YOU'RE A CARNIVORE. DON'T YOU KNOW THAT...
...A BUNCH OF CARNIVORE STUDENTS ARE PLANNING TO LYNCH LOUIS?
RUMOR HAS IT LOUIS IS GOING TO BECOME THE SCHOOL'S BEASTAR AFTER THE METEOR FESTIVAL.
IF THE LEADER OF CHERRYTON ACADEMY IS AN HERBIVORE, THE STATUS OF CARNIVORE STUDENTS WILL PLUMMET.

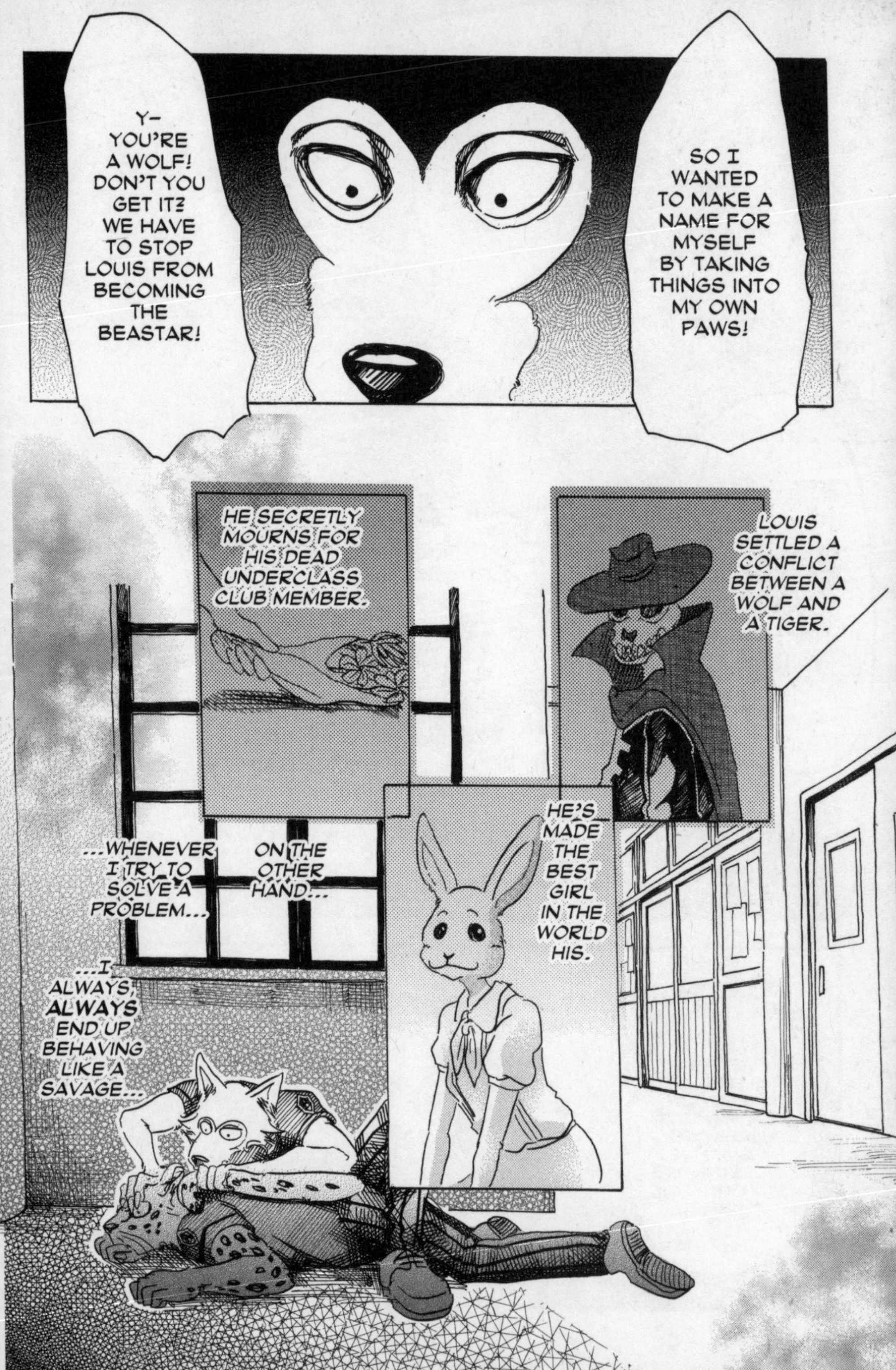
Y— YOU'RE A WOLF! DON'T YOU GET IT? WE HAVE TO STOP LOUIS FROM BECOMING THE BEASTAR!
SO I WANTED TO MAKE A NAME FOR MYSELF BY TAKING THINGS INTO MY OWN PAWS!
LOUIS SETTLED A CONFLICT BETWEEN A WOLF AND A TIGER.
HE SECRETLY MOURNS FOR HIS DEAD UNDERCLASS CLUB MEMBER.
HE'S MADE THE BEST GIRL IN THE WORLD HIS.
ON THE OTHER HAND...
...WHENEVER I TRY TO SOLVE A PROBLEM...
...I ALWAYS, ALWAYS END UP BEHAVING LIKE A SAVAGE...

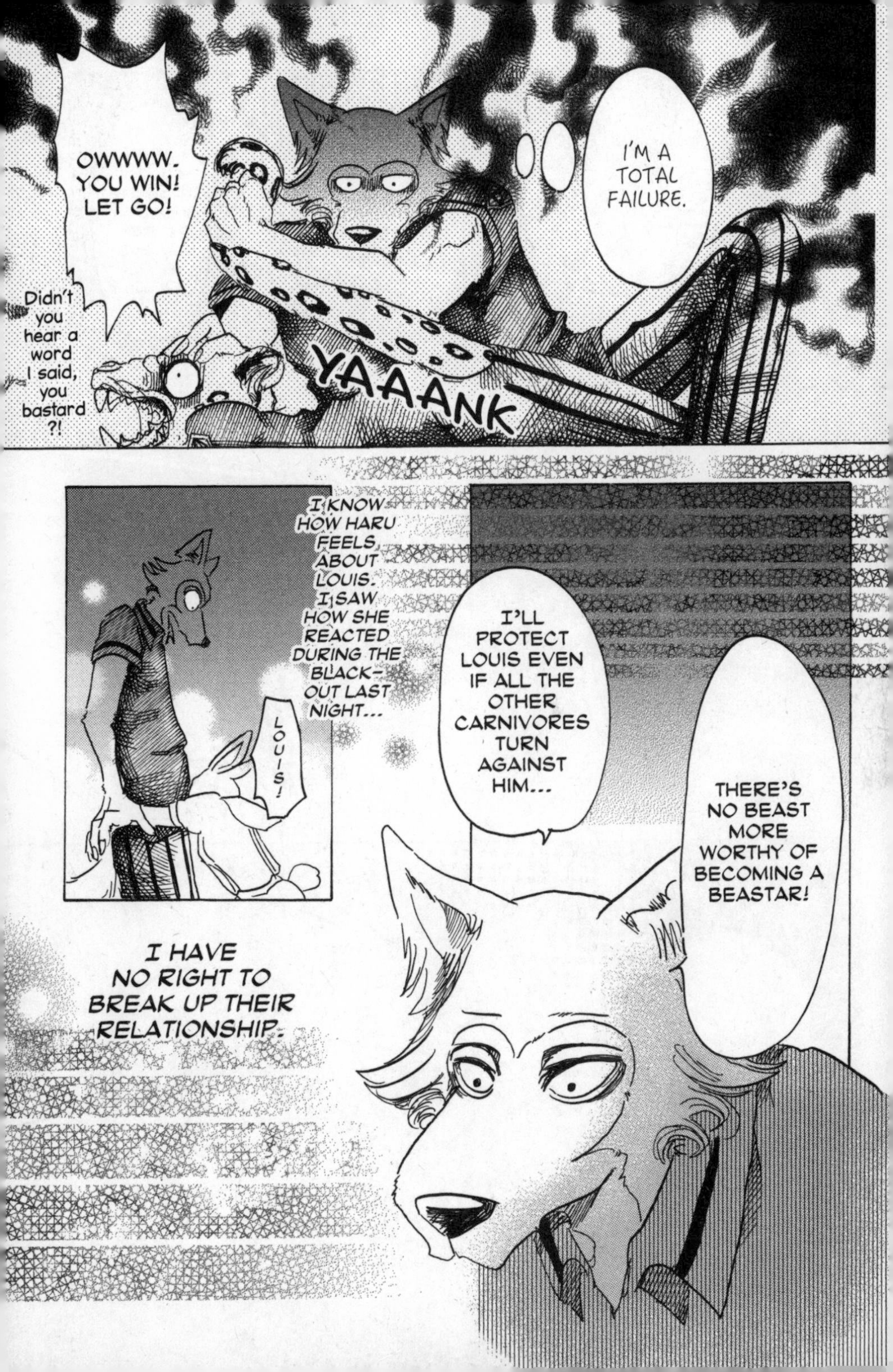
I'M A TOTAL FAILURE.
OWWWW. YOU WIN! LET GO!
YAAANK
Didn't you hear a word I said, you bastard?!
I'LL PROTECT LOUIS EVEN IF ALL THE OTHER CARNIVORES TURN AGAINST HIM...
THERE'S NO BEAST MORE WORTHY OF BECOMING A BEASTAR!
I KNOW HOW HARU FEELS ABOUT LOUIS. I SAW HOW SHE REACTED DURING THE BLACK-OUT LAST NIGHT...
LOUIS!
I HAVE NO RIGHT TO BREAK UP THEIR RELATIONSHIP.

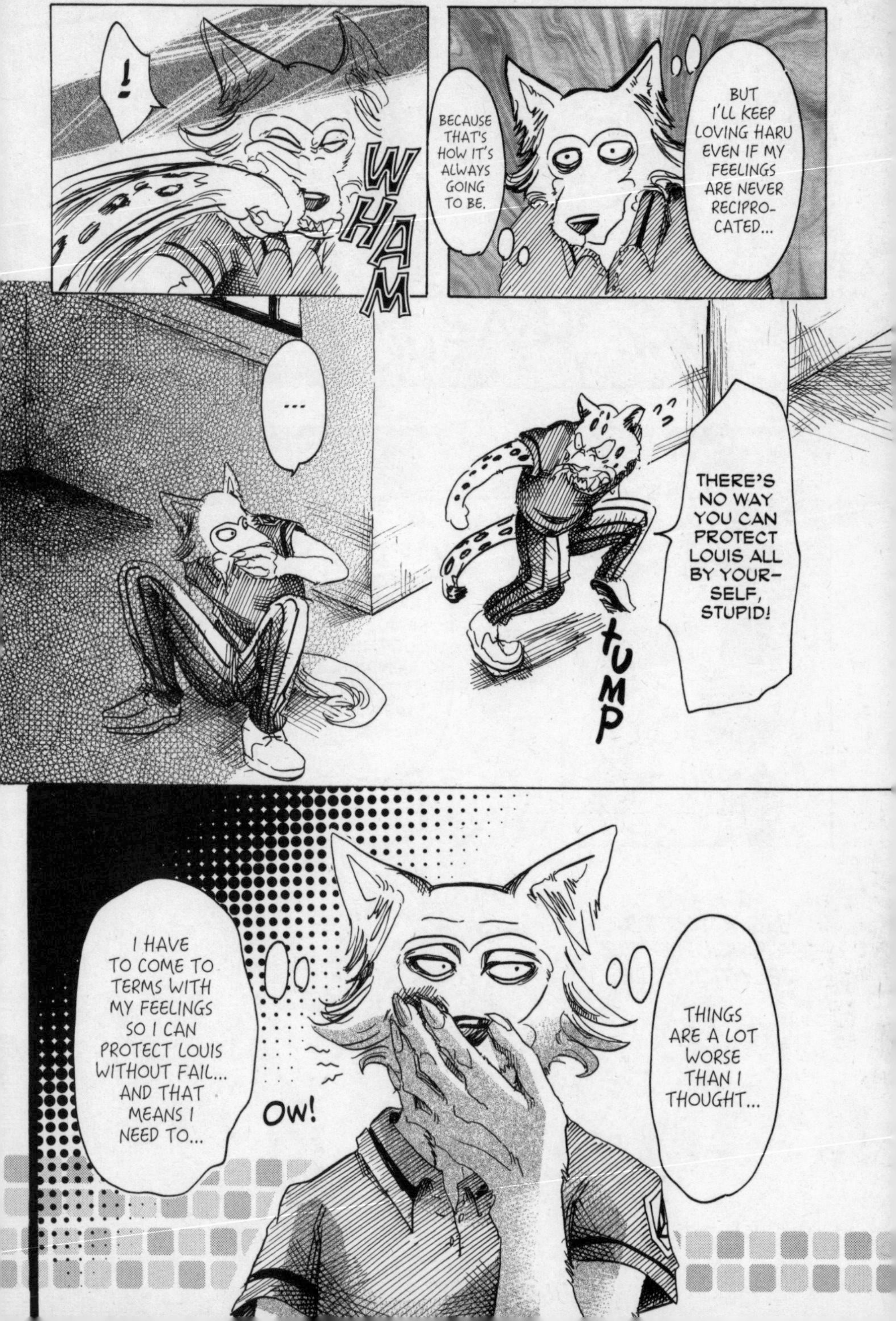
BUT I'LL KEEP LOVING HARU EVEN IF MY FEELINGS ARE NEVER RECIPRO-CATED...
BECAUSE THAT'S HOW IT'S ALWAYS GOING TO BE.
!
WHAM
THERE'S NO WAY YOU CAN PROTECT LOUIS ALL BY YOUR-SELF, STUPID!
TUMP
...
THINGS ARE A LOT WORSE THAN I THOUGHT...
I HAVE TO COME TO TERMS WITH MY FEELINGS SO I CAN PROTECT LOUIS WITHOUT FAIL... AND THAT MEANS I NEED TO...
OW!

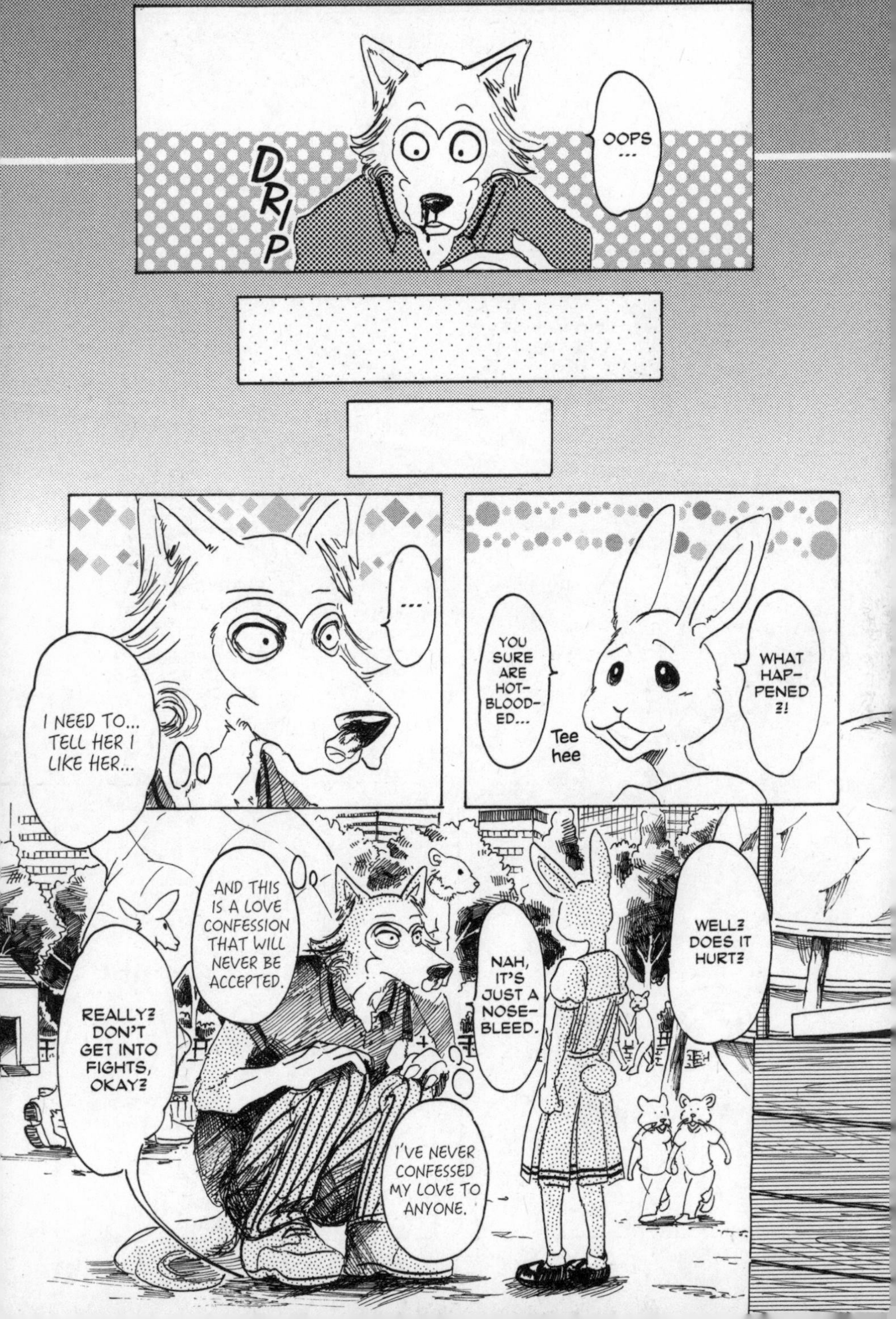
DRIP
OOPS...
WHAT HAPPENED?!
YOU SURE ARE HOT-BLOODED...
Tee hee
...
I NEED TO... TELL HER I LIKE HER...
WELL? DOES IT HURT?
NAH, IT'S JUST A NOSEBLEED.
REALLY? DON'T GET INTO FIGHTS, OKAY?
I'VE NEVER CONFESSED MY LOVE TO ANYONE.
AND THIS IS A LOVE CONFESSION THAT WILL NEVER BE ACCEPTED.

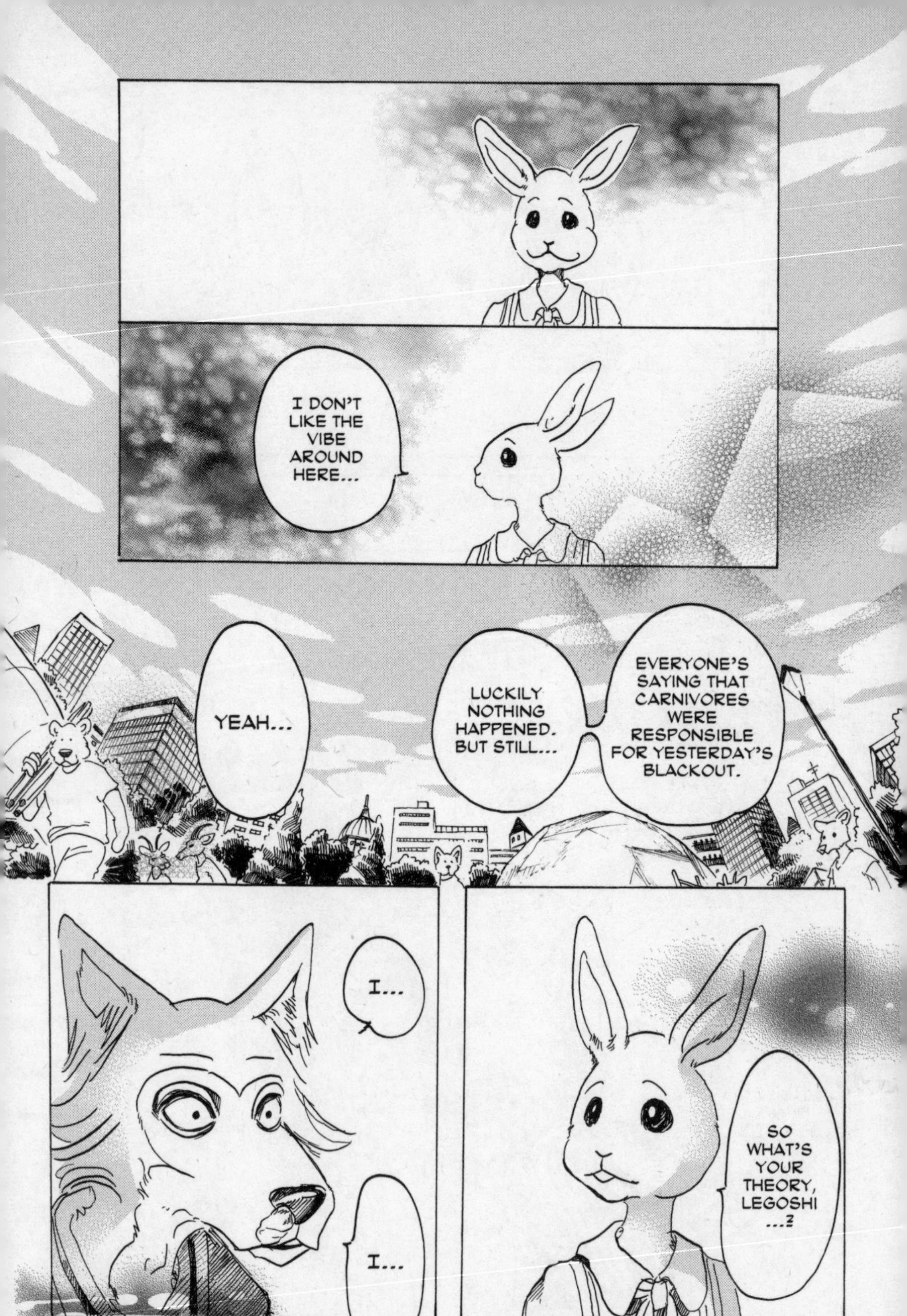
I DON'T LIKE THE VIBE AROUND HERE...
EVERYONE'S SAYING THAT CARNIVORES WERE RESPONSIBLE FOR YESTERDAY'S BLACKOUT.
LUCKILY NOTHING HAPPENED. BUT STILL...
YEAH...
SO WHAT'S YOUR THEORY, LEGOSHI ...?
I...
I...

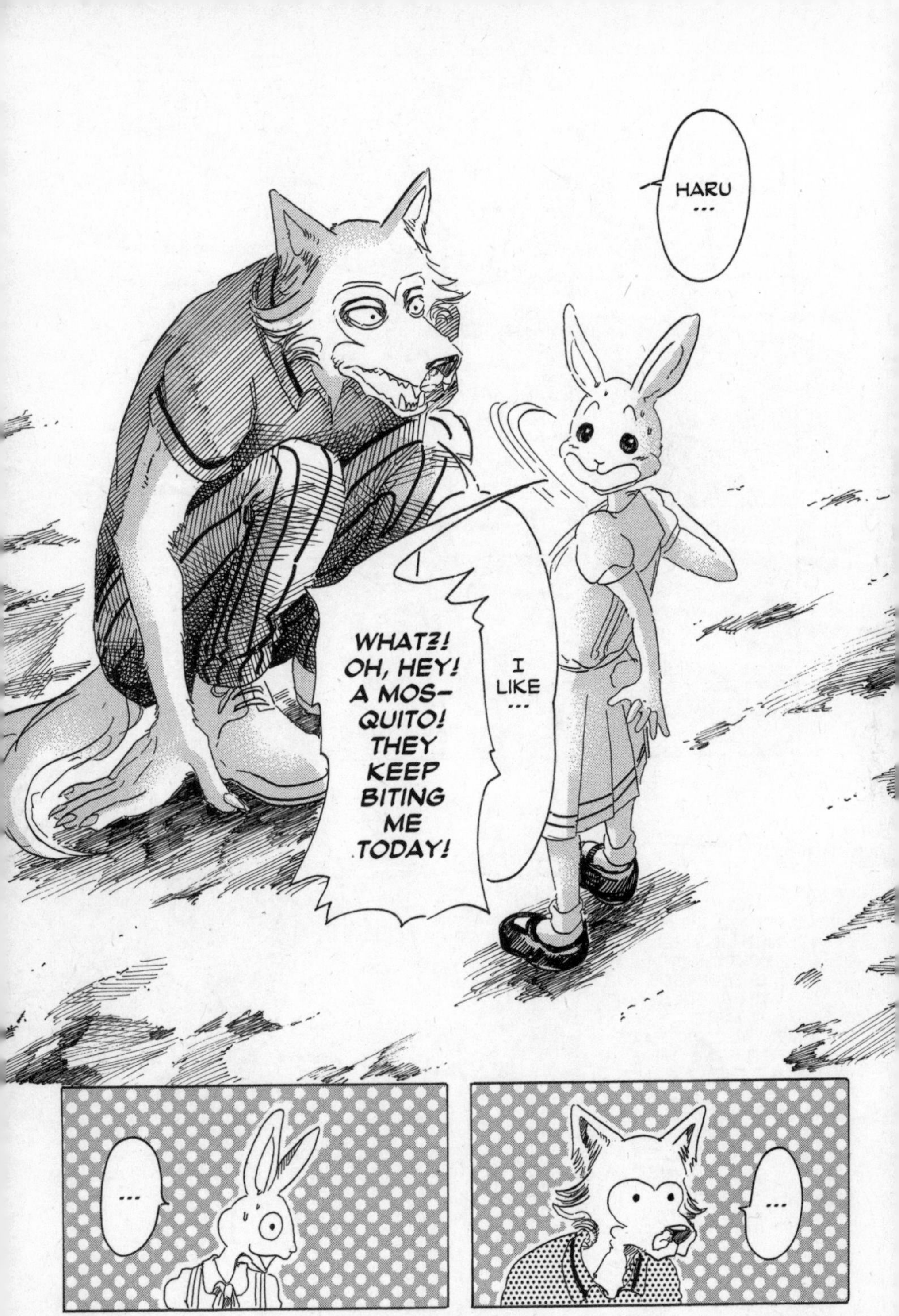
HARU...
I LIKE...
WHAT?! OH, HEY! A MOS-QUITO! THEY KEEP BITING ME TODAY!
...
...

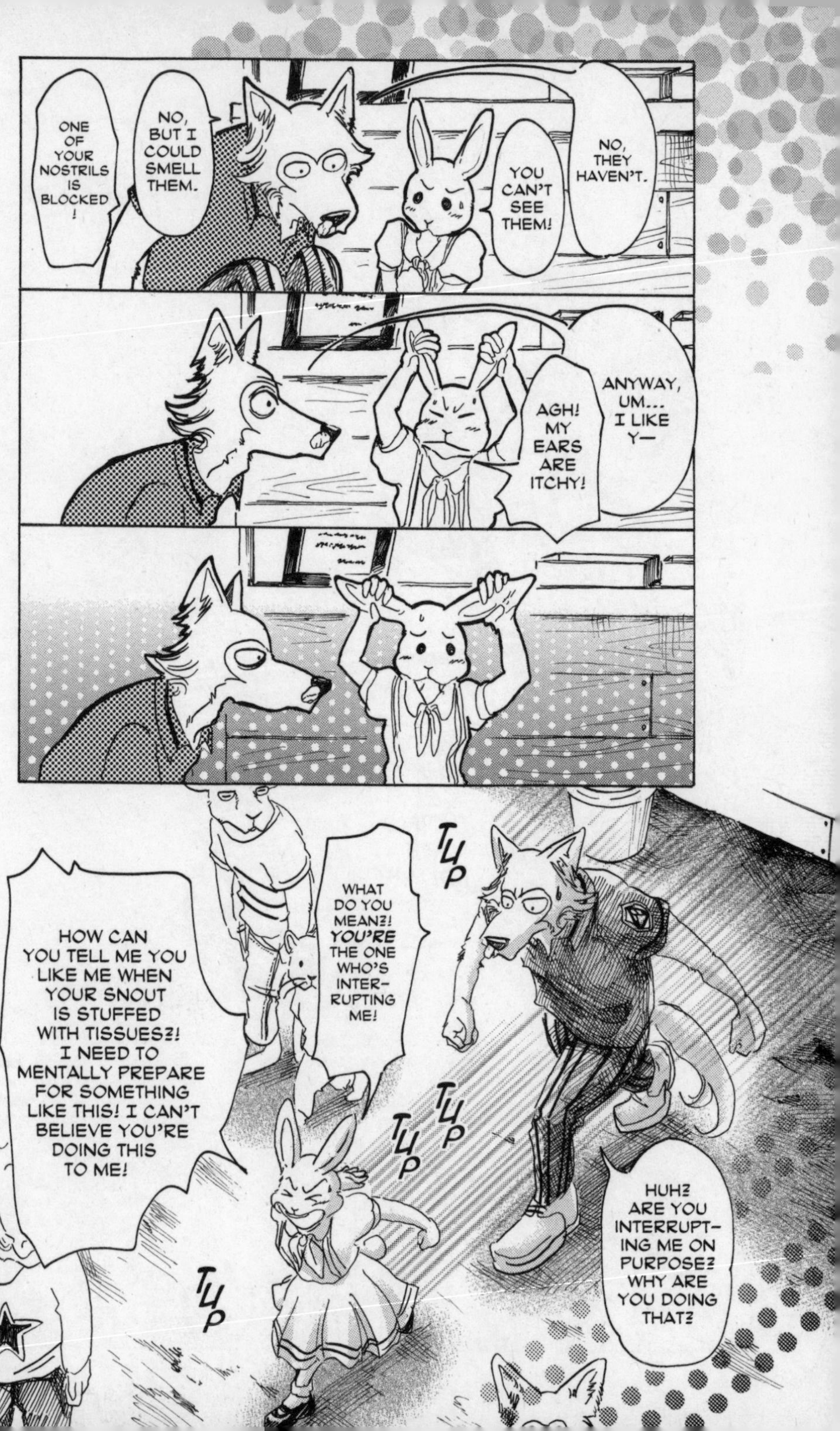
NO, THEY HAVEN'T.
YOU CAN'T SEE THEM!
NO, BUT I COULD SMELL THEM.
ONE OF YOUR NOSTRILS IS BLOCKED!
ANYWAY, UM... I LIKE Y—
AGH! MY EARS ARE ITCHY!
TUP
HUH? ARE YOU INTERRUPTING ME ON PURPOSE? WHY ARE YOU DOING THAT?
TUP
TUP
WHAT DO YOU MEAN?! *YOU'RE* THE ONE WHO'S INTERRUPTING ME!
HOW CAN YOU TELL ME YOU LIKE ME WHEN YOUR SNOUT IS STUFFED WITH TISSUES?! I NEED TO MENTALLY PREPARE FOR SOMETHING LIKE THIS! I CAN'T BELIEVE YOU'RE DOING THIS TO ME!
TUP

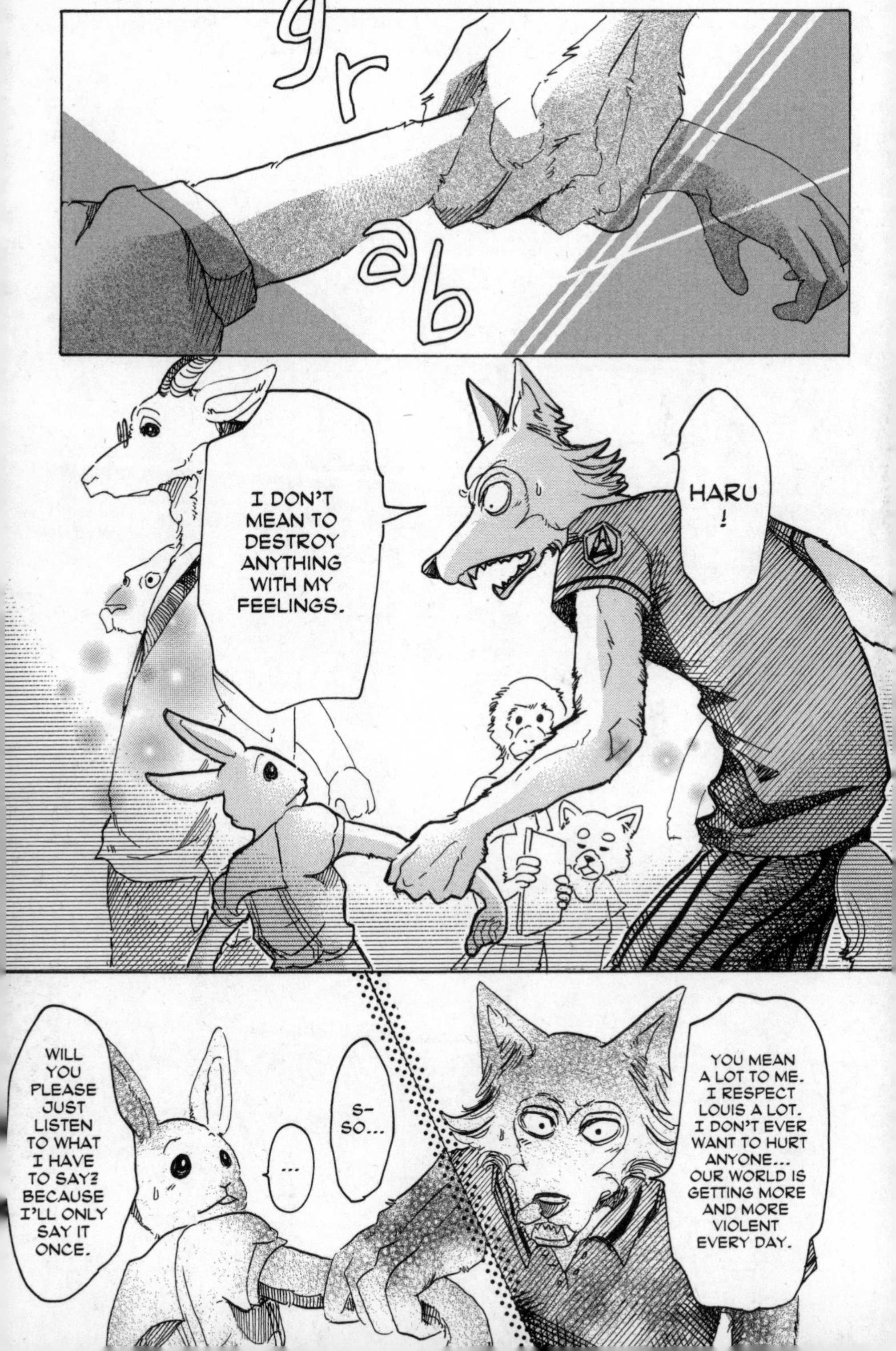
grab
HARU!
I DON'T MEAN TO DESTROY ANYTHING WITH MY FEELINGS.
YOU MEAN A LOT TO ME. I RESPECT LOUIS A LOT. I DON'T EVER WANT TO HURT ANYONE... OUR WORLD IS GETTING MORE AND MORE VIOLENT EVERY DAY.
S-SO...
...
WILL YOU PLEASE JUST LISTEN TO WHAT I HAVE TO SAY? BECAUSE I'LL ONLY SAY IT ONCE.

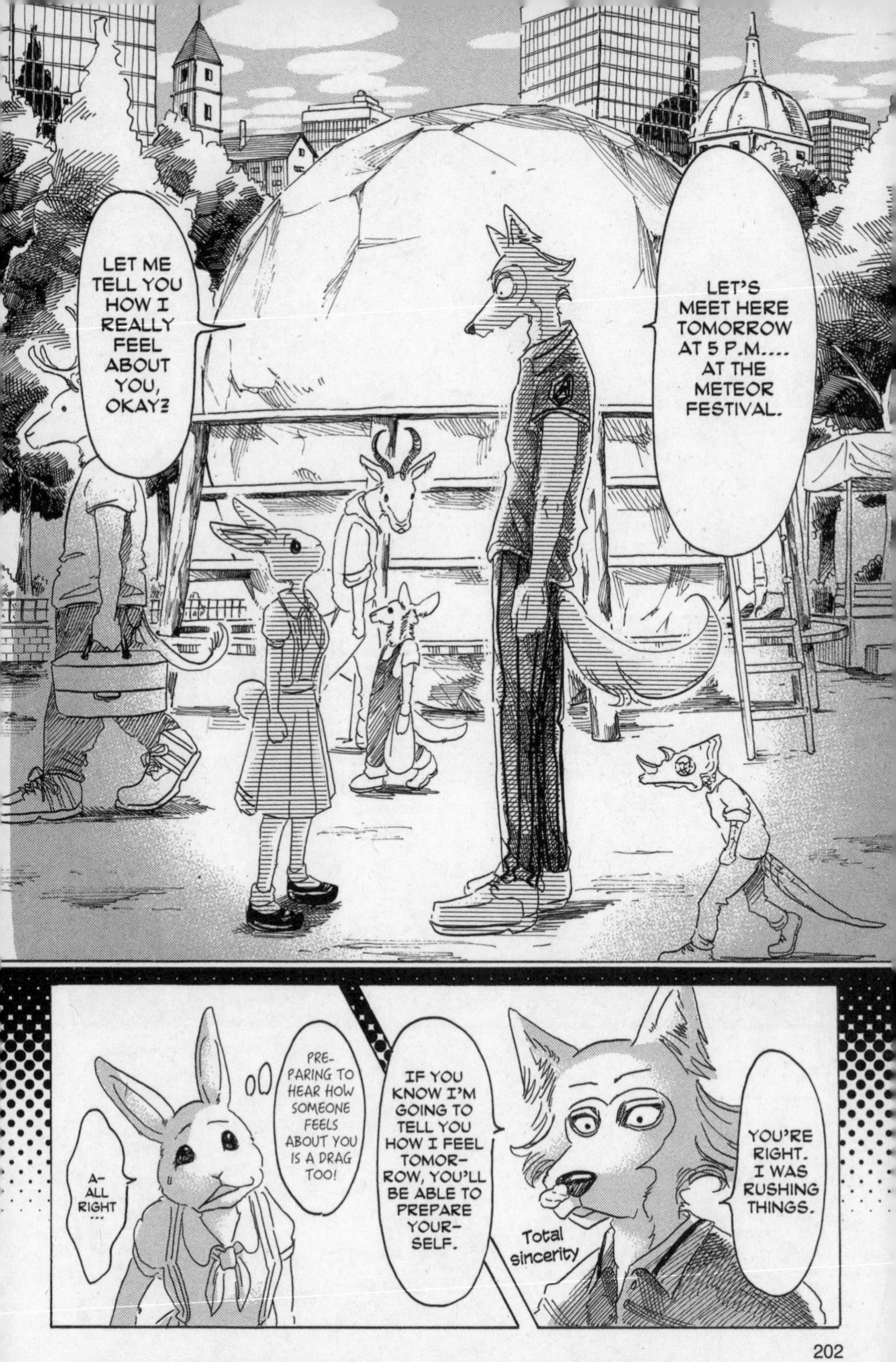
LET'S MEET HERE TOMORROW AT 5 P.M.... AT THE METEOR FESTIVAL.
LET ME TELL YOU HOW I REALLY FEEL ABOUT YOU, OKAY?
YOU'RE RIGHT. I WAS RUSHING THINGS.
Total sincerity
IF YOU KNOW I'M GOING TO TELL YOU HOW I FEEL TOMORROW, YOU'LL BE ABLE TO PREPARE YOURSELF.
PREPARING TO HEAR HOW SOMEONE FEELS ABOUT YOU IS A DRAG TOO!
A-ALL RIGHT...

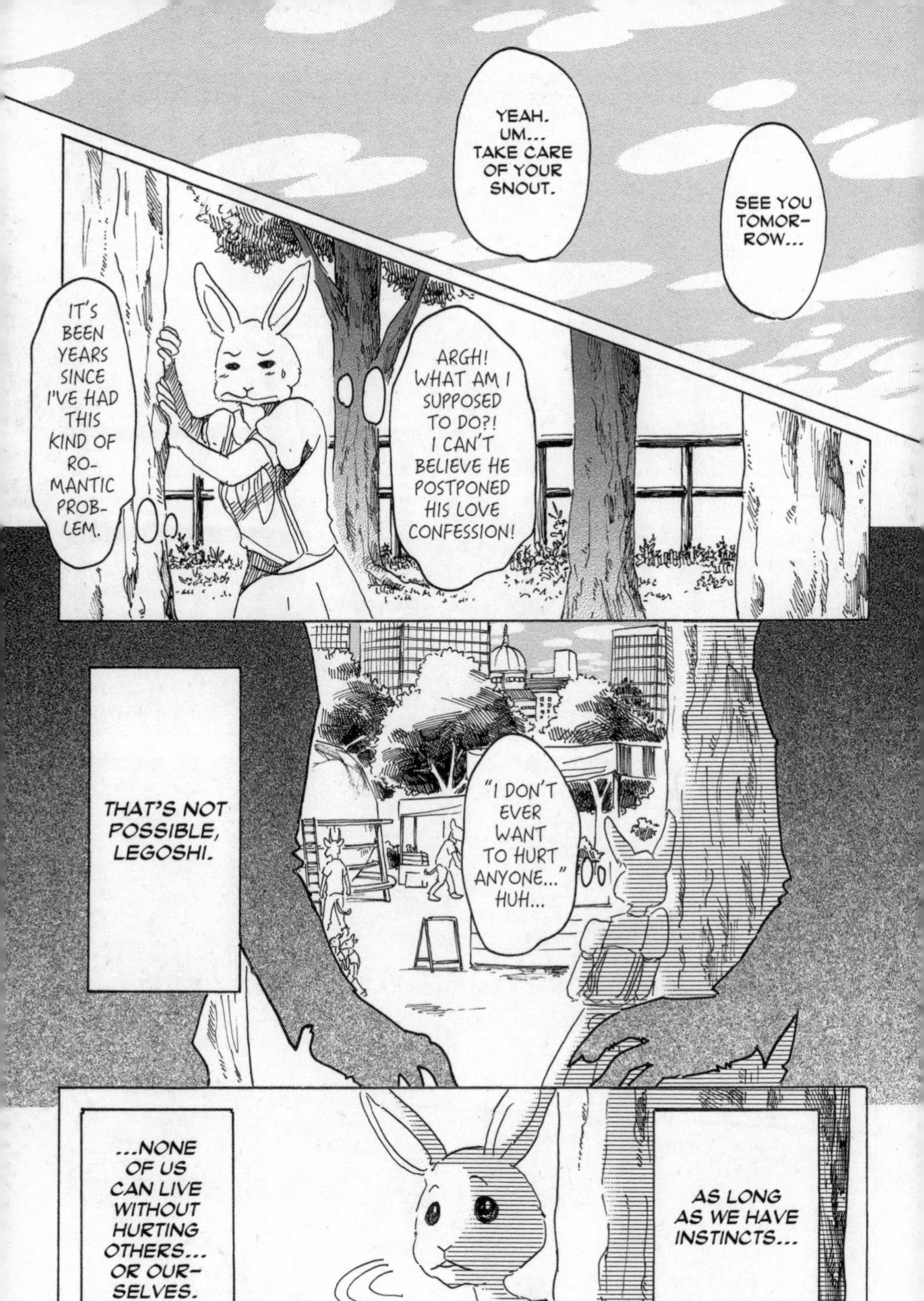
SEE YOU TOMOR-ROW...
YEAH. UM... TAKE CARE OF YOUR SNOUT.
ARGH! WHAT AM I SUPPOSED TO DO?! I CAN'T BELIEVE HE POSTPONED HIS LOVE CONFESSION!
IT'S BEEN YEARS SINCE I'VE HAD THIS KIND OF RO-MANTIC PROB-LEM.
"I DON'T EVER WANT TO HURT ANYONE..." HUH...
THAT'S NOT POSSIBLE, LEGOSHI.
AS LONG AS WE HAVE INSTINCTS...
...NONE OF US CAN LIVE WITHOUT HURTING OTHERS... OR OUR-SELVES.

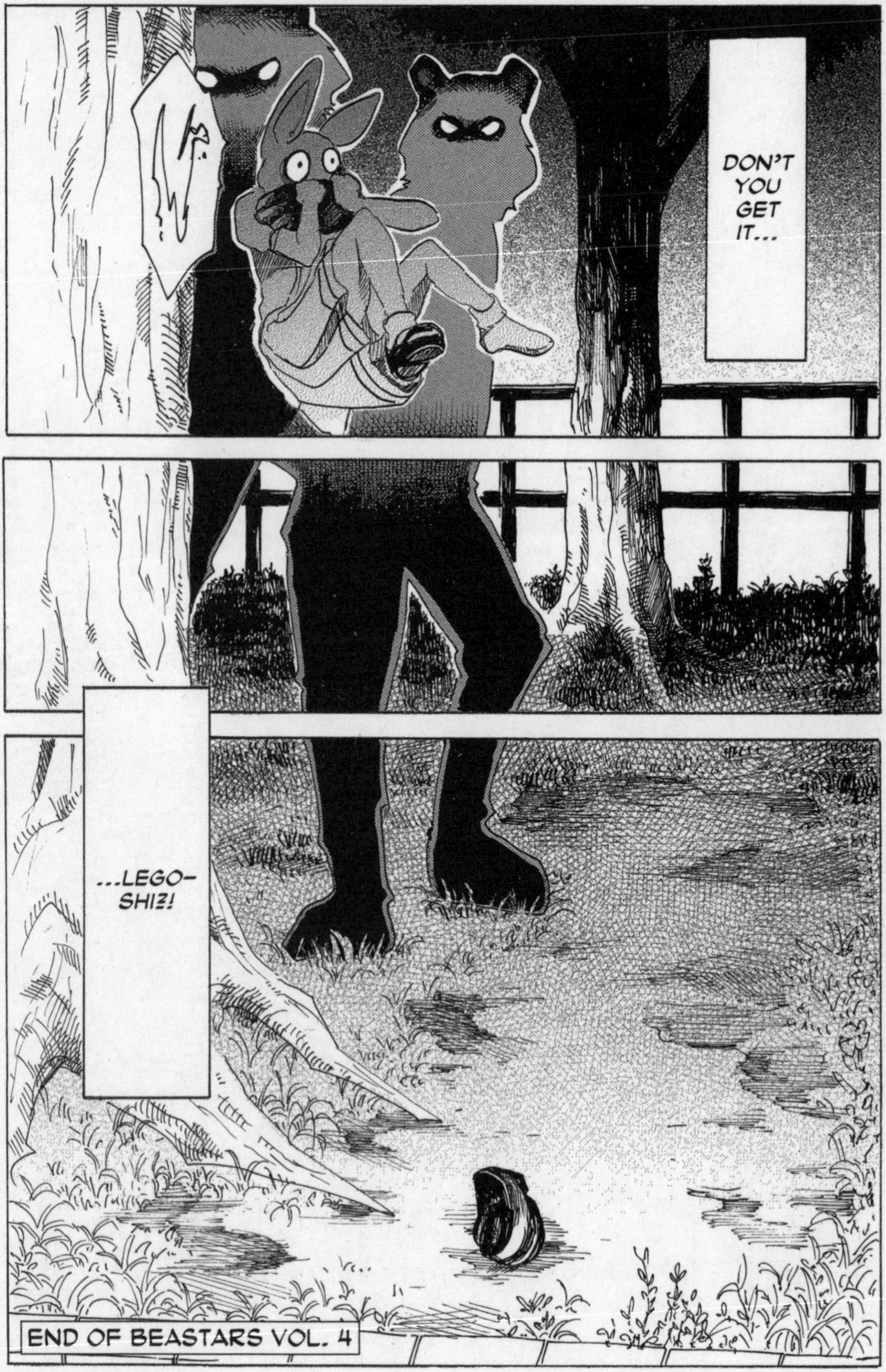
DON'T YOU GET IT...
...LEGOSHI?!
END OF BEASTARS VOL. 4

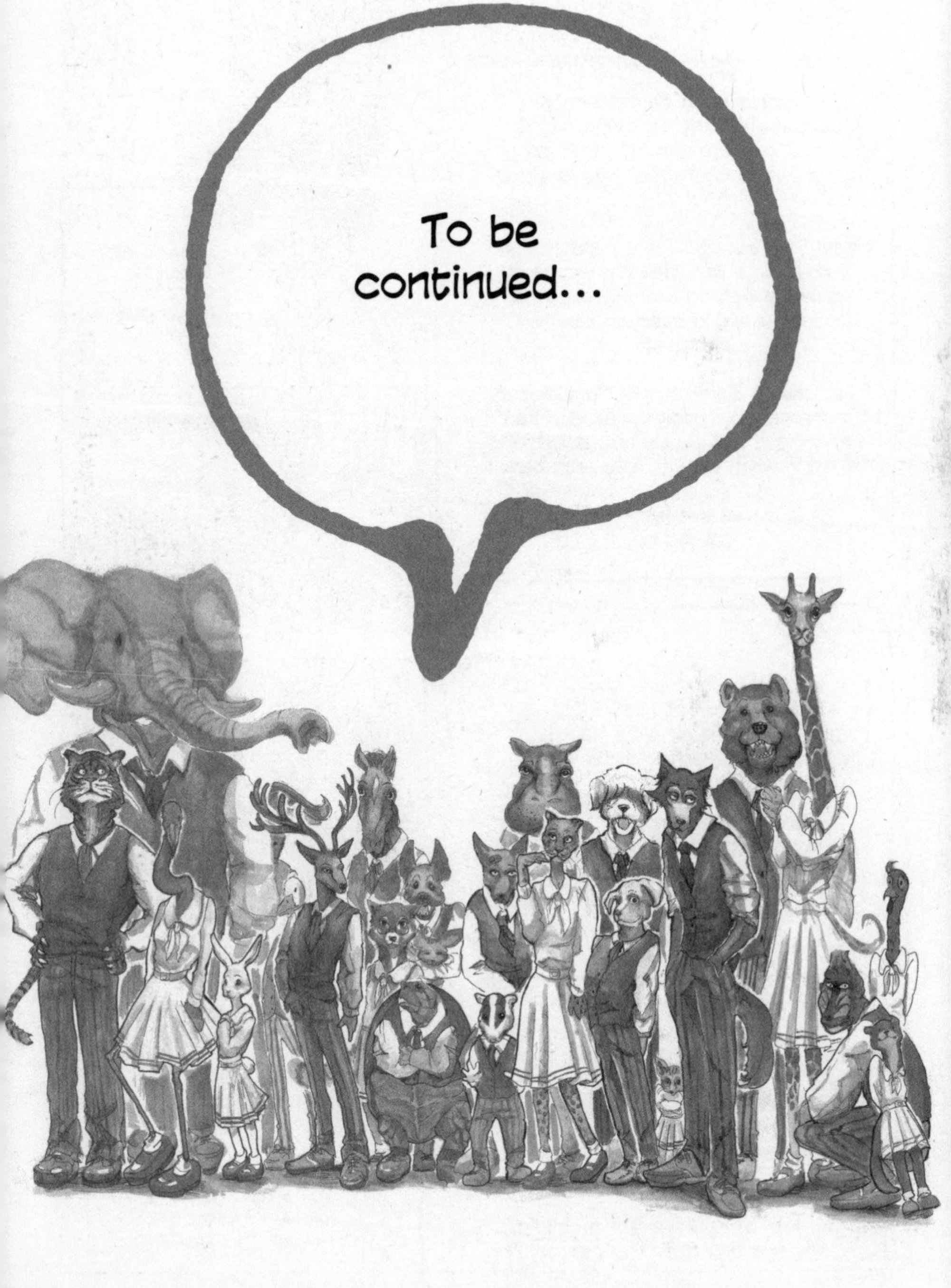
To be continued...

Juno Character Design Notes

Juno's personality

I added Juno to the story because Haru is so complicated both outside and in. I wanted a female character who is a classic beauty.

When I created Juno's personality, I thought a beautiful girl wouldn't grow up warped and complicated because she'd been so blessed all her life.

But then I didn't like her character anymore, so I took a risk and had her behave differently in chapter 31. That's when I fell in love with her.

This was the lesson Juno taught me.

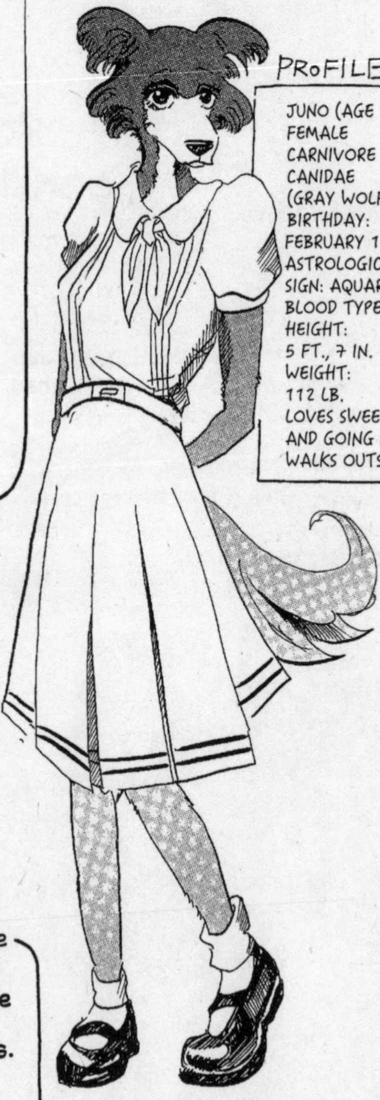

PROFILE

JUNO (AGE 16)
FEMALE
CARNIVORE
CANIDAE
(GRAY WOLF)
BIRTHDAY: FEBRUARY 12
ASTROLOGICAL SIGN: AQUARIUS
BLOOD TYPE: AB
HEIGHT: 5 FT., 7 IN.
WEIGHT: 112 LB.
LOVES SWEETS AND GOING FOR WALKS OUTSIDE

How did you come up with her name?

I wanted it to sound juicy. My impression of beautiful girls is that their skin, hair and lips are fresh and dewy.

If you say Legoshi's and Juno's name together, they sound like a beautiful power carnivore couple. Ha ha ha.

Juno's appearance

I designed her to complement Haru. She has dark-brown fur. Her body is fully mature, with prominent breasts and hips.

Her face looks like a young Winona Ryder's.

Her eyes shine like a child's, yet she has a strong personality.

I'M PARTICULAR ABOUT THESE DETAILS:

- SHE HAS A SLENDER GIRLISH FRAME BUT THE STRENGTH OF A WOLF.

Responsible Mating Practices Exist in Their World Too

(*Not for readers under the age of 18. Actually, I guess they can read this too...)

The contraceptives section is the biggest one in the drugstores of this world, because they need to be available in a wide range of sizes.

Most species have similar penis shapes, but there are slight differences, just like between Japanese and Americans.

Practicing birth control is very important in this world because beasts can conceive even when mating with a different species.

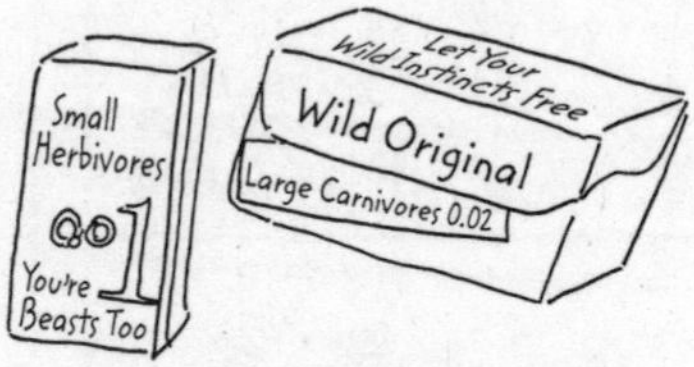

Small Herbivores
0.01
You're Beasts Too
Let Your Wild Instincts Free
Wild Original
Large Carnivores 0.02

Breeding with members of different species is strongly disapproved of, so intermarriage is frowned upon. I'll stop here because I might end up touching upon the core of this story. But seriously, birth control is important—whether you're a beast or a hominidae!

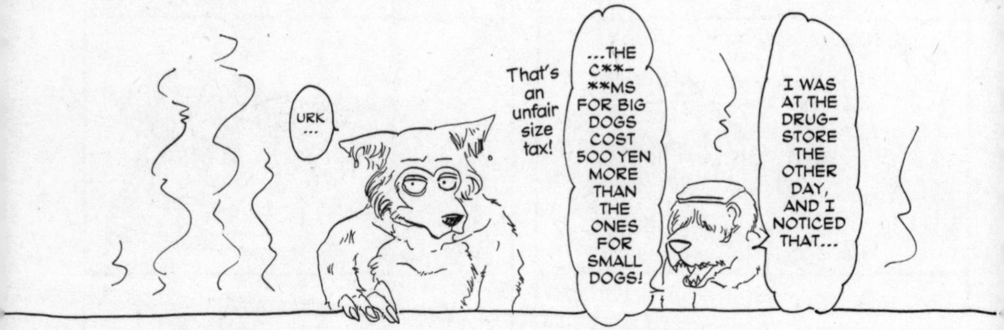

I WAS AT THE DRUGSTORE THE OTHER DAY, AND I NOTICED THAT...
...THE C**-**MS FOR BIG DOGS COST 500 YEN MORE THAN THE ONES FOR SMALL DOGS!
That's an unfair size tax!
URK...

Do you prefer cats? Or dogs?

Let's compare a similar situation with both (males, in this case).

Subject: Els

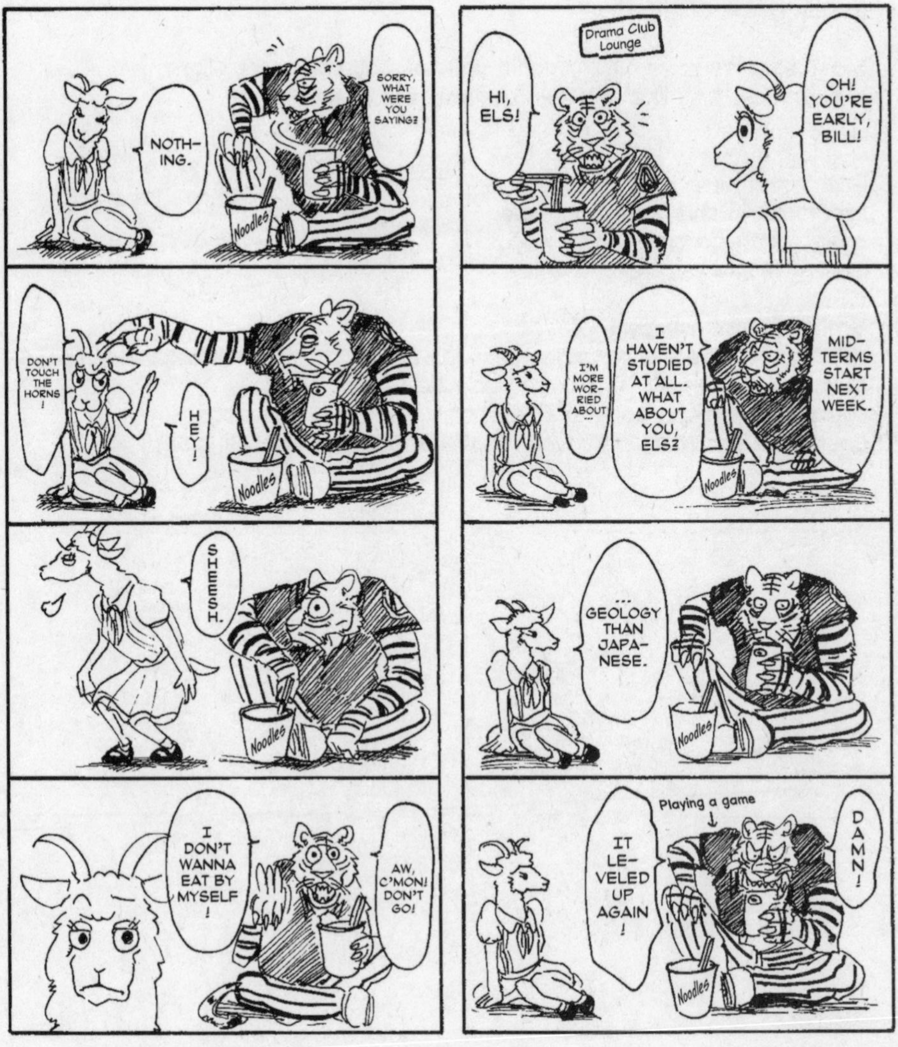

Drama Club Lounge
OH! YOU'RE EARLY, BILL!
HI, ELS!
MID-TERMS START NEXT WEEK.
I HAVEN'T STUDIED AT ALL. WHAT ABOUT YOU, ELS?
I'M MORE WOR-RIED ABOUT...
Noodles
...GEOLOGY THAN JAPA-NESE.
Noodles
DAMN!
Playing a game
IT LE-VELED UP AGAIN!
Noodles
SORRY, WHAT WERE YOU SAYING?
NOTH-ING.
Noodles
HEY!
DON'T TOUCH THE HORNS!
Noodles
SHEESH.
Noodles
AW, C'MON! DON'T GO!
I DON'T WANNA EAT BY MYSELF!

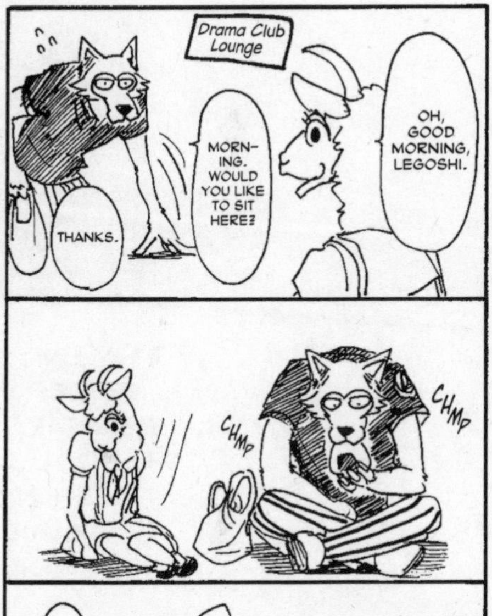
Drama Club Lounge
OH, GOOD MORNING, LEGOSHI.
MORNING. WOULD YOU LIKE TO SIT HERE?
THANKS.
CHMP
CHMP
DID YOU SWITCH TO A NEW SOAP?
HUH? WHAT?!
YOUR LAUNDRY DETERGENT, I MEAN.
HOW DID YOU KNOW?!
YOU SMELL DIFFERENT.
WHOA...
YOU CAN TELL?!
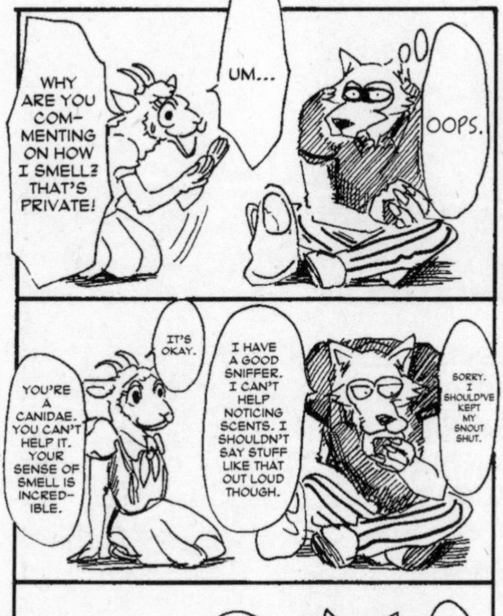
OOPS.
UM...
WHY ARE YOU COMMENTING ON HOW I SMELL? THAT'S PRIVATE!
SORRY. I SHOULD'VE KEPT MY SNOUT SHUT.
I HAVE A GOOD SNIFFER. I CAN'T HELP NOTICING SCENTS. I SHOULDN'T SAY STUFF LIKE THAT OUT LOUD THOUGH.
IT'S OKAY.
YOU'RE A CANIDAE. YOU CAN'T HELP IT. YOUR SENSE OF SMELL IS INCREDIBLE.
YOU TH-THINK SO?
YEAH. NO OTHER ANIMAL COMES CLOSE.
YOU SWITCHED TO NIFLAN'S PURE SOAP!
Detergent...
...

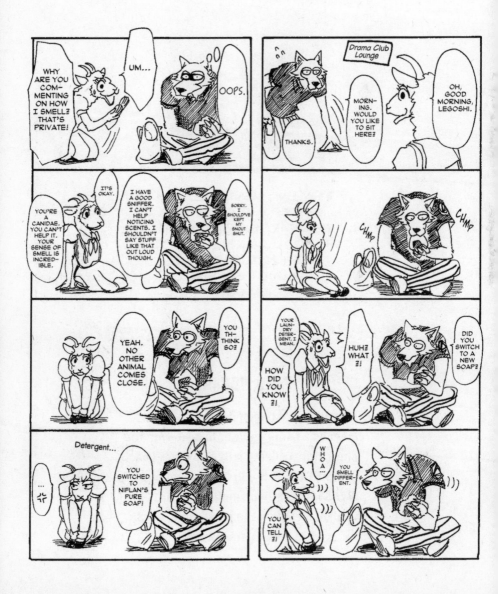

I HAVEN'T MENTIONED THIS
BEFORE, BUT THERE ARE
BEASTARS EXTRAS UNDER
THE BOOK JACKETS. THEY'VE
BEEN INCLUDED SINCE
VOLUME 1, SO CHECK
THEM OUT.*

*In the English version, the extras are printed on the two pages before the author's note.

PARU ITAGAKI

Paru Itagaki began her professional
career as a manga author in 2016 with the
short story collection **BEAST COMPLEX**.
BEASTARS is her first serialization.
BEASTARS has won multiple awards in
Japan, including the prestigious 2018
Manga Taisho Award.

BEASTARS
VOL. 4
VIZ Signature Edition

Story & Art by
Paru Itagaki

Translation/Tomoko Kimura
English Adaptation/Annette Roman
Touch-Up Art & Lettering/Susan Daigle-Leach
Cover & Interior Design/Yukiko Whitley
Editor/Annette Roman

Published by VIZ Media, LLC
P.O. Box 77010
San Francisco, CA 94107

10 9 8 7 6 5 4 3 2
First printing, January 2020
Second printing, February 2020

viz.com   vizsignature.com

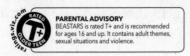

PARENTAL ADVISORY
BEASTARS is rated T+ and is recommended
for ages 16 and up. It contains adult themes,
sexual situations and violence.

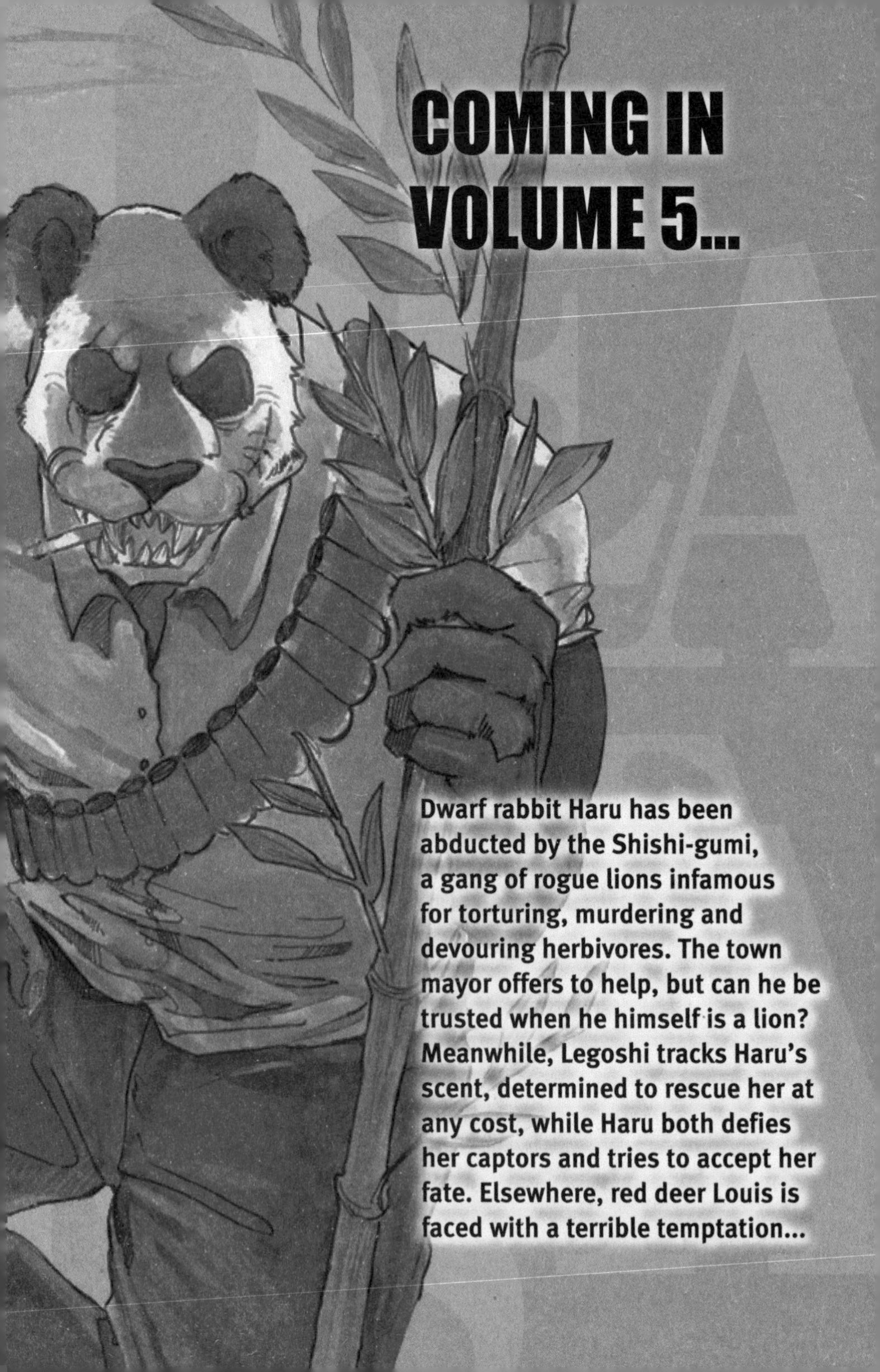

COMING IN VOLUME 5...

Dwarf rabbit Haru has been abducted by the Shishi-gumi, a gang of rogue lions infamous for torturing, murdering and devouring herbivores. The town mayor offers to help, but can he be trusted when he himself is a lion? Meanwhile, Legoshi tracks Haru's scent, determined to rescue her at any cost, while Haru both defies her captors and tries to accept her fate. Elsewhere, red deer Louis is faced with a terrible temptation...

CHILDREN OF THE WHALES

In this postapocalyptic fantasy, a sea of sand swallows everything but the past.

In an endless sea of sand drifts the Mud Whale, a floating island city of clay and magic. In its chambers a small community clings to survival, cut off from its own history by the shadows of the past.

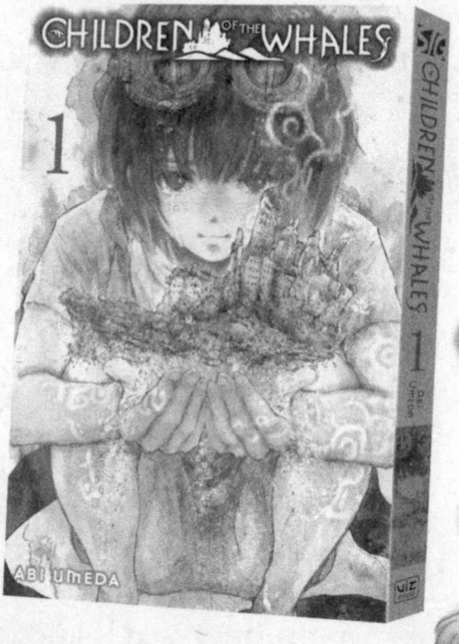
CHILDREN OF THE WHALES
1
CHILDREN OF THE WHALES
1
ABI UMEDA

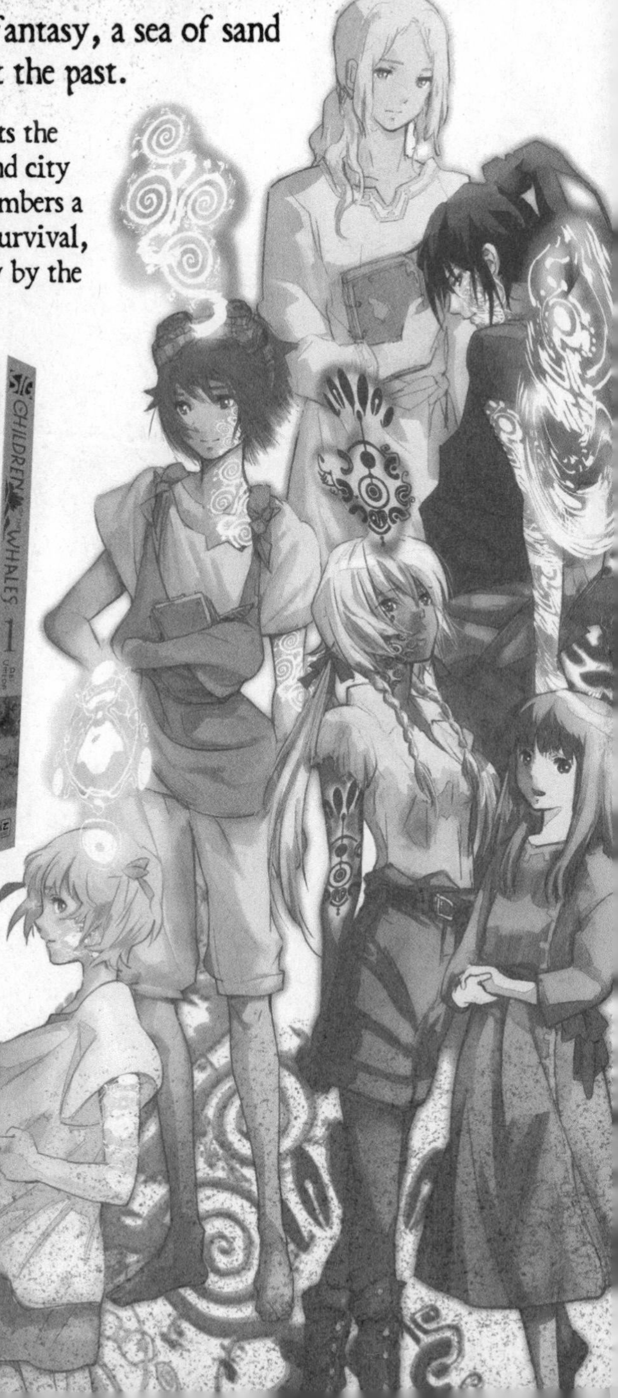

viz.com

RATED T+ OLDER TEEN

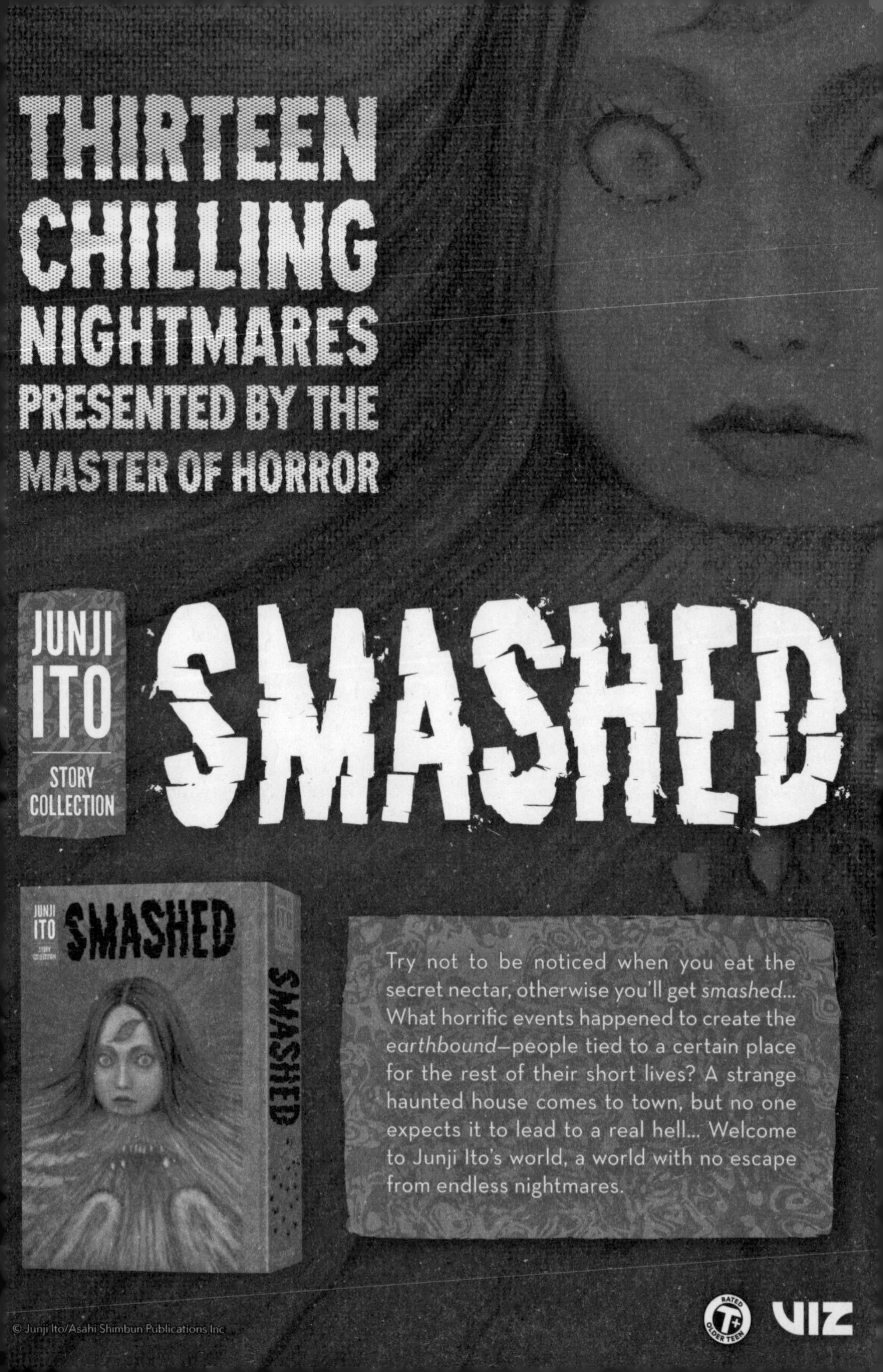
THIRTEEN CHILLING NIGHTMARES PRESENTED BY THE MASTER OF HORROR
JUNJI ITO
STORY COLLECTION
SMASHED
JUNJI ITO SMASHED STORY COLLECTION
SMASHED
Try not to be noticed when you eat the secret nectar, otherwise you'll get *smashed*... What horrific events happened to create the *earthbound*—people tied to a certain place for the rest of their short lives? A strange haunted house comes to town, but no one expects it to lead to a real hell... Welcome to Junji Ito's world, a world with no escape from endless nightmares.
© Junji Ito/Asahi Shimbun Publications Inc.
RATED T+ OLDER TEEN
VIZ

TOKYO GHOUL

C O M P L E T E B O X S E T STORY AND ART BY SUI ISHIDA

KEN KANEKI is an ordinary college student until a violent encounter turns him into the first half-human, half-Ghoul hybrid. Trapped between two worlds, he must survive Ghoul turf wars, learn more about Ghoul society and master his new powers.

Box set collects all fourteen volumes of the original *Tokyo Ghoul* series. Includes an exclusive double-sided poster.

COLLECT THE COMPLETE SERIES

This is the last page.

BEASTARS reads from right to left to preserve the orientation of the original Japanese artwork.